International Handbook of Shared Parenting

International Handbook of Shared Parenting

Francis Jacob

STATES
ACADEMIC PRESS
www.statesacademicpress.com

States Academic Press,
109 South 5th Street,
Brooklyn, NY 11249, USA

Visit us on the World Wide Web at:
www.statesacademicpress.com

ISBN: 978-1-63989-703-2

Cataloging-in-publication Data

International handbook of shared parenting / Francis Jacob.
p. cm.
Includes bibliographical references and index.
ISBN 978-1-63989-703-2
1. Joint custody of children. 2. Parenting, Part-time--Law and legislation.
3. Parenting--Law and legislation. I. Jacob, Francis.

K7190 .I58 2023
346.017 3--dc23

Table of Contents

Preface

Shared parenting (SP) or joint physical custody refers to a child custody arrangement after divorce or separation of the child's parents. In this type of arrangement, both the parents share the responsibility of raising their child or children with equal or close to equal parenting time. The underlying idea in shared parenting is that children have the right to benefit from a close relationship with both their parents, and that no child should be separated from either of the parents. There are various themes that are studied under the concept of shared parenting. It studies whether SP provides real benefits to children whose parents separate and seeks persuasive evidence related to it. It also highlights the specific factors that make SP beneficial and the symbolic value of SP. This book is a valuable compilation of topics related to shared parenting. It will serve as a reference to a broad spectrum of readers.

This book is a comprehensive compilation of works of different researchers from varied parts of the world. It includes valuable experiences of the researchers with the sole objective of providing the readers (learners) with a proper knowledge of the concerned field. This book will be beneficial in evoking inspiration and enhancing the knowledge of the interested readers.

In the end, I would like to extend my heartiest thanks to the authors who worked with great determination on their chapters. I also appreciate the publisher's support in the course of the book. I would also like to deeply acknowledge my family who stood by me as a source of inspiration during the project.

Francis Jacob

1

Shared Physical Custody: Interdisciplinary Perspectives

Laura Bernardi and Dimitri Mortelmans

Abstract This introductory chapter provides the rationale for adopting an interdisciplinary approach to study the implications of shared physical custody arrangements for families and their members. The Chapter gives a rapid overview of the current state of the literature on shared physical custody in the legal, sociological and psychological literature and highlights the uncertainties and controversial aspects still open to exploration in this field. It addresses the specific research needs in order to move forward from the current situation, where evidence on shared physical custody produce results that are scattered across disciplines and hard to compare across contexts. It concludes by arguing that the complexity of shared physical custody implications in terms of health, educational, relational and living standards requires research from different disciplinary fields in order to agree on a comprehensive theoretical perspective, standardize definitions and collect longitudinal and comparable data on the custody arrangements and their normative environments.

Keywords Interdisciplinary · Care arrangements · Comparative · Longitudinal · Shared custody

---

L. Bernardi (✉)
LIVES Centre, Swiss Centre of Expertise in Life Course Research and Institute of Social Sciences, University of Lausanne, Lausanne, Switzerland
e-mail: laura.bernardi@unil.ch

D. Mortelmans
Centre for Population, Family and Health (CPFH), University of Antwerp, Antwerp, Belgium
e-mail: dimitri.mortelmans@uantwerpen.be

1.1 An Interdisciplinary Approach to Shared Physical Custody

Shared physical custody (SPC)[1], the care arrangement in which a child lives from 30% to 70% of the time with each parent after their separation or divorce, has been on the rise in most Western regions in the last two decades (Smyth 2017). Prevalence and incidence of SPC vary substantively by context though. While the percentage of SPC among divorced and separated parents grew from 12% to 50% between 1989 and 2010 in some contexts like in the US state of Wisconsin (Meyer et al. 2017), it remains mostly a minority arrangement, ranging from 12% in the UK to 40% as in Belgium and Quebec in 2017 (Steinbach et al. 2020).

The emergence of SPC can be related to increasing aspirations to gender equality among parents, where mothers are increasingly active on the labour market and engaged in demanding professional careers as well as wanting equality in housework shares, while, at the same time, fathers want to care more for their children (Goldscheider et al. 2015; Hook 2016; Westphal et al. 2014). The daily time that both residential and non-residential fathers report to spend in childcare increased substantially over the last decade (Klünder and Meier-Gräwe 2018; Schoppe-Sullivan and Fagan 2020), indicating that many separated fathers increasingly engage with their children. The introduction of more gender-neutral family policies facilitating active fatherhood (e.g., longer parental and paternal leave Thevenon 2011) contributed to this shift (Bartova and Keizer 2020).

In addition, shared physical custody is also seen as a way to counteract the negative consequences of separation and divorce for children. Several social and psychological studies addressing this issue have pointed out the multiple risks of children when losing contact with one of their parents (in the large majority of cases fathers). Economic and psychological hardships would threaten children's adjustment, their future development and life chances (Amato 2000, 2010; Amato and Cheadle 2005; Härkönen et al. 2017).

Last, and relatedly to these societal developments and scientific evidence, the exponential increase in SPC care arrangements depends on changes in the principles guiding courts' and judges' decisions. These have shifted from an implicit preference for mothers' physical custody, to an encouragement to prefer shared physical custody or to hold a presumption in its favor (Goubau 2009). Change started with shared legal custody granting unmarried parents, as well as married ones, equal say in important decisions concerning child development and living conditions (health, education, residence and religion). The demand for shared physical custody was a logical next step as the shared responsibility of legal custody would have to match the parental experience of raising the children. Nowadays, legal custody is

[1]Such arrangement is also known as joint physical custody, shared parenting, shared (dual) residence; or in French-speaking countries as *résidence alternée* (alternating residence). From now on in this volume we define it as shared physical custody as this is the less ambivalent term among such alternatives.

widespread but it is not always followed up by shared physical custody despite the strong advocacy it has received.

The key turning point in shared physical custody occurred when juridical guidelines for decisions regarding post separation custody arrangements began to be constructed as if the "best interest of the child" was something different from the interest of the child's primary caregiver (the mother until then). The notion is tricky though as the best interest of the child as an autonomous person seems to be at odds with the fact that the child depends on at least one of its parents and the interest of both parents may not overlap with the child's interests. When parents disagree on custody arrangements, judges often have to evaluate a complex set of factors in order to identify the best interest of the child.

The societal and legal debate on the best interest of the child is often informed by ideological positions (Kruk 2012). On the one hand, the need for the continuity of the relationship with both parents has been contrasted to the idea that mothers are the primary carers and therefore shall have priority in shared physical custody. On the other hand, the issue of equal treatment among parents questions the moral basis on which fathers are charged for financing children that they could visit and not live with. Father's movement have been vocal about more equality, to an extent the issue has come to dominate both the legal and political landscape. Fathers' rights groups identified the fact of ensuring justice and equality between parents with the presumption of a post separation SPC, possibly a 50/50 one, unless the child's wellbeing suggested otherwise (Spruijt and Duindam 2002).

As a consequence, in the last few decades, maintaining the relationship with both parents after the marital separation or divorce through co-parenting has evolved into a political as much as an emotional debate (Harris-Short 2010). The idea is that both parent-child relationships shall continue despite the fact that the conjugal relationship has broken apart, replacing the non-substitutability of the mother as primary carer. Debates are still hot on whether this is also the case for babies and toddlers, in case of absent or conflictual communication among parents and in cases of severe precarious living conditions. In addition, parents' ability to establish cooperative co-parenting after separation seems to clash, at least in the short term, with the fact that they have put an end to their alliance as a couple. Newly published research shows, for instance, that it is not SPC that may benefit adolescent children but rather the family characteristics that led them to prefer such arrangements (Steinbach et al. 2020). As a matter of fact, empirical evidence is still to be solid and reliable, as often based on heterogeneous studies involving selective populations of higher educated and low-conflict parents or smaller scale studies, as we will discuss in the next section.

And yet, when evaluating the reasons leading to prefer a care arrangement for children or its consequences, we are immediately confronted with the complexity of mechanisms at work. Reasons can be based on parents' or judges' belief that continuity shall be privileged with the pre-separation care habits, or on the possibilities of offering the child a better living standard, or, still, on the child preference for spending more time in one household rather than the other (not changing the social environment, not getting along with possible step parents and siblings etc.).

Outcomes are also a multidimensional realm ranging from short term cognitive and emotional health, physical health, economic and housing conditions, educational and relational opportunities to longer term consequences including life course development of children and their success in adult life. With such a complex picture, defining what is in the child's best interest seems to be a challenging task, where priorities shall be established and shorter and longer outcomes weighed against each other. A comprehensive theoretical perspective addressing the complexity of such mechanisms is currently missing, contributing to a wealth of diverging empirical results concerning determinants and consequences of SPC.

In addition to the lack of clarity in whether SPC is desirable and under what circumstances, there is also some fuzziness in the definition on what constitutes enough custodial time so that it can be defined as "shared". While 50% would correspond to equal sharing, among professionals, policy makers and social scientists the interpretation of the term "shared" converges on something in between the time accorded for usual visiting rights to a non-residential parent (usually every two weekends and half of school holidays) and the full custody. Mostly, in research and practice, 30–50% of the time is considered sufficiently substantial to be SPC, with a primary and a secondary carer when time is not exactly equal (Meyer et al. 2017). The development over time of such percentage is unclear though. Couples may be constantly re-evaluating and changing it or even suspending it for a period without any chance for researchers to track such dynamics too closely.

Against this background of contradicting theoretical predictions, diverging empirical evidence and lack of precise definitions of care arrangements forms of post separation families involving children, this volume gives a multidisciplinary view of SPC, hoping to contribute to a substantive and constructive research dialogue to advance knowledge in this domain and offer a better guidance both for future research and for legal and social policy professionals. Psychological adjustment and development studies address the short and longer term risks for children and parents involved in such arrangements. At the same time, sociological and demographic awareness include attention to the heterogeneity of processes across social groups and gender. In addition, shifting care arrangements are looked at in terms of changes for family relationships but also, in the longer run, for family diversity and the distribution of family forms in the society. The dynamics of obligations and interdependency of individuals' support beyond the nuclear family is affected by children's care and residential arrangements. Both legal and social policy scholarships have to be involved in the definition of what the boundaries of the state intervention are in such dynamics. Similarly, there is a need to clearly indicate the empirical basis and the guiding value principles shaping such intervention.

1.2 Insights on Shared Physical Custody Outcomes

The field that covers the outcomes of shared physical custody is characterized by a huge number of studies and an almost equal number of reviews summarizing these studies. Some of these reviews focus on the outcomes for children (Baude et al.

2019; Braver and Votruba 2018), others take parents into account (Fransson et al. 2016). Some aim specifically at informing practice (e.g. the legal field: Nielsen 2015), while others only focus on empirical evidence (Nielsen 2018b; Steinbach 2019). And finally, meta-analyses (Baude et al. 2016; Bauserman 2012) are developed next to classic literature overviews (Nielsen 2014b). These meta-analyses are important since they allow to compare the (often small) effect sizes. The analyses also show the direction and size of the effects under study. The huge amount of reviews shows that this is a controversial topic that raises great concerns (especially concerning children) and touches basic societal processes like parenthood and basic human attachment.

In this introduction, we do not aim to give a review of all reviews. Nor do we want to present a new all-encompassing literature review on the empirical evidence on outcomes of shared physical custody. We rather aim to point at the research interests that have been developed in this field to provide the reader with some directions through the literature. As this book aims to give new insights in shared physical custody from an interdisciplinary perspective, we will point to research interests from psychology, demography, sociology and law research. The fields of psychology and sociology have produced knowledge on the outcomes of SPC and the potential gains and losses for both children and parents adopting this custody regime. Demography adds a focus on gendered union and fertility dynamics that may derive from different custodial practices (e.g. van der Wiel et al. 2020). Law research on the other hand looks for ways to apply these results in legal procedures that mould the outcomes in the best possible way. For more detailed overviews in these fields, we refer to Chaps. 2, 3 and 4 where more elaborate disciplinary introductions are provided.

The overall burning question in the literature is whether or not the outcomes for children and parents are better when shared physical custody is chosen over single physical custody. Multiple factors have been explored to study a wide variety of possible outcomes. As we will discuss, parental education and income are the most important factors identified in this field and wellbeing is the outcome that received the most attention. Baude et al. (2016) and Nielsen (2018b) classify children's outcomes in five broad categories: (1) general adjustment or cognitive outcomes, (2) emotional or psychological adjustment, (3) behavioural adjustment, (4) social adjustment, and (5) family relations. In all these domains, results point to a general tendency of positive outcomes on children in joint physical custody (except in conflictual or violent situations which we will elaborate on later). Even though effects are usually small, they point to a higher wellbeing of children in shared care arrangements compared to sole physical custody. Mental health of children is better (e.g. Bergström et al. 2014), stress measures turn out to be lower (e.g. Turunen 2017) and their self-esteem is higher (e.g. Bastaits and Mortelmans 2016). Also behavioural and health components turn out to score better in shared physical custody: risk behaviour is lower than children in sole physical custody (e.g. Carlsund et al. 2012) and the children in joint physical custody tend to have less health related problems (Fabricius and Luecken 2007).

When family relations are concerned, the focus lies exclusively on the bond with the father as traditional custody arrangements entailed living with the mother and visiting the father (e.g. once every two weeks). Shared physical custody almost automatically implies an increased contact with the father (Bauserman 2012; Cheadle et al. 2010; Westphal et al. 2014). This increased presence in the lives of children also results in closer bonds between the father and his children (Spruijt et al. 2004). The higher contact intensity also leads to better wellbeing in children after divorce (Bastaits and Pasteels 2019). But despite the positive outcomes in the literature, Poortman (2018) warns for a selection effect as pre-divorce involvement matters more to outcomes for children than the custody arrangement in itself.

Not only positive outcomes for children are found, also parents with a shared custody arrangement show improved outcomes on many domains. In his meta review, Bauserman (2012) reports lower levels of conflict both reported from the fathers and the mothers side. Some studies on relitigation show that parents in SPC less often return to court than other ex-partners even though some studies have found no difference or opposite effects (Bauserman 2012). Also labour market related factors turn out to be more favourable among parents in SPC compared to lone parents (Bernardi and Mortelmans 2018). For mothers, SPC enables them to gain a better access to the labour market and to focus on their career when their child resides with the father (Kruyfhooft and Mortelmans 2011). Women no longer have the full ‘second shift’ (Hochschild and Machung 1989) leaving room for leisure time, repartnering and labour market choices (Sodermans et al. 2015; van der Heijden et al. 2016).

Throughout these results, three main topics stand out as dividing the specialists the most: the role of parental resources (education and income), the role of conflict and the potential harm of SPC for young children. In the remainder of this book, the reader will find many expressions of the dominance of these three leitmotivs. The first controversy concerns parental resources. Studies have shown that parents in joint physical custody turn out to be higher educated and have higher incomes (Nielsen 2015; Steinbach 2019). Comparable to the classic observation of Goode (1962, 1963) that divorce rates start with the avantgarde of the wealthy and the higher educated, also SPC is selective in its parental demographic background. Comparable to Goode, also SPC is also expected to become less selective when more ex-couples prefer this care regime (Sodermans et al. 2013). Despite the selection effect, income differences turn out to be more limited than expected and even when controlling for education or income, SPC is systematically more beneficial than sole custody (Nielsen 2018a).

For conflict, the general assumption is that the lack of destructive parental conflict (Cummings and Davies 2010) is a crucial determinant in the success of SPC. The first question again is whether or not there is a selection effect of lower conflict families into SPC. The meta-analysis of Bauserman (2012) suggests that studies more often report lower levels of conflict in SPC. These results are confirmed from both the father’s and the mother’s side. But again, as SPC is rising among divorced couples, the more important question is whether conflict is more detrimental for children’s outcomes in high conflict SPC compared to good interparental contacts among ex-spouses. Here, the evidence points to a rather limited effect of conflict on children's outcomes, contrary to general belief (Nielsen 2017).

Nielsen (2018b) asserts that we need to take into account selectivity or at least try to go beyond income and conflict to see whether the outcomes are really better in SPC *despite* these two crucial factors. Garriga and Bernardi (2019) show that SPC can translate in an additional source of inequality among children of non intact families given that more disadvantaged children profit less of its benefits than advantaged children, all other things equal. Other recent studies show that it is much more important for children to have a good relationship with their parents and have authoritative parents (Bastaits and Mortelmans 2016; Sobolewski and Amato 2007). The selection effect is clear in countries that introduce increased possibilities for SPC but as the phenomenon spread across society, the effect of class is likely to wane.

The last domain of controversy concerns the appropriateness for SPC for very young children (toddlers and babies). This domain is probably the most heavily debated field in this literature leading to scientific woozles, i.e. the misrepresentation and misuse of research by advocacy groups for their own political purposes (Nielsen 2014c). A first observation to be made is that the number of studies with babies or toddlers is very limited (Nielsen 2014a). Second, specialists often refer to attachment theory, or at least old concepts from attachment theory like monotrophy (attachment related to a single caregiver) (Warshak 2018) to defend care regimes with one dominant care giver. Time spent with a parent is taken as a main indicator for attachment while social interaction and expression of affection and a parent's responsiveness are far more critical to a secure attachment of children (Main et al. 2011). This leads to a mother-centered perspective and prohibiting laws for (overnight) stays at the father's house (Lamb and Kelly 2001). Third, even though time spent with parents is taken as the point of departure, overnights are considered as more "salient" in the debate on negative consequences than the overall frequency of stays. Also here, little or no empirical evidence exists for this claim (Warshak 2018). In summary, at present studies showing negative effects of SPC on young children are not only limited in number, they are often also handicapped in their methodological rigour as a control group is often absent. It strengthens advocates of SPC at any age in their claim that there is no scientific proof that SPC would harm infants in their development (Warshak 2018).

1.3 Research Needs

As our short overview of the literature has shown, many uncertainties and controversies remain in this field. Psychologists and sociologists debate on consequences of SPC, law researchers debate the best way to incorporate the best interest of the child in custody laws incorporating the wishes of both parents. For future research, it is clear that both new theoretical and empirical work is necessary. The confusion for practitioners is great and courts decide in many directions on the lives of parents and children. This volume aims to shed new insights from psychology, law and sociology and collects the major new insights in the field.

One issue that the volume cannot resolve is the lack of good and representative data. In order to make progress in the field, new empirical research on nationally representative data is crucial to gain nuanced insights in the outcomes for both children and parents. Too often, the debate is on the border of an ideological fight between advocates and contestants of SPC. Positive results from one review are interpreted by the next review in an opposite way to prove the adversary effects of SPC (Smyth cited in: Nielsen 2018b). Not seldomly, research is done on small samples acquired with convenience sampling techniques.

Even though small scale studies (for an overview, see: Bauserman 2012) and qualitative inquiry (e.g. Markham and Coleman 2012) contribute to new insights on the processes and mechanisms involved in SPC arrangements, nationally representative surveys are necessary to obtain more reliable knowledge with valid conclusions for subpopulations under study and practical recommendations to be applied by field workers. Too often, small samples lead to insignificant or small effects sizes jeopardizing firm conclusions. Fortunately, several nationally representative surveys have already been used in the US (Stanford Custody Project – Maccoby et al. 1993), Sweden (ULF – Survey on Swedish Living Conditions – Fransson et al. 2016), Australia[2] (HILDA, LSAC & LSSF – Cashmore et al. 2010), Belgium (DIF – Divorce in Flanders – Bastaits and Mortelmans 2016), Switzerland (SHP – Swiss Household Panel, this volume) and the Netherlands (NFN – New Families in the Netherlands – van der Heijden et al. 2016).

Most studies are cross-sectional in design. Only some studies have a longitudinal set-up and even then, it usually concerns a two-wave follow-up study (Guidubaldi and Perry 1985; Solomon and George 1999). Except for the Australian panel studies (see above), these longitudinal studies are also rather small in sample size. This lack in longitudinal analyses is problematic as SPC is a highly dynamic process (Bastaits et al. 2018). Throughout the life course of children not only the care regime change, but also the outcomes of the custody arrangements are not stable. Custody arrangements get adapted as children age or as parents ask courts to make adaptions. Also, the arrival of new-borns in blended families can have an influence on the SPC of the older children.

A quick gain in longitudinal analyses can be found in the use of register data (see Claessens and Mortelmans, Chap. 7, in this volume). As fiscal data become increasingly available, tax reductions for SPC arrangements lead to official identifications of this care regime in governmental data. Being longitudinal by nature, register data can provide us with large scale samples with a wide variety in family forms. It can also take the linked lives of former partners into account and follow their life courses as they unfold. Even though legal requirements on data linkage are challenging and not all countries will allow to match data from population registers with fiscal

[2]HILDA – Household Income and Labour Dynamics in Australia; LSAC – Longitudinal Study of Australian Children; LSSF – Longitudinal Study of Separated Parents.

registers, exciting and complex life course research on SPC becomes possible in some countries. As the advantages of large-scale longitudinal data without attrition are clear, the registers do not have any subjective measures on parents or children. Health outcomes might be measurable but other indicators like problematic child behaviour, insecure attachment, or parenting styles lie beyond the scope of the registers.

A last empirical issue is the lack of comparable data to start comparative cross-country analyses. To our knowledge, only one large scale comparative study on 37 Western countries has been done, using WHO data (Bjarnason and Arnarsson 2011). The main problem is the availability of indicators on the custody arrangement of children in large, nationally representative (panel) surveys. A lot of classic household surveys take "living under the same roof" as a holy principle for household composition. In such case, everybody in a household is assumed to live in it full time. With more and more children living in two households, the classic household grid needs adaptation to encompass new family forms in all its complexity. Register data is also no solution for the lack of comparable studies as most of these registers cannot be combined in pooled international databases due to privacy regulations of most countries and the aforementioned difficulty in linking fiscal data with general population registers. Also, outcome measures need more standardisation. Even though several validated tests are used in several studies, there still is debate on which boundaries to take to identify SPC (see elsewhere in this book) or which indicators are the best to measure child and parental outcomes. We hope this book will contribute in standardizing indicators to take the longitudinal and comparative leap forward in the field of SPC.

1.4 Outline of the Book

Chapter 2, *Thompson and Turunen* is a much needed sociological and demographic perspective on shared physical custody which complements perfectly the psychological and legal scholarships about such family arrangements. The authors make a compelling analysis of the structural features that are specific of SPC families and their implications for family relationships and family dynamics. One important observation among others is that the nature of the relationship between (step)parents and (step)children, (step)siblings and (step)grandparents requires more explicit recognition than in intact families and solo families since each other's agendas and needs cross and shall be negotiated upon more frequently. Crucially related to these aspects are the transformations in the gendered division of labour and the gendered character of family life and the recursive positive loop between gender equity and shared custody. Not only more gender equal couples are more likely to adopt SPC in case of separation, but also children in alternate residence also means more gender equal work, leisure and family trajectories after separation than parents with solo custody. The chapter clearly shows how SPC has the potential to revolutionize the gender contract and concludes with a pledge to monitor the longer run implications for the conceptualization and representations of family and gender at large.

In Chapter 3, *Emery* presents an extensive overview of research from a psychological perspective. The chapter focuses on the wellbeing of children living in SPC. A first part in the chapter deals with defining SPC and brings up the question of the wide range of family forms in which children live after the break-up of their parents. Defining SPC relies on determining a minimum amount of time that children spend with their both parents. Emery puts this on at least 25% independent of how the days and nights in a month are divided among the two parental homes. Whether equal time sharing or specific schedules are more or less beneficial is currently unknown in the literature. The second part of the chapter summarizes the insights from studies that look at how children fare in SPC situations. Also here, Emery concludes that a lot of work needs to be done. There is not enough evidence yet to determine the benefit of SPC versus sole custody. Four factors appear to be of importance in the outcomes for children: logistics, parental conflict, the age of the children and their personality and mental health. The chapter concludes with a plea for larger, methodologically sound studies to further develop our insights in the effects of SPC on children's wellbeing.

Building upon the work of the Commission on European Family Law (CEFL), *Boele-Woelki* presents in Chapter 4 an overview of comparative legal work regarding parental responsibilities. In total 39 principles regarding Parental Responsibilities have been gathered by 26 legal experts. The definition of parental responsibilities is a broad one encompassing both taking care of the child's person and its property. The parental duties stretch from the birth of a child to the child reaching majority, without determining a fixed upper age limit. From the parent's perspective, not only the two biological parents are holders of the parental responsibilities. Also other persons and public bodies can be attributed parental responsibilities which could results in more than just two persons exercising these responsibilities. The (romantic) relationship or (absence of) the legal bond between the parents should have no influence in the joint execution of parental responsibilities by both parents. Parents can make agreements on the shared exercise of the responsibilities and in case of disagreement see an external authority decide about them. In these cases, alternative conflict resolution procedures should be available to parents in order to solve their disagreement. The CEFL principles are presented as a frame of reference for national legislators.

Switzerland is seeing rapid changes in family life after divorce. For the first time, *Recksiedler* and *Bernardi* present an insight in the distribution of SPC among Swiss parents. A second focus in Chapter 5 concerns the correlates of having children in SPC and the parent's health. The share of SPC arrangements in Switzerland turned out to be quite low (11%) and when looking at a 50-50 division, only 6.5% of all post-divorce families share the children in an equal way. There was an overrepresentation of higher educated parents and older children residing in the Swiss SPC families. With respect to health, the authors report that custody arrangements are neither associated with better physical health, nor with higher levels of emotional wellbeing. Economic factors like labour market attachment and financial situation turned out to be strong predictors of the parent's health situation. For gender, a surprising negative effect on SPC father's health was observed. The conclusion therefore leads to the observation that parents in SPC are neither healthier, nor happier. The high labour market attachment and the lower educational level might explain these results, as well as the overall burden of combining work and family life among the Swiss forerunners in SPC.

Is the father-child relationship quality related to the living arrangement of the children? That is the central research question in Chapter 6. *Vrolijk* and *Keizer* consider self-selection as an important factor that drives previous results in this domain. By controlling for interparental conflict before the divorce and SES, the potential self-selecting influences on the linkage between living arrangement and the quality of the father-child relationship are strongly reduced. As mediating factors, the authors take father involvement and the co-parental relationship into account. The results show that living in SPC indeed has a positive effect on the father-child relationship (even though the amount of time is unrelated to this link). The effect was mediated by parental involvement and (to a lesser degree) by the co-parental relationship. The sex of the child also played a role in that the father-son relationship was more easily influenced in SPC than the father-daughter one. The results are strengthened by the fact that the Divorce in Flanders multi-actor data allowed to perform the analyses both from the father's and from the child's perspective. The two perspectives were not always in accordance with each other but the use of both perspectives allowed to explore the complexity of the father-child relationship, and its link with children's living arrangements, to a greater extent.

Chapter 7, by *Claessens and Mortelmans* taps into pre- and post-separation life courses of men and women formerly living as a nuclear family with common children and specifically focuses on three postseparation dynamics affecting changes in the type of children's custody arrangements: financial position, labour force participation and repartnering. One of the most interesting gendered effects is that produced by union dynamics on custody choices. While repartnering fathers tend to drop out of SPC, repartnering mothers join in the SPC group. While apparently different, these are movements of the same kind because for both men and women repartnering translates in less time with their own biological children, fathers because the shift from SPC to sparser visiting rights and mothers because they move out of lone parenthood and sole custody towards SPC. The authors optimistically conclude that their results show some evidence of a ideational shift towards more egalitarian parenting preferences given that higher income from men and higher labour force participation for women, indicator of higher bargaining power, are not any longer predictive of higher shares of custody but rather of SPC.

Merla, Dedonder, Nobels and Murru in Chapter 8 address the underexplored question of the sense of home for children experiencing shared custody arrangements. Post-divorce arrangements where children alternate between two distinct family dwellings challenge the nuclear family ideal of home and raise questions about whether the sense of belonging and identity of such children is challenged by such complex family configurations. The authors discuss the theoretical impetus underlying such question and develop a parsimonious survey instrument, The Sense of Home Instrument (SOHI), to capture material and behavioural-relational dimensions of children' sense of home, by measuring the level of material comfort, the quality of parent-child relations, the level of conflict between ex-partners, and the continuity of communication across households. On the basis of survey data from Belgium, they then illustrate its validity and propose it as a useful tool to test new hypotheses on the consequences of divorce and separation for children.

The socioeconomic gradient in SPC arrangements is the focus of Chapter 9. The chapter uses two repeated cross section datasets from the Spanish and the Swedish *Health Behavior of School Children* (HBSC) by the World Health Organisation. The paper compares the changes in socioeconomic gradient of SPC over time and across welfare states. *Garriga, Bernardi and Turunen* test two competing hypotheses. First, the *diffusion hypothesis* that states that SPC will spread among all social strata given the changes in family law incrementally favouring the view that SPC is the preferred arrangement for children to grow up after parental separation. Second, the *diverging destinies hypothesis* that states that union dissolutions are increasingly socially stratified, with higher strata separating to a lesser degree than lower classes. Since SPC arrangements are more expensive than sole custody, such social difference in the likelihood to separate might make SPC even more selective among higher social classes who can afford it. The authors test both hypotheses while considering also the difference between former cohabiters versus married couples as well as the influence of the welfare state in Spain and in Sweden. The results show that the diffusion hypothesis seems to correspond to the Spanish trends in SPC while in Sweden is rather the diverging destinies hypothesis, with little or no diffusion across social strata across time, that is closer to the data. The authors conclude that the role of legal institutions regulating SPC might have been so far underestimated in social research.

In Chapter 10, by *Poortman* the main focus is on the role of the interplay between geographical distance between parents' home, the frequency of home-commuting and the parent child contact on a variety of children outcomes: psychological wellbeing, social integration and educational performance. Drawing on the original Dutch data from the New Families in the Netherlands Survey, the author finds differential effects of the interaction of various aspects of post separation arrangements not only depending of the outcome but also on the kind of interaction between such aspects. For instance, a frequent parent child contact (either because of SPC or because of frequent father visitations) improve the psychological wellbeing of children only in cases in which the commuting time and frequency between parents' home is lower, calling for a more nuanced understanding of what arrangements are more or less disruptive for children of separation and divorce. Shared physical custody and frequent commutes may be positive for children if parents live sufficiently close to each other.

The contribution by *Hachet,* in Chapter 11 analyses the negotiation process leading to shared physical custody arrangements in France around the 2002 law that begins to regulate SPC in the country. Making use of the exceptional data of the French National Funds for Family Allowances data, he shows that the large majority of couples separating agree on SPC and do not need any external intervention while in one third of the cases either SPC issues from a court decision or it is the result of a mediation operated by third parties like the children themselves, the judges or the family mediators. The qualitative analyses of 55 in-depth interviews of parents who equally share their children's custody result in a fine picture of who, for what reasons request shared physical custody in cases of disagreement and under which conditions. Even more interestingly, the Chapter discusses the majority of "obvious agreements", which seem to be related to the history of the relationship (e.g the pre-separation division of tasks within the couple) and of its breakup (e.g. having initiated separation makes the responsible partner more vulnerable and likely to accept the other's requests).

Chapter 12 by *Darwiche, Eira Nunes, El Ghaziri, Imesch* and *Bessero* is based on a developmental psychological approach to co-parenting. If coparenting is understood as the way in which parents support and undermines each other in relation to their parental duties, shared physical custody gives parents an opportunity to coparent their children after parental separation. In a first part of the Chapter, the authors identify a limited number of intervention programs that explicitly include SPC either as topic of discussion during the treatment or as an outcome of it. The second part of the Chapter illustrates, through a Swiss case study, the way in which SPC emerges during a therapy of a separating couple. The clinical case analysis shows that severe personal distress and acute suffering of the separating parents can coexist with effective coparenting. The authors conclude with a strong practice-oriented message in favour for more training of professional family therapists in matters related to legal decisions and child custody arrangements and for more concerted action between married and divorced couples therapists. Such suggestions seem crucial to support parents in raising their children in the contemporary context of complexification and fluidity of family arrangements.

Chapter 13, *Walper, Entleitner-Phleps and Langmeyer* aims at defining the prevalence and predictors of SPC in Germany, where this living arrangement is still "a rare exception" (5% in 50–50% arrangements and 10% in 30–70% arrangements), suggesting once more that a gendered division of labour within couple time has consequences for children custody after separation and divorce. Regression analyses on cross-sectional data indicate that mother's higher education and employment status as well as parents' short residential distance and good cooperation associate strongly with SPC when compared to sole custody. Less intuitively the level of conflict among SPC parents seems to be higher, which the authors explain by the need for more frequent interaction or by the fact that anticipating conflict on other issues these parents try to minimize by having an equal share of time with the children. The chapter ends with a call for more systematic longitudinal data collection on changing families arrangements.

In Chapter 14, *Hakovirta and Skinner* address the adaptation of child maintenance policies to the diffusion of SPC in an international comparative perspective. Adopting the model family approach, the study draws on original vignette data collected from topic experts in thirteen countries in 2017. The experts had to calculate the child maintenance due by parents depending on whether they have a 50% SPC arrangements versus a situation in which one parent has usual visiting rights and the other sole custody. Despite that countries vary according to what is the locus of formal decision about child maintenance (an administrative agency, the court, or an hybrid form of the two), no relation was found between such differences and the differences in maintenance under similar custody conditions. The result of this fine-grained comparison shows that there is no international standard practice in dealing with SPC maintenance policies, with most countries providing a partial reduction in the amount child maintenance if custody is shared equally, one third requiring no obligation to maintenance even in case of different parental incomes, and only two countries not offering any reduction of maintenance duties despite equal custody time. The study reveals the need for further collaborative investigations on the matter implying sociologists, public policy and legal scholars and well as professionals.

References

Amato, P. R. (2000). The consequences of divorce for adults and children. *Journal of Marriage and Family, 62*(4), 1269–1287. https://doi.org/10.1111/j.1741-3737.2000.01269.x.

Amato, P. R. (2010). Research on divorce: Continuing trends and new developments. *Journal of Marriage and Family, 72*(3), 650–666. https://doi.org/10.1111/j.1741-3737.2010.00723.x.

Amato, P. R., & Cheadle, J. (2005). The long reach of divorce: Divorce and child well-being across three generations. *Journal of Marriage and Family, 67*(1), 191–206. https://doi.org/10.1111/j.0022-2445.2005.00014.x.

Bartova, A., & Keizer, R. (2020). How well do European child-related leave policies support the caring role of fathers? In R. Nieuwenhuis & W. van Lancker (Eds.), *Handbook of family policy* (pp. in press). Palgrave.

Bastaits, K., & Mortelmans, D. (2016). Parenting as mediator between post-divorce family structure and children's well-being. *Journal of Child and Family Studies, 25*(7), 2178–2188. https://doi.org/10.1007/s10826-016-0395-8.

Bastaits, K., & Pasteels, I. (2019). Is joint physical custody in the best interests of the child? Parent–child relationships and custodial arrangements. *Journal of Social and Personal Relationships, 36*(11–12), 3752–3772. https://doi.org/10.1177/0265407519838071.

Bastaits, K., Pasteels, I., & Mortelmans, D. (2018). How do post-divorce paternal and maternal family trajectories relate to adolescents' subjective well-being? *Journal of Adolescence, 64*, 98–108. https://doi.org/10.1016/j.adolescence.2018.02.005.

Baude, A., Pearson, J., & Drapeau, S. (2016). Child adjustment in joint physical custody versus sole custody: A meta-analytic review. *Journal of Divorce & Remarriage, 57*(5), 338–360. https://doi.org/10.1080/10502556.2016.1185203.

Baude, A., Drapeau, S., Lachance, V., & Ivers, H. (2019). Adjustment of children in joint custody and associated variables: A systematic review. *Journal of Child Custody, 16*(4), 313–338. https://doi.org/10.1080/15379418.2019.1691106.

Bauserman, R. (2012). A meta-analysis of parental satisfaction, adjustment, and conflict in joint custody and sole custody following divorce. *Journal of Divorce & Remarriage, 53*(6), 464–488. https://doi.org/10.1080/10502556.2012.682901.

Bergström, M., Fransson, E., Hjern, A., Köhler, L., & Wallby, T. (2014). Mental health in Swedish children living in joint physical custody and their parents' life satisfaction: A cross-sectional study. *Scandinavian Journal of Psychology, 55*(5), 433–439. https://doi.org/10.1111/sjop.12148.

Bernardi, L., & Mortelmans, D. (Eds.). (2018). *Lone parenthood in the life course*. Springer. https://doi.org/10.1007/978-3-319-63295-7

Bjarnason, T., & Arnarsson, A. (2011). Joint physical custody and communication with parents: A cross-national Study of children in 36 Western countries. *Journal of Comparative Family Studies, 42*(6). https://doi.org/10.2307/41604494.

Braver, S. L., & Votruba, A. M. (2018). Does joint physical custody "cause" children's better outcomes? *Journal of Divorce & Remarriage, 59*(5), 452–468. https://doi.org/10.1080/10502556.2018.1454203.

Carlsund, Å., Eriksson, U., Löfstedt, P., & Sellström, E. (2012). Risk behaviour in Swedish adolescents: Is shared physical custody after divorce a risk or a protective factor? *European Journal of Public Health, 23*(1), 3–8. https://doi.org/10.1093/eurpub/cks011.

Cashmore, J., Parkinson, P., Weston, R., Patulny, R., Redmond, G., Qu, L., Baxter, J., Rajkovic, M., Sitek, T., & Katz, I. (2010). *Shared care parenting arrangements since the 2006 family law reforms: Report to the Australian government attorney-general's department*. Social Policy Research Centre, University of New South Wales. https://www.arts.unsw.edu.au/sites/default/files/documents/2_AG_Shared_Care.pdf

Cheadle, J. E., Amato, P. R., & King, V. (2010). Patterns of nonresident father contact. *Demography, 47*(1), 205–225. https://doi.org/10.1353/dem.0.0084.

Cummings, E. M., & Davies, P. T. (2010). *Marital conflict and children: An emotional security perspective*. New York: Guilford Press.

Fabricius, W. V., & Luecken, L. J. (2007). Postdivorce living arrangements, parent conflict, and long-term physical health correlates for children of divorce. *Journal of Family Psychology, 21*(2), 195–205. https://doi.org/10.1037/0893-3200.21.2.195.

Fransson, E., Turunen, J., Hjern, A., Ostberg, V., & Bergstrom, M. (2016). Psychological complaints among children in joint physical custody and other family types: Considering parental factors. *Scandinavian Journal of Public Health, 44*(2), 177–183. https://doi.org/10.1177/1403494815614463.

Garriga, A., & Bernardi, L. (2019). Custody arrangements and social inequalities among children. *Revue des politiques sociales et familiales, 131–132*, 207–221.

Goldscheider, F. K., Bernhardt, E., & Lappegård, T. (2015). The gender revolution: A framework for understanding changing family and demographic behavior. *Population and Development Review, 41*(2), 207–239. https://doi.org/10.1111/j.1728-4457.2015.00045.x.

Goode, W. J. (1962). Marital satisfaction and instability. A cross-cultural class analysis of divorce rates. In R. Bendix & S. M. Lipset (Eds.), *Class, status, and power. Social stratification in comparative perspective* (pp. 377–387). New York: The Free Press.

Goode, W. J. (1963). *World revolution and family patterns*. New York: Free Press Glencoe.

Goubau, D. (2009). L'évolution de la place de l'enfant au sein du droit de la famille séparée au Canada. In FAJEF & AIFI (Eds.), *Du droit de l'enfant à l'intérêt de la famille séparée* (pp. 1–20). Toronto: Éditions Yvon Blais.

Guidubaldi, J., & Perry, J. D. (1985). Divorce and mental health sequelae for children: A two-year follow-up of a nationwide sample. *Journal of the American Academy of Child Psychiatry, 24*(5), 531–537.

Härkönen, J., Bernardi, F., & Boertien, D. (2017). Family dynamics and child outcomes: An overview of research and open questions [article]. *European Journal of Population, 33*(2), 163–184. https://doi.org/10.1007/s10680-017-9424-6.

Harris-Short, S. (2010). Resisting the march towards 50/50 shared residence: Rights, welfare and equality in post-separation families. *Journal of Social Welfare and Family Law, 32*(3), 257–274. https://doi.org/10.1080/09649069.2010.520519.

Hochschild, A., & Machung, A. (1989). *The second shift: Working families and the revolution at home*. New York: Penguin.

Hook, J. L. (2016). Care in context: Men's unpaid work in 20 countries, 1965–2003. *American Sociological Review, 71*(4), 639–660. https://doi.org/10.1177/000312240607100406.

Klünder, N., & Meier-Gräwe, U. (2018). Caring, Cooking, Cleaning – repräsentative Zeitverwendungsmuster von Eltern in Paarbeziehungen. *Zeitschrift fur Familienforschung, 30* (1), 9–29. https://doi.org/10.3224/zff.v30i1.02.

Kruk, E. (2012). Arguments for an equal parental responsibility presumption in contested child custody. *The American Journal of Family Therapy, 40*(1), 33–55. https://doi.org/10.1080/01926187.2011.575344.

Kruyfhooft, M., & Mortelmans, D. (2011). Gezin en arbeid in je eentje: combinatiestrategieën van alleenstaande moeders en vaders. *Tijdschrift voor arbeidsvraagstukken, 27*(4), 487–506.

Lamb, M. E., & Kelly, J. B. (2001). Using the empirical literatureto guide the development of parenting plans for young children. *Family Court Review, 39*(4), 365–371. https://doi.org/10.1111/j.174-1617.2001.tb00618.x.

Maccoby, E. E., Buchanan, C. M., Mnookin, R. H., & Dornbusch, S. M. (1993). Postdivorce roles of mothers and fathers in the lives of their children. *Journal of Family Psychology, 7*(1), 24–38. https://doi.org/10.1037/0893-3200.7.1.24.

Main, M., Hesse, E., & Hesse, S. (2011). Attachment theory and research. Overview with suggested aplications to child custody. *Family Court Review, 49*(3), 426–463. https://doi.org/10.1111/j.1744-1617.2011.01383.x.

Markham, M. S., & Coleman, M. (2012). The good, the bad, and the ugly: Divorced mothers' experiences with coparenting. *Family Relations, 61*(4), 586–600. https://doi.org/10.1111/j.1741-3729.2012.00718.x.

Meyer, D. R., Cancian, M., & Cook, S. T. (2017). The growth in shared custody in the United States: Patterns and implications. *Family Court Review, 55*(4), 500–512. https://doi.org/10.1111/fcre.12300.

Nielsen, L. (2014a). Parenting plans for infants, toddlers, and preschoolers: Research and issues. *Journal of Divorce & Remarriage, 55*(4), 315–333. https://doi.org/10.1080/10502556.2014.901857.

Nielsen, L. (2014b). Shared physical custody: Summary of 40 studies on outcomes for children. *Journal of Divorce & Remarriage, 55*(8), 613–635. https://doi.org/10.1080/10502556.2014.965578.

Nielsen, L. (2014c). Woozles: Their role in custody law reform, parenting plans, and family court. *Psychology, Public Policy, and Law, 20*(2), 164–180. https://doi.org/10.1037/law0000004.

Nielsen, L. (2015). Shared physical custody: Does it benefit most children. *Journal of the American Academy of Matrimonial Lawyers, 28*, 79–138.

Nielsen, L. (2017). Re-examining the research on parental conflict, coparenting, and custody arrangements. *Psychology, Public Policy, and Law, 23*(2), 211–231. https://doi.org/10.1037/law0000109.

Nielsen, L. (2018a). Joint versus sole physical custody: Children's outcomes independent of parent–child relationships, income, and conflict in 60 studies. *Journal of Divorce & Remarriage, 59*(4), 247–281. https://doi.org/10.1080/10502556.2018.1454204.

Nielsen, L. (2018b). Joint versus sole physical custody: Outcomes for children independent of family income or parental conflict. *Journal of Child Custody, 15*(1), 35–54. https://doi.org/10.1080/15379418.2017.1422414.

Poortman, A.-R. (2018). Postdivorce parent–child contact and child well-being: The importance of predivorce parental involvement. *Journal of Marriage and Family, 80*(3), 671–683. https://doi.org/10.1111/jomf.12474.

Schoppe-Sullivan, S. J., & Fagan, J. (2020). The evolution of fathering research in the 21st century: Persistent challenges, new directions. *Journal of Marriage and Family, 82*(1), 175–197. https://doi.org/10.1111/jomf.12645.

Smyth, B. M. (2017). Special issue on shared-time parenting after separation. *Family Court Review, 55*(4), 494–499. https://doi.org/10.1111/fcre.12299.

Sobolewski, J. M., & Amato, P. R. (2007). Parents' discord and divorce, parent-child relationships and subjective well-being in early adulthood: Is feeling close to two parents always better than feeling close to one? *Social Forces, 85*(3), 1105–1124. https://doi.org/10.1353/sof.2007.0056.

Sodermans, A. K., Matthijs, K., & Swicegood, G. (2013). Characteristics of joint physical custody families in Flanders [Article]. *Demographic Research, 28*, 821–848, Article 29. https://doi.org/10.4054/DemRes.2013.28.29

Sodermans, A. K., Botterman, S., Havermans, N., & Matthijs, K. (2015). Involved fathers, liberated mothers? Joint physical custody and the subjective well-being of divorced parents. *Social Indicators Research, 122*(1), 257–277. https://doi.org/10.1007/s11205-014-0676-9.

Solomon, J., & George, C. (1999). The effects on attachment of overnight visitation on divorced and separated families: A longitudinal follow up. In J. Solomon & C. George (Eds.), *Attachment disorganization in atypical populations* (pp. 243–264). New York: Guilford Press.

Spruijt, E., & Duindam, V. (2002). Was there an increase in caring fatherhood in the 1990s? Two Dutch longitudinal studies. *Social Behavior and Personality: An International Journal, 30*(7), 683–695. https://doi.org/10.2224/sbp.2002.30.7.683.

Spruijt, E., de Goede, M., & Vandervalk, I. (2004). Frequency of contact with nonresident fathers and adolescent well-being: A longitudinal analysis. *Journal of Divorce & Remarriage, 40*(3–4), 77–90. https://doi.org/10.1300/J087v40n03_05.

Steinbach, A. (2019). Children's and parents' well-being in joint physical custody: A literature review. *Family Process, 58*(2), 353–369. https://doi.org/10.1111/famp.12372.

Steinbach, A., Augustijn, L., & Corkadi, G. (2020). Joint physical custody and adolescents' life satisfaction in 37 North American and European countries. *Family Process*. https://doi.org/10.1111/famp.12536.

Thevenon, O. (2011). Family policies in OECD countries: A comparative analysis. *Popululation and Development Review, 37*(1), 57–87. https://doi.org/10.1111/j.1728-4457.2011.00390.x.

Turunen, J. (2017). Shared physical custody and children's experience of stress. *Journal of Divorce & Remarriage, 58*(5), 371–392. https://doi.org/10.1080/10502556.2017.1325648.

van der Heijden, F., Poortman, A.-R., & van der Lippe, T. (2016). Children's postdivorce residence arrangements and parental experienced time pressure. *Journal of Marriage and Family, 78*(2), 468–481. https://doi.org/10.1111/jomf.12283.

van der Wiel, R., Mulder, C. H., & de Valk, H. A. G. (2020). From living apart to living together: Do children born before the current partnership matter? *Comparative Population Studies, 45*, 115–142. https://doi.org/10.12765/CPoS-2020-07en.

Warshak, R. A. (2018). Night shifts: Revisiting blanket restrictions on children's overnights with separated parents. *Journal of Divorce & Remarriage, 59*(4), 282–323. https://doi.org/10.1080/10502556.2018.1454193.

Westphal, S. K., Poortman, A.-R., & van der Lippe, T. (2014). Non-resident father-child contact across divorce cohorts: The role of father involvement during marriage. *European Sociological Review, 30*(4), 444–456. https://doi.org/10.1093/esr/jcu050.

Laura Bernardi is Full Professor of Life Course Demography and Sociology at the University of Lausanne and President of the Social Sciences and Humanities Division of the Swiss National Research Foundation. She is also Associate Editor and former co-Editor in Chief of the journal Advances in Life Course Research and of the Springer book series Life Course and Social Policies. Her research interests are in the field of life course sociology and family demography. Her publications range from the cultural determinants of fertility and family behaviours, the role of social influence on fertility and family transitions to spillover and crossover processes in the life course and their effects on wellbeing. She has extensively published in a wide range of peer-reviewed articles in international journals, in the field of demography, sociology and gender, contributed several chapters in collective volumes and has co-edited the books Lone parenthood in the Life Course (Springer); Situating Children of Migrants (Springer); The Demography of Europe (Springer).

Dimitri Mortelmans is Full Professor of Sociology at the Faculty of Political and Social Sciences of the University of Antwerp, Belgium. He is head of the Centre for Population, Family, and Health (CPFH). His research concentrates on family sociology and sociology of labour. He has published on divorce, new constituted families, gendered labour careers and work–life balance. He is also the main author of the Step in Statistics book series of which six volumes have been published (in Dutch). On qualitative methodology, he published the Handbook of Qualitative Research Methods and Qualitative Analysis with NVivo. In demography, he (co-)edited Changing Family Dynamics and Demographic Evolution. The Family Kaleidoscope (Edward Elgar), Lone parenthood in the Life Course (Springer) and Divorce in Europe (Springer).

Part I
Cross-Disciplinary Views

2

Families with Shared Custody: Structural Features

Elizabeth Thomson and Jani Turunen

Abstract In this chapter, we identify structural features of families with shared physical custody that differ from those of nuclear families or those of families where one parent has sole physical custody, and discuss the implications for family and kin relationships. We pay particular attention to the ways in which shared physical custody alters the gendered nature of parenting and kinship. We argue that the structural features of shared physical custody create distinct contexts for parent-child and sibling relationships and produce differences in shared understandings of obligations between family members. The unique context for relationships and obligations together constitute a new family form. Our analysis generates an agenda for future research on the nature and consequences of shared physical custody.

Keywords Shared physical custody · Divorce · Gender · Stepfamily · Kinship

Shared physical custody, where children live alternately in their mother's and father's homes[1], produces a new family form (Melli and Brown 2008). In contrast

[1]Occasionally children stay in one home while their parents move in and out; such arrangements usually occur only immediately after separation until each parent has a stable residence (Masardo 2009).

E. Thomson (✉)
Stockholm University Demography Unit (SUDA), Stockholm University, Stockholm, Sweden

Center for Demography and Ecology, University of Wisconsin-Madison, Madison, WI, USA
e-mail: elizabeth.thomson@sociology.su.se

J. Turunen
Department of Social Work, School of Social Sciences, Södertörn University, Huddinge, Sweden

Stockholm University Demography Unit (SUDA), Stockholm University, Stockholm, Sweden

Centre for Research on Child and Adolescent Mental Health, Karlstad University, Karlstad, Sweden
e-mail: jani.turunen@sh.se

to nuclear families, parents live apart; in contrast to families with sole physical custody, each parent is both resident and non-resident at different times. In this chapter, we identify structural features of families with shared physical custody that differ from those of nuclear families or those of families where one parent has sole physical custody, and discuss the implications for family and kin relationships. Our analysis generates an agenda for future research on the nature and consequences of shared physical custody.

The context for the emerging family form produced by shared physical custody is the conjugal kinship system in which parents and minor children typically live in a their own household separate from extended kin; the parents' relationship is characterized by emotional as well as economic bonds; and obligations to conjugal family members are expected to be stronger than those to more distant kin (Parsons 1943). In this system, the boundaries of the conjugal family and the nuclear household are identical, and family relationships are constructed and maintained within a fixed space. Coresidence also means that interactions with extended kin usually occur at the same time for all family members and kin support is provided to family members as a group through their common household and economy.

In a conjugal family system, separated parents retain responsibilities to their children and children retain rights to both parents' resources and care.[2] The parent-child relationships remain primary, in comparison to relationships with extended kin. The establishment of two households, however, changes the dynamics of the relationship between the two parents, the relationships between each parent and the children, and contact and exchange with extended kin. Children rarely interact with both parents or with both sets of extended kin at the same time and place. They experience their relationship with each parent and with each parent's extended kin in a different time and place. Until the recent past, the new maternal household was privileged over the new paternal household as the locus for family and kin relationships, i.e., children lived primarily with their mothers and periodically visited their fathers and his kin. When separated parents share physical custody, neither parent's household is primary.

We begin our analysis below with this transformation in the gendered character of household and family life. We then analyze the structural features of family living that are uniquely produced by shared physical custody (in contrast to nuclear families and sole physical custody), and how they might influence relationships among family members. We further examine the implications of such arrangements for parents' re-partnering, step-family relationships, and kinship. We cite what scarce evidence exists for our theoretical speculations, noting here that such evidence is currently available only for a limited number of societal contexts.

---

[2]This is not to say that parents always enact those responsibilities and rights, but it is rare that the parent-child relationship is terminated by law.

2.1 Transformations in the Gendered Division of Labor

The most noticeable feature of families with shared physical custody is the parents' division of labor. Several scholars have argued that the second stage of the gender revolution requires fathers to take on the same types of responsibility as mothers, i.e., be responsible for 24/7 care and parenting (Bianchi et al. 2012; DeRose et al. 2019). Shared physical custody demands that level of commitment from fathers.

It is not surprising, then, that shared physical custody is most common in Sweden (Bjarnason and Arnarsson 2011), where maternal employment (Oláh and Bernhardt 2008) and men's family work (Ferrarini and Duvander 2010) have also been in the forefront. Gender-egalitarian norms are strongest in Sweden and more than in other countries emphasize parents' equal responsibility for earning and caring (Edlund and Öun 2016). Sweden was the first country to allow fathers and mothers to equally share parental leave (Duvander and Lammi-Taskula 2011) and fathers' responsibilities for child care in Sweden are viewed as critical for making shared physical custody work (Harris-Short 2011).

Gender arrangements are also associated at the micro-level with shared physical custody. The transition from parents and children living together to children living alternatively with each parent is facilitated when couples have achieved relatively high levels of gender equality in paid work and childrearing before separation. Shared physical custody is more likely when the mother has been working full-time before separation (Bonnet et al. 2017; Cancian et al. 2014; Juby et al. 2005; Pelletier 2016; Poortman and van Gaalen 2017; Smyth et al. 2004), even though it also depends to a considerable extent on fathers' economic contributions (Cashmore et al. 2010; Le Bourdais et al. 2002; Maccoby and Mnookin 1992). Fathers with shared physical custody are more likely to have been engaged in child care and family work and to have expressed more enjoyment of parenting prior to separation compared to fathers without physical custody (Juby et al. 2005; Kitteröd and Wiik 2017; Masardo 2009; Pelletier 2016). Couples with shared physical custody place high value on each parent's identity as both earner and carer (Bakker and Karsten 2013).

Regardless of a couple's ideologies, preferences and arrangements prior to separation, shared physical custody in and of itself imposes a high degree of gender equality. In France, for example, mother's labor force participation is greater when separated parents share physical custody of their children, becoming more similar to that of fathers (Bonnet et al. 2017). Shared physical custody also has implications for the types of work that mothers and fathers do. Mothers are typically expected to require flexibility in their employment conditions in order to care for children; fathers are not. Thus, fathers with shared physical custody may need to change jobs or occupations or may be viewed as problem employees when they take full responsibility for their children (Eriksson 2018). Parents with shared physical custody are more likely than parents without physical custody but less likely than parents with sole physical custody to report that their work interferes with family responsibility (Van den Eynde and Mortelmans 2017). Separated mothers remain more likely to report such conflicts than separated fathers, however, regardless of the residential arrangement.

Because few coresident couples achieve full equality in parenting, shared physical custody provides greater opportunities and demands for father-child interaction than before separation and certainly more than for nonresident fathers. Several studies have demonstrated that children who live alternately with each parent have closer relationships with their fathers than those living primarily with their mothers (Bastaits and Mortelmans 2016; Bastaits et al. 2012; Cashmore et al. 2010; Melli and Brown 2008; Sodermans et al. 2015; Spruijt and Duindam 2010; Vanassche et al. 2013). All of this evidence is cross-sectional and much of the association could result from the selection (as noted above) of the most engaged fathers into sharing physical custody. The potential effect of shared physical custody on father-child relationships therefore remains to some extent theoretical.

Shared physical custody should also generate greater quality between mothers and fathers in leisure, given that each parent has extended periods of time without childcare responsibilities. Limited evidence shows that mothers who share physical custody of their children report more social activities than mothers with sole physical custody; although no such differences are reported for fathers, the result is greater equality for parents who share physical custody in comparison to those who don't (Botterman et al. 2015; Sodermans et al. 2015).

Overall, then, the family and household lives of parents who share physical custody are much more similar than are those of separated parents who do not, and are likely more similar than parents in nuclear households. In the latter case, there are possibilities to divide earning and caring in unequal ways that are not available to parents whose children live alternately with each of them. As discussed in later sections, the gender transformation in households where children live part but not all of the time also has implications for the gendered character of stepfamilies and relationships with extended kin.

2.2 Household Structure and Family Relationships

The distinction between weekday and weekend/vacation living is critical to the new family form produced by shared physical custody.[3] A weekend parent has periods of 24-hour responsibility, but may not have to juggle the simultaneous demands of child care and work. It is possible for children to keep their clothing and other necessities in one place, packing a travel bag for visits to the other parent. When both parents have children during the weekday, each must juggle childcare with other

[3]Some scholars limit the definition of shared physical custody to equal amounts of time in each home, while others include families where children live as little as 25% with one parent, and/or not during the week (e.g., Bakker and Mulder 2013; Meyer et al. 2017). The emerging definition for research purposes is at least 35%, a level that cannot be achieved with only weekend or vacation visits.

activities at least some of the time and children must have everything they need in both homes. These structural features of daily life appear to be reflected in family members' perceptions of where the children live; members of families in which children live alternately with each parent view the children as living with both parents; members of families with visiting arrangements are more likely to identify the children's home as that of the parent with sole physical custody (Bakker and Mulder 2013; Sodermans et al. 2014).

A second structural element of shared physical custody is the "cycle of care" (Steinbach 2018:3), how often children move back and forth. The most common cycle in studies to date is weekly (Bakker and Karsten 2013; Berman 2015; Sodermans et al. 2014). One study found that transitions between homes were most likely to occur in conjunction with the weekend (Sodermans et al. 2014). Thus, children have a stable home-to-school commute during any given week and transfers between homes occurs at breaks in the school and work week. In comparison with families where weekends are typically visiting time with one of the parents, both parents have leisure and work days with children in the home.

The nature of parents' and children's time together is fundamentally different in families where children commute between homes than where they live with both parents in the same home or primarily with one parent. In comparison to a two-parent coresidential family, one parent is always there during the time in residence, engaged in everything from mealtime to bedtime, from comfort to discipline, in the same way as for parents with sole physical custody. Each parent-child relationship is constructed more directly, rather than one parent mediating the child's relationship with the other, giving children greater autonomy and bargaining power (Berman 2015). Full-time engagement may increase feelings of closeness with parents, especially fathers who would otherwise have only visits with their children (Fransson et al. 2018). Children may even spend *more* time with each parent than do children whose parents live together (Berman 2015). On the other hand, children living alternately with each parent may be exposed to more conflict associated with more frequent contact of the two separated parents (Drapeau et al. 2017).

The sibling experience is also likely to be altered by shared physical custody. When separated parents have more than one child, the siblings generally commute together; residential arrangements where siblings live full-time with different parents are rare (Berman 2015; Meyer et al. 2017). Thus, time with a sibling will not differ across household arrangements. With shared physical custody, however, the siblings share more of daily life with each other than they do with either parent (Winther et al. 2015). Thus, the sibling relationship may gain in importance relative to the parent-child relationships (Berman 2015).

The daily lives of parents with shared physical custody are dramatically different from those of nuclear family parents, parents with sole physical custody, or parents without physical custody. Parents with shared physical custody report their lives as divided into two parts, one in which they are intensely engaged with caring for children and less engaged in work, and the other in which they work long hours with freedom from the scheduling constraints of child care (Bakker and Karsten 2013; Berman 2015). This division also produces a stronger demarcation between family and work, perhaps contributing to overall balance in everyday life. Parents with shared physical custody experience less time pressure than parents with sole physical custody, though more than parents without physical custody (Van der Heijden et al. 2016).

It goes almost without saying that separated parents' relationship with each other must be of a different character than when both rather than one or the other has primary responsibility for children. The structure of shared physical custody increases the number of conditions to negotiate and the frequency of contact between separated parents. Elements of cooperation as well as conflict will likely be greater than for parents where one has physical custody and the other does not, though cooperation would likely be less than for a nuclear family couple. Parents who do not have a sufficiently cooperative relationship to communicate and coordinate the regular exchange and different living conditions for children are less likely to share physical custody (Pelletier 2016). Most studies find that parents with shared physical custody have less conflict than those where only one parent has physical custody (Maccoby and Mnookin 1992; Pelletier 2016; Spruijt and Duindam 2010; Sodermans et al. 2013; Turunen 2017). The evidence here is, however, cross-sectional, measured after the union dissolution, and could therefore be due entirely to the positive effect of cooperation on sharing physical custody. When shared physical custody is encouraged by a court or by legislation, more high conflict couples are likely to end up with the arrangement (Sodermans et al. 2013). Whether shared physical custody might improve or worsen the separated couple's relationship is an open question.

2.3 Household and Family Stability

A key dimension of family life after parental separation is the stability of children's households. Geographic constraints mean that shared physical custody could increase stability by reducing each parent's ability to move after separation. A child alternating between homes may therefore be less likely to experience residential moves, school changes and other forms of spatial instability compared to a child living with one or the other parent. A recent study in France found that mothers with sole physical custody were more likely than those with shared physical custody to remain in the couple's home, but that when the mother moved, the distance was less for those with shared than for those with sole physical custody (Ferrari et al. 2019). Later residential stability might still, however, favor families with shared physical custody.

The economic and organizational demands of shared physical custody may in themselves produce an element of instability, i.e., children or parents decide it takes too much time and effort to sustain. A considerable share of children who live alternately with each parent eventually live only with their mother (Cloutier and Jacques 1997; Kline et al. 1989; Maccoby and Mnookin 1992; Pearson and Thoennes 1990; Pelletier 2016; Smyth et al. 2008; but see Berger et al.

2008). Important to consider, however, is the fact that the maternal household remains a stable part of the child's life.

Household instability is also a function of who moves in or out. Parental separation is often the first in a series of family changes experienced by children, often followed by entering a stepfamily and sometimes by the birth of half-siblings (Andersson et al. 2017; Thomson et al. 2014). It is not clear whether shared physical custody is likely to alter the stability of children's households in comparison to maternal or paternal physical custody. Resident children may reduce opportunities for the separated parent to find a new partner, and/or increase the costs for a new couple to live together (Ivanova et al. 2013). Thus, it is not surprising that mothers with shared physical custody are more likely to re-partner than mothers with sole physical custody, while fathers with shared physical custody are less likely to re-partner than fathers without physical custody (Bakker and Mulder 2013; Juby et al. 2005; Schnor et al. 2017). Chances for children to acquire a step-parent would therefore not necessarily change with shared physical custody, but the children would be more likely to acquire a step-father and less likely to acquire a step-mother, compared to children whose mother has sole physical custody. Children's coresidence could increase the costs of childbearing in stepfamilies, but evidence for an association between children's coresidence and stepfamily births is mixed (Vanassche et al. 2015; Vikat et al. 2004).

We might expect shared physical custody to cement the child's relationship with each parent, and therefore minimize any changes associated with a parent's re-partnering or births of younger half-siblings. When mothers have sole physical custody, father-child relationships appear to be weakened when the father re-partners or has children in a new partnership (Cooksey and Craig 1998; McGene and King 2012; Seltzer 1991; Swiss and Le Bourdais 2009). Findings are mixed with respect to re-partnering of mothers with sole physical custody (Berger et al. 2012; McGene and King 2012; Seltzer and Bianchi 1988; Seltzer et al. 1989).[4] Poortman and van Gaalen (2017) reported that father's re-partnering was associated with a shift from shared to maternal physical custody, but mother's re-partnering had no parallel effect, suggesting that even when physical custody is shared, the maternal household may be somewhat privileged.

Because coresidence is a critical element in the establishment of family ties, the roles of step-mother and step-father are transformed by shared physical custody. Both step-mothers and step-fathers will be expected to provide material support to the step-children who live with them a substantial part of the time (Ganong et al. 1995; Maclean et al. 2016). Children living alternately with each parent will also be more likely to live with their father's step-children than if they were living only with their mother. And if their step-father shares physical custody of his children, they share a household at least some of the time with another set of step-siblings. With the

[4]Juby et al. (2007) report little difference related to either parent's re-partnering, but their models control for child support payments that are likely endogenous to relationships between nonresident fathers and children.

birth of half-siblings, the older children moving back and forth will live part of the time with a younger half-sibling, part of the time without; or they may live part of the time with one half-sibling (from the mother) and part of the time with another (from the father). Relationships with and obligations to step-parents, step-siblings and half-siblings have been shown to be more similar to their biological counterparts, the longer the period of coresidence (Arránz Becker et al. 2013; Bressan et al. 2009; Kalmijn 2013; Pollet 2007; van Houdt et al. 2018). Thus, shared physical custody has the potential to strengthen ties between children and all members of their larger and complex family, despite the potential negative effects of household and family instability.

2.4 Coresidence and Kinship

The effects of coresidence on family relationships also extend to the wider kinship network. Of course, children remain biologically related to both parents' kin after separation. Because children's kin relationships are mediated by their parents (Chan and Elder 2000; Whitbeck et al. 1993), however, their contact with extended kin depends on where they live and on the nature of relationships between former in-laws.

Most research finds that parental separation reduces contacts and close relationships between children and their paternal grandparents, while contacts and relationships with maternal grandparents remain the same or are increased (see review in Jappens and van Bavel 2016). The difference arises, of course, from the fact that most children live with their mothers. The shift toward maternal kin is exacerbated by the fact that women are traditional kin-keepers even in nuclear families (Chan and Elder 2000). Maintenance of relationships with paternal kin therefore depend on the mother's relationships with her former in-laws, especially the mother-in-law (Coleman et al. 1997; Doyle et al. 2010; Goetting 1990).

The reverse occurs when children live full-time with fathers, i.e., they have more contact with their paternal than maternal kin (Hilton and Macari 1997; Lussier et al. 2002; Weston 1992). This suggests that families with shared physical custody would have equal opportunities for maintaining relationships between children and both sets of kin. A few studies have shown that this is indeed the case, and that contact is similar to that of children living in nuclear families (Jappens 2018; Jappens and van Bavel 2016; Westphal et al. 2015).

2.5 Conclusions

We claimed at the start of this essay that shared physical custody produces a new family form, different of course from nuclear families, but distinct in organization and relationships from separated families where one parent has physical custody and the other does not.[5] One might argue that the gender egalitarian structure inherent in shared physical custody can be found among coresident parents. Or that parents without physical custody may provide considerable support and relief from childcare responsibilities for the parent with sole physical custody. And that parents and their kin may make extra efforts to maintain contact and relationships with the parent who does not have physical custody.

It is difficult to argue, however, that children's commuting from one home to another is anything like living in one home. Or that each parent having the full-time responsibility for children while the other has time off from childcare is anything like the egalitarian nuclear family where both parents are simultaneously earning and caring, and trading off only occasionally or by the hour rather than the week. As we argued, these structural features of shared physical custody create distinct contexts for parent-child and sibling relationships and produce differences in shared understandings of obligations between family members. The unique context for relationships and obligations together constitute a new family form.

Shared physical custody highlights the distinctions between family relationships and household membership that become salient when parents separate. When children reside in and feel at home in both parents' households, their relationships with stepparents and step-siblings are altered. Shared physical custody places more demands on step-mothers and fewer on step-fathers, compared to arrangements where children live with their mothers (and step-fathers) but not with their fathers (and step-mothers). Shared physical custody also provides greater opportunities to develop relationships with the father's as well as the mother's step-children (step-siblings). Relationships with both paternal and maternal half-siblings are developed in a shared household. Beyond the two households, children's ties to paternal as well as maternal kin, and even to step-kin, are likely to be stronger. From the child's point of view, the boundaries of the two households may be viewed as the boundaries of their family, parallel to the coincidence of household and family boundaries in a nuclear family.

Parents with shared physical custody are to some extent rewriting the gender contract, i.e. "social agreements on what men and women are, what they think and expect, and what they do" (Duncan 1995: 265). Whether they are motivated or not by gender equality in earning and caring, they are de facto in the vanguard of completing the gender revolution (DeRose et al. 2019). Shared physical custody appears to generate the best of both traditionally 'male' (access to paid work) and 'female' (access to children) worlds.

Some have argued that shared physical custody may be increasing too fast. The political and legal shift toward shared physical custody was initially driven not by mothers seeking more engagement from fathers, but by fathers seeking more rights over their children (Masardo 2009). Shared physical custody may also have outpaced increases in nuclear-family gender equality. When mothers have been

[5]Melli and Brown (2008) also noted that shared physical custody produced a new family form but did not draw attention to its unique structure.

primary parents before separation, the assumption that fathers should become equal parents afterwards can be viewed as unrealistic and unfair (Fransson et al. 2016; Harris-Short 2011). As Harris-Short (2010) puts it: "... equality cannot be conjured out of nothing at the point of separation. It must be firmly rooted in the practices of the intact family" (p. 270).

Nevertheless, shared physical custody is now the experience of a rapidly increasing proportion of separated parents and their children. Where it is most common, societal institutions are already in place or relatively easily modifiable to make it work. The ability to afford two homes and to manage children's commutes between homes is made easier by direct payments to parents; ubiquitous and affordable preschool and after-school care; leave to care for sick children; and housing subsidies for low-income parents. Other policies related to labor markets and conditions of work (employers, shifts, hours, etc.) may also provide opportunities or constraints for shared physical custody (Bakker and Mulder 2013). Where occupations are highly gender-segregated such that female-dominated occupations allow more work-family balance than male-dominated occupations, sharing care responsibilities will be more difficult for many heterosexual couples (Eriksson 2018).

Housing availability may also constrain parents' possibilities to provide two homes for children. If housing is scarce, it is not simply the double cost of housing, but the possibility of dramatically increasing prices in an area that make it impossible to find another household of similar quality nearby. Shared physical custody is inversely associated with distance between parental homes (Bakker and Mulder 2013; Kitteröd and Lyngstad 2012), and shifts from shared to sole physical custody are more likely to occur when parents live further apart (Poortman and van Gaalen 2017). Housing costs also underlie the positive association between parents' education or income and shared physical custody (Fransson et al. 2018; Kitteröd and Lyngstad 2012; Pelletier 2016).

Although research on shared physical custody has burgeoned in the past several years, its primary concern has been with the implications of such arrangements for children's and parents' wellbeing. Investigations into the structure of daily life, the development and maintenance of parent-child and sibling relationships, implications for step-families and extended kin, have only begun. The theoretical implications of shared physical custody for conceptualizations of households and families and for gender contracts are only beginning to be understood. Empirical research is concentrated in a relatively small number of societal contexts, limiting understandings of how social policies and institutions facilitate or hinder the construction and maintenance of family life when separated parents share physical custody and children move back and forth between two parental homes. This essay provides, we hope, a roadmap for further investigations of the new family form.

References

Andersson, G., Thomson, E., & Duntava, A. (2017). Life-table representations of family dynamics in the 21st century. *Demographic Research, 37*, 1081–1230.

Arránz Becker, O., Salzburger, V., Lois, N., & Nauck, B. (2013). What narrows the stepgap? Closeness between parents and adult (step)children in Germany. *Journal of Marriage and Family, 75*, 1130–1148.

Bakker, W., & Karsten, L. (2013). Balancing paid work, care and leisure in post-separation households: A comparison of single parents with co-parents. *Acta Sociologica, 56*, 173–187.

Bakker, W., & Mulder, C. H. (2013). Characteristics of post-separation families in the Netherlands: Shared residence versus resident mother arrangements. *GeoJournal, 78*, 851–866.

Bastaits, K., & Mortelmans, D. (2016). Parenting as mediator between post-divorce family structure and children's well-being. *Journal of Child and Family Studies, 25*, 2178–2188.

Bastaits, K., Ponnet, K., & Mortelmans, D. (2012). Parenting of divorced fathers and the association with children's self-esteem. *Journal of Youth and Adolescence, 41*, 1643–1656.

Berger, L. M., Brown, P. R., Joung, E., Melli, M. S., & Wimer, L. (2008). The stability of child physical placements following divorce: Descriptive evidence from Wisconsin. *Journal of Marriage and Family, 70*, 273–283.

Berger, L. M., Cancian, M., & Meyer, D. R. (2012). Maternal re-partnering and new-partner fertility: Associations with nonresident father investments in children. *Children and Youth Services Review, 34*, 426–436.

Berman, R. (2015). (Re)doing parent-child relationships in dual residence arrangements: Swedish children's narratives about changing relations post-separation. *Journal of Family Research, 10*, 123–142.

Bianchi, S. M., Sayer, L. C., Milkie, M. A., & Robinson, J. P. (2012). Housework: Who did, does or will do it, and how much does it matter? *Social Forces, 91*(1), 55–63.

Bjarnason, T., & Arnarsson, Á. (2011). Joint physical custody and communication with parents in 37 western societies. *Journal of Comparative Family Studies, 42*, 871–890.

Bonnet, C., Garbinti, B., & Solaz, A. (2017). *Does part-time mothering help get a job? The role of shared custody on women's employment after divorce*. Paper presented at the Workshop on Family Dynamics and the Changing Landscape of Shared Custody in Europe, Lausanne, Switzerland, December 14–15.

Botterman, S., Sodermans, A. K., & Matthijs, K. (2015). The social life of divorced parents. Do custody arrangements make a difference in divorced parents' social participation and contacts? *Leisure Studies, 34*, 487–500.

Bressan, P., Colarelli, S. M., & Cavalieri, M. B. (2009). Biologically costly altruism depends on emotional closeness among step but not half or full sibling. *Evolutionary Psychology, 7*, 118–132.

Cancian, M., Meyer, D. R., Brown, P. R., & Cook, S. T. (2014). Who gets custody now? Dramatic changes in children's living arrangements after divorce. *Demography, 51*(4), 1381–1396.

Cashmore, J., Parkinson, P., Weston, R., Patulny, R., Redmond, G., Qu, L., Baxter, J., Rajkovic, M., Sitek, T., & Katz, I. (2010). *Shared care parenting arrangements since the 2006 family law reforms: Report to the Australian government attorney-general's department*. Sydney: Social Policy Research Centre, University of New South Wales.

Chan, C. G., & Elder, G. H., Jr. (2000). Matrilineal advantage in grandchild-grandparent relations. *Gerontologist, 40*, 179–190.

Cloutier, R., & Jacques, C. (1997). Evolution of residential custody arrangements in separated families. *Journal of Divorce & Remarriage, 28*(1–2), 17–33.

Coleman, M., Ganong, L., & Cable, S. M. (1997). Beliefs about women's intergenerational family obligations to provide support before and after divorce and remarriage. *Journal of Marriage and Family, 49*, 165–176.

Cooksey, E. C., & Craig, P. H. (1998). Parenting from a distance: The effects of paternal characteristics on contact between the nonresidential fathers and their children. *Demography, 35*(2), 187–200.

DeRose, L.F., Goldscheider, F., Brito, J. R., Salazar-Arango, A., Corcuera, P., Corcuera, P. J., & Gas-Aixendri, M. (2019). Are children barriers to the gender revolution? International comparisons. *European Journal of Population*, Published online 23 January.

Doyle, M., O'Dywer, C., & Timonen, V. (2010). "How can you just cut off a whole side of the family and say move on?" The reshaping of paternal grandparent–grandchild relationships following divorce or separation in the middle generation. *Family Relations, 59*, 587–598.

Drapeau, S., Baude, A., Quellet, J., Godbout, E., & Ivers, H. (2017). Relations between postdivorce custody arrangements, family contexts and children's adjustment. *Journal of Child Custody, 14*, 1–23.

Duncan, S. (1995). Theorizing European gender systems. *Journal of European Social Policy, 5*(4), 263–284.

Duvander, A.-Z., & Lammi-Taskula, J. (2011). Parental leave. In I. V. Gislason & G. Björk Eydal (Eds.), *Parental leave childcare and gender equality in the Nordic countries*. TemaNord, Copenhagen: Nordic Council of Ministers.

Edlund, J., & Öun, I. (2016). Who should work and who should care? Attitudes towards the desirable division of labour between mothers and fathers in five European countries. *Acta Sociologica, 59*, 151–169.

Eriksson, H. (2018). *Fathers and mothers taking leave from paid work to care for a child: Economic considerations and occupational conditions of work.* Stockholm research reports in demography 2018:12. Stockholm University Demography Unit, Stockholm, Sweden.

Ferrari, G., Bonnet, C., & Solaz, A. (2019). Will the one who keeps the children keep the house? Residential mobility after divorce by parenthood status and custody arrangements in France. *Demographic Research, 40*, 359–394.

Ferrarini, T., & Duvander, A.-Z. (2010). Earner-carer model at the crossroads: Reforms and outcomes of Sweden's family policy in comparative perspective. *International Journal of Health Services, 40*(3), 373–398.

Fransson, E., Sarkadi, A., Hjern, A., & Bergström, M. (2016). Why should they live more with one of us when they are children to us both? Parents' motives for practicing equal joint physical custody for children aged 0–4. *Children and Youth Services Review, 66*, 154–160.

Fransson, E., Låftman, S. B., Östberg, V., Hjern, A., & Bergström, M. (2018). The living conditions of children with shared residence – The Swedish example. *Child Indicators Research, 11*, 861–883.

Ganong, L. H., Coleman, M., & Mistina, D. (1995). Normative beliefs about parents' and step-parents' financial obligations to children following divorce and remarriage. *Family Relations, 44*, 306–315.

Goetting, A. (1990). Patterns of support among in-laws in the United States: A review of research. *Journal of Family Issues, 11*, 67–90.

Harris-Short, S. (2010). Resisting the march towards 50/50 shared residence: Rights, welfare and equality in post-separation families. *Journal of Social Welfare & Family Law, 32*, 257–274.

Harris-Short, S. (2011). Building a house upon sand: Post-separation parenting, shared residence and equality – Lessons from Sweden. *Child and Family Law Quarterly, 23*, 344–369.

Hilton, J. M., & Macari, D. P. (1997). Grandparent involvement following divorce: A comparison in single-mother and single-father families. *Journal of Divorce and Remarriage, 28*, 203–224.

Ivanova, K., Kalmijn, M., & Uunk, W. (2013). The effect of children on men's and women's chances of re-partnering in a European Context. *European Journal of Population, 29*, 417–444.

Jappens, M. (2018). Children's relationships with grandparents in shared versus sole physical custody families. *Journal of Divorce & Remarriage, 59*(5), 359–371.

Jappens, M., & van Bavel, J. (2016). Parental divorce, residence arrangements and contact between grandchildren and grandparents. *Journal of Marriage and Family, 78*, 451–467.

Juby, H., Le Bourdais, C., & Marcil-Gratton, N. (2005). Sharing roles, sharing custody? Couples' characteristics and children's living arrangements at separation. *Journal of Marriage and Family, 67*, 157–172.

Juby, H., Billette, J.-M., Laplante, B., & Le Bourdais, C. (2007). Nonresident fathers and children: Parents' new unions and frequency of contact. *Journal of Family Issues, 28*(9), 1220–1245.

Kalmijn, M. (2013). Adult children's relationships with married parents, divorced parents, and stepparents: Biology, marriage or residence? *Journal of Marriage and Family, 75*(5), 1181–1193.

Kitteröd, R., & Lyngstad, J. (2012). Untraditional caring arrangements among parents living apart: The case of Norway. *Demographic Research, 27*, 121–152.

Kitteröd, R., & Wiik, K. A. (2017). Shared residence among parents living apart in Norway. *Family Court Review, 55*(4), 556–571.

Kline, M., Tschann, J. M., Johnston, J. R., & Wallerstein, J. S. (1989). Children's adjustment in joint and sole physical custody families. *Developmental Psychology, 23*, 430–434.

Le Bourdais, C., Juby, H., & Marcil-Gratton, N. (2002). Keeping in touch with children after separation: The point of view of fathers. *Canadian Journal of Community Mental Health, 21*(4), 109–130.

Lussier, G., Deater-Deckard, K., Dunn, J., & Davies, L. (2002). Support across two generations: Children's closeness to grandparents following parental divorce and remarriage. *Journal of Family Psychology, 16*, 363–376.

Maccoby, E. E., & Mnookin, R. H. (1992). *Dividing the child: Social and legal dilemmas of custody*. Cambridge, MA: Harvard University.

Maclean, M. J., Drake, D., & Mckillop, D. (2016). Perceptions of stepfathers' obligations to financially support stepchildren. *Journal of Family Economic Issues, 37*, 285–296.

Masardo, A. (2009). Managing shared residence in Britain and France: Questioning a default primary carer model. In K. Rummery, I. Greener, & C. Holden (Eds.), *Social policy review 21: Analysis and debate in social policy* (pp. 197–214). Bristol: The Policy Press.

McGene, J., & King, V. (2012). Implications of new marriages and children for coparenting in nonresident father families. *Journal of Family Issues, 33*(12), 1619–1641.

Melli, M., & Brown, P. (2008). Exploring a new family form – The shared time family. *International Journal of Law, Policy and the Family, 22*, 231–269.

Meyer, D. R., Cancian, M., & Cook, S. T. (2017). The growth in shared custody in the United States: Patterns and implications. *Family Court Review, 55*, 500–512.

Oláh, L., & Bernhardt, E. (2008). Sweden: Combining childbearing and gender equality. *Demographic Research, 19*, 1105–1144.

Parsons, T. (1943). The kinship system of the contemporary United States. *American Anthropologist, 45*, 22–38.

Pearson, J., & Thoennes, N. (1990). Custody after divorce: Demographic and attitudinal patterns. *American Journal of Orthopsychiatry, 60*, 233–249.

Pelletier, D. (2016). *Prévalence, déterminants et dynamique des arrangements de temps parental postséparation chez les enfants québécois nés à la fin des années 1990*. Montrèal: Université de Montréal.

Pollet, T. V. (2007). Genetic relatedness and sibling relationship characteristics in a modern society. *Evolution and Human Behavior, 28*, 176–185.

Poortman, A., & van Gaalen, R. (2017). Shared residence after separation: A review and new findings from the Netherlands. *Family Court Review, 55*, 531–544.

Schnor, C., Pasteels, I., & Van Bavel, J. (2017). Sole physical custody and mother's repartnering after divorce. *Journal of Marriage and Family, 79*, 879–890.

Seltzer, J. (1991). Relationships between fathers and children who live apart: The father's role after separation. *Journal of Marriage and the Family, 53*, 79–101.

Seltzer, J. A., & Bianchi, S. M. (1988). Children's contact with absent parents. *Journal of Marriage and Family, 50*, 663–677.

Seltzer, J. A., Schaeffer, N. C., & Chang, H. W. (1989). Family ties after divorce: The relationship between visiting and paying child support. *Journal of Marriage and the Family, 51*(4), 1013–1032.

Smyth, B., Qu, L., & Weston, R. (2004). The demography of parent-child contact. In B. Smyth (Ed.), *Parent-child contact and post-separation parenting arrangements* (Research report no. 9) (pp. 111–122). Melbourne: Australian Institute of Family Studies.

Smyth, B., Weston, R., Moloney, L., Richardson, N., & Temple, J. (2008). Changes in patterns of postseparation parenting over time: Recent Australian data. *Journal of Family Studies, 14*, 23–36.

Sodermans, A., Matthijs, K., & Swicegood, G. (2013). Characteristics of joint physical custody families in Flanders. *Demographic Research, 28*(29), 821–848.

Sodermans, A., Vanassche, S., Matthijs, K., & Swicegood, G. (2014). Measuring post-divorce living arrangements: Theoretical and empirical validation of the residential calendar. *Journal of Family Issues, 35*, 125–145.

Sodermans, A. K., Botterman, S., Havermans, N., & Matthijs, K. (2015). Involved fathers, liberated mothers? Joint physical custody and the subjective well-being of divorced parents. *Social Indicators Research, 122*(1), 257–277.

Spruijt, E., & Duindam, V. (2010). Joint physical custody in the Netherlands and the well-being of children. *Journal of Divorce & Remarriage, 51*, 65–82.

Steinbach, A. (2018). Children's and parents' well-being in joint physical custody: A literature review. *Family Process*. Published online: 02 July 2018. https://doi.org/10.1111/famp.12372

Swiss, L., & Le Bourdais, C. (2009). Father–child contact after separation: The influence of living arrangements. *Journal of Family Issues, 30*(5), 623–652.

Thomson, E., Lappegård, T., Carlson, M., Evans, A., & Gray, E. (2014). Childbearing across partnerships in Australia, the United States, Norway and Sweden. *Demography, 51*, 485–508.

Turunen, J. (2017). Shared physical custody and children's experience of stress. *Journal of Divorce & Remarriage, 58*, 371–392.

Van den Eynde, A., & Mortelmans, D. (2017). *The effect of children's residence arrangements on the work-family balance of divorced families*. Paper presented at the Workshop on Family Dynamics and the Changing Landscape of Shared Custody in Europe, Lausanne, Switzerland, December 14–15.

Van der Heijden, F., Poortman, A., & Van der Lippe, T. (2016). Children's postdivorce residence arrangements and parental experienced time pressure. *Journal of Marriage and Family, 78*, 468–481.

van Houdt, K., Kalmijn, M., & Ivanova, K. (2018). Family complexity and adult children's obligations: The role of divorce and co-residential history in norms to support parents and step-parents. *European Sociological Review, 34*(2), 169–183.

Vanassche, S., Sodermans, A., & Matthijs, K. (2013). Commuting between two parental households: The association between joint physical custody and adolescent well-being following divorce. *Journal of Family Studies, 19*(2), 139–158.

Vanassche, S., Corijn, M., Matthijs, K., & Swicegood, G. (2015). Repartnering and childbearing after divorce: Differences according to parental status and custodial arrangements. *Population Research and Policy Review, 34*, 761–784.

Vikat, A., Thomson, E., & Prskawetz, A. (2004). Childrearingresponsibility and stepfamily fertility in Finland and Austria. *European Journal of Population, 20*, 1–21.

Weston, R. (1992). Families after marriage breakdown. *Family Matters, 32*, 41–45.

Westphal, S. K., Poortman, A., & Van der Lippe, T. (2015). What about the grandparents? children's postdivorce residence arrangements and contact with grandparents. *Journal of Marriage and Family, 77*(2), 424–440.

Whitbeck, L. B., Hoyt, D. R., & Huck, S. M. (1993). Family relationship history, contemporary parent-grandparent relationship quality, and the grandparent-grandchild relationship. *Journal of Marriage and the Family, 55*(4), 1025–1035.

Winther, I. W., Palludan, C., Gulløv, E., & Rehder, M. M. (2015). *Siblings – Practical and sensitive relations*. Copenhagen: Akademisk Forlag.

Elizabeth Thomson is Professor of Demography Emerita, Stockholm University, Professor of Sociology Emerita, University of Wisconsin-Madison, and past director of the Linnaeus Center for Social Policy and Family Dynamics in Europe. She has conducted research on family behaviors across the life course, including couple childbearing decisions, implications of family structure for child well-being, and childbearing in cohabitation and stepfamilies. In recent years, much of her research has focused on comparative European family demography. Current projects focus on the relationship between cohabitation and family complexity, i.e., the formation of stepfamilies and childbearing with more than one partner, and the consequences of joint physical custody for parents and children. Professor Thomson is a member of the Royal Swedish Academy of Sciences.

Jani Turunen is Associate Professor and Senior Lecturer of Social Work at Södertörn University, Stockholm, and an affiliate of the Stockholm University Demography Unit. He holds a PhD in Sociological Demography from Stockholm University. His research focuses on different aspects of children's family structure and wellbeing, and on historical change in family structure and kinship. He currently directs a research project on shared physical custody in Sweden.

3

Joint Physical Custody: Major Questions, Findings and Controversies

Robert E. Emery

Abstract This overview discusses key findings, questions, and controversies about joint physical custody (JPC) emphasizing psychological issues for research and practice. Children living in JPC are slightly better adjusted, on average, but it is not clear whether this is a consequence of the arrangement or due to nonrandom selection into it. Moreover, no consistent evidence links specific variations in JPC to better or worse child adjustment, including equal or some other pattern of shared time. Parental conflict/cooperation is the factor most firmly, if still somewhat tenuously, established as a moderator of JPC effects. Other important moderators include logistics (e.g., geographical distance between parents), developmental stage (very young children and older adolescents may fare less well), and personality (a factor only beginning to be explored). The clearest implication for policy and practice is that children will fare better if their parents cooperate in crafting a parenting plan designed to meet their individual needs.

Keywords Joint physical custody · Selection or causation · Logistics · Conflict/cooperation · Developmental stage · Child personality

Psychological perspectives on joint physical custody (JPC) are critically important to parents who live apart and to the mental health and legal professionals who work with, influence, and perhaps decide children's living arrangements for parents. Questions and positions about JPC also raise broad social questions about the roles of men and women not only as parents but also as workers. While JPC could be analyzed from each of these points of view, the focus of this chapter is the well-being of children living in JPC, a topic of concern for parents, professionals, and society.

This chapter offers a broad overview of research on key psychological topics, questions, and controversies concerning how JPC affects children. It should be noted

---

R. E. Emery (✉)
Department of Psychology, University of Virginia, Charlottesville, VI, USA
e-mail: ree@virginia.edu

at the outset that, given limited research, this summary raises more questions than it answers. The review of studies is more illustrative than definitive, reflecting limited, current understanding and suggesting an agenda for future research. While emphasizing research, the chapter also should be of practical value to mental health and legal professionals by highlighting questions parents often ask, while hopefully also inoculating practitioners against premature claims that research on JPC is definitive.

The chapter is divided into two major sections. The first considers the definition of JPC, JPC in different family forms, evidence on how children fare in JPC generally, and the all-important question of selection versus causation. The second section asks when JPC may help children, and when it may harm them, with a specific focus on logistical considerations, parental conflict and cooperation, children's age, and children's personality and mental health.

3.1 What Is JPC and Does it Benefit Children?

Joint physical custody is defined here, as it often is defined in research (e.g., Bauserman 2002; Smyth 2017), as an arrangement where children spend at least 25% of their time with each of their parents who live apart. Functionally, this definition includes equal time, for example, swapping homes every other week, or the 2-2-5-5 schedule, where children spend every Monday and Tuesday overnight with one parent, Wednesday and Thursday with the other, and alternate three-day weekends with each. However, the 25–50% definition also includes many other arrangements, such as weekdays with one parent and weekends with the other, or even the school year with one parent and summers and most school vacations with the other (Emery 2016).

3.2 Variations in JPC Schedules

The very task of defining JPC raises two central and often controversial considerations about the arrangement. First, some advocacy groups assert that equal time is the best, perhaps the only, true form of JPC. In fact, fathers' rights organizations have been lobbying to make equal custody time the guiding legal standard, and laws promoting equal time have been adopted in a few countries, including Australia (Smyth and Chisholm 2017) and Belgium (Vanassche et al. 2017), as well as some smaller jurisdictions. Demographic evidence shows a dramatic increase over recent decades in both unequal (25–49% time) and particularly equal JPC, at least in the U.S. state of Wisconsin where unequal JPC grew from 7% to 15% between 1989 and

2010, while equal went from 5% to 35%[1] (Meyer et al. 2017). At this time, however, there is no clear evidence on the relative benefits for children of equal versus unequal JPC, so this debate remains philosophical, not empirical.

This brings us to the second issue: Are different JPC schedules more or less beneficial to children? In addition to the equal versus unequal question, issues of importance include (a) whether more transitions affect children adversely (e.g., alternating homes every day versus every week), (b) whether longer separations from each parent harm younger children (e.g., babies may benefit from more transitions and shorter separations from either parent, while school-age children benefit from fewer transitions and longer separations), (c) whether flexible, evolving custody arrangements work better for both children and parents (e.g., babies may spend most of their time with the primary attachment figure, but more equal time with both parents as they grow older), and (d) whether JPC is more beneficial, harmful, or desirable to children of different ages (e.g., a teenager's own, busy schedule may make JPC less desirable to adolescents).

At present, the field lacks even basic demographic research[2] on how many parents follow the above or the many other variations in JPC, let alone on whether, at what ages, and under what circumstances different schedules benefit or harm children and families. Of course, many parents agonize over these questions and more, as they try to craft the best arrangements for their children and themselves, and they often turn to practicing professionals for advice. In an effort to respond to parents' concerns, some have offered research-informed, developmental-based guidelines to help parents in their decision making (e.g., Emery 2016). While experience with JPC and knowledge about child development suggest reasonable answers to many of parents' pressing questions, research is a long way from supporting those answers definitively.

3.3 Relationship Status

Another broad consideration about JPC concerns the status of the relationship between parents. Parents who have made a commitment to each other (whether married or cohabiting), lived together for years, and both been involved in rearing multiple children are very different from parents who have had a brief relationship,

[1]Sole mother custody dropped from 76% to 42% and sole father custody from 9% to 6% over the same time period. At both time points, a very small percentage of cases resulted in split custody, with each parent having custody of at least one child.

[2]In the U.S., no national demographic data exist even on the prevalence of JPC, however it is defined. In Belgium, JPC prevalence has been estimated to be 37% among separated parent families (Vanassche et al. 2017), with slightly lower rates found in the Netherlands (Poortman and van Gaalen 2017) and Norway (Kitterod and Wiik 2017). However, JPC was defined differently across counties (33–66% in Belgium; mostly equal in Norway), a fact that complicates comparisons and underscores the need for demographic details on variations in JPC schedules.

never cohabited, and have a newborn. These latter parents need to build a relationship with each other, as well as with their children, a circumstance that raises questions for them, and for courts, about whether JPC is a healthy or even viable arrangement. Few custody studies have focused on these families.

3.4 Average Adjustment in JPC

While important variations in JPC have yet to be studied, a few dozen studies of varying methodological quality have compared the well-being of groups of children living in JPC versus sole custody. Most but not all of these studies find that children in JPC are somewhat better adjusted, on average, as indexed by a variety of psychological measures of personal, social, and academic adjustment (Baude et al. 2016; Bauserman 2002; Smyth et al. 2016; Steinbach 2018). While some wish to interpret this result as supporting the conclusion that JPC *causes* children to adjust better to divorce – and that equal custody therefore should be the guiding legal principle (Nielsen 2018), in fact, research shows that the difference in children's well-being in JPC versus sole custody is small, .109 standard deviation units according to a recent meta-analysis (Baude et al. 2016). Moreover, the number of existing studies is modest, their methodological quality is uneven, and most work focuses only on adolescents or school-aged children (Smyth et al. 2016; Steinbach 2018).

Perhaps the clearest conclusion from existing research is that the back and forth of JPC does not, in and of itself, appear to create significant, observable problems for most children[3]. Yet, two additional and critical considerations further cloud the appropriate interpretation of research on the modest benefits associated with JPC: (1) nonrandom selection and (1) individual variations around the average.

3.5 Selection into JPC

Families do not select JPC at random. Evidence indicates that, on average, parents with JPC are wealthier, better educated, have better co-parenting relationships, and include more involved fathers than families with sole custody (Smyth et al. 2016; Steinbach 2018). Each of these factors also is linked with better well-being among children (Smyth et al. 2016), which leads to the question: Is the small difference in child adjustment found between sole and shared custody due to better adjusted families (and children) *selecting* JPC, or does the arrangement *cause* children (and

[3]Perhaps even this conclusion can be questioned. The unpopularity of bird nesting – where children remain in one home but parents move in and out – would seem to speak to the disruption JPC can cause, despite its other benefits.

families) to be better adjusted? Methodologically careful reviewers view this as a critical and unanswered question (Smyth et al. 2016; Steinbach 2018).

The importance of selection considerations is underscored by a recent study of father's involvement in parenting both before and after JPC (Poortman 2018). Using a population-based sample of 3694 separated parents with minor children in the Netherlands, this investigation found that the benefits of post-separation father involvement (including both JPC and the frequency of father contact in mother custody) were moderated by *pre-separation* father involvement. Children living in JPC (or who had more father contact) fared better than children in sole custody (or who had less contact) when their fathers had been involved parents prior to the separation. Importantly, however, children living in JPC (or who had more father contact) had *more* problems when fathers were low on parental involvement before the separation (Poortman 2018).

This study is one of the first to consider pre-separation factors and JPC, and the findings underscore the need for more longitudinal research. In order to distinguish correlation from causation, researchers need to study changes associated with JPC from before to after separation. In the present context, perhaps the most critical question is: Does children's well-being improve from before to after separation if they live in JPC, or does the slightly better functioning found among children in JPC actually predate the separation and therefore cannot be caused by JPC?

3.6 Boundaries of the Benefits of JPC

A second, critical consideration about association between JPC and somewhat better child adjustment concerns variation around the mean. Even if JPC does causally increase children's well-being, on average, the arrangement still may harm some children in some circumstances, while helping others. Four factors are of particular importance to consider in relation to whether JPC helps or harms children: logistics, parental conflict and cooperation, children's age, and children's personality and mental health.

3.7 Logistics

The viability of JPC, as well as its potential benefits, would seem to be constrained by basic logistical considerations, particularly the ability of parents to provide children with two reasonable homes and the geographic distance between the parents' residences. Evidence indicates that the frequency of children's contact with one parent declines if the parents live an hour's travel or more apart (Furstenberg et al. 1983). Practical considerations like getting children to school – and the need to get children's "stuff" from one home to another – make proximity an even more prominent consideration. Indeed, living near one another, even in the same neighborhood, is frequently discussed in the practice literature as helping to make JPC successful (Emery 2016).

Notwithstanding such obvious logistical considerations, the author routinely is contacted by parents who have been ordered by judges to follow seemingly harmful schedules in order to maintain JPC. One recent example involved a two-year-old child who was ordered to spend two and one-half months in the geographically distant residences of her mother followed by two and one-half months with her father. Due to concerns about maintaining secure attachments to both parents, mental health professionals worry about separations of more than a day or two at this tender age (Emery 2016; Lamb and Kelly 2001). In a second recent example, a fourteen-year-old was ordered to move across the U.S. each year in order to live equal time with each of his parents. Yet, one wonders about how this adolescent would adjust to – or simply feel about – a yearly change in schools and peer groups, in addition to his family.

How often do judges make orders like these, and what are the consequences for children and families? To the author's knowledge, there is no data on this question. However, the often contentious issue of whether a parent can relocate with the children away from the other parent, and the potentially deleterious effects of relocation, highlight the importance of geographical proximity if children are to maintain close relationships with both parents (Austin 2008)[4].

3.8 Parental Conflict and Cooperation

Another key consideration in deciding when JPC benefits or harms children is the degree and nature of conflict and cooperation between their parents. A few commentators claim that JPC benefits children whether parental conflict is controlled or raging (Nielsen 2018). This, however, is an unusual position. Many researchers, and legal and mental health practitioners, conclude that JPC benefits children when conflict is contained, but harms children when parent conflict is poorly managed (e.g., Kasipiew et al., 2009; Lee 2002; Spruijt and Duindam 2010). The logic of this latter position seems intuitive. After all, no fault divorce and other efforts to minimize parent conflict such as divorce mediation were premised on research showing that children fare better in low-conflict divorced families than in a high-conflict two-parent families (Emery 1982; Emery and Wyer 1987). The same logic would seem to apply to JPC: Faced with the alternative, children should fare better in low-conflict sole custody than in high conflict JPC.

Empirical research on the moderating effects of conflict is stronger than for other factors considered in this section. Several studies have found that JPC is linked to

[4]Today, children and parents can maintain contact using telephones, computers, and other electronic devises. The extent to which such contact is a viable substitute for face-to-face interaction is both controversial and understudied. See Merla et al. (this volume) and Poortman (this volume).

worse child adjustment when parent conflict is high. For example, a study of 1570 Belgian adolescents found that, when adolescents reported more parental conflict, JPC (versus sole custody) was linked to lower life satisfaction (for boys and girls) and to increased depression (for girls) (Vanassche et al. 2013). Similarly, Modecki et al. (2015) found that moderate contact with fathers combined with low parental conflict, measured during adolescence, predicted higher academic achievement and fewer externalizing problems in young adulthood in a sample of 156 U.S. teenagers followed longitudinally. The teenagers from moderate contact, low conflict families fared better than those from either low contact and moderate conflict families or high contact and high conflict families (the three subgroups identified through latent profile analysis). Young adults in the high contact, high conflict group were no better adjusted than those in low contact, moderate conflict families, again pointing to the importance of conflict over contact (Modecki et al. 2015).

Not every study has found that conflict predicts worse adjustment in JPC (Mahrer et al. 2018). It may be that children's problems in high conflict JPC become more evident as time passes (Mahrer et al. 2018). The definition of high conflict also varies between studies. Given that conflict is expected in divorce, this raises the important question: How much conflict is too much?

The present author has argued that one index of too much conflict is when parents are so acrimonious that they resort to litigation, asking a judge to decide custody for them (Emery 1999, 2011, 2016). Ordering JPC in contested custody cases, roughly 10% of all divorces (Maccoby and Mnookin 1992), may be unhealthy for children, even though JPC might appear to be fair to parents.

Evidence from Australian courts suggests that many judges share this concern. An Australian national law enacted in 2006 encouraged equal, and if not equal, significant and substantial contact with both parents. However, an extensive analysis of legal decisions under the law found that Australian judges ordered JPC in only 3% of contested cases in 2011–2012, a lower percentage than in earlier years under the law (Smyth et al. 2014)[5]. Another analysis in this same report showed far higher rates of JPC (largely reached as a result of parental agreement) when parents described their relationship as friendly versus either distant or having lots of conflict (Smyth et al. 2014).

3.9 Children's Age or Developmental Stage

Children's age or developmental stage is a third factor that may influence whether JPC benefits or harms children. The school-age years, and perhaps the preschool years, may be the "sweet spot" for JPC (Emery 2016). Adolescents may find that

[5]A subsequent analysis using somewhat different methods found a somewhat higher level of judicial orders of JPC in contested cases, but they still represented a small minority of cases – 9.7% (Smyth and Chisholm 2017).

their schedule with each parent disrupts a third, more critical schedule, their own (Maccoby and Mnookin 1992), while very young children's attachment security may be undermined by too long or frequent separations from their primary attachment figure (McIntosh 2011).

The question of what is the best schedule for infants and toddlers has become a topic of considerable debate in recent years (Lamb 2012; McIntosh 2011). Both sides of this controversy focus on the importance of infant-parent attachments (Main et al. 2011) to the current and future well-being of very young children. One attachment-based position highlights the importance of a secure, primary attachment, usually but not always with the mother (Sroufe and McIntosh 2011). The other attachment-based position highlights the importance of multiple attachments, to both the mother and the father (Lamb and Kelly 2001).

Interestingly, the opposing positions both acknowledge the benefits of both attachment security and multiple attachments, but the primacy placed on one over the other has led to very different recommendations about schedules. For example, experts who prioritize attachment security suggest that babies should reside primarily with one parent to promote attachment security, but the same experts also want babies to have frequent contact with the other parent (several visits weekly plus occasional overnights) so they can also develop an attachment to their other parent (Sroufe and McIntosh 2011). Experts who prioritize multiple attachments want babies to have equal or near equal contact with both parents, including overnights, but the same experts would have children switching homes every day or two in an effort to maintain secure attachments by keeping separations from either parent relatively short (Lamb and Kelly 2001).

By now, the reader will not be surprised to learn that research on this topic is inadequate. In fact, only four studies in the world have directly addressed the question of overnight frequency and infant attachment security. The largest study was conducted by the author and his graduate students and included 1023 one-year-olds and 1547 two- and three-year-olds in a sample representative of 20 U.S. cities with a population of 200,000 or more. Overnights of once a week or more during the first year of life predicted a significantly higher rate of attachment insecurity at age 3 in comparison to infants who had some but less frequent overnights (Tornello et al. 2013). Two- and three-year-olds who had 5 or more overnights every 2 weeks, that is, JPC, also had higher attachment insecurity, but comparisons with other father contact classifications were not statistically significant for this age group.

It should be noted that (a) the sample in this study included disproportionate numbers of poor, never married minority parents, consistent with the population of large U.S. cities; (b) the measure of attachment security was a variation on the attachment Q-sort completed by mothers; and (c) the majority of the weekly overnight group (57%) did *not* have insecure attachments. On the other hand, higher rates of attachment insecurity were found in the weekly overnight group even though, in comparison to less frequent contact groups, mothers rated the co-parenting relationship and the father's parenting more positively. Moreover, the study broadly replicated a large Australian study (McIntosh et al. 2013), as it was intended to do, by using identical definitions of overnight frequency but a better, if still imperfect, measure of attachment security. Finally, another, small scale study also found some indications of more attachment problems associated with more frequent infant overnights (Solomon and George 1999a, b), while a fourth study found that having any overnights (more than one, ever) was neither positively nor negatively associated with measures of infants and toddlers well-being (Pruett et al. 2004).

The polarized and political nature of the debate about overnights for very young children is apparent in the publication of a so-called "consensus report" that claimed to review a wider range of the relevant literature and included endorsements from 110 researchers and practitioners (Warshak 2014). However, (1) the report was never peer reviewed (as noted in the publication, the paper was submitted and accepted on the same day), (2) it contained no information on number of professionals contacted who did *not* endorse the author's recommendations or even on the population that was sampled, (3) none of the authors of any of the four direct studies of overnights and very young children (i.e, those cited above) were contacted about their "consensus," and (4) shortly before the "consensus" report was published, the author of the report, as well as the present author, both participated along with 30 other family law experts in a conference designed to reach consensus about JPC hosted by the Association of Family and Conciliation Courts. This diverse group explicitly did *not* reach consensus (Pruett and DiFonzo 2014), yet shortly after this meeting, the author of the controversial report nevertheless went on to claim "consensus." Finally, the review (Warshak 2014) included 16 studies, 12 of which either were not empirical studies, included older children, did not directly study overnights and attachment, or contained all three problems. Yet, the reviewer repeatedly labeled three of the four direct studies cited above as "outliers" (McIntosh et al. 2013; Solomon and George 1999a, b; Tornello et al. 2013). In short, the so-called "consensus" report is an example of what the present author and other in experts have called "scholar-advocacy bias," where evidence gets "bent" in order to promote a cause, the fathers' rights cause in this case (Emery et al. 2016).

Despite consensus claims, there is no clear evidence-based conclusion about frequent overnights away from the primary attachment figure and attachment insecurity. In the absence of definitive research – and given the cautions raised by 3 of the 4 direct studies, the present author believes that the risk of infants being securely attached to no parent is greater than the risk of being securely attached to only one parent. This conclusion leads him to favor schedules that promote and preserve a primary, secure attachment, while also building a secure second attachment in the first year of life. However, the schedule should evolve to more equally shared parenting time as infants become toddlers and preschoolers (Emery 2016).

3.10 Children's Personality and Mental Health

A number of practicing mental health professionals have suggested that the JPC is contraindicated or at least more challenging when children suffer from certain psychological problems, particularly Attention-Deficit/Hyperactivity Disorder (ADHD) or Autism Spectrum Disorder (ASD) (Pickar and Kaufman 2015). Surprisingly, no high quality, empirical research has examined whether children with these disorders actually are less likely to be placed in JPC, and if they are, whether they have more problems than children with the same problems and are living in sole custody.

Beyond psychological disorders, parents and professionals wonder, and worry, if some children's personalities allow them to thrive in JPC, while other children's personalities make sole custody a better option. A recent study instructively addressed this concern. The investigation included 506 adolescents aged 14 to 21 drawn from a national sample of families in Flanders (Sodermans and Matthijs 2014). Results revealed an interaction between adjustment to JPC and youth's conscientiousness. Youths who rated themselves lower on conscientiousness were significantly less depressed and had a higher sense of mastery if they lived in JPC versus sole mother custody. The opposite was found for youth high in conscientiousness, who were less depressed and had a higher sense of mastery when living in sole mother custody versus JPC. The investigators speculated that JPC may be disruptive for orderly, conscientious youth, but attractive to more laid back adolescents (Sodermans and Matthijs 2014).

Like other research on JPC, this finding is more illustrative than definitive. No one should be deciding custody based on adolescent's "Big Five" personality scores. But the research underscores the general idea that JPC may be a good or a bad fit for some children based their individual personality or mental health needs.

3.11 Where Do We Go from Here?

This overview clearly establishes the need for more research on a great many facets of JPC. Fortunately, some high quality studies are being conducted in Europe, Australia, and Singapore, while U.S. efforts lag behind as no federal or private agency has prioritized funding research on JPC or related topics. Hopefully, the U.S. research investment will grow, given the large number of children affected, the controversies involved, and the importance of clear answers to children's (and parents') well-being (Emery 2019).

In the meantime, how can practitioners answer the questions so many parents ask? Perhaps the most honest answer, particularly for legislators and policy-makers, is that research is complicated, JPC requires careful consideration in terms of the issues outlined here, and research certainly is not definitive, despite some claims that it is. In short, there are no quick and easy empirically-based answers about JPC for legal policy.

For practicing legal and mental health professionals, the unanswered questions comprise a series of concerns to share with parents who are seeking to construct a JPC arrangement that will work for their family. Toward that end, parents, and the professionals who work with them, are wise to attempt to resolve their differences in mediation or some other, more cooperative forum for dispute resolution. Mediation has been demonstrated to lead to improved long-term parenting and co-parenting, and the sustained involvement of both parents in children's lives (Emery et al. 2001).

Working together cooperatively also gives parents a way to answer unanswered research questions individually for their own children and family. Parents can experiment to see what actually *does* work for their children, rather than guessing what *might* work based limited research on average child and family well-being. That is, parents can try what they believe is a good schedule for several weeks or months. If the plan is not working, however, they can change it and try something else.

Working together also gives parents other opportunities to individualize JPC. For one, cooperative parents can construct somewhat different schedules for their different children. Differing schedules might be based on factors such as children's age, personality, and/or preferences. For example, a very young child might have more overnights with one parent, while older children have a more equal number of overnights with each parent. Alternatively, parents might devise schedules that vary a bit from child to child simply to give children and parents some one-on-one time. Once a month, for example, one child might transition from one home to the other on a Friday afternoon, while the other transitions Saturday at noon. If parents alternate this arrangement between children, every parent-child pair gets some regular one-on-one time. The schedule also has the advantage of making the parenting time "pie" bigger (Emery 2016).

Parents who cooperate also can be more flexible in changing schedules over time, so a plan can grow and change along with children's and parents' changing developmental needs. The schedule for an infant might change when she becomes a toddler, for example, and then again when she becomes a preschooler. Custody schedules often do change as children grow older. Recognition of this fact in advance not only prepares parents for the likelihood of change, but also can help parents accept a less than ideal current schedule in the present.

In contrast to cooperative parents, parents who fail to work together close out options for themselves and for the children. As noted earlier, in fact, parents who fail to contain their understandable anger may undermine the success of or even the possibility of JPC.

References

Austin, W. G. (2008). Relocation, research, and forensic evaluation: Part I: Effects of residential mobility on children of divorce. *Family Court Review, 46*, 136–149.

Baude, A., Pearson, J., & Drapeau. (2016). Child adjustment in joint physical custody versus sole custody: A meta-analytic review. *Journal of Divorce and Remarriage, 57*, 338–360.

Bauserman, R. (2002). Child adjustment in joint-custody versus sole custody arrangements: A meta-analytic review. *Journal of Family Psychology, 16*, 91–102.

Emery, R. E. (1982). Interparental conflict and the children of discord and divorce. *Psychological Bulletin, 92*, 310–330.

Emery, R. E. (1999). *Marriage, divorce, and children's adjustment* (2nd ed.). Thousand Oaks: Sage.

Emery, R. E. (2011). *Renegotiating family relationships: Divorce, child custody, and mediate* (2nd ed.). New York: Guilford.

Emery, R. E. (2016). *Two homes, one childhood: A parenting plan to last a lifetime*. New York: Avery.

Emery, R. E. (2019). More research is needed. *Family Court Review, 57*, 10–12.

Emery, R. E., & Wyer, M. M. (1987). Divorce mediation. *American Psychologist, 42*, 472–480.

Emery, R. E., Laumann-Billings, L., Waldron, M., Sbarra, D. A., & Dillon, P. (2001). Child custody mediation and litigation: Custody, contact, and co-parenting 12 years after initial dispute resolution. *Journal of Consulting and Clinical Psychology, 69*, 323–332.

Emery, R. E., Holtzworth-Munroe, A., Kline-Pruett, M., Johnston, J., Pedro-Carroll, J. P. C., Saini, M., & Sandler, I. (2016). Scholar-advocacy bias in family law. *Family Court Review, 54*, 134–149.

Furstenberg, F. F., Peterson, J. L., Nord, C. W., & Zill, N. (1983). The life course of children of divorce: Marital disruption and parental contact. *American Sociological Review, 48*, 656–668.

Kaspiew, R., Gray, M., Weston, R., Moloney, L., Hand, K., Qu, L., & the Family Law Evaluation Team. (2009). *Evaluation of the 2006 family law reforms*. Melbourne: Australian Institute of Family Studies.

Kitterod, R., & Wiik, K. A. (2017). Shared residence among parents living apart in Norway. *Family Court Review, 55*, 556–571.

Lamb, M. E. (2012). A wasted opportunity to engage with the literature on the implications of attachment research for family court professionals. *Family Court Review, 50*, 481–485.

Lamb, M. E., & Kelly, J. B. (2001). Using the empirical literature to guide the development of parenting plans for young children. *Family Court Review, 39*, 365–371.

Lee, M.-Y. (2002). A model of children's postdivorce behavioral adjustment in maternal- and dual-residence arrangements. *Journal of Family Issues, 23*, 672–697.

Maccoby, E. E., & Mnookin, R. H. (1992). *Dividing the child: Social and legal dilemmas of custody*. Cambridge, MA: Harvard University Press.

Mahrer, N. E., O'Hara, K. L., Sandler, I. N., & Wolchik, S. A. (2018). Does shared parenting help or hurt children in high-conflict divorced families? *Journal of Divorce and Remarriage, 59*, 324–347.

Main, M., Hesse, E., & Hesse, S. (2011). Attachment theory and research: Overview and suggested applications to child custody. *Family Court Review, 49*, 426–463.

McIntosh, J. E. (2011). Guest editor's introduction to special issue on attachment theory, separation, and divorce: Forging coherent understandings for family law. *Family Court Review, 49*, 418–425.

McIntosh, J. E., Smyth, B. M., & Kelaher, M. (2013). Overnight care patterns following parental separation: Associations with emotion regulation in infants and young children. *Journal of Family Studies, 19*, 224–239.

Merla, L., Dedonder, J., Murru, S., & Nobels, B. (this volume). Sense of home, digital communication and quality of parent-child relations in post-divorce families. In L. Bernardi & D. Mortelmans (Eds.), *Shared physical custody*. Cham: Springer.

Meyer, D. R., Cancian, M., & Cook, S. T. (2017). The growth in shared custody in the United States: Patterns and implications. *Family Court Review, 55*, 500–512.

Modecki, K. L., Hagan, M., Sandler, I. N., & Wolchik, S. (2015). Latent profiles of nonresidential father engagement six years after divorce predict long-term offspring outcomes. *Journal of Clinical Child & Adolescent Psychology, 44*, 123–136.

Nielsen, L. (2018). Joint versus sole physical custody: Children's outcomes independent of parent-child relationships, income, and conflict in 60 studies. *Journal of Divorce and Remarriage, 59*, 247–281.

Pickar, D. B., & Kaufman, R. L. (2015). Parenting plans for special needs children: Applying the risk-assessment model. *Family Court Review, 53*, 113–133.

Poortman, A. (2018). Postdivorce parent-child contact and child Well-being: The importance of predivorce parental involvement. *Journal of Marriage and Family, 80*, 671–683.

Poortman, A. (this volume). Postdivorce parent-child contact and child outcomes: The role of spatial mobility. In L. Bernardi & D. Mortelmans (Eds.), *Shared physical custody*. Cham: Springer.

Poortman, A., & van Gaalen, R. (2017). Shared residence after separation: A review and new findings from the Netherlands. *Family Court Review, 55*, 531–544.

Pruett, M. K., & DiFonzo, J. H. (2014). Closing the gap: Research. *Policy, Practice, and Shared Parenting, Family Court Review, 52*, 152–174.

Pruett, M. K., Ebling, R., & Insabella, G. (2004). Critical aspects of parenting plans for young children: Interjecting data into the debate about overnights. *Family Court Review, 42*, 39–59.

Smyth, B. (2017). Special issue on shared-time parenting after separation. *Family Court Review, 55*, 494–499.

Smyth, B., & Chisholm, R. (2017). Shared-time parenting after separation in Australia: Precursors. *Prevalence, and Postreform Patterns, Family Court Review, 55*, 586–603.

Smyth, B., Chisholm, R., Rodgers, B., & Son, V. (2014). Legislating for shared-time parenting: Insights from Australia? *Journal of Law and Contemporary Problems, 77*, 108–149.

Smyth, B. M., McIntosh, J. E., Emery, R. E., & Higgs Howarth, S. L. (2016). Shared-time parenting: Evaluating the evidence of risks and benefits to children. In L. Drozd, M. Saini, & N. Olesen (Eds.), *Parenting plan evaluations: Applied research for the family court* (2nd ed.). New York: Oxford University Press.

Sodermans, A. K., & Matthijs, K. (2014). Joint physical custody and adolescents' subjective well-being: A personality × environment interaction. *Journal of Family Psychology, 28*, 346–356.

Solomon, J., & George, C. (1999a). The development of attachment in separated and divorced families: Effects of overnight visitation, parent and couple variables. *Attachment & Human Development, 1*, 2–33. https://doi.org/10.1080/14616739900134011.

Solomon, J., & George, C. (1999b). The effects of overnight visitation in divorced and separated families: A longitudinal follow-up. In J. Solomon & C. George (Eds.), *Attachment disorganization* (pp. 243–264). New York: Guilford.

Spruijt, E., & Duindam, V. (2010). Joint physical custody in the Netherlands and the well-being of children. *Journal of Divorce & Remarriage, 51*, 65–82.

Sroufe, A., & McIntosh, J. (2011). Divorce and attachment relationships: The longitudinal journey. *Family Court Review, 49*, 464–473.

Steinbach, A. (2018). Children's and parents well-being in joint physical custody: A literature review. *Family Process*, zx, zx.

Tornello, S. L., Emery, R. E., Rowen, J., Potter, D., Ocker, B., & Xu, Y. (2013). Overnight custody arrangements, attachment, and adjustment among very young children. *Journal of Marriage and the Family, 75*, 871–885.

Vanassche, S., Sodermans, A. K., Matthijs, K., & Swicegood, G. (2013). Commuting between two parental households: The association between joint physical custody and adolescent wellbeing following divorce. *Journal of Family Studies, 19*, 139–158.

Vanassche, S., Sodermans, A. K., Declerck, C., & Matthijs, K. (2017). Alternating residence for children after parental separation: Recent findings from Belgium. *Family Court Review, 55*, 545–555.

Warshak, R. A. (2014). Social science and parenting plans for young children: A consensus report. *Psychology, Public Policy, and Law, 20*, 46–67.

Robert E. Emery is Professor of Psychology and Director of the Center for Children, Families, and the Law at the University of Virginia, USA. He has authored over 150 scientific publications, and several books on divorce, including, Two Homes, One Childhood (2016), The Truth about Children and Divorce (2004), and Renegotiating Family Relationships (2012, 2nd Ed). He is a practicing clinical psychologist and divorce mediator, as well as an academic investigator.

4

Harmonization of Family Law: A European Model

Katharina Boele-Woelki

Abstract Since 2001 the academic Commission on European Family Law (CEFL) has drafted Principles of European Family Law that are thought to be most suitable for the harmonization of family law within Europe. The CEFL Principles are non-binding rules. They can be considered to be a model law which national legislators can take into account.

This contribution explains methodological aspects of the drafting process of the Principles on Parental Responsibilities. It informs about the huge amount of international and European instruments. Although each of these instruments only addresses some specific aspects of the law regarding parental responsibilities, they collectively built the general framework which to a considerable extent has also determined the national systems in Europe. Before focussing on the concept of parental responsibilities, as well as on those Principles which specifically address the situation upon divorce and separation of the parents (joint and sole exercise, (dis-)agreement on exercise, residence of the child, relocation, maintenance of personal relationships, hearing of the child, representing the child), information about the structure of the Principles is provided. Finally, more than 10 years after the publication of the Parental Responsibilities Principles it makes sense to take stock and explore how they have been perceived.

Keywords Europe · Parental responsibilities · Harmonization · Methodology · Comparative family law

K. Boele-Woelki (✉)
Bucerius Law School, Hamburg, Germany
e-mail: Katharina.Boele-Woelki@law-school.de

4.1 Comparative Research-Based Drafting of Principles of European Family Law

Family law in Europe consists of two sets of legal rules: national substantive family law on the one hand and their respective private international law rules for family matters on the other. The latter apply in cross-border family relations, for instance, if a couple who both have Portuguese nationality but live in Belgium want to obtain a divorce. The substantive family law systems largely differ. No one system is the same as another. These dissimilarities between the family law systems create problems for the increasing number of families who have links with more than one State, due to their nationality or habitual residence. They must cope with two problems: firstly, the internationality of their relationship is disregarded since, according to the traditional rules of private international law, their cross-border relationship (e.g. marriage, divorce) must be located within the territory of one State, whereas such a relationship is, by definition, connected to more than one State. Secondly, case law of the European countries indicates that crossing borders often results in the loss of rights (e.g. civil status) or the creation of financial obligations. The international couple may 'shop' for the specific jurisdiction which provides the most favourable results for themselves as individuals (e.g. a quick divorce or a lifelong maintenance claim). Since in particular within the European Union the European Commission has no competence to harmonize or unify the family law systems of the Member States it is up to legal scholars to provide solutions which might lead to the further harmonization of family laws in Europe.

Some 18 years ago the Commission on European Family Law (CEFL) started its academic work through drafting Principles of European Family Law that are thought to be most the suitable for the harmonization of family law within Europe. This has resulted in Principles regarding Divorce and Maintenance between Former Spouses (2004), Parental Responsibilities (2007) and Property Relations between Spouses (2013). The next set of Principles regarding *de facto* Unions will be finalised in 2019. The Principles on European Family Law are non-binding rules. They function like Model Laws. First and foremost, they are addressed towards national legislators, however, it is for them to decide whether they reform their family laws according to the proposals of the CEFL. Eventually, the CEFL Principles can function as a source of inspiration for both the European and international legislator.

The aim of this contribution[1] is twofold. It explains the methodological aspects of the drafting process and it informs the reader about the content of the Principles on Parental Responsibilities, about CEFL's considerations as to why the various rules were adopted and about the huge amount of international and European instruments that are relevant in the context of parental responsibilities. Although each of these instruments only addresses some specific aspects of the law regarding parental

[1] See also Boele-Woelki, The CEFL Principles regarding parental responsibilities: Predominance of the common core, in Boele-Woelki/ Sverdrup (eds), *European Challenges in Contemporary Family Law*, European Family Law series no. 19, Intersentia 2008, pp. 63–91.

responsibilities, they collectively build the general framework which to a considerable extent has also determined the national systems in Europe. In no other field of family law have so many agreements between states been drafted, concluded, adopted and have become binding. This development which started some 50 years ago and which culminated in 1989 with the adoption of the Convention on the Rights of the Child can be classified as a spontaneous harmonisation of the law regarding the parent-child relationship. It forms the very foundation on which the CEFL Principles were drafted. Before focussing on the concept of parental responsibilities, as well as on those Principles which specifically address the situation upon divorce and the separation of the parents (joint and sole exercise, (dis)agreement on exercise, residence of the child, relocation, maintenance of personal relationships, hearing of the child, representing the child), information about the structure of the Principles is provided. Finally, 12 years after the publication of this set of Principles it makes sense to take stock and explore how they have been perceived. Did they have any impact on the process of the harmonization of family law?

4.2 Working Method

The establishment of the CEFL in 2001 and its drafting of common Principles have led to a widespread and intensive debate among family law comparatists about the working method to be applied. Over the years the CEFL has applied its own method which in short consists of six steps. The *first* step is to select the fields of family law that are most suitable for harmonization. The *second* step is to draft a questionnaire which proceeds from the functional approach. According to this problem-oriented approach questions are posed in purely functional terms without any reference to the concepts of a specific legal system, thus asking what is the underlying problem that a certain legal provision aims to redress. The *third* step is to draw up national reports which not only take the law in the books into account, but also the law in practice. Each legal system may prescribe its list of official sources, but this list, which is only designed to bind judges and courts internally, does not necessarily bind a comparatist. The practical importance of the law as it appears in action also holds true in the field of family law. The national reports are aimed at discovering what practitioners are actually doing with the legal rules. The *fourth* step is to collect and to disseminate the comparative material. In addition to the country-by-country reports which are accessible on the CEFL's website, an integrated and printed version laid out according to the numbers of the questions has been published. This integrated version provides a rapid overview and a straightforward simultaneous comparison of the different solutions within the national systems. The *fifth* step is to draft the Principles of European Family Law. Proposals are made by the members of the Organizing Committee which are discussed with the authors of the national reports (the Expert Group). At this stage a decision must be made between either the 'common core' or the 'better law' approach. The *sixth* and final step is to publish the Principles.

Similarities and differences, convergence and divergence, common law and/or better law are the key expressions which are discussed in the process of indicating the various findings. The main questions boil down to the following: When and why should we build on similarities, convergence and, finally, the common core and how can we cope with differences and divergences, as well as when and why do we opt for the better law approach? In drafting the Principles of Parental Responsibilities these questions were repeatedly posed and finally answered for each specific subject. Many similarities, a great deal of converging tendencies and a common core regarding numerous issues could be detected.

4.3 International and European Instruments

In the field of parental responsibilities, the differences among the European systems are considerably less strong than in other fields of family law. Hence, in the majority of issues CEFL's Principles only restate the common solutions that are generally applied. The harmonisation of the law regarding parental responsibilities within Europe has gradually taken place through the many international and European instruments. In drafting the Principles on Parental Responsibilities 16 conventions by respectively the United Nations, the Hague Conference on Private International Law, the Council of Europe and the European Union, 1 EU Regulation, 4 Declarations of the United Nations, 13 Recommendations and, additionally, the White Paper of the Council of Europe were taken into account.[2] Although each of these instruments only addresses some specific aspects of the law regarding parental responsibilities, they collectively built the general framework which to a considerable extent has also determined the national systems in Europe. In no other field of family law have so many agreements between states been drafted, concluded, adopted and have become binding.

[2]BOELE-WOELKI, K./FERRAND, F./GONZÁLEZ BEILFUSS, C./JÄNTERÄ-JAREBORG, M./ LOWE, N./MARTINY, D./PINTENS, W., *Principles of European Family Law Regarding Parental Responsibilities*, European Family Law Series no. 16 (2007), 15–19.

4.4 Structure

The publication of 39 Principles regarding Parental Responsibilities,[3] including the compilation of the comparative material,[4] are the result of teamwork to which 26 legal experts from 22 European jurisdictions in the field of comparative family law have contributed. Each section containing a Principle consists of four parts. The text of the Principle itself[5] is followed by an overview of the relevant international and/or European provisions regarding the issue addressed in the Principle in order to recall the international commitments that have previously been achieved. The international obligations built the framework along which the Principles have been drafted. The comparative overviews and the comments do not only refer to the 22 national reports by the CEFL experts, but include, in addition, the related international and/or European instruments. All four parts belong together.

Preamble
Chapter I: Definitions
Chapter II: Rights of the child
Chapter III: Parental responsibilities of parents and third persons
Chapter IV: Exercise of parental responsibilities

Section A: Parents
Section B: Third persons

Chapter V: Content of parental responsibilities

Section A: The child's person and property
Section B: Maintenance of personal relationships

Chapter VI: Termination of parental responsibilities
Chapter VII: Discharge and restoration of parental responsibilities
Chapter VIII: Procedure

The table of contents indicates which issues are addressed. Essentially, a distinction is made between three different areas. Chapters I, II and VIII contain general rules. To these general rules belong four different parts: first, the Preamble, second, two Principles which define, first, the concept of parental responsibilities and, second, the holders of parental responsibilities. The choice for a broad concept of parental responsibilities necessitates indicating who can be attributed with parental responsibilities and can exercise the necessary rights and duties. CEFL's concept explicitly makes a distinction between parents and third persons. Primarily parents

[3]BOELE-WOELKI, K./FERRAND, F./GONZÁLEZ BEILFUSS, C./JÄNTERÄ-JAREBORG, M./ LOWE, N./MARTINY, D./PINTENS, W., *Principles of European Family Law Regarding Parental Responsibilities*, European Family Law Series no. 16 (2007).

[4]BOELE-WOELKI, K./BRAAT, B./CURRY-SUMNER, I. (eds.), *European Family Law in Action, Volume III: Parental Responsibilities*, European Family Law Series no. 9 (2005).

[5]Enclosed in the Appendix at the end of this contribution.

are in charge of exercising parental responsibilities. However, persons other than parents as well as public bodies can also have parental responsibilities. The relevant international and European human rights cinstruments have profoundly influenced Chap. 2 which is devoted to the rights of the child. With its five Principles this Chapter forms the main general part of the CEFL Principles. The rights of the child are always to be taken into account in all matters of parental responsibilities. They constitute the principal point of departure along which all other issues should be addressed. Also the procedural aspects are of a general nature. Chapters 3, 4 and 5 address three aspects: the position of parents and third persons, the exercise of parental responsibilities and their content. Chapters 6 and 7, finally, deal with the termination of parental responsibilities and being discharged therefrom.

4.5 Concept of Parental Responsibilities

What are parental responsibilities and who are its holders? In accordance with international and European instruments the CEFL opted for a broad concept of parental responsibilities consisting of a collection of rights and duties that embody the concept of taking care of the child's person and property (Principle 3:1). Concepts like guardianship and custody that are still used in national systems have been abandoned. CEFL's concept of parental responsibilities applies to children from the moment of their birth until they have reached the age of majority. A difference between younger and adolescent children has been recognized, although the indication of an age limit has intentionally been avoided. It not only depends on the child's age but also upon his/her maturity whether his/her opinion should be taken into account.

The Principles refer to the rather long-winded term "holders of parental responsibilities". Normally, the child has two parents who are the holders of parental responsibilities. However, also a person other than a parent, who has no legal ties with the child, can be attributed with and exercise parental responsibilities. Principle 3:2 clarifies this distinction. Primarily, the parents, whose legal parentage has been established, are in charge of the exercise of parental responsibilities. However, physical persons other than the parents as well as public bodies can also have parental responsibilities. According to the CEFL Principles it is thus possible that there might be even more than two holders of parental responsibilities.

4.6 Divorce and Separation

In the case of divorce or the separation of the parents they continue to hold parental responsibilities jointly. Principle 3:10 states that parental responsibilities should neither be affected by the dissolution or annulment of the marriage or other formal relationship nor by the legal or factual separation between the parents. Hence a divorce or separation has no influence on the attribution of parental responsibilities. The Principle is in accordance with the common core of the legal systems that were surveyed by the CEFL. Consequently, parents who have parental responsibilities should have a continuous equal right and duty to exercise such responsibilities jointly. Exceptions to the joint and equal exercise of parental responsibilities are however recognized because it is realized that parental responsibilities should be exercised by the parents together "whenever possible". This is expressed in Principle 3:11. The fact that parental responsibilities should be exercised jointly does not mean that parents must act together in all circumstances. This issue is further developed under Principle 3:12(1) which grants the authority to act alone in daily matters. However, Principle 3:12(2) requires that important decisions concerning matters such as education, medical treatment, the child's residence, or the administration of his or her property should be taken jointly. The Principle contains a non-exhaustive list which serves as an illustration. Not all matters in these areas require a joint decision; this is only so if the matter is important. The Principles do not provide a criterion in order to evaluate whether or not an issue is important. Decisions with a long-lasting effect for the child should, however, be considered as being important. For example, whereas authorizing a child to attend a language course will not be deemed to be an important decision on education requiring the consent of both parents, a change of school would probably be regarded as such. Much, however, depends on the circumstances of the case. Irrespective of whether a matter is to be considered important, a parent should have the right to act alone in urgent matters. In this case the other parent should be informed without undue delay (Principle 3:12 (2)).

Given the fact that the joint exercise of parental responsibilities becomes more complicated after divorce or the separation of the parents, they are encouraged to agree on how to arrange their rights and duties. Principle 3:13(1) lays down the generally acknowledged principle that the parents can make agreements concerning the exercise of parental responsibilities. This means that they may agree on several matters or on a specific issue. The scope of an agreement can cover all aspects of parental responsibilities listed in Principle 3:1, in particular care, protection and education. An agreement between the holders of parental responsibilities may also lead to the sole exercise of parental responsibilities by one of the parents according to Principle 3:15(a); however, both the agreement on joint exercise as well as on sole exercise are subject to the best interests of the child. As a result, the competent authority, usually a court, should scrutinize the agreement from this perspective.

In many cases, however, the parents disagree on their joint exercise of parental responsibilities. This situation has been addressed in Principle 3:14. In the case of a disagreement they may apply to the competent authority, but only if they cannot agree on an important matter, such as the child's residence or educational matters. If the competent authority is requested to decide the dispute, it should first attempt to attain an agreement between the parties. The competent authority can decide the dispute itself or it can authorize one of the parents to act alone with regard to one or more issues. The second alternative avoids any unnecessary intervention in family life. However, the practical result will often be the same, because deciding on the most competent parent will be difficult without taking into account the disputed issue itself. Therefore, Principle 3:14(3) leaves it open whether parental responsibilities may be exercised by one holder of parental responsibilities alone or the dispute itself may be decided by the competent authority. Authorizing one of the parents to act alone will be preferable where it can be established that a specific, separable issue must be resolved and one of the holders of parental responsibilities has a sufficient degree of competence or knowledge to pursue the best interests of the child concerning this question. In any case the competent authority must observe the principle of the best interests of the child and also has to take into account the former practice of the parents.

The majority of the Principles which belong to Chap. 4 on the exercise of parental responsibilities are based on the common core which can be found in both the national systems and the international and European instruments. These general rules to be applied were selected as the best solutions. In respect of a few, but important, aspects it was not possible to discover a common approach. Regarding these aspects, a solution was selected which is applied in only a few countries. They are practicable and in line with CEFL's objectives in creating a flexible and efficient system which is also based on equality. This applies to the power of the parents having joint parental responsibilities to act alone in daily matters (Principles 3:12 (1)), the obligation of the parent who acted in urgent cases to inform the other parent without undue delay (Principles 3:12(2)), the competence of the competent authority to decide on a dispute or to authorize one of the parents having joint parental responsibilities in case of a disagreement between them (Principles 3:14(3)), the exercise of parental responsibilities by one parent if both parents have made an agreement to that end (Principle 3(15)) and the recognition that parental responsibilities may be exercised by third persons in addition to or instead of the parents (Principle 3:17). Hence, in respect of these issues the CEFL applied the better law approach in order to establish a coherent regulatory scheme.

4.7 Maintenance of Personal Relationships, Residence of the Child and Relocation

The maintenance of personal relationships between the child and his or her parents forms a part of parental responsibilities. Such a maintenance of personal relationships is established by contact. Principle 3:25 prefers contact to "access" because this term is broader and better expresses the bilateral nature of personal relationships. Because the maintenance of personal relationships exists mainly in the child's interests, the child should have his or her own right of contact whereas the parents should have a right and a corresponding duty. Principle 3:25(1) therefore expressly establishes that contact is a right and it implicitly declares that it is also a duty for the parents.

Principle 3:25(2) states that a child should also have a right of contact with relatives other than his or her parents. This includes mainly his or her grandparents. In these cases, there exist close family ties and grandparents can fulfil an important role for the development of the child. Grandparents are not expressly mentioned despite the fact that they enjoy a privileged status according to many family systems. Also with siblings, personal relationships should be maintained. However, Principle 3:25(2) does not establish a list of such relatives. This is in accordance with Article 5 § 1 of the Convention on Contact Concerning Children 2003. This right to contact should exist even against the will of the parent(s). The child's right to maintain relationships with persons other than a parent does create an obligation for parents to enable and support such contact. The question of whether these persons have an actionable right allowing them to have contact even in opposition to the wishes of the parents has not been dealt with in the CEFL Principles. There are good reasons for not enforcing such contact if it seriously disturbs the parent-child relationship. This is recognized by some national systems which do not grant such a right to persons other than parents or which allow more restrictions on this right than they do when the issue at stake is contact between the child and a parent.

Principle 3:25(3) recognizes also that with third persons who are not relatives, close ties can exist. This group embraces a great variety of persons (step-parents, foster parents). Particularly when these persons have fulfilled social family functions, the maintenance of personal relationships is appropriate and generally in the best interests of the child. However, Principle 3:25(3) only states that there "may" be contact; there is no automatic maintenance of personal relations. Since the factual circumstances and the degree of closeness may differ greatly, in these cases there should only be a right for these persons but not an obligation.

Two issues deserve special attention when the parents divorce or separate. Where will the residence of the child be and under which circumstances should it be possible to relocate to a different place or country? In many national systems, the determination of the child's residence is not a separate issue. The child's residence falls under the exception that no common core could be found. The lack of a common core regarding this aspect is due to the fact that, on the one hand, we are witnessing a greater mobility of persons not only within Europe but all around the globe, and, on the other hand, that joint parental responsibilities increasingly lead to equal parenting which eventually results in an alternating residence for the child. These developments are new and are approached differently in the systems surveyed. Legislation is exceptional and judicial decisions differ to a great extent. In this area, the CEFL Principles provide new solutions which to a certain extent are based on the legal practice of some countries. These solutions may function as guidelines not only for legislatures but primarily for the courts and other administrative bodies which are requested to decide on disputes concerning the child's residence.

In accordance with CEFL's approach the decision with whom the child should reside is left to the parents. Principle 3:20(1) recalls that any determination of the child's residence requires the parents to reach an agreement to this effect if they cease to live together. This is consistent with Principle 3:10 which establishes that parental responsibilities are as such unaffected by the fact that the parents divorce or separate. If they fail to agree on the child's residence, the matter will be deferred to the competent authority which will proceed according to Principle 3:14.

At the time the CEFL Principles regarding Parental Responsibilities were drafted, none of the jurisdictions surveyed had legislated the concept of shared or alternating residence which entails that the child lives with both parents on an alternate basis for a specific period of time.[6] Other terms that are commonly used to indicate this situation are: joint custody, joint parental responsibility, shared care, shared parenting, co-parenting and residential co-parenting. It started some 20 years ago. Ex-partners who had a very co-operative relationship with each other shared the daily care of the child due to flexible work times and the geographical proximity of their residences. However, when fathers (and fathers' rights organizations) were starting to see alternating residence less as an alternative way of arranging post-separation care, and more as an equality issue, the call for more arrangements regarding alternative residence, even in less appropriate situations, increased.[7] Principle 3:20(2) deals with alternating residence. Whether an alternating residence should be the rule or an exception is not decided by Principle 3:20(2). It merely establishes that an alternating residence should be possible if this is agreed upon by the holders of parental responsibilities and the competent authority approves such an agreement. The criteria which should be considered by the competent authority are factors such as (a) the age and opinion of the child; (b) the ability and willingness of the parents to cooperate with each other in matters concerning the child as well as their personal situation and (c) the distance between the residences of the parents and to the child's school. Principle 3:20(2) also contemplates the possibility that an alternating residence will be decided upon by the competent authority failing an agreement by the holders of parental responsibilities, if this is considered to be in the child's best interests taking into account the factors mentioned under Principle 3:20 (2). Since the ability and willingness of the holders of parental responsibilities is one of the criteria mentioned, an alternating residence should only be ordered by the competent authority failing an agreement in exceptional cases. Undoubtedly, an alternating residence should only be possible if it is in the best interests of the child. The list of factors provides guidelines for scrutinizing any agreement on an alternating residence for the child between the parents. It is also useful when there is no such agreement, but the competent authority is considering whether to decide on an alternating residence. The factors listed reflect the CEFL's concern that notwithstanding the fact that an alternating residence may promote personal relationships with both parents, it may also deprive the child of a stable environment and thus be

[6]NIKOLINA, *Divided Parents – Shared Children, Legal Aspects of (Residential) Co-Parenting in England, the Netherlands and Belgium*, European Family Law series no. 39, Intersentia 2015.

[7]ANTOKOLSKAIA, Solomo's oordeel nieuwe stijl: verblijfsco-ouderschap in België en Nederland. Over de rol van de wetenschap, invloed van de politiek, en nattevingerwerk in het wetgevingsproces, Rede uitgesproken bij de aanvaarding van de Marcel Storme leerstoel te Universiteit Gent op 12 mei 2010, p. 7.

harmful for the child. Each case is different. The final decision is to be taken by the competent authority.

Another issue that at the time of the drafting of the CEFL Principles regarding Parental Responsibilities was not statutorily regulated in any family law system of the jurisdictions surveyed by the CEFL concerns the wish of one of the parents to change the child's residence within or outside the jurisdiction. The CEFL decided to introduce a Principle specifically dealing with relocation in order to respond to an ever-increasing mobility in European society which is closely linked to EU citizenship. Relocation is emerging as an important issue in the context of European integration and the free movement of persons and is likely to lead to many disputes. Changing the child's residence within or outside the jurisdiction is such an important matter that it requires the other parent to be informed in advance. Since the determination of the child's residence is considered to be an important matter requiring that parents should act in agreement, the duty to inform is in fact implicit when parental responsibilities are held jointly by the parents. Principle 3:21(2) partially recalls Principle 3:14. When there is no agreement on relocation, the matter must be deferred to the competent authority. Principle 3:21(3) contains a non-exhaustive list of factors which have to be taken into consideration by the competent authority in order to take a decision on relocation. This decision requires that the competent authority tries to find a balance between the right of the child to maintain personal relationships with the non-residential parent and close relatives and persons with whom the child has a close relationship (Principle 3:25) and the right of the residential parent to move in pursuit of a valid purpose, in order to, for example, improve his or her professional situation or to accompany a new partner (free movement rights). Geographical distance and accessibility as well as the personal, particularly the financial, situation of the holders of parental responsibilities are crucial factors. As always, due weight should be given to the child's opinion, having regard to his or her age and maturity.

4.8 Procedural Issues

All five Principles in the Chapter on Procedure are based on the common core. These concern the following issues: It is generally acknowledged and practised that in deciding on or intervening in matters of parental responsibilities the situation of the child should be investigated. To that end, the competent authority should, where necessary, appoint any suitable person or body in order to obtain a clear view of the child's situation. In addition to this more traditional approach the increasing importance of alternative dispute resolution, which is being recognized by all national laws, is acknowledged by the Principles. Also in this field the common core is apparent. Consequently, in all disputes regarding parental responsibilities alternative dispute resolution mechanisms should be available (Principle 3:36). Principle 3:37 (1) stresses that the child should be heard in the context of proceedings that affect him or her. It is recognized, however, that there are situations where such a hearing could result in more harm than good. If the authority decides not to hear the child it should give specific reasons for this. In this respect a common core is not available and therefore the best solution was selected instead. There is no uniform approach in the national systems as to whether the hearing of the child should take place directly before the competent authority or indirectly before a person or body appointed by the competent authority. The Principles prefer a direct hearing; the court should use the knowledge of experts but should form its own impression. Additionally, the child should be heard in a manner which is appropriate to his or her age and maturity (Principle 3:37 (3)). No specific age limit is given. It is the common core of the majority of the jurisdictions represented in the CEFL that the child should have a special representative appointed in all cases in which the child's interest could be in conflict with those of the holders of PR or in which the welfare of the child is otherwise at risk. This guarantee is provided in Principle 3:38. The appointment of a special representative should take place ex officio by an order of the competent authority or may be requested by the child subject to the condition that he or she has sufficient understanding. Finally, the principle of the expeditious and effective enforcement of a decision by the competent authority or an agreement concerning parental responsibilities is approved in Principle 3:39. This is the main rule. Exceptionally, the enforcement may not take place if it is obviously irreconcilable with the child's best interests. Consequently, and subject to the condition that the child has sufficient understanding, a residence or contact order, for instance, should not be enforced against the wishes of the child.

4.9 Impact of the CEFL Principles

By and large, the Parental Responsibilities Principles form a frame of reference which is useful for any legislator. Comparative research has been carried out in the respective field, the material is easily accessible and widely disseminated, similarities and differences are determined, explanations are provided and, finally, while evaluating the solutions common Principles are proposed. They are based on the comparative findings. CEFL's final goal will have been achieved if in the end the final result will acquire a decent standing within the plethora of international and European instruments addressing the parent-child relationship. Additionally, by the empirical testing of the Principles in a number of legal systems one can demonstrate whether they are indeed acceptable and/or are regarded as an improvement on existing national laws. This has been done by Esin Örücü and Jane Mair in respect of the Principles discussed in this contribution.[8] Finally, to date the CEFL Principles regarding Parental Responsibilities inspired the Portuguese (Lei do divórcio 2008), Norwegian (Children Act 2010), Croatian (Family Law Act 2013) and Czech (2014)

[8]ÖRÜCÜ, E./MAIR, J. (eds), *Juxtaposing Legal Systems and the Principles of European Family Law on Parental Responsibilities*, European Family Law Series no. 27, 2010.

legislators in reforming the law of divorce and parental responsibilities respectively. More references to the CEFL Principles are to be expected. Recently, the Estonian legislator has been provided with information about CEFL's Principle on alternating residence, however, only after the general elections there in March 2019 the legislative process will be resumed.

Further research might include more extensive comparisons between national provisions on parental responsibilities which are not represented in CEFL's comparative material and the CEFL Model. Since the latter have only partially been incorporated into the law of a few national jurisdiction, it is not possible to test them as a whole from, for example, a social science perspective. The CEFL Principles as such are black letter rules belonging to the law in the books, whereas national parental responsibilities rules are applied in practice. In respect of these rules, qualitative and/or quantitative research can be undertaken, which might reveal that the law is in accordance with the needs of parents and their children, or that the law should be changed. When the latter is the case, the CEFL Principles might provide a better solution than the national system. For example, regarding the issue of the alternating residence of the child after divorce, or that of the relocation of the child, many national systems have not yet provided any legislative guidelines. It will depend on the courts how each individual case will be decided. This creates uncertainty and inequality. In its Explanatory Memorandum on the Recommendation of 2015 on Preventing and Resolving Disputes on Child Relocation, the Council of Europe has acknowledged this lack of guidance. It rightly refers to the CEFL Principle 3:21 in this respect. As stated in the introduction to this contribution, legislative measures will not be taken by the European Commission, since it lacks competence in the field of substantive family law.

Appendix: Principles of European Family Law Regarding Parental Responsibilities

Preamble

Recognising that, notwithstanding the existing diversities of national family law systems, there is nevertheless a growing convergence of laws;

Recognising that the free movement of persons within Europe is hindered by the remaining differences;

Desiring to contribute to common European values regarding the child's rights and welfare;

Desiring to contribute to the harmonisation of family law in Europe and to further facilitate the free movement of persons within Europe;

The Commission on European Family Law recommends the following Principles:

Chapter I: Definitions

Principle 3:1 Concept of Parental Responsibilities

Parental responsibilities are a collection of rights and duties aimed at promoting and safeguarding the welfare of the child. They encompass in particular:

(a) care, protection and education;
(b) maintenance of personal relationships;
(c) determination of residence;
(d) administration of property, and
(e) legal representation.

Principle 3:2 Holder of Parental Responsibilities

(1) A holder of parental responsibilities is any person having the rights and duties listed in Principle 3:1 either in whole or in part.
(2) Subject to the following Principles, holders of parental responsibilities are:
    (a) the child's parents, as well as
    (b) persons other than the child's parents having parental responsibilities in addition to or instead of the parents.

Chapter II: Rights of the Child

Principle 3:3 Best Interests of the Child

In all matters concerning parental responsibilities the best interests of the child should be the primary consideration.

Principle 3:4 Autonomy of the Child

The child's autonomy should be respected in accordance with the developing ability and need of the child to act independently.

Principle 3:5 Non-discrimination of the Child

Children should not be discriminated on grounds such as sex, race, colour, language, religion, political or other opinion, national, ethnic or social origin, sexual orientation, disability, property, birth or other status, irrespective of whether these grounds refer to the child or to the holders of parental responsibilities.

Principle 3:6 Child's Right to Be Heard

Having regard to the child's age and maturity, the child should have the right to be informed, consulted and to express his or her opinion in all matters concerning the child, with due weight given to the views expressed by him or her.

Principle 3:7 Conflict of Interests

The interests of the child should be protected whenever they may be in conflict with the interests of the holders of parental responsibilities.

Chapter III: Parental Responsibilities of Parents and Third Persons

Principle 3:8 Parents

Parents, whose legal parentage has been established, should have parental responsibilities for the child.

Principle 3:9 Third Persons

Parental responsibilities may in whole or in part also be attributed to a person other than a parent.

Principle 3:10 Effect of Dissolution and Separation

Parental responsibilities should neither be affected by the dissolution or annulment of the marriage or other formal relationship nor by the legal or factual separation between the parents.

Chapter IV: Exercise of Parental Responsibilities

SECTION A: PARENTS

Principle 3:11 Joint Exercise

Parents having parental responsibilities should have an equal right and duty to exercise such responsibilities and whenever possible they should exercise them jointly.

Principle 3:12 Daily Matters, Important and Urgent Decisions

(1) Parents having joint parental responsibilities should have the right to act alone with respect to daily matters.
(2) Important decisions concerning matters such as education, medical treatment, the child's residence, or the administration of his or her property should be taken jointly. In urgent cases a parent should have the right to act alone. The other parent should be informed without undue delay.

Principle 3:13 Agreement on Exercise

(1) Subject to the best interests of the child, parents having joint parental responsibilities may agree on the exercise of parental responsibilities.
(2) The competent authority may scrutinize the agreement.

Principle 3:14 Disagreement on Exercise

(1) Where parents having joint parental responsibilities cannot agree on an important matter they may apply to the competent authority.
(2) The competent authority should promote agreement between the parents.
(3) Where agreement cannot be reached the competent authority should divide the exercise of parental responsibilities between the parents or decide the dispute.

Principle 3:15 Sole Exercise upon Agreement or Decision

Subject to the best interests of the child a parent may exercise parental responsibilities alone.

(a) upon agreement between the parents according to Principle 3:13, or
(b) upon a decision of the competent authority.

Principle 3:16 Sole Exercise by One Parent

If only one parent has parental responsibilities he or she should exercise them alone.

SECTION B: THIRD PERSONS

Principle 3:17 Exercise in Addition to or Instead of the Parents

A person other than a parent may exercise some or all parental responsibilities in addition to or instead of the parents.

Principle 3:18 Decisions in Daily Matters

The parent's partner living with the child may take part in decisions with respect to daily matters unless the other parent having parental responsibilities objects.

Chapter V: Content of Parental Responsibilities

Section A: The CHILD'S Person and Property

Principle 3:19 Care, Protection and Education

(1) The holders of parental responsibilities should provide the child with care, protection and education in accordance with the child's distinctive character and developmental needs.
(2) The child should not be subjected to corporal punishment or any other humiliating treatment.

Principle 3:20 Residence

(1) If parental responsibilities are exercised jointly the holders of parental responsibilities who are living apart should agree upon with whom the child resides.
(2) The child may reside on an alternate basis with the holders of parental responsibilities upon either an agreement approved by a competent authority or a decision by a competent authority. The competent authority should take into consideration factors such as:

    (a) the age and opinion of the child;
    (b) the ability and willingness of the holders of parental responsibilities to

cooperate with each other in matters concerning the child, as well as their personal situation;
(c) the distance between the residences of the holders of the parental responsibilities and to the child's school.

Principle 3:21 Relocation

(1) If parental responsibilities are exercised jointly and one of the holders of parental responsibilities wishes to change the child's residence within or outside the jurisdiction, he or she should inform the other holder of parental responsibilities thereof in advance.
(2) If the other holder of parental responsibilities objects to the change of the child's residence, each of them may apply to the competent authority for a decision.
(3) The competent authority should take into consideration factors such as:
   (a) the age and opinion of the child;
   (b) the right of the child to maintain personal relationships with the other holders of parental responsibilities;
   (c) the ability and willingness of the holders of parental responsibilities to cooperate with each other;
   (d) the personal situation of the holders of personal responsibilities;
   (e) the geographical distance and accessibility;
   (f) the free movement of persons.

Principle 3:22 Administration of the child's Property

(1) The holders of parental responsibilities should administer the child's property with due care and diligence in order to preserve and where possible increase the value of the property.
(2) In administering the child's property the holders of parental responsibilities should not make gifts unless the gifts are deemed to be made under a moral obligation.
(3) The income derived from the child's property which is not needed for the proper management of the property or for the maintenance and education of the child may, where necessary, be used for the needs of the family.

Principle 3:23 Restrictions

(1) The holders of parental responsibilities should not administer property acquired by a child through a testamentary disposition or a gift, if the testator or the donor so instructed.

(2) Similarly the earnings by the child should not be administered by the holders of parental responsibilities unless the child is not of sufficient age and maturity to decide himself or herself.
(3) Where transactions can have significant financial consequences for the child the authorisation of the competent authority should be necessary.

Principle 3:24 Legal Representation

(1) The holders of parental responsibilities should legally represent the child in matters concerning the child's person or property.
(2) Legal representation should not take place where there is a conflict of interest between the child and the holders of parental responsibilities.
(3) Having regard to the child's age and maturity, the child should have the right to self-representation in legal proceedings concerning himself or herself.

SECTION B: MAINTENANCE OF PERSONAL RELATIONSHIPS

Principle 3:25 Contact with Parents and Other Persons

(1) The child and the parents should have the right to obtain and maintain regular contact with each other.
(2) Contact should be established between the child and his or her close relatives.
(3) Contact may be established between the child and persons with whom the child has close personal relations.

Principle 3:26 Content of Contact

(1) Contact comprises the child staying for a limited period of time with or meeting a parent or person other than a parent with whom he or she is not usually living; and any form of communication between the child and such person.
(2) Such contact should be in the best interests of the child.

Principle 3:27 Agreement

(1) Subject to the best interests of the child, the parents and the other persons identified under Principle 3:25(2) and (3) may agree on contact.
(2) The competent authority may scrutinize the agreement.

Principle 3:28 Restrictions

Contact may be restricted, terminated or made subject to conditions by the competent authority if the best interests of the child so require.

Principle 3:29 Information to Parents

A parent should have the right to be informed about matters concerning the personal situation of the child.

Chapter VI: Termination of Parental Responsibilities

Principle 3:30 Termination

(1) Parental responsibilities should be terminated in the case of the child:

(a) reaching majority;
(b) entering into a marriage or registered partnership;
(c) being adopted;
(d) dying.

(2) If a parent's partner adopts the child of the parent the parental responsibilities in relation to the other parent should be terminated.

Principle 3:31 Death of the Parents

(1) If parents have joint parental responsibilities and one of them dies the parental responsibilities should belong to the surviving parent.
(2) If a parent having sole parental responsibilities dies, responsibilities should be attributed to the surviving parent or a third person upon a decision by the competent authority.
(3) On the death of both parents, of whom at least one parent had parental responsibilities, the competent authority should take protective measures in respect of the person and the property of the child.

Chapter VII: Discharge and Restoration of Parental Responsibilities

Principle 3:32 Discharge of Parental Responsibilities

The competent authority should discharge the holder of parental responsibilities, wholly or in part, where his or her behaviour or neglect causes a serious risk to the person or the property of the child.

Principle 3:33 Request for Discharge of Parental Responsibilities

(1) The discharge of parental responsibilities may be requested by:

(a) any parent having parental responsibilities;
(b) the child, and.
(c) any institution protecting the interests of the child.

(2) **The competent authority may also order the discharge of parental responsibilities of its own motion.**

Principle 3:34 Restoration of Parental Responsibilities

Having regard to the best interests of the child, the competent authority may restore parental responsibilities if the circumstances that led to the discharge no longer exist.

Chapter VIII: Procedure

Principle 3:35 Competent Authority

(1) All decisions on parental responsibilities should be taken by the competent authority which can either be a judicial or an administrative body.
(2) Where necessary, the competent authority should appoint any suitable person or body to investigate the child's circumstances.

Principle 3:36 Alternative Dispute Resolution

In all disputes regarding parental responsibilities alternative dispute resolution mechanisms should be available.

Principle 3:37 Hearing of the Child

(1) Subject to Principle 3:6, the competent authority should hear the child in all proceedings concerning parental responsibilities but if it decides not to hear the child it should give specific reasons.
(2) The hearing of the child should take place either directly before the competent authority or indirectly before a person or body appointed by the competent authority.
(3) The child should be heard in a manner appropriate to his or her age and maturity.

Principle 3:38 Appointment of a Special Representative for the Child

In proceedings concerning parental responsibilities in which there could either be a serious conflict of interests between the child and the holders of parental responsibilities or in which the welfare of the child is otherwise at risk, the competent authority should appoint a special representative for the child.

Principle 3:39 Enforcement

(1) Failing voluntary compliance, a decision by the competent authority and an enforceable agreement concerning parental responsibilities should be enforced without delay.
(2) Enforcement should not take place if it is manifestly contrary to the best interests of the child.

Katharina Boele-Woelki is President of Bucerius Law School, the first private law school in Germany, where she also serves as the Claussen Simon Foundation Professor of Comparative Law. Until September 2015, she was Professor of Private International Law, Comparative Law and Family Law at Utrecht University, the Netherlands. In 2017 she has been appointed Extraordinary Professor at the University of Stellenbosch, South Africa. She established the Commission on European Family Law (CEFL) and the Utrecht Centre for European Research into Family Law (UCERF). She is president of the International Academy of Comparative Law, member of the Curatorium of The Hague Academy for International Law and was awarded honorary doctorates from Uppsala University, the University of Lausanne and the University of Antwerp, as well as the Anneliese Maier-Forschungspreis from the Alexander von Humboldt Foundation. She is an elected member of the Akademie der Wissenschaften in Hamburg.

Part II
Shared Physical Custory from the Parents' Perspective

5

A Study of Parents in Shared Physical Custody

Claudia Recksiedler and Laura Bernardi

Abstract Changing legal and parental practices across Europe led to a higher share of parents practicing shared physical custody (SPC) upon separation, who tended to be more affluent and less conflict-ridden. Since SPC became more prevalent, profiles of SPC parents pluralized. Far from these developments, no clearly defined legal pathways toward SPC existed in Switzerland before 2017. Profiling the Swiss case, we examine the prevalence of SPC families, and its associations with parental health and well-being before these legislative changes. Among 875 separated parents of 1,269 minors, SPC (i.e., child alternates between parental homes at least 30% of the time) was practiced by about 11% of the sample. A higher share of SPC parents was highly-educated, yet more financially strained compared to other parents. Although no overall differences in health and well-being emerged between SPC and other separated parents (e.g., with sole custody), SPC-health-linkages varied by gender and education. We conclude that lacking institutional support for SPC and gender-biased employment practices reinforce traditional custody models. Because of costly childcare and more skewed time splits among Swiss SPC parents, SPC may represent more of a resource drain—at least economically—than a relief for the parent shouldering more care duties and expenses.

Keywords Shared care · Parental well-being · Health disparities · Switzerland

C. Recksiedler (✉)
German Youth Institute, Munich, Germany
e-mail: recksiedler@dji.de

L. Bernardi
LIVES Centre, Swiss Centre of Expertise in Life Course Research and Institute of Social Sciences, University of Lausanne, Lausanne, Switzerland
e-mail: laura.bernardi@unil.ch

5.1 Introduction and Study Aims

The landscape of family forms and living arrangements with and without children is changing rapidly in Switzerland similar to the trends in many other Western nations (Bernardi et al. 2018; Sánchez Gassen and Perelli-Harris 2015; Goldschneider et al. 2015). Steady increases in divorce rates and non-marital childbirth across many European countries have, among other reasons, led to growing numbers of lone parents and blended families. For example, crude divorce rates have more than doubled in Switzerland and Belgium from 0.9 and 0.5 per 1,000 inhabitants in 1960 to 2.0 and 2.1 per 1,000 inhabitants in 2016, respectively (Eurostat 2018). Due to the growing numbers of lone parents and blended families, minors are at a higher risk of growing up without the presence of both biological parents in one household (Sobotka and Toulemon 2008; Smyth and Moloney 2008). Even though children are still more likely to stay with their mothers after a separation, changes in legal and cultural practices across Europe have led to a higher share of parents who opt for *shared physical custody* (hereafter, 'SPC'; Cancian et al. 2014; Juby et al. 2005; Kitterød and Lyngstad 2012). SPC is hereby defined as a post-separation custody arrangement where children spend time at two alternating places of residence—one at each of the parents' homes—and parents are able share daily responsibilities and routines compared to other non-residential parents with sparse contact to their children (i.e., no physical custody; hereafter, 'NC'). How SPC parents decide to split children's time between the two households, however, can vary widely from equal amounts of time (50%:50%) to up to at least one-quarter of time (75%:25%) across families and legislative contexts (Baude et al. 2016; Meyer et al. 2017).

Prior studies documented that the low prevalence of SPC families meant higher levels of selectivity. Children in SPC families tended to have parents with higher levels of education, higher income, and lower reported levels of relationship conflict compared to children in more traditional sole (physical) custody (hereafter, 'SC') arrangements (Bauserman 2012; Nielsen 2018; Steinbach 2019). In countries where SPC was legally regulated, either as default or as the priority custody arrangement, such as many of the Nordic countries, the share of SPC increased. Consequently, profiles of SPC families became less selective, at least in terms of parental education and income (Cancian et al. 2014). Far from these developments, in Switzerland, clearly defined legal regulations for SPC were lacking until 2017. Although separation and divorce among Swiss parents is rising at a similar rate to other Western countries, no prior study has yet examined the spread and profiles of families practicing novel post-separation custody arrangements, such as SPC, in the Swiss context to our knowledge. In addition, while the majority of research on correlates and consequences of SPC has so far focused on children's adjustment to SPC, little research has devoted attention to the correlation of SPC arrangements with parental health. This is all the more surprising given that previous studies established a reciprocal dependence of union separation, family structure, parenting, and parental health across the life course more generally (Amato 2010; Osborne et al. 2012; Umberson et al. 2010). To fill these research gaps, the aim of this chapter is twofold.

First, we aim at providing a comprehensive overview of the prevalence and characteristics of SPC families in Switzerland before the legislative change of 2017. Second, we examine whether SPC is associated with Swiss parents' physical health and well-being.

5.1.1 Spread and Characteristics of SPC Families

More involved and active fathering has been on the political agenda of many Western countries with the introduction of more gender-neutral family polices—particularly in the Scandinavian countries—and a societal re-definition of manhood that encourages men to engage in multiple social roles besides the traditional breadwinner role (Goldschneider et al. 2015). For example, legal changes facilitating the establishment of longer parental and paternal leave were introduced in many European countries (Thévenon 2011), which may have contributed to the substantial daily time increase coupled fathers reported to spend with their children over the last decade (e.g., 57% increase in time spent with children from 2001/2002 to 2012/2013 among German men; Klünder and Meier-Gräwe 2018). The majority of fathers also wish to continue their engagement with their biological (or step-) children upon the separation from a former partner or spouse indicating shifting social norms related to parenting and fatherhood that may consequently impact changes on the social policy-level (Bengtson and Allen 2009). However, the implementation of post-separation legislation that fosters father involvement in custody arrangements, such as SPC, varies considerably across Europe. Note that, throughout the chapter, SPC and other custody arrangements are referring to decisions concerning children's living arrangements only (e.g. SPC, SC) and not to legal custody, which defines which parent can make decisions about a child's life such as schooling, religious upbringing, or medical care.

In countries where SPC was introduced as the legally preferred solution for married couples seeking divorce or separation early-on (e.g., 1998 in Sweden and 2006 in Belgium), incident rates of parents utilizing shared-time custody models have risen to nearly 50% in Sweden (Bergström et al. 2013) and 37% in Belgium (Vanassche et al. 2017). In contrast, countries without a clear legal framework for SPC, such as in Germany, only about 5% of post-separation families reported to practice SPC (Walper 2016). Changes can also occur rather rapidly. In Spain, where similar legal changes happened in 2010, SPC almost tripled in just the space of a few years but with considerable regional variation in rates of SPC (ranging from 13% to up to 32% in some regions in 2013; Steinbach 2019). Studies have shown that at the initial stage of SPC diffusion, separated parents opting for this custody arrangement, tended to be more affluent, highly educated, practiced greater gender role equality, and reported lower levels of marital or post-separation conflict compared to ex-couples with SC arrangements (e.g., Bauserman 2012; Juby et al. 2005; Kitterød and Lyngstad 2012; Nielsen 2018; Schier and Hubert 2015). Since SPC arrangements became more common after strengthening the legal pathways toward SPC, however, profiles of SPC parents pluralized as well (Cancian et al. 2014; Sodermans et al. 2013). Even though the share of high-conflict and average to low educated SPC couples increased in response to the legal changes, the prevalence among the lowest educational groups—particularly families with two lower-educated parents—remained relatively low. Reasons for this development are most likely the financial means necessary for practicing SPC, such as maintaining two rooms for a child, or coordinating commutes between parental residences, which limit the feasibility of SPC particularly for less resourceful parents (Melli and Brown 2008; Steinbach 2019). Furthermore, parents' ability to find non-conflictual custody agreements that are beneficial and acceptable for all parties involved, or to seek help to negotiate respective solutions (e.g., with a counsellor), may also be strongly correlated with one's educational attainment.

In Switzerland, similarly to Germany, no explicit legal framework for SPC was available before 2017 and SPC arrangements could only be formalized if both parents demanded and agreed to it. Only since 2014, the Swiss Family law no longer differentiates between children born to married and non-marital unions with regard to parental responsibilities and duties, which particularly strengthened the rights of post-separation fathers to a child born out of wedlock upon separation. Nevertheless, judges were only advised to investigate the possibility of SPC routinely regardless of parents' demands or disagreements since 2017. Additionally, gender-biased employment practices in the labor market and the lack of widespread, affordable childcare, despite some institutional efforts to promote gender equality at the policy level, encourage Swiss women to reduce their time in paid labor once they became mothers (Le Goff et al. 2009). It is important to note, however, that rates of childcare coverage vary across Switzerland's multilingual cantons with higher coverage in French-speaking cantons and urban centers (Bonoli 2008). Working part-time, and often in lower-paying, less career-oriented jobs has, in turn, shown to contribute to the emergence of more traditional role distributions among Swiss couples prior and after a separation (Bernardi et al. 2013; Bühlmann et al. 2009; Le Goff et al. 2009). The lack of explicit family policies to support women's full-time engagement in the workforce may further reinforce the establishment of (female-headed) SC arrangements upon separation (Davis and Greenstein 2009; Juby et al. 2005), despite recent advances in fostering legal pathways toward SPC.

Examining the Swiss case more closely—a late and only partial adopter of gender-neutral parenting policies—our study is the first attempt to provide a comprehensive overview of the prevalence of families who opted into SPC before the 2014 and 2017 legislative change, as well as to describe the sociodemographic make-up of those families. We expect SPC arrangements to represent a small proportion of custody arrangements among separated parents because of Switzerland's lack of legal guidance at the time of data collection. Relatedly, we expect that SPC parents are rather selective in terms of education and socioeconomic standing (SES) compared to parents with NC, SC, or visitation rights only (hereafter, 'VR'; **Hypothesis 1**).

5.1.2 SPC and Parents' Health

Prior research on SPC has largely focused on child adjustment, such as the perceived stress or emotional well-being of SPC children compared to their peers in SC arrangements or those growing up with both parents in one household (e.g., Bergström et al. 2013; Baude et al. 2016; Nielsen 2018; Turunen 2017). Going through a divorce or separation has shown to have—at least temporarily—detrimental effects on the physical health and mental well-being of former spouses or partners due to the expose to multiple stressors, such as shouldering sole parenting responsibilities, losing of emotional support, being exposed to continuing relational conflict, or experiencing economic decline (Amato 2010; Cooper et al. 2009; Osborne et al. 2012). Changing social roles of and relationships between the linked lives of family members need to be re-assigned and re-negotiated in response to such an impactful life event, which may have lasting ripple effects on parents' subsequent life course (Bengtson and Allen 2009). Even though parenting stress has generally shown to weigh on parents' well-being—at least when children are young—separated families may be particularly prone to the negative impact of parenting stress because they encounter more life strains related to parenting duties (e.g., through potentially stressful, yet constant consultation and negotiation with the former partner or spouse; Umberson et al. 2010). Findings further suggest that well-being and health penalties for parents having gone through union dissolution and potentially re-formation, such as lone parents, were substantially larger in countries with less generous policy support for families and lower levels of gender equality (Burstrom et al. 2010; Hübgen 2018; Pollmann-Schult 2018).

Despite the well-established linkages between family structure, parenting, and health, the associations between SPC and parental outcomes have rarely been examined. Apart from potential selectivity effects into SPC after a separation, splitting parenting duties may enable both parents, and particularly fathers, to enjoy time with their children and maintain supportive and positives ties to them—particularly father-child contact—which, in turn, could foster parents' health and well-being (Baranowska-Rataj et al. 2014; Steinbach 2019; Vogt Yuan 2016). SPC parents may further benefit from having more time for activities unrelated to parenting, such as work, dating, or leisure activities, which may decrease parenting stress for both mothers and fathers compared to lone parents. On the flip side, SPC may also increase parenting stress and therefore curb parental health and well-being—especially for those with sparse resources to fall back on or for conflictual couples—because practicing SPC is rather costly compared to traditional SC arrangements (e.g., paying for commutes between parental homes and maintaining the child's rooms in each of these home or duplicate sets of cloth, school supplies, etc.), and requires constant communication with the ex-spouse or partner. These additional burdens may outweigh potential benefits from reduced parenting duties. For example, the challenges of negotiating parenting roles and responsibilities in complex family configurations with residential stepchildren, whether they reside in the household full- or part-time, have shown to weigh particularly on stepmothers' perceived parenting stress (Guzzo et al. 2019). Yet the role strain of separated fathers has also shown to be higher compared to married fathers (Umberson and Williams 1993), even though fathers' psychological distress generally seemed to be diminished by higher-quality father-child contact after a separation (Vogt Yuan 2016).

In a review of 50 empirical studies primarily based on data from the 1980s to 1990s, Bauserman (2012) found that only SPC fathers were more satisfied with custody arrangements compared to SC parents. SPC mothers experienced less parenting burden and stress and both, SPC fathers and mothers, reported more emotional support and less conflict in their relationship with their former partners or spouses. Recent studies also found that SPC mothers had a more active social life, more time for leisure activities, and better employment opportunities compared to lone mothers (Bonnet et al. 2018; van der Heijden et al. 2015; Schnor et al. 2017; Steinbach 2019; Vanassche et al. 2017), presumably because of the freed time and resources due to sharing parenting responsibilities. Whereas reduced time pressure that allows for participation in gainful employment and networking seems to be the main benefit of SPC for mothers, SPC fathers experienced higher levels of time pressure compared to nonresidential fathers among a sample of Dutch divorced or separated parents (Van der Heijden et al. 2016). Findings on the overall psychological adjustment and health of SPC parents compared to SC parents, however, are inconsistent. Melli and Brown (2008) reported that, among a sample of U.S. divorced mothers and fathers, SPC parents were better off in terms of their physical and psychological health compared to SC parents. Other studies using data from Belgium and the Netherlands, however, did not find a direct association between SPC and parents' well-being (Sodermans et al. 2015; Spruijt and Duindam 2009). Potential reasons for these surprising null effects—particularly given the highly selective nature of SPC parents' characteristics—could be related to the gap between official arrangements (legal and declared) and daily practices. Some research showed that rather unequal time splits are often common practice in SPC arrangements, which still leave one parent shouldering the majority of childcare costs and responsibilities.

To address inconsistencies in prior findings, we further examine the association between SPC and parents' well-being and physical health, as well as potential variations in these links by gender and educational attainment. Overall, we expect that SPC parents report better health and well-being than lone parents, who generally tend to suffer from poorer health and well-being outcomes compared to their partnered peers and particularly in less generous and more gender-biased family policy regimes such as Switzerland (**Hypothesis 2**). However, we also expect mothers' health and well-being to benefit more from SPC compared to fathers because mothers, as traditional caregivers, stand more to gain from stronger father involvement in care duties in terms of freed up resources for employment and leisure time (**Hypothesis 2a**). Lastly, we expect SPC parents with higher levels of education attainment to report better health and well-being compared to their lower-educated peers because, in addition to being more likely to opt for SPC, higher-educated parents may have the sufficient resources and problem-solving skills to implement

SPC successfully, particularly with limited institutional support for SPC, and can benefit from it subsequently (**Hypothesis 2b**).

5.2 Method

5.2.1 Data

Data were drawn from the cross-sectional *Families and Generations Survey* (FGS) conducted by the Swiss Federal Office of Statistics in 2013 (*N* = 17,298; 53% females), which collected information on respondents' current household composition, employment and partnership characteristics, fertility, and well-being. In addition, the FGS includes retrospective information on the respondents' union and fertility histories. The survey randomly sampled permanent Swiss residents aged 15 to 80 years. Survey interviews were conducted in one of the three official languages, depending on the respondents' preferences (German, French, and Italian), during computer assisted telephone interviews and via complementary online or paper questionnaires. Retention rate was 50% and 82% of the sample were Swiss nationals.

For the purpose of this study, we drew a subsample of respondents with at least one biological child aged 18 years or younger (*N* = 5,002), where both biological parents were not living in the same household at the time of data collection. Note that the parent that took part in the survey also provided basic socio-demographic information (e.g., sex and educational attainment) about the other biological parent of their child, but that this parent was not contacted to participate in the survey as well. Thus, the sample consisted of full-time residential parents with children in their household (i.e., lone parents), non-residential parents with children outside of the household providing information about their children and the parent taking care of them, and parents splitting parenting duties with children alternating between the parental residences. The final analytic sample consisted of 875 post-separation parents (59.8% females; M_{age} (SD) = 43.90 (7.69)) of 1,269 minors (49.2% females; M_{age} (SD) = 12.12 (4.59)).

5.2.2 Measures

SPC, again referring to children's living arrangements and not legal custody, was assessed with two questions asking whether another parent takes care of the child on a regular basis (0 = no, 1 = yes), and if so, for how many days per month (M (SD) = 8.52 (5.44)). Based on this information, we differentiated four custody arrangements: no custody (i.e., non-residential parents; 'NC'; *0 days)*, sole custody (i.e., full-time residential parents; 'SC'; 0 days), visitation rights ('VR'; 1–9 days per month), and shared physical custody ('SPC'; *for at least 30% of the time, i.e.,* 10 days or more per months). We chose a 70%:30% time split, rather than equal time splits, as the cut-off criteria to be classified as SPC because of the left-skewed distribution of the time spent in the other parents' household.

We measured respondents' own overall evaluation of their physical health, which is a commonly used and validated single-item health indicator (Idler and Benyamini 1997), by asking: "In general, would you say your health is . . .?" on a scale from 1 (very bad) to 5 (very good). Emotional well-being was measured with a shortened version of the Positive and Negative Affect Schedule (Watson et al. 1988). Participants were asked to rate how often they generally felt the following emotions on a scale from 1 (never) to 6 (always): happy, tired, lonely, energetic, sad, and nervous. Items were recoded so that higher values indicate higher levels of emotional well-being and a mean composite score was formed (Cronbach's $\alpha = 0.73$).

Lastly, information about respondents' sex (0 = female; 1 = male), age (in full years), mother's and father's educational attainment (1 = primary [basic schooling]; 2 = secondary [vocational training]; 3 = tertiary [advanced vocational training or university degree]), children's age (in full years), respondents' employment status (0 = unemployed; 1 = employed), perceived economic difficulties (0 = no; 1 = yes), current partnership status (0 = single; 1 = partnered), time since the separation or divorce (in full years), whether child support payments were received or made (0 = no; 1 = yes), and the linguistic region of residence (1 = German-speaking cantons; 2 = French-speaking cantons; 3 = other [Italian or Romansh]) were available.

5.3 Results

5.3.1 Descriptive Results

Table 5.1 displays summary statistics of the sample and key study variables for parents and children. Descriptive results showed that, as expected, SPC was only reported for 10.9% of the children in post-separation families (vs. 32.6% of children outside of the parental household (NC), 35.9% of children in SC households, and 20.6% of children in VR arrangements). When a 50:50% time split is used, the share of SPC children even dropped to 6.5% (vs. 25.0% of children in VR arrangements). Not surprisingly, the majority of post- separation households with children were female-headed. For example, 87.5% of the SC parents were female compared to 10.5% of non-residential (NC) mothers with minors outside of their household. Furthermore, 92.6% of residential mothers granted another parent VR and 59.8% of SPC parents were female. SPC parents were overrepresented in the French-speaking Swiss cantons (55.8% vs. 28.4% of NC parents, 37.3% of SC parents, and 37.8% of parents with VR arrangements).

SPC parents, both mother and father, reported higher levels of education (41.7–48.2% with the highest level of education, respectively) compared to

Table 5.1 Descriptive statistics of the key study variables by custody arrangements

Indicator	NC	SC	VR	SPC
N (%)	413 (32.6)	456 (35.9)	262 (20.6)	138 (10.9)
Age, *M* (*SD*)	45.27 (8.39)	43.75 (7.59)	42.21 (6.65)	43.22 (6.30)
Male, *n* (%)	255 (89.5)	44 (12.5)	14 (7.4)	52 (54.7)
Education mother, *n* (%)				
Primary	42 (17.6)	44 (13.1)	14 (7.4)	10 (11.9)
Secondary	131 (54.8)	215 (63.8)	128 (68.1)	39 (46.4)
Tertiary	66 (27.6)	78 (23.1)	46 (24.5)	35 (41.7)
Education father, *n* (%)				
Primary	33 (12.0)	39 (14.8)	10 (6.1)	6 (6.7)
Secondary	143 (52.2)	134 (51.2)	93 (57.1)	46 (51.1)
Tertiary	98 (35.8)	89 (34.0)	60 (36.8)	42 (48.2)
Linguistic region, *n* (%)				
German	162 (56.8)	178 (50.7)	97 (51.6)	35 (36.8)
French	81 (28.4)	131 (37.3)	71 (37.8)	53 (55.8)
Other[a]	42 (14.8)	42 (12.0)	20 (10.6)	7 (7.4)
Currently partnered, *n* (%)	203 (71.4)	190 (54.1)	102 (54.3)	55 (57.9)
Time since separation[b], *M* (*SD*)	7.16 (4.87)	7.70 (4.79)	5.65 (4.15)	5.37 (3.95)
Number of children, *M* (*SD*)	1.82 (0.72)	1.72 (0.86)	1.84 (0.70)	1.89 (0.77)
Age of youngest child, *M* (*SD*)	11.01 (4.82)	12.03 (4.67)	9.70 (4.39)	10.04 (4.08)
Age of children, *n* (%)				
Infants/toddlers (0–2 years)	13 (3.7)	11 (2.7)	11 (4.2)	4 (2.9)
Pre-school (3–5 years)	29 (8.2)	24 (6.1)	23 (8.8)	12 (8.7)
Elementary school (6–8 years)	34 (9.7)	45 (11.2)	47 (17.9)	22 (15.9)
Tweens (9–12 years)	95 (27.0)	74 (18.4)	79 (30.2)	46 (33.3)
Teens (13–18 years)	181 (51.4)	247 (61.6)	102 (38.9)	54 (39.2)
Days per months at other Parents' home, *M* (*SD*)	–	–	5.14 (2.07)	14.93 (3.81)
Received child support, *n* (%)	9 (3.8)	131 (55.5)	210 (82.3)	42 (31.1)
Paid child support, *n* (%)	183 (78.2)	4 (1.7)	2 (0.8)	68 (51.6)
Employment, *n* (%)				
Full-time	210 (73.9)	115 (32.9)	43 (22.9)	52 (54.7)
Part-time	27 (9.5)	165 (47.1)	116 (61.7)	23 (24.2)
Unemployed	47 (16.6)	70 (20.0)	29 (15.4)	20 (21.1)
Financial difficulties, *n* (%)	133 (48.5)	194 (56.1)	105 (56.8)	57 (62.0)
Self-rated health[c], *M* (*SD*)	3.93 (0.94)	3.89 (0.78)	4.01 (0.82)	4.13 (0.90)
Well-being[d], *M* (*SD*)	3.29 (0.60)	3.24 (0.56)	3.34 (0.57)	3.34 (0.58)

Notes. NC = no (physical) custody, *SC* = sole (physical) custody, *VR* = visitation rights, *SPC* = shared physical custody

[a]Includes Italian and Romansh

[b]In years

[c]Higher values indicate better health

[d]Higher values indicate higher ratings of well-being. Range of variables was as follows: Age of parents in years 21–71; Number of children 1–6; Age of youngest child in years 0–18; Days per month at the second parental residence 0–30; Self-rated health 1–5; Well-being 1–5

respondents in the NC, SC, and VR groups (27.6–35.8%, 23.1–34.0%, and 24.5–36.8% with the highest levels of education, respectively). Yet at the same time, a larger share of SPC parents reported to have financial difficulties (62.0% vs. 48.5% of NC parents, 56.1% of SC parents, and 56.8% of parents with VR). Most post-separation parents reported to be employed across all custody arrangements, even though the share of unemployed parents was highest among SPC parents (21.1% vs. 16.6% of NC parents, 20.0% of SC parents, and 15.4% of parents with VR). Note that within the SC and VR groups, most parents reported to work part-time (47.1% part-time vs. 32.9% full-time for SC parents and 61.7% part-time vs. 22.9% full-time for VR parents) compared to NC parents who worked predominantly full-time (73.9% vs. 9.5% part-time).

Lastly, SPC was most frequent in families with high-school aged children (33.3% for children aged 9–12 years and 39.2% for children aged 13–18 years) compared to other families. The share of SPC actually increases with children's age: being the least in families with infants aged 0–2 years (2.9%) and growing gradually for children aged 3–5 years (8.7%) and those aged 6–8 years (15.9%).

5.3.2 Regression Results

In order to address the first hypothesis on the relatively privileged positon of SPC parents compared to NC, SC parents, or parents with VR, we employed multinomial regression models predicting the likelihood of belonging to each custody arrangement. Our data is hierarchical with potentially multiple children (Level 2) nested within families (Level 1), and yet the number of siblings did not allow the use of multilevel modeling ($M_{\text{children in families}}$ (SD) = 1.80 (0.69)). Therefore, we estimated stepwise regression models with cluster robust standard errors that allow for intragroup correlation. SC served as reference category in all regression models. Model 1 included basic socio-demographic characteristics of the surveyed parent (e.g., age), as well as mothers' and fathers' education, and children's age. Model 2 added partnership characteristics, such as time since the separation of the parents, and whether surveyed parents were currently partnered. In Model 3, we introduce employment status and the financial situation of the surveyed parent.

To ease interpretation and allow comparability across nested models, we report discrete differences in average marginal effects (AME) of the multinomial regression models in Table 5.2 (Long 2015). AME represent the average impact of the independent variable on the likelihood of each outcome category (i.e., belonging to each respective custody arrangement in our case). For continuous variables, the table shows average discrete change in the predicted probabilities for a one-unit increase in the predictor and, for categorical variables, it represents average differences in predicted probabilities for pairs of levels of the predictor.

Results revealed some gender differences in the likelihood of belonging to different custody arrangements. Compared to women, men were more likely to belong the NC group (56–69%) and less likely to belong to the SC and VR groups

Table 5.2 Discrete differences in average marginal effects for multinomial regression models predicting custody arrangements

	Model 1				Model 2				Model 3			
Predictors	NC	SC	VR	SPC	NC	SC	VR	SPC	NC	SC	VR	SPC
Age	−0.00 (0.01)	0.00 (0.00)	0.00 (0.00)	−0.00 (0.00)	−0.00 (0.00)	−0.00 (0.00)	0.01 (0.00)	−0.00 (0.00)	−0.00 (0.00)	−0.00 (0.00)	0.00 (0.00)	−0.00 (0.00)
Male	0.69*** (0.03)	−0.38*** (0.03)	−0.35*** (0.03)	0.04 (0.03)	0.67*** (0.03)	−0.36*** (0.03)	−0.36*** (0.03)	0.05 (0.03)	0.56*** (0.08)	−0.36*** (0.04)	−0.25** (0.07)	0.05 (0.06)
Secondary education mother[a]	0.01 (0.04)	−0.01 (0.06)	−0.00 (0.06)	0.00 (0.04)	0.00 (0.04)	0.00 (0.06)	−0.01 (0.06)	0.01 (0.04)	0.03 (0.04)	−0.03 (0.07)	−0.02 (0.07)	0.02 (0.04)
Tertiary education mother[a]	0.04 (0.05)	−0.02 (0.07)	−0.08 (0.06)	0.06 (0.04)	0.03 (0.05)	−0.02 (0.07)	−0.08 (0.07)	0.07 (0.05)	0.06 (0.04)	−0.06 (0.07)	−0.08 (0.07)	0.08 (0.05)
Secondary education father[a]	−0.05 (0.05)	−0.13* (0.06)	0.14*** (0.04)	0.04 (0.04)	−0.06 (0.05)	−0.14* (0.06)	0.17*** (0.04)	0.04 (0.04)	−0.01 (0.04)	−0.21** (0.07)	0.16*** (0.04)	0.06 (0.05)
Tertiary education father[a]	−0.04 (0.05)	−0.14* (0.07)	0.14** (0.04)	0.04 (0.04)	−0.05 (0.05)	−0.16* (0.07)	0.17*** (0.04)	0.04 (0.04)	−0.01 (0.05)	−0.23** (0.07)	0.18** (0.05)	0.06 (0.05)
Age of children	0.01 (0.03)	0.02*** (0.00)	−0.02*** (0.00)	−0.00 (0.00)	0.01 (0.00)	0.02*** (0.00)	−0.02*** (0.00)	−0.00 (0.00)	0.01 (0.00)	0.00 (0.00)	−0.01* (0.00)	0.00 (0.00)
French[b]	−0.05 (0.03)	0.01 (0.04)	−0.00 (0.03)	0.05 (0.03)	−0.03 (0.03)	0.00 (0.04)	−0.01 (0.03)	0.04 (0.03)	−0.04 (0.03)	0.00 (0.04)	0.00 (0.04)	0.03 (0.04)
Other[b]	0.10*** (0.03)	−0.01 (0.05)	−0.04 (0.05)	−0.05 (0.03)	0.11*** (0.03)	−0.00 (0.05)	−0.05 (0.05)	−0.06 (0.03)	0.07* (0.03)	0.01 (0.06)	0.01 (0.06)	−0.09** (0.03)
Currently partnered					0.02 (0.03)	−0.04 (0.04)	−0.01 (0.03)	0.02 (0.03)	0.01 (0.03)	−0.01 (0.03)	−0.03 (0.03)	0.02 (0.03)
Time since separation					0.00 (0.00)	0.01 (0.00)	−0.00 (0.00)	−0.01* (0.00)	−0.00 (0.00)	0.01** (0.00)	−0.01 (0.00)	−0.01 (0.00)
Received child support									−0.21** (0.06)	−0.03 (0.05)	0.23** (0.06)	0.01 (0.05)
Part-time employed[c]									−0.01 (0.04)	−0.08 (0.06)	0.10 (0.05)	−0.01 (0.04)

(continued)

Table 5.2 (continued)

Predictors	Model 1 NC	SC	VR	SPC	Model 2 NC	SC	VR	SPC	Model 3 NC	SC	VR	SPC
Full-time employed[c]									−0.04 (0.04)	−0.01 (0.06)	0.01 (0.06)	0.03 (0.04)
Financial difficulties									−0.02 (0.03)	0.01 (0.03)	−0.00 (0.03)	0.01 (0.03)

Notes. *NC* = no (physical) custody, *SC* = sole (physical) custody, *VR* = visitation rights, *SPC* = shared physical custody

$^{*}p < 0.05$. $^{**}p < 0.01$. $^{***}p < 0.001$

[a]*Reference category is primary education*

[b]*Reference category is German-speaking cantons*

[c]*Reference category is unemployed*

(36–38% and 25–36%, respectively) across all of the models. Higher paternal education, both secondary and tertiary, compared to primary levels of educational attainment, were related to lower chances to belong to the SC group (13–21% and 14–23%, respectively) and higher chances to belong to the VR group (14–17% and 14–18%, respectively). Yet, there was no significant association between SPC and education. Children's age was positively related to the likelihood of belonging to the SC group and negatively to the VR group, but again there was no significant link between children's age and SPC across the models. Model 2 revealed that the more time had passed since the parental separation, chances was greater to belong to the SC group and lower to belong to the SPC group. However, the latter effect faded when employment and financial characteristics were introduced in the final model. Respondents in Italian- or Romansh-speaking cantons were less likely to belong to the SPC group and more likely to belong to the NC group in Model 3.

A second set of regression models predicting self-rated health and emotional well-being examined Hypothesis 2 on the positive link between physical and mental health and SPC compared to more traditional custody arrangements. We estimated stepwise regression models with basic socio-demographic characteristics and custody arrangements in Model 1, partnership characteristics in Model 2, and employment and financial characteristics in Model 3. Again, SC served as the reference category for the custody arrangements in all models. To explore the gender and educational differences in the link between physical or mental health and custody arrangements, we also examined interaction terms between custody arrangements and gender (Hypothesis 2a; Model 4) and custody arrangements and parental education (Hypothesis 2b; Model 5). In order to address potential selectivity effects into custody arrangements based on parents' characteristics, we used the predicted probabilities (i.e., 1 – P(custody arrangement)) from the fully-adjusted multinomial model as regression weights for the these models. Again, a cluster robust standard error estimator was employed to account for the hierarchical structure of the data.

Table 5.3 shows that, contrary to our expectations, custody arrangements were neither significantly associated with self-rated health nor with emotional well-being across all models. Most of parents' socio-demographic characteristics, such as age, gender, and educational attainment, were also not associated with self-rated health and emotional well-being across all models (expect for a negative link between parents' age and well-being in Model 1, and a positive link between fathers' tertiary vs. primary education and health in Model 1 and 2). For emotional well-being only, being partnered was related to higher ratings (Model 2–5) and living in a French-speaking canton (compared to German-speaking cantons; Model 1–2) to lower ratings of emotional well-being. The employment status and financial situation of the surveyed parent entered in Model 3, however, were significantly related to both health and well-being. More specifically, part- and full-time employed parents reported better health and higher ratings of emotional well-being compared to their unemployed peers (Model 3–5). Having financial difficulties was also linked to lower ratings of self-rated health and well-being (Model 3–5). Lastly, a significant SPC by gender interaction term for health only (Model 4) suggests that, contrary to our expectations, SPC fathers reported significantly poorer health compared to SPC

Table 5.3 Regression results predicting self-rated health and emotional well-being

Predictors	Model 1		Model 2		Model 3		Model 4		Model 5	
	Health	Well-Being	Health	Well-Being	Health	Well-Being	Health	Well-Being	Health	Well-Being
NC[a]	−0.06 (0.12)	−0.01 (0.08)	−0.10 (0.12)	−0.10 (0.08)	−0.04 (0.16)	−0.07 (0.10)	−0.03 (0.26)	−0.10 (0.16)	−0.07 (0.39)	0.23 (0.33)
VR[a]	0.01 (0.10)	0.11 (0.06)	0.02 (0.10)	0.12 (0.06)	0.07 (0.12)	0.08 (0.07)	0.08 (0.12)	0.08 (0.08)	−0.33 (0.48)	0.43 (0.41)
SPC	0.15 (0.13)	0.11 (0.09)	0.13 (0.14)	0.10 (0.09)	0.22 (0.15)	0.12 (0.09)	0.32 (0.16)	0.15 (0.11)	−0.11 (0.39)	−0.14 (0.35)
Age	−0.01 (0.01)	−0.01* (0.00)	−0.01 (0.01)	−0.01 (0.00)	−0.00 (0.01)	−0.01 (0.00)	−0.01 (0.01)	−0.01 (0.00)	−0.00 (0.01)	−0.01 (0.00)
Male	0.02 (0.11)	0.08 (0.07)	0.04 (0.11)	0.10 (0.07)	−0.22 (0.16)	0.12 (0.10)	0.27 (0.22)	0.06 (0.23)	−0.17 (0.16)	0.14 (0.10)
Secondary education mother[b]	0.16 (0.14)	0.04 (0.11)	0.17 (0.14)	0.05 (0.11)	−0.02 (0.14)	−0.05 (0.11)	0.01 (0.13)	−0.04 (0.11)	0.02 (0.27)	0.06 (0.22)
Tertiary education mother[b]	0.19 (0.15)	0.14 (0.11)	0.19 (0.15)	0.14 (0.11)	−0.08 (0.15)	0.03 (0.11)	−0.06 (0.14)	0.03 (0.11)	−0.02 (0.31)	0.06 (0.25)
Secondary education father[b]	0.08 (0.12)	0.16 (0.12)	0.07 (0.11)	0.14 (0.11)	0.04 (0.12)	0.12 (0.12)	0.05 (0.12)	0.12 (0.12)	−0.14 (0.15)	0.20 (0.16)
Tertiary education father[b]	0.28* (0.12)	0.22 (0.12)	0.25* (0.13)	0.19 (0.11)	0.22 (0.13)	0.17 (0.12)	0.24 (0.13)	0.18 (0.12)	0.12 (0.21)	0.24 (0.19)
Age of children	0.00 (0.01)	0.02* (0.01)	0.01 (0.01)	0.01 (0.01)	0.00 (0.01)	0.01 (0.01)	0.00 (0.01)	0.01 (0.01)	0.00 (0.01)	0.01 (0.01)
French[c]	−0.15 (0.09)	−0.20*** (0.06)	−0.16 (0.09)	−0.17** (0.06)	−0.10 (0.10)	−0.12 (0.06)	−0.10 (0.10)	−0.12 (0.06)	−0.11 (0.10)	−0.09 (0.06)
Other[c]	−0.02 (0.11)	−0.05 (0.09)	−0.03 (0.11)	−0.04 (0.08)	−0.02 (0.12)	0.05 (0.09)	−0.01 (0.12)	0.04 (0.09)	−0.03 (0.12)	0.05 (0.09)
Currently partnered			0.09 (0.08)	0.28*** (0.06)	0.06 (0.09)	0.23*** (0.06)	0.06 (0.09)	0.23*** (0.06)	0.04 (0.09)	0.23*** (0.06)

Time since separation			−0.01 (0.01)	0.01 (0.01)	−0.01 (0.01)	0.01 (0.01)	−0.01 (0.01)	0.01 (0.01)	−0.01 (0.01)	0.01 (0.01)
Received child support					−0.02 (0.12)	0.16* (0.08)	−0.02 (0.12)	0.15 (0.08)	−0.01 (0.12)	0.13 (0.07)
Part-time employed[d]					0.41* (0.16)	0.29** (0.10)	0.40* (0.16)	0.29** (0.10)	0.40* (0.16)	0.29** (0.10)
Full-time employed[d]					0.56** (0.16)	0.28** (0.10)	0.55** (0.16)	0.28** (0.10)	0.54** (0.17)	0.28** (0.10)
Financial difficulties					−0.21* (0.09)	−0.15* (0.06)	−0.21* (0.09)	−0.15* (0.06)	−0.21* (0.09)	−0.15* (0.06)
NC × Male							−0.46 (0.31)	0.09 (0.27)	–	–
VR × Male							−0.37 (0.23)	0.18 (0.26)	–	–
SPC × Male							−0.69* (0.30)	−0.02 (0.25)	–	–
NC × Secondary education mother[b]									−0.26 (0.33)	−0.27 (0.26)
VR × Secondary education mother[b]									0.30 (0.41)	0.06 (0.37)
SPC × Secondary education mother[b]									−0.09 (0.37)	−0.06 (0.28)
NC × Tertiary education mother[b]									−0.14 (0.38)	−0.10 (0.28)
VR × Tertiary education mother [b]									0.27 (0.47)	0.03 (0.39)
SPC × Tertiary education mother[b]									−0.34 (0.42)	0.13 (0.30)
NC × Secondary education father[b]									0.23 (0.30)	−0.23 (0.26)

(continued)

Table 5.3 (continued)

Predictors	Model 1		Model 2		Model 3		Model 4		Model 5	
	Health	Well-Being	Health	Well-Being	Health	Well-Being	Health	Well-Being	Health	Well-Being
VR × Secondary education father[b]									0.18 (0.47)	−0.40 (0.43)
SPC × Secondary education father[b]									0.69* (0.32)	0.23 (0.27)
NC × Tertiary education father[b]									0.22 (0.33)	−0.07 (0.28)
VR × Tertiary education father[b]									0.09 (0.50)	−0.46 (0.44)
SPC × Tertiary education father[b]									0.41 (0.34)	0.23 (0.29)

Notes. NC = no (physical) custody, *SC* = sole (physical) custody, *VR* = visitation rights, *SPC* = shared physical custody

$^{*}p < 0.05$. $^{**}p < 0.01$. $^{***}p < 0.001$

[a]*Reference category is SC*

[b]*Reference category is primary education*

[c]*Reference category is German-speaking cantons*

[d]*Reference category is unemployed*

mothers. In Model 5, a significant SPC by secondary (vs. primary) paternal education interaction term emerged for health only, which indicates that SPC parents where fathers had secondary schooling reported better health compared to SPC parents where fathers had primary schooling. Yet there was no difference in reported health between SPC fathers with secondary vs. tertiary schooling.

5.4 Discussion

Non-traditional custody arrangements, such as SPC, are on the rise among separated or divorced parents due to changes in cultural and legal practices across many Western nations (e.g., Bauserman 2012; Cancian et al. 2014; Kitterød and Lyngstad 2012). While the profile of SPC parents has pluralized in terms socio-demographic characteristics in countries where SPC has become a legal default or is institutionally-encouraged, SPC parents tend to be more educated and affluent compared to lone parents or those with VR arrangements in countries where SPC is less prevalent (Vanassche et al. 2017; Sodermans et al. 2013). Our study is, to our knowledge, the first to examine the socio-demographic make-up of SPC parents in Switzerland, which is a rather late and only very partial adopter of gender-neutral parenting policies, and adds to the sparse and contradicting findings on SPC and parents' health and well-being.

In line with our expectations, SPC was practiced by a rather small share of post-separation parents with about 11%, even though a relative low cut-off point was used to define SPC (i.e., at least 30% of the time at the other parents' home). When we used an equal-time sharing model, the percentage of SPC parents was closer to the incidence rate of about 5% reported from German survey data, where clear-cut legal pathways to SPC are equally sparse as in Switzerland (Walper 2016). We therefore conclude that opting for SPC upon separation still represents the exception rather than the rule in Switzerland, which could be attributed to the lack of legal and institutional support for SPC at the time of data collection in 2013. Gender-biased cultural practices in the workforce and, in turn, the private lives of young couples—particularly the traditional role distributions in the division of household and childcare tasks upon entry into parenthood (e.g., Bernardi et al. 2013; Bühlmann et al. 2009)—may further increase the likelihood of establishing more traditional (female-headed SC) post-separation custody arrangements upon separation (Juby et al. 2005). For example, we did observe descriptively that the household head in SC and VR arrangements was pre-dominantly female, which highlights persisting gender disparities in parental involvement and the shouldering of childcare duties in post-separation families (Bernardi et al. 2018; Bjarnason and Arnarsson 2011).

We also anticipated that Swiss SPC parents would represent a more privileged group in terms of educational attainment and financial assets compared to lone parents and those with VR arrangement because they would need to voluntarily seek out SPC given the lack of legal guidance and have the available resources to implement it (e.g., maintaining the child's room at both parental homes or having duplicate sets of cloths, school supplies, etc.; Nielsen 2018; Schier and Hubert 2015; Steinbach 2019). Again descriptively, SPC parents tended to be more highly educated compared to the parents with other childcare arrangements, which was in line with our expectation. Yet, the share of parents reporting financial difficulties and unemployed parents was also highest among SPC parents in our descriptive statistics. The discrepancy between parents' higher educational attainment on the one hand, and higher perceived economic strain on the other hand, may be related to the still more unevenly distributed time that children alternate between the parental households and the higher costs of SPC compared to other custody arrangements, as we outlined before. First, the 70%:30% time split could indicate that a bulk of care duties and child-related expenses still needs to be shouldered by one parent (Steinbach 2019), which, in addition to potentially reduced institutional support due to the (formally) higher contribution to parenting duties from both parents, could contribute to the higher perceived economic strain of SPC parents. The high costs of childcare in Switzerland, which could subsequently lead to more precarious work situations for parents unable to afford childcare expenses (Struffolino and Bernardi 2017), on top of the costs related to SPC, could also erode any gains from SPC, such as freed up time and resources to invest in other life domains such as work, dating, or leisure (e.g., Van der Heijden et al. 2015). Thus, SPC could represent more of an economic resource drain than a relief for the more involved parent, when the time is not truly shared equally.

Lastly, we predicted that overall SPC parents would be healthier and happier parents compared to NC, SC, and VR parents because of their more privileged position in terms of SES (Bauserman 2012; Vanassche et al. 2017) and because SPC parents may experience less parental role strain and related stressors (Umberson et al. 2010; Van der Heijden et al. 2016). This expectation was not confirmed in our models. It could be the case that experiencing such fundamental changes in social roles and the reconfiguration of relationships between family members after a divorce or separation (Amato 2010; Bengtson and Allen 2009) may have the effect of 'leveling' or reducing social differentiation between parents (Leopold and Leopold 2016). Or, in other words, union dissolution itself may leave a more permanent mark on or represent a "turning point" for all families, regardless of prior SES or subsequently chosen custody arrangement, which would explain the lack of differences between the custody arrangements. Additionally, we also anticipated that SPC mothers may experience more health and well-being benefits compared to SPC fathers because shared parenting would alleviate mothers from their more traditional role as full-time custodial caretaker and may free up time and energy to invest into other life domains (Bonnet et al. 2018; Bauserman 2012; Schnor et al. 2017), which could in turn foster mothers' health and well-being. Our models partially supported that notion because SPC fathers tended to report poorer health compared to SPC mothers. It could be the case that SPC fathers may perceive health impairments because, in the Swiss context, SPC was still relatively rare and a rather non-traditional post-separation custody arrangement at the time of data collection for which fathers may receive little institutional support or social acceptance (Bjork 2013; Haas and Hwang 2019).

Because SPC fathers may be likely and expected to continue their engagement in full-time employment compared to mothers who often work part-time only, family-work-conciliation issues and parental role strain may weigh harder on their health (e.g., Umberson and Williams 1993). At the same time, we found that only SPC parents where fathers have secondary levels of schooling reported better health compared to SPC parents where fathers had primary levels of schooling only. It could therefore be the case that the positive link between higher levels of paternal education and parental health may buffer with the previously outlined gendered effects that may contribute to SPC fathers' poorer health ratings. For example, SPC families where fathers have higher levels of education may simply have more resources to outsource some care responsibilities (e.g., paying for costly childcare), which may facilitate fathers' family-work-conciliation, or to seek professional help in light of conflict (e.g., seeing a counselor to establish mutually beneficial SPC routines), while still enjoying the health benefits of maintaining father-child bonds (Vogt Yuan 2016). There may not have been a further gain from fathers' tertiary vs. secondary schooling because of ceiling effects or because fathers' potential outsourcing of care duties may in turn contribute financial difficulties, which we observed descriptively.

Nevertheless, involvement in the labor market—whether part- or full-time—seemed to be overall a driving force of the physical health and emotional well-being of post-separation parents, which is in line with previous research on lone mothers (Struffolino et al. 2016). Because the presence of a new partner was related to higher levels of well-being as well, one could argue that both being able to repartner and to engage in gainful employment may indirectly be facilitated by SPC because these parents simply have more time to be engaged in life domains other than parenting (van der Heijden et al. 2015; Vanassche et al. 2017). However, in a plausible inversed causal relation, more well-adjusted parents may also simply be more likely to take up employment and find a new partner.

5.4.1 Limitations and Future Research

Our study has several limitations. First, we used a rather low cut-off point to define SPC for our sample due to low case numbers for SPC and a left-skewed distribution of the amount of shared time between households. With our criteria, children needed to spend at 30% of the time alternating between parental homes to be grouped into SPC. Even though definitions and criteria of SPC vary widely between studies (i.e., ranging from equal amounts of time up to at least one-quarter of time; Bauserman 2012), unequal time sharing still implies that one parent—often the mother (Bjarnason and Arnarsson 2011)—is likely shouldering the majority of daily childcare task and responsibilities. It could therefore be the case that some SPC parents and those with VR are more similar than we anticipated in terms of sharing parental roles and duties, which could explain the lack of significant differences in health and well-being by custody arrangements. Results may have looked somewhat different if we could have used a stricter criteria for SPC with a larger sample of post-separation and SPC parents specifically.

Second, custody arrangements among post-separation families are likely to evolve and change over time (Poortman and van Gaalen 2017; Smyth and Moloney 2008). Schedules and routines that parents agreed on upon separation or divorce—even if court mandated—may be revised if deemed not feasible in practice, altered to the child's needs or wishes, or adapted to new realities such as the emergence of a new partner in a parents' romantic life or even new-partner fertility. Our cross-sectional measure of custody arrangements, however, only provided a single snap-shot into the routines of separated parents and was therefore not able to capture any dynamic changes over time. Targeted longitudinal data collection will be needed to explore temporal dynamics in the establishment and development of SPC and other custody arrangements among post-separation families. Our dataset also captures parents at different stages after their separation or divorce because the time since separation or divorce varied considerably between former couples. Future research based on these longitudinal follow-ups will need to examine the stability of SPC because prior research has suggested that particularly fathers' investment in non-residential children has shown to fade over time (Berger et al. 2012). It would also have been interesting to look at SPC parents' division of childcare-related task or their ratings of satisfaction with SPC, yet this information was not available in the secondary dataset that was not specifically designed with a focus on studying post-separation custody arrangements. Unfortunately, using existing panel data for Switzerland was still not an option because of the relatively small number of observations available in each wave for this subpopulation, which makes it difficult to apply time-lagged models. As SPC diffuses further among the Swiss population and the panel progresses, future research will be able to exploit bigger sample sizes and should be able to address and disentangle causal paths.

Despite these limitations we are confident that our study provides some first evidence of the characteristics of SPC parents as well as correlates of SPC (or the lack thereof) for separated parents in Switzerland, which was still a rather gender-biased and traditional family policy context that promoted more traditional childcare arrangements at the time of data collection in 2013. We therefore argued that the lack of institutional support for SPC and the rather traditional role distribution among Swiss couples hindered the spread of SPC and reinforced gendered SC models. Furthermore, because of the high costs of childcare in Switzerland, SPC may represent more of a resource drain than a relief for the parent shouldering the majority of the care responsibilities, when time is not shared equally between caregivers. Nevertheless, SPC did neither seem to diminish nor foster parents' health and well-being. Future data collection and research will need to monitor the spread of SPC and its' potential ripple effects of the 2017 legislative change in Switzerland that established SPC as a routinely investigated option for post-separation custody arrangements.

References

Amato, P. R. (2010). Research on divorce: Continuing trends and new developments. *Journal of Marriage and Family, 72*(3), 650–666. https://doi.org/10.1111/j.1741-3737.2010.00723.x.

Baranowska-Rataj, A., Matysiak, A., & Mynarska, M. (2014). Does lone motherhood decrease women's happiness? Evidence from qualitative and quantitative research. *Journal of Happiness Studies, 15*(6), 1457–1477. https://doi.org/10.1007/s10902-013-9486-z.

Baude, A., Pearson, J., & Drapeau, S. (2016). Child adjustment in joint physical custody versus sole custody: A meta-analytic review. *Journal of Divorce & Remarriage, 57*(5), 338–360. https://doi.org/10.1080/10502556.2016.1185203.

Bauserman, R. (2012). A meta-analysis of parental satisfaction, adjustment, and conflict in joint custody and sole custody following divorce. *Journal of Divorce & Remarriage, 53*(6), 464–488. https://doi.org/10.1080/10502556.2012.682901.

Bengtson, V. L., & Allen, K. R. (2009). The life course perspective applied to families over time. In P. Boss, W. J. Doherty, R. LaRossa, W. R. Schumm, & S. K. Steinmetz (Eds.), *Sourcebook of family theories and methods* (pp. 469–504). Boston: Springer. https://doi.org/10.1007/978-0-387-85764-0_19.

Berger, L. M., Cancian, M., & Meyer, D. R. (2012). Maternal re-partnering and new-partner fertility: Associations with nonresident father investments in children. *Children and Youth Services Review, 34*(2), 426–436. https://doi.org/10.1016/j.childyouth.2011.11.012.

Bergström, M., Modin, B., Fransson, E., Rajmil, L., Berlin, M., Gustafsson, P. A., & Hjern, A. (2013). Living in two homes-a Swedish national survey of wellbeing in 12 and 15 year olds with joint physical custody. *BMC Public Health, 13*(1), 868–876. https://doi.org/10.1186/1471-2458-13-868.

Bernardi, L., Ryser, V. A., & Le Goff, J. M. (2013). Gender role-set, family orientations, and women's fertility intentions in Switzerland. *Swiss Journal of Sociology, 39*(1), 9–31.

Bernardi, L., Mortelmans, D., & Larenza, O. (2018). Changing lone parents, changing life courses. In L. Bernardi & D. Mortelmans (Eds.), *Lone parenthood in the life course* (pp. 5–30). New York: Springer. https://doi.org/10.1007/978-3-319-63295-7_16.

Bjarnason, T., & Arnarsson, A. M. (2011). Joint physical custody and communication with parents: A cross-national study of children in 36 western countries. *Journal of Comparative Family Studies, 42*(6), 871–890.

Bjork, S. (2013). Doing morally intelligible fatherhood: Swedish fathers' accounts of their parental part-time work choices. *Fathering, 11*(2), 221–238. https://doi.org/10.3149/fth.1102.221.

Bonnet, C., Garbinti, B., & Solaz, A. (2018). *Does part-time mothering help get a job? The role of shared custody in women's employment.* CASE papers 209: Centre for Analysis of Social Exclusion. Retrieved from http://sticerd.lse.ac.uk/dps/case/cp/casepaper209.pdf

Bonoli, G. (2008). The impact of social policy on fertility: Evidence from Switzerland. *Journal of European Social Policy, 18*(1), 64–77. https://doi.org/10.1177/0958928707081074.

Bühlmann, F., Elcheroth, G., & Tettamanti, M. (2009). The division of labour among European couples: The effects of life course and welfare policy on value–practice configurations. *European Sociological Review, 26*(1), 49–66. https://doi.org/10.1093/esr/jcp004.

Burstrom, B., Whitehead, M., Clayton, S., Fritzell, S., Vannoni, F., & Costa, G. (2010). Health inequalities between lone and couple mothers and policy under different welfare regimes: The example of Italy. *Sweden and Britain. Social Science & Medicine, 70*(6), 912–920. https://doi.org/10.1016/j.socscimed.2009.11.014.

Cancian, M., Meyer, D. R., Brown, P. R., & Cook, S. T. (2014). Who gets custody now? Dramatic changes in children's living arrangements after divorce. *Demography, 51*(4), 1381–1396. https://doi.org/10.1007/s13524-014-0307-8

Cooper, C. E., McLanahan, S. S., Meadows, S. O., & Brooks-Gunn, J. (2009). Family structure transitions and maternal parenting stress. *Journal of Marriage and Family, 71*(3), 558–574. https://doi.org/10.1111/j.1741-3737.2009.00619.x.

Davis, S. N., & Greenstein, T. N. (2009). Gender ideology: Components, predictors, and consequences. *Annual Review of Sociology, 35*, 87–105. https://doi.org/10.1146/annurev-soc-070308-115920.

Eurostat. (2018). *Marriage and divorce statistics*. Retrieved from http://ec.europa.eu/eurostat/statistics-explained/index.php/Marriage_and_divorce_statistics#Fewer_marriages.2C_more_divorces

Goldscheider, F., Bernhardt, E., & Lappegård, T. (2015). The gender revolution: A framework for understanding changing family and demographic behavior. *Population and Development Review, 41*(2), 207–239. https://doi.org/10.1111/j.1728-4457.2015.00045.x.

Guzzo, K. B., Hemez, P., Anderson, L., Manning, W. D., & Brown, S. L. (2019). Is variation in biological and residential ties to children linked to mothers' parental stress and perceptions of coparenting? *Journal of Family Issues, 40*(4), 488–517. https://doi.org/10.1177/0192513X18812172.

Haas, L., & Hwang, C. P. (2019). Workplace support and European fathers' use of state policies promoting shared childcare. *Community, Work & Family, 22*(1), 1–22. https://doi.org/10.1080/13668803.2018.1556204.

Hübgen, S. (2018). Only a husband away from poverty'? Lone mothers' poverty risks in a European comparison. In L. Bernardi & D. Mortelmans (Eds.), *Lone parenthood in the life course* (pp. 167–189). New York: Springer. https://doi.org/10.1007/978-3-319-63295-7_8.

Idler, E. L., & Benyamini, Y. (1997). Self-rated health and mortality: A review of twenty-seven community studies. *Journal of Health and Social Behavior, 38*(1), 21–37.

Juby, H., Le Bourdais, C., & Marcil-Gratton, N. (2005). Sharing roles, sharing custody? Couples' characteristics and children's living arrangements at separation. *Journal of Marriage and Family, 67*(1), 157–172. https://doi.org/10.1111/j.0022-2445.2005.00012.x.

Kitterød, R. H., & Lyngstad, J. (2012). Untraditional caring arrangements among parents living apart: The case of Norway. *Demographic Research, 27*, 121–152. https://doi.org/10.4054/DemRes.2012.27.5.

Klünder, N., & Meier-Gräwe, U. (2018). Caring, cooking, cleaning – repräsentative Zeitverwendungsmuster von Eltern in Paarbeziehungen [Caring, cooking, cleaning – Representative time use patterns in two-parent households]. *ZfF–Zeitschrift für Familienforschung/Journal of Family Research, 30*(1), 9–28. https://doi.org/10.3224/zff.v30i1.02.

Le Goff, J. M., Levy, R., Sapin, M., & Camenisch, M. (2009). Devenir parent. Changer de vie [Becoming a parent: Changing a life]. In M. Oris, E. Widmar, A. de Ribaupierre, D. Joye, D. Spini, G. Labouvie-Vief, & J.-M. Falter (Eds.), *Transitions dans les parcours de vie et construction des inégalités* (pp. 211–232). Lausanne: Presses Polytechniques et Universitaires Romandes.

Leopold, L. & Leopold, T. (2016). *Maternal education, divorce, and change in economic resources: Evidence from Germany*. SOEPpaper no. 836. Available from: https://ssrn.com/abstract=2778090.

Long, J. S. (2015). Regression models for nominal and ordinal outcomes. In H. Best & C. Wolf (Eds.), *The Sage handbook of regression analysis and causal inference* (pp. 173–204). London: Sage.

Melli, M. S., & Brown, P. R. (2008). Exploring a new family form–The shared time family. *International Journal of Law, Policy and the Family, 22*(2), 231–269. https://doi.org/10.1093/lawfam/ebn002.

Meyer, D. R., Cancian, M., & Cook, S. T. (2017). The growth in shared custody in the United States: Patterns and implications. *Family Court Review, 55*(4), 500–512. https://doi.org/10.1111/fcre.12300.

Nielsen, L. (2018). Joint versus sole physical custody: Children's outcomes independent of parent-child relationships, income, and conflict in 60 studies. *Journal of Divorce & Remarriage, 59*(4), 247–281. https://doi.org/10.1080/10502556.2018.1454204.

Osborne, C., Berger, L. M., & Magnuson, K. (2012). Family structure transitions and changes in maternal resources and well-being. *Demography, 49*(1), 23–47. https://doi.org/10.1007/s13524-011-0080-x.

Pollmann-Schult, M. (2018). Single motherhood and life satisfaction in comparative perspective: Do institutional and cultural contexts explain the life satisfaction penalty for single mothers? *Journal of Family Issues, 39*(7), 2061–2084. https://doi.org/10.1177/0192513X17741178.

Poortman, A. R., & van Gaalen, R. (2017). Shared residence after separation: A review and new findings from the Netherlands. *Family Court Review, 55*(4), 531–544. https://doi.org/10.1111/fcre.12302.

Sánchez Gassen, N., & Perelli-Harris, B. (2015). The increase in cohabitation and the role of union status in family policies: A comparison of 12 European countries. *Journal of European Social Policy, 25*(4), 431–449. https://doi.org/10.1177/0958928715594561.

Schier, M., & Hubert, S. (2015). Alles eine Frage der Opportunität, oder nicht? Multilokalität und Wohnentfernung nach Trennung und Scheidung [It's all a question of opportunity, isn't it? Multi-locality and residential distance in post-separation families]. *Zeitschrift für Familienforschung, 27*(1), 3–31.

Schnor, C., Pasteels, I., & Van Bavel, J. (2017). Sole physical custody and mother's repartnering after divorce. *Journal of Marriage and Family, 79*(3), 879–890. https://doi.org/10.1111/jomf.12389.

Smyth, B., & Moloney, L. (2008). Changes in patterns of post-separation parenting over time: A brief review. *Journal of Family Studies, 14*(1), 7–22. https://doi.org/10.5172/jfs.327.14.1.7.

Sobotka, T., & Toulemon, L. (2008). Changing family and partnership behaviour: Common trends and persistent diversity across Europe. *Demographic Research, 19*, 85–138. https://doi.org/10.4054/DemRes.2008.19.6.

Sodermans, A. K., Matthijs, K., & Swicegood, G. (2013). Characteristics of joint physical custody families in Flanders. *Demographic Research, 28*, 821–848. https://doi.org/10.4054/DemRes.2013.28.29.

Sodermans, A. K., Botterman, S., Havermans, N., & Matthijs, K. (2015). Involved fathers, liberated mothers? Joint physical custody and the subjective well-being of divorced parents. *Social Indicators Research, 122*(1), 257–277. https://doi.org/10.1007/s11205-014-0676-9.

Spruijt, E., & Duindam, V. (2009). Joint physical custody in the Netherlands and the Well-being of children. *Journal of Divorce & Remarriage, 51*(1), 65–82. https://doi.org/10.1080/10502550903423362.

Steinbach, A. (2019). Children's and parents' Well-being in joint physical custody: A literature review. *Family Process, 58*(2), 353–369. https://doi.org/10.1111/famp.12372.

Struffolino, E., & Bernardi, L. (2017). Vulnerability of lone mothers in Switzerland from a life course perspective. *Zeitschrift für Soziologie der Erziehung und Sozialisation, 37*(2), 123–141.

Struffolino, E., Bernardi, L., & Voorpostel, M. (2016). Self-reported health among lone mothers in Switzerland: Do employment and education matter? *Population, 71*(2), 187–213. https://doi.org/10.3917/popu.1602.0193.

Thévenon, O. (2011). Family policies in OECD countries: A comparative analysis. *Population and Development Review, 37*(1), 57–87. https://doi.org/10.1111/j.1728-4457.2011.00390.x.

Turunen, J. (2017). Shared physical custody and children's experience of stress. *Journal of Divorce & Remarriage, 58*(5), 371–392. https://doi.org/10.1080/10502556.2017.1325648.

Umberson, D., & Williams, C. L. (1993). Divorced fathers: Parental role strain and psychological distress. *Journal of Family Issues, 14*(3), 378–400. https://doi.org/10.1177/019251393014003003.

Umberson, D., Pudrovska, T., & Reczek, C. (2010). Parenthood, childlessness, and Well-being: A life course perspective. *Journal of Marriage and Family, 72*(3), 612–629. https://doi.org/10.1111/j.1741-3737.2010.00721.x.

Van der Heijden, F., Gähler, M., & Härkönen, J. (2015). Are parents with shared residence happier? Children's Postdivorce residence arrangements and parents' life satisfaction. *Stockholm Research Reports in Demography, 17*, 1–35.

Van der Heijden, F., Poortman, A. R., & Van der Lippe, T. (2016). Children's postdivorce residence arrangements and parental experienced time pressure. *Journal of Marriage and Family, 78*(2), 468–481. https://doi.org/10.1111/jomf.12283.

Vanassche, S., Sodermans, A. K., Declerck, C., & Matthijs, K. (2017). Alternating residence for children after parental separation: Recent findings from Belgium. *Family Court Review, 55*(4), 545–555. https://doi.org/10.1111/fcre.12303.

Vogt Yuan, A. S. (2016). Father–child relationships and nonresident fathers' psychological distress: What helps and what hurts? *Journal of Family Issues, 37*(5), 603–621. https://doi.org/10.1177/0192513X14526394.

Walper, S. (2016). Arrangements elterlicher Fürsorge nach Trennung und Scheidung: Das Wechselmodell im Licht neuer Daten aus Deutschland [Parental care arrangements after separation and divorce: Shedding light on joint physical custody with new data from Germany]. In Deutscher Familiengerichtstag e.V. (Ed.), Brühler Schriften zum Familienrecht Band 19 (pp. 99–143). Bielefeld: Gieseking Verlag.

Watson, D., Clark, L. A., & Tellegen, A. (1988). Development and validation of brief measures of positive and negative affect: The PANAS scales. *Journal of Personality and Social Psychology, 54*(6), 1063–1070.

Claudia Recksiedler is a senior research fellow at the German Youth Institute in the Department of Social Monitoring and Methodology. She received her Ph.D. in Human Development and Family Sciences from Oregon State University and subsequently completed post-doctoral training at the University of Lausanne focusing on the link between single parents' re-partnering choices and health, as well as the emergence and effects of alternative post-separation childcare arrangements on parents. Her research interests further comprise social influences on the adaptation to transition experiences across the life course, such as in the transition to adulthood and to later-life divorce and widowhood.

Laura Bernardi is Full Professor of Life Course Demography and Sociology at the University of Lausanne and co-Editor in Chief of the journal Advances in Life Course Research, co-Editor of the Springer book series Life Course and Social policies, and a member of the Research Council of the Swiss National Research Foundation. Her research interests are in the field of life course sociology and family demography. Her publications range from the cultural determinants of fertility and family behaviours, the role of social influence on fertility and family transitions to spillover and crossover processes in the life course and their effects on wellbeing. She has extensively published in a wide range of peer-reviewed articles in international journals, in the field of demography, sociology and gender, contributed several chapters in collective volumes and has co-edited the books Lone parenthood in the Life Course (Springer); Situating Children of Migrants (Springer); The Demography of Europe (Springer).

6

Post Divorce Father-Child Relationship Quality and Children's Living Arrangements

Paula Vrolijk and Renske Keizer

Abstract Using data from the multi-actor Divorce in Flanders survey, this study aimed to provide a more comprehensive understanding of linkages between children's living arrangements after divorce and father-child relationship quality. First, we tested whether father involvement and co-parental relationship quality explained linkages between living arrangements and father-child relationship quality. Second, we examined whether child's loyalty conflicts and child's sex moderated associations between living arrangements and father-child relationship quality. Finally, we explored whether results differed when fathers or children reported on their relationship. Results show that father-child relationship quality (irrespectively of the reporter) was significantly higher for children living in JPC but only compared to children who live solely with their mother. Furthermore, father involvement explained the association between living arrangements and father-child relationship quality (again irrespectively of the reporter). The co-parental relationship also explained part of this association, but only when children reported on father-child relationship quality. The association between children's living arrangement and father-child relationship quality was stronger for sons than daughters. This association did not differ by loyalty conflicts. These findings highlight the importance of enabling fathers to remain involved after divorce and having a positive co-parental relationship for maintaining high quality relationships between fathers and children.

Keywords Living arrangements · Father-child relationship quality · Joint physical custody · Father involvement · Co-parental relationship

---

P. Vrolijk (✉) · R. Keizer
Department of Public Administration and Sociology, Erasmus University Rotterdam, Rotterdam, Netherlands
e-mail: vrolijk@essb.eur.nl; keizer@essb.eur.nl

6.1 Introduction

Recent trends show an increasing number of children in Europe who have experienced a parental divorce (Eurostat Statistics Explained 2016). While research suggests that a good relationship with *both* parents has short and long-term beneficial consequences for children's mental well-being (Stafford et al. 2016), in divorced families there is on average less father-child contact and a weaker father-child relationship compared to intact families (Dunlop et al. 2001; Peters and Ehrenberg 2008; Shapiro and Lambert 1999). Even though part of this effect is likely due to selection (i.e. fathers who are less involved in childrearing and who have weaker father-child relationship quality are more likely to experience divorce), longitudinal studies reveal that the divorce itself weakens the father-child relationship (Amato and Booth 1996; Shapiro and Lambert 1999). Given the importance of strong father-child relationship quality for child's well-being, it is important to obtain a comprehensive understanding of the conditions under which the father-child relationship is weaker after divorce and what factors may help maintain high quality father-child relationships.

Living arrangement of the child seems to play a crucial role in the association between divorce and father-child relationship quality. Although the majority of children live with their mother after divorce, there is a growing number of children that lives in joint physical custody (JPC), meaning that children live at least one-third of the time with each parent. Many researchers stress that this type of arrangement enables fathers and children to maintain positive father-child relationships after divorce (Baude et al. 2016; Bauserman 2012; Spruijt and Duindam 2009; Vanassche et al. 2017). In the current chapter, we investigate linkages between children's living arrangements after divorce and the quality of the father-child relationship. We contribute to the literature in four ways. First, we differentiate between three different types of living arrangements reflecting children's actual living situation: JPC arrangements, arrangements in which the child lives mainly with the mother (with visitation arrangements for fathers) and arrangements in which the child lives solely with the mother. All recent review studies collapse the latter two categories into one (Baude et al. 2016; Nielsen 2018), although this distinction has important consequences for what opportunities there are for the continuation of the father-child relationship. Second, we move beyond the question *whether* living arrangements have an effect on father-child relationship quality after divorce. We elaborate on and test different mechanisms that might explain this association, namely the level of father involvement and the quality of the co-parental relationship. Third, we aim to investigate under what conditions JPC is more or less beneficial for father-child relationship quality than living solely or mainly with mother. We examine to what extent the association between living arrangements after divorce and the quality of the father-child relationship is influenced by (a) experienced loyalty conflicts by the child (i.e. feeling caught in the middle between parents), and (b) child's sex. Fourth, the multi-actor nature of our dataset allows us to explore if linkages between living arrangements and the father-child relationship are different depending on whether the father or the child reports on the quality of the father-child relationship. Previous studies that have investigated father-child relationship quality within different living arrangement have only made use of child reports (e.g., Bjarnason and Arnarsson 2011; Carlsund et al. 2013; Låftman et al. 2014), while per definition, relationships consist of (at least) two persons whom both have their own perceptions on and views of the relationship (Harach and Kuczynski 2005). We made use of family systems theory to develop our hypotheses. According to family systems theory, it is important to study individuals within the context of their larger family, which consists of individuals and subsystems (e.g., parental subsystem, parent-child subsystem) that are constantly influencing each other (Cox and Paley 2003; Minuchin 1985).

6.1.1 Linkages Between Living Arrangements After Divorce and Father-Child Relationship Quality: The Issue of Self-Selection

As previously mentioned, the father-child relationship appears to be stronger in JPC compared to other living arrangements, in particular in comparison to sole maternal custody (e.g., Carlsund et al. 2013; Låftman et al. 2014; Nielsen 2018; Spruijt and Duindam 2009; Vanassche et al. 2017). Although there are strong reasons to believe that living arrangements after divorce shape the quality of the relationship children have with their father, we need to take the possibility of self-selection into account, that is, the possibility that characteristics of the different family members and their relationships influence the family's choice for a certain living arrangement. For instance, highly involved fathers who have stronger bonds with their children are more likely to obtain a JPC arrangement. Also, parents who have better co-parental relationships may be more likely to choose for JPC. While self-selection might play a role in research on living arrangements, recent evidence indicates that it does not largely accounts for the benefits of JPC for children (Braver and Votruba 2018).

We made two choices in the current chapter in our attempt to rule out part of the self-selection. First, we decided to control for two important self-selection factors (Braver and Votruba 2018). We controlled for interparental conflicts before the divorce, since low-conflict families are overrepresented in JPC (Sodermans et al. 2013), and interparental conflicts can have a negative effect on the father-child relationship (Kalmijn 2015). We also controlled for parents' socioeconomic status (SES), because highly educated parents have on average a better relationship with their children (Conger et al. 2010) and are more likely to have JPC (Sodermans et al. 2013) compared to lower educated parents.

Second, we decided to use Flemish data to answer our research questions. In Belgium, the percentage of children living in JPC after divorce rose from 7% (couples who divorced before 1995) to 27% (couples who divorced after 2006) (Sodermans et al. 2011). This increase is associated with the tendency towards equal parental rights after divorce and the accompanying changes in laws and policy in

Belgium. Since 2006, JPC is introduced as the default residential model after divorce in the Belgian law. So, when parents do not agree on the child arrangements after divorce, the judge must investigate and seriously consider the possibility of an equally divided alternating residence (Vanassche et al. 2017). Due to this change in law, JPC living arrangements are also presented as the default starting option for families in which there are conflicts between the ex-partners or in which the father was relatively weaker involved in childcare during the marriage (Sodermans et al. 2013). As a consequence, since 2006, self-selection into different types of living arrangements after divorce might play a smaller role within the Belgian context. Therefore, and because of the high divorce rate (Eurostat Statistics Explained 2016), Belgium makes an interesting setting to study the effects of different living arrangements after divorce.

6.1.2 Linkages Between Living Arrangements After Divorce and Father-Child Relationship Quality: Causal Relationships

Because parenting time predicts a better father-child relationship (Fabricius et al. 2010), researchers suggest that the more equal children spend their time between mother and father, the higher the quality of the father-child relationship. Research shows that even weak father-child relationships improve when father and child spent more time together (Fabricius et al. 2010). Below we elaborate on two factors that may explain these linkages between children's living arrangements and father-child relationship quality: the level of father involvement and the quality of the co-parental relationship.

6.1.3 Linkages Between Living Arrangements After Divorce and Father-Child Relationship Quality: The Mediating Role of Father Involvement

From a family systems perspective, living under the same roof as your child helps fathers to maintain their role as an involved parent which contributes to a strong father-child relationship (Fabricius et al. 2010; Melli and Brown 2008; Vanassche et al. 2013). Overnight stays enable the father to move beyond the recreational role which he might have had with only daytime contact, and fulfil a more caregiving role (Cashmore et al. 2008; Stewart 1999). It permits the father to be involved in children's everyday lives and routines, like transitions to and from school, or helping with homework. This higher level of father involvement is associated with higher quality father-child relationships (Cashmore et al. 2008).

6.1.4 Linkages Between Living Arrangements After Divorce and Father-Child Relationship Quality: The Mediating Role of the Co-parental Relationship

After divorce, parents end their relationship with each other as spouses, but maintain their relationship as co-parents. Family system theory states that the whole family has to adjust to these new roles, expectations, and boundaries (Ahrons 1980; Carroll et al. 2007). Parents need to jointly make decisions regarding their child(ren), need to share information about their child(ren)'s life, and need to decide on what level they will align their parenting activities which means they have to manage their conflicts (when present). In sum, ex-spouses need to find a way of cooperating in their new roles within their co-parental relationship. Studies show that JPC predicts stronger co-parental relationships characterized by more emotional support and positive feelings compared to sole custody (Bauserman 2012; Spruijt and Duindam 2009). In turn, this co-parental relationship is shown to benefit the quality of the father-child relationship. Research shows that when mothers and non-residential fathers have positive co-parental relationships, the father-child relationship is stronger (Sobolewski and King 2005).

6.1.5 Linkages Between Living Arrangements After Divorce and Father-Child Relationship Quality: The Moderating Influence of Loyalty Conflicts

Although the quality of the father-child relationship is generally highest in families with JPC, this might not be the case in all circumstances, in particular when there is high interparental conflict (see the review of Smyth et al. 2016). One of the main concerns about JPC is that this type of living arrangement might not be beneficial when children are being exposed to interparental conflicts (Pruett et al. 2014; Smyth et al. 2016; but please note that other scholars argue that JPC is always the best living arrangement, e.g. Kruk 2012; Warshak 2014). Children who experience many conflicts between their parents often experience loyalty conflicts and feel they have to 'choose' between their parents. Children who feel caught in the middle are less able to freely express their love for one parent without the feeling of hurting the other parent or themselves (Afifi and Schrodt 2003). In line with this reasoning, scholars have shown that feeling caught in the middle is associated with low quality parent-child relationships (Afifi and Schrodt 2003; Amato and Afifi 2006). The behavior in the parental subsystem (i.e. interparental conflicts) seems to spill over to the parent-child subsystem (i.e. weaker father-child relations). As such, linkages between children's living arrangements after divorce and the quality of the father-child relationship might differ by the extent to which the child reports to feel caught in the middle.

6.1.6 *Linkages Between Living Arrangements After Divorce and Father-Child Relationship Quality: The Moderating Influence of Child's Sex*

The second possible moderating influence for the relationship between living arrangements and father-child relationship quality is the child's sex. An advantage of JPC (compared to arrangements were children live solely or mainly with their mother) is that fathers can more easily maintain close bonds with their children. Studies showed that fathers are more likely to stay in contact and maintain a strong relationship with sons than with daughters after divorce (Marsiglio 1991; Peters and Ehrenberg 2008; Sobolewski and King 2005). This is probably because fathers are typically more involved with their sons than daughters. In addition, studies show that the father-daughter relationship is at greater risk after divorce compared to the father-son relationship (for a review see Nielsen 2011). These results suggest that the father-son bond might be strong irrespectively of living arrangement, while for daughters, it especially important to live with their father to ensure a high-quality father-child relationship.

6.1.7 *The Present Study*

The aim of the current study is to provide a comprehensive understanding of linkages between children's living arrangements and the quality of the father-child relationship by differentiating between three living arrangements. Further we empirically test two underlying mechanisms and examine under what conditions linkages between children's living arrangements and the quality of the father-child relationship differ. We aim to test the following hypotheses:

1. The quality of the father child relationship is highest in JPC, somewhat lower in families in which children live mainly with mother, and lowest in families in which children live solely with mother.
2. Fathers whose children live solely with their mother, and to a lesser extent fathers of children who live mainly with mother, show less involvement with their children compared to fathers in JPC, which explains the relation between living arrangements and the quality of the father-child relationship.
3. Parents whose children live solely with their mother, and to a lesser extent parents of children that live mainly with mother, have worse co-parental relationships compared to parents with JPC, which explains the relation between living arrangements and the quality of the father-child relationship.
4. The effect of living arrangements on the quality of the father-child relationship is weaker for children who experience loyalty conflicts.
5. The effect of living arrangements on the quality of the father-child relationship is stronger for daughters compared to sons.

Further, we explore whether the results of our study differ depending on the person who reports on father-child relationship quality. We make use of structural equation modelling (SEM) to answer our research questions.

6.2 Methods

6.2.1 *Data*

We made use of the cross-sectional 'Divorce in Flanders' study, which was conducted in 2009–2010 (Mortelmans et al. 2011). This multi-actor study includes information on 4550 first marriages (reference marriages) contracted between 1971 and 2008 that were drawn from the Belgian National Register. Respondents were one or both (ex)-spouses of each reference marriage. Furthermore, one child, the target child, was randomly selected to participate. We only focused on divorced families with a participating minor target child between 10 and 17 years old, living with at least one of the parents at the time of the interview ($n = 414$). Next, we excluded families who had other arrangements (i.e. living solely with father, living mainly with father, or a flexible arrangement) than our three arrangements of interest ($n = 57$). Sample sizes within these living arrangements were too small to draw meaningful conclusions from comparisons. Finally, we excluded families whereby the child did not have any face-to-face contact with father, because these children were not asked about the relationship with their father ($n = 35$). Our final sample contains information on 322 divorced families. Participants were interviewed by face-to-face Computer Assisted Personal Interviews (CAPI).

In total, 780 family members were part of our research sample, consisting of 173 fathers ($M_{age} = 43.62$, $SD = 4.52$), 285 mothers ($M_{age} = 41.42$, $SD = 4.06$), and 322 children. The mean age of the participating children (51.2% boys) was 13.71 ($SD = 2.16$). The majority of the parents was highly educated (fathers = 37.0%, mothers = 43.5%) or moderately educated (fathers = 41.6%, mothers = 44.2%). Almost all fathers (87.9%) and half of the mothers (50.9%) had a full-time job. Approximately one third of the mothers was working a part-time job (35.1%). At the time of the interview half of the parents was living with a new partner (fathers = 54.9%, mothers = 44.9%).

6.2.2 *Measures*

Living Arrangements To categorize the families into living arrangements we used information on children's actual residency. This information was collected using the month-calendar (Sodermans et al. 2014). A residential calendar was presented to the parent, corresponding with a regular month. The parent indicated for every day and night whether the child resided with him/her or with the

Table 6.1 Percentages of children, mothers, and fathers per living arrangement

	Total	Solely	Mainly	JPC
Respondents	780 (100%)	24.7%	36.9%	38.3%
Children	322 (100%)	26.4%	36.6%	37.0%
Mothers	285 (100%)	29.8%	38.2%	31.9%
Fathers	173 (100%)	13.3%	35.3%	51.4%

ex-partner. When answers of parents were not identical, a mean score was calculated. Next, we distinguished three different living arrangements based on regularly used cut-off criteria (e.g., Fabricius et al. 2012; Smyth et al. 2008): (1) living solely with mother (100% at mother's residence), (2) living merely with mother (child lives 66–99% of the time with mother and less than 33% of the time with father), and (3) living in JPC (child lives at least 33% of the time with each parent). This resulted in 85 children (26.4%) who were living solely with mother, 118 children (36.6%) who were living merely with mother, and 119 children (37.0%) who were living in JPC. Table 6.1 shows how all family members were divided among the living arrangements.

Father-Child Relationship Quality Father-child relationship quality was reported by fathers and children separately. Relationships are defined as dyads that accumulate a history of interactions over time (Hinde 1976). In the most recent review on living arrangements and children's outcomes (Nielsen 2018), the quality of parent-child relationship was described as how well parents and children communicate and how close they feel to each other. To tap into the specific concept of father-child relationship, most researchers use different items. For example, scholars assess both affection as well as conflicts between parents and children (e.g., Fauchier and Margolin 2004), or both care as well as control (e.g., Dunlop et al. 2001). In the current study, in a similar line, we aimed to tap into both an affective and an evaluative component of the father-child relationship. First, children and fathers were asked to rate the quality of their father-child relationship ('How good or how bad is the relationship with your father/child?') on a 5-point scale from (1) *very bad* to (5) *very good.* Second, we assessed parent-adolescent communication by the Parent-Adolescent Communication Scale (PACS) (Barnes and Olson 1985). Children and fathers answered 9 items on a 7-point scale from (1) *strongly disagree* to (7) *strongly agree.* An example item is 'I openly show affection to my father/My child openly shows his or her affection for me'. The communication scale showed a good reliability for children ($\alpha = .83$) and fathers ($\alpha = .78$). Finally, because the relationship-item and communication scale was significantly correlated for both fathers, $r(169) = .48$, $p < .001$, and children, $r(315) = .68$, $p < .001$, we decided to compute their mean to indicate the quality of father-child relationship quality. Father-child relationship quality from father's perspective and from child's perspective were analyzed separately. Father and child report on father-child relationship were significantly related, $r(169) = .45$, $p < .001$.

Father Involvement Father involvement is a quantitative measure reported by fathers. This scale consists of 6 questions concerning how often the father undertakes certain activities with his child (i.e. helping with homework, talking about his/her problems, having fun together, taking part in leisure activities, taking to/from school, going to parent evenings). Fathers could answer on a 7-point scale, ranging from (1) *never* to (7) *daily*. The scale showed an acceptable reliability, $\alpha = .70$.

Co-parental Relationship Co-parenting refers to interactions of parents regarding their children, or the ways that parents work together in their roles as parents (Feinberg 2003). This is somewhat different from the interparental or marital relationship. Van Egeren and Hawkins (2004) state there are 4 co-parenting dimensions; co-parenting solidarity, co-parenting support, undermining co-parenting, and shared parenting. By incorporating different items that tap into these different dimensions, we aimed to obtain a multidimensional concept of co-parenting. To measure the co-parental relationship, both parents reported on three items. First, both parents were asked to rate the quality of their relationship at time of the interview ('How would you describe the relationship with [ex-spouse] at the moment?') on a 5 point scale from (1) *very bad* to (5) *very good*. Second, parents filled in two questions that were related to the co-parenting practices, (1) 'My ex-spouse and I agree on how to share the responsibilities of parenting', and (2) 'My ex-spouse and I have difficulty discussing financial matters involving the children' (reversed). Items are answered on a 5-point scale ranging from (1) *never* to (5) *almost always*. These three questions together with the relationship question had an acceptable reliability for fathers ($\alpha = .71$) and mothers ($\alpha = .72$). The mean of the three items was computed to indicate the co-parental relationship according to fathers and mothers separately. Higher scores are corresponding to a better co-parental relationship. Reports of fathers and mothers were strongly correlated, $r(134) = .55$, $p < .001$. This was true within all living arrangements (ranging from $r = .47$, to $r = .62$). When both parents ($n = 136$) reported on the co-parental relationship, we decided to compute the mean.

Loyalty Conflicts Children were asked whether they experienced conflicts between the parents (i.e. blamed each other, yelled at each other, used violence, broke things deliberately, did not want to talk to each other) during the last 12 months. Children who indicated that they never experienced interparental conflicts, were not asked about their loyalty conflicts ($n = 129$). Children who did indicate that they experienced interparental conflicts could answer on a 5-point scale ranging from (1) *Completely false* to (5) *Completely true* whether they feel caught in the middle when their parents argue. Because data was not normally distributed, we decided to create three categories; (1) children who never experienced interparental conflicts ($n = 129$), (2) children who did experience interparental conflicts, but indicated the statement about loyalty conflicts was completely false, false, or neither true nor false ($n = 113$), and (3) children who did experience interparental conflicts and who indicated the statement about loyalty conflicts was true or completely true ($n = 61$).

Conflicts Before Separation Conflicts during the year before separation were reported both by fathers and mothers. Parents were asked how frequently they blamed each other, yelled at each other, used physical violence, threw or broke things deliberately or not wanted to talk to each other for a while. They could answer on a 7-point scale, ranging from (1) n*ever* to (7) *daily*. These five items had a good reliability for fathers ($\alpha = .72$) and mothers ($\alpha = .78$).

Child's Sex The sex of the child was indicated by the interviewer whereby male was coded as 0 and female as 1.

6.2.3 Data Analysis

To answer our research questions, structural equation modeling in *Mplus* version 8 (Muthén and Muthén 2017) was used. We tested our hypotheses by using three models: (1) a saturated model for the direct effect of living arrangements on father-child relationship quality, (2) a model for testing the mediation effects, and (3) a saturated model for testing the moderation effects. All models were computed two times; once for child-reported father-child relationship quality, and once for father-reported father-child relationship quality.

First, we tested whether there was a main effect of living arrangements on the quality of the father-child relationship, in which we treated JPC as the reference category. To examine this direct effect, we used a saturated model that included all control variables. We controlled for the previously mentioned self-selection factors: father's SES, mother's SES, father-reported and mother-reported interparental conflicts before separation. Further we controlled for children's age at the time of the interview, as father's involvement is shown to vary by child's age (Lamb 2000; Marsiglio 1991). Next, we controlled for the child's age at separation since previous research suggests that the older the child was at time of separation, the more opportunities the father and child had to develop a strong father-child relationship (Cheadle et al. 2010). We also controlled for the effect of re-partnering (0 = no partner, 1 = new partner), because re-partnering of both mothers and fathers might have an influence on father-child relationship quality (e.g., Kalmijn 2012; Noël-Miller 2013; Tach et al. 2010). Finally, we included the effects of loyalty conflicts and child's sex since these variables may be related to father-child relationship quality.

Second, when there was a significant main effect, we tested the indirect effects. We included both father involvement and the co-parental relationship to the model. We added the effect of living arrangements on both variables. We also added the effect of both variables on father-child relationship quality. Then, to improve model fit, we included more parameters and compared each model by a chi-square difference test. When model fit did not significantly improve, we tested for the indirect effects.

Finally, the moderation effects of loyalty conflicts and child's sex were examined by adding six latent variables to the first saturated model, without father involvement and the co-parental relationship in the model. Two latent variables represented the interaction between child's sex and dummy coded living arrangements (0 = JPC). The other four latent variables represented the interaction between dummy coded loyalty conflicts (0 = no interparental conflicts) and dummy coded living arrangements. Father-child relationship quality was regressed on these latent variables.

Within the 322 families, 149 fathers and 37 mothers did not participate. Some important differences were found between parents who were missing and parents who were not missing from the data. Fathers who did not participate ($M = 4.23$, $SD = 0.94$) had children who reported a lower father-child relationship quality compared to fathers who were not missing ($M = 4.53$, $SD = 0.90$), $t(315) = 2.88$, $p = .004$, $d = 0.32$. When the mother had missing data ($M = 4.71$, $SD = 0.64$), children reported higher father-child relationship quality compared to families where the mother was not missing ($M = 4.35$, $SD = 0.96$), $t(60) = 3.07$, $p = .003$, $d = 0.45$. Mothers who did not participate had more often an equally divided living arrangement ($V(1, 322) = .30$, $p < .001$), while fathers who did not participate had more often children who lived solely with mother ($V(1, 322) = .38$, $p < .001$). Parents with missing data did not differ on child-reported loyalty conflicts, partner-reported conflicts before divorce, partner-reported co-parental relationship or father-reported father-child relationship quality. Little's (1988) Missing Completely at Random test produced a norm χ^2 (χ^2/df) of 1.51. This indicates that it is likely that data was missing at random and it is safe to impute missing items (Bollen 1989). Missing data was imputed using the missRanger package in R (Mayer, 2019). Maximum likelihood estimation with robust standard errors (MLR) was used as the estimator, since it takes into account non-normality (Satorra and Bentler 1994). Because MLR is used, the chi-square difference test is not reliable due to the scaling correction. Therefore, the scaling correction factor is accounted for by using the Satorra-Bentler Scaled Chi-Square. RMSEA's smaller than .05, and CFI's larger than .95 indicated an adequate model fit (Hu and Bentler 1999).

6.3 Results

6.3.1 Descriptives

The frequencies, percentages, means and standard deviations of all variables are represented in Table 6.2 and 6.3 for each living arrangement separately. Also results of one-way between analyses of variances (ANOVA's) and Cramer's *V*'s are represented, to compare the different living arrangements on all variables. Regarding the key variables, the groups differed significantly on child-reported father-child relationship quality, father involvement and the co-parental relationship. Post-hoc tests revealed that children who lived solely with their mother reported lower father-child relationship quality compared to children who lived mainly with mother

Table 6.2 Frequencies, means, standard deviations of measures, and ANOVA statistics

	Living arrangement										
	Solely			Mainly			JPC			ANOVA	
	N	*M*	*SD*	*N*	*M*	*SD*	*N*	*M*	*SD*	*F*	η^2
Father-child relationship (child-reported)	80	$4.03^{b,c}$	0.99	118	4.46^{a}	0.90	119	4.56^{a}	0.86	8.65**	.05
Father-child relationship (father-reported)	23	4.58	0.73	59	4.93	0.67	89	4.89	0.61	2.64	.03
Father involvement (father-reported)	23	$2.43^{b,c}$	0.79	60	$3.00^{a,c}$	0.88	89	$3.60^{a,b}$	0.91	19.18**	.18
Co-parental relationship (parent-reported)	81	3.23^{c}	1.17	118	3.46	1.00	118	3.61^{a}	0.99	3.18*	.02
Age child	85	14.33^{c}	2.26	118	13.83^{c}	2.03	119	$13.14^{a,b}$	2.08	8.14**	.05
Age at separation	76	6.12	3.94	108	6.23	3.46	107	7.25	3.55	2.96	.02
Co-parental conflicts (father-reported)	23	2.72	1.26	61	2.74	1.03	89	2.45	0.89	1.72	.02
Co-parental conflicts (mother-reported)	85	$3.44^{b,c}$	1.43	109	2.77^{a}	1.25	91	2.88^{a}	1.27	6.89*	.05

[a]Different from solely, [b]Different from mainly, [c]Different from JPC, * = $p < .05$, ** = $p < .001$

Table 6.3 Frequencies, percentages, and Cramer's *V* statistics

		Living arrangement								
		Solely		Mainly		JPC		Total		Cramer's *V*
		N	%	*N*	%	*N*	%	*N*	%	
Loyalty conflicts	No parental conflicts	37	50.7	50	43.5	42	36.5	129	42.6	.09
	No loyalty conflicts	22	30.1	46	40.0	45	39.1	113	37.3	
	Loyalty conflicts	14	19.2	19	16.5	28	24.3	61	20.1	
Child's sex	Boys	40	47.1	62	52.5	63	52.9	165	51.2	.05
	Girls	45	52.9	56	47.5	56	47.1	157	48.8	
Father's SES	Low	6	26.1	23	37.7	8	9.0	37	21.4	.24**
	Middle	12	52.2	20	32.8	40	44.9	72	41.6	
	High	5	21.7	18	29.5	41	46.1	64	37.0	
Mother's SES	Low	20	23.5	7	6.4	8	8.8	35	12.3	.17*
	Middle	33	38.8	55	50.5	38	41.8	126	44.2	
	High	32	37.6	47	43.1	45	49.5	124	43.5	

* = $p < .05$, ** = $p < .001$

(d = 0.37, p = .003) and children in JPC (d = 0.45, p < .001). Further, in JPC families, fathers reported more father involvement compared to families whereby the child lived mainly with mother (d = 0.62, p < .001) or solely with mother (d = 0.87, p < .001). There was also significantly more father involvement in families whereby the child lived mainly with mother compared to families whereby the child lived solely with mother (d = 0.41, p = .025). Finally, within JPC parents had a better co-parental relationship compared to living arrangements in which the child lived solely with mother (d = 0.28, p = .037). We did not find any significant differences between the three types of living arrangements on father-reported father-child relationship quality, child's sex, and loyalty conflicts. Correlations between all concepts are shown in Table 6.4.

6.3.2 *Child-Reported Father-Child Relationship Quality*

First, we tested the main effect of living arrangements on the child-reported father-child relationship quality in a saturated model including all control variables. There was only a difference between children who live in JPC and children who live solely with mother (β = −0.38, p = .008). Children in JPC reported higher father-child relationship quality compared to children who lived solely with mother. There was no difference between children in JPC and children who live mainly with mother on their father-child relationship quality (β = 0.03, p = .790).

In order to answer the mediation questions, we included father involvement and the co-parental relationship to the saturated model. We added parameters until model fit did not significantly improve (see Table 6.5). After the eighth model, model fit did not significantly improve so we decided to use that model for the mediation analyses

Table 6.4 Correlations between measures

Variable	1	2	3	4	5	6	7
1. Father child relationship (child-reported)							
2. Father-child relationship (father-reported)	.45**						
3. Father involvement (father-reported)	.26*	.32**					
4. Co-parental relationship (parent-reported)	.32**	.06	.01				
5. Age child	−.22**	−.28**	−.39**	−.05			
6. Age at separation	−.12*	−.16*	−.00	−.11	.34**		
7. Conflicts (father-reported)	−.15	−.16*	−.05	−.25**	.22**	.07	
8. Conflicts (mother-reported)	−.21**	.05	.11	−.27**	−.00	.05	.21*

* = $p < .05$, ** = $p < .001$

($\chi^2(13) = 16.07$, $p = .246$, RMSEA = 0.03, CFI = 0.99). Table 6.6 represents the parameters of this final model.

For the first mediation analysis (father involvement), we found that fathers whose child lived solely or mainly with mother reported less father involvement compared to fathers with JPC. Further, more father involvement predicted higher father-child relationship quality. We tested whether father involvement explained the difference we found in father-child relationship quality between children in JPC and children who lived solely with mother. Results showed that father involvement indeed explained this difference. Children living solely with mother reported lower levels of father-child relationship compared to children in JPC, because their fathers were less involved.

For the second mediation analysis (co-parental relationship) results indicate that parents with JPC had a better co-parental relationship compared to parents whose children lived solely with mother, and (approaching borderline significance) parents whose children lived mainly with mother. Further, a better co-parental relationship predicted a stronger father-child relationship quality. The indirect effect of the co-parental relationship was also significant. Results show that children in JPC have a stronger father-child relationship quality compared to children living only with mother, because their parents have a better co-parental relationship.

Next we analyzed whether the effect of living arrangements was the same for boys and girls and across different levels of loyalty conflicts. We added the four latent variables that represent the interaction of the dummy coded loyalty conflicts and the dummy coded living arrangements to the saturated model. We also added the interaction effects between child's sex and dummy coded living arrangements to the model. Parameters of this saturated model are shown in Table 6.7.

First, the model shows a main effect of loyalty conflicts on father-child relationship quality. Children who experience loyalty conflicts reported lower father-child relationship quality compared to children that experienced no interparental conflicts. Also, children who indicated they experienced interparental conflicts but no loyalty conflicts, reported lower father-child relationship quality compared to children that experienced no interparental conflicts. The interaction terms concerning the moderation effects of loyalty conflicts were not significant. So, the relationship between living arrangements and father-child relationship quality did not differ by level of loyalty conflicts.

Second, the model shows that girls reported a lower father-child relationship quality compared to boys. One interaction effect of child's sex was significant, indicating that the difference between JPC and living solely with mother in father-child relationship quality was less strong for girls compared to boys. The other interaction effects showed that boys and girls did not differ on the difference between JPC and living mainly with mother in father-child relationship quality.

6.3.3 Father-Reported Father-Child Relationship Quality

Also, for father-reported father-child relationship quality we first examined the direct effect of children's living arrangements after divorce on the quality of the father-child relationship in a saturated model, while including all control variables. Similar to the results found when we used child reports, results indicated there was only a difference between fathers in JPC and father whose child lived solely with mother in father-child relationship quality ($\beta = -0.28$, $p = .048$). So, when all control variables included in the model, fathers in JPC reported higher father-child relationship quality compared to fathers whose child lived solely with mother. There was no difference between fathers in JPC and fathers whose children lived mainly with mother ($\beta = 0.14$, $p = .334$).

In order to check whether father involvement and the co-parental relationship mediated the effect of living arrangements on father-child relationship quality we computed a new model containing father involvement and the co-parental relationship. Again, we added parameters until model fit did not significantly improve (see Table 6.8). This resulted in the same final model as the model we used for child-reported father-child relationship with the same model fit, ($\chi^2(13) = 16.07$, $p = .246$, RMSEA $= 0.03$, CFI $= 0.99$). All parameters for this model can be found in Table 6.9.

Similar to the results we found when we relied on child-reports, children's living arrangements after divorce were a significant predictor for the level of father involvement. In line with our expectations, our results showed that fathers whose child lived solely or mainly with mother reported less father involvement compared to fathers with JPC. More father involvement in turn, predicted better father-child relationship quality reported by fathers. The difference between JPC and living solely with mother in father-reported father-child relationship quality was also significantly explained by father involvement. So, more father involvement explained why fathers in JPC reported higher father-child relationship quality compared to fathers whose children lived solely with mother.

Next, regarding the co-parental relationship, there was a significant effect from living arrangements on the co-parental relationship. Parents in JPC had a better co-parental relationship compared to parents whose children lived only with mother. However, in contrast to the child reports, the co-parental relationship did not predict father-child relationship quality. The indirect effect of the co-parental relationship was also not significant, meaning that the co-parental relationship did not explain the difference between JPC and living only with mother in father-reported father-child relationship quality.

Next we analyzed whether the effect of living arrangements on father-reported father-child relationship quality differed by level of loyalty conflicts and by child's sex. We added the interaction effects between dummy coded loyalty conflicts and dummy coded living arrangements and the interaction effects between child's sex and dummy coded living arrangements to the saturated model.

Within this model (see Table 6.10), we found no effect of child's loyalty conflicts on father-reported father-child relationship quality. Further, the relationship between living arrangements and father-reported father-child relationship quality did not significantly differ for different levels of loyalty conflicts experienced by children.

Second, there was no main effect of child's sex on father-reported father-child relationship. Finally, the relationship between living arrangements and father-reported father-child relationship did not significantly differ for sons and daughters.

6.3.4 Control Variables

Finally, regarding control variables, models show that mother-reported interparental conflicts before separation have a negative effect on child-reported father-child relationship quality while it was positively related to father involvement. Next, higher levels of interparental conflicts before separation reported by fathers predict a lower father-child relationship quality reported by fathers. When their father had a new partner, this was related to a weaker child-reported father-child relationship. However, when their mother had a new partner, this was related to a higher quality of child-reported father-child relationship. Mother's re-partnering was also related to a better co-parental relationship. Further, parents' SES was predicting father-child relationship quality reported by children. When their father had a higher SES, this was related to higher child-reported father-child relationship quality, while higher levels of mother's SES were related to lower child-reported father-child relationship quality. When fathers were more highly educated, they were also more likely to be more involved. Finally, older children had less involved fathers compared to younger children.

6.4 Discussion

In this study, we examined the effect of children's living arrangements after divorce on father-child relationship quality. We made a distinction between three living arrangements: JPC, living mainly with mother, and living solely with mother. We examined two mechanisms that may underlie linkages between children's living arrangements after divorce and father-child relationship quality, namely the level of father involvement and the quality of the co-parental relationship. Furthermore, we tested to what extent these linkages were conditioned by the level of loyalty conflicts experienced by the child or the child's sex. Finally, we examined to what extent our results differed by the person reporting on the quality of the father-child relationship (father or child).

Our first hypothesis about the effect of living arrangements on father-child relationship quality is partly confirmed. Father-child relationship quality was higher in JPC compared to families in which children lived solely with mother, while controlling for self-selection factors (i.e. parents' SES and interparental conflicts before separation), child's age, child's age at separation, child's sex and loyalty conflicts. Nevertheless, even though previous research suggest that time spend more equally between parents will lead to better father-child relationships (Fabricius et al. 2010), there was no difference between JPC and families in which children lived mainly with mother. This result suggests that living in two parental households matters more for father-child relationship quality than the actual time spent together for maintaining a high father-child relationship quality (Vanassche et al. 2013).

Next, we hypothesized that father involvement would explain the effect of living arrangements on father-child relationship quality. This hypothesis was confirmed for the difference we found between families in JPC and families with children living only with mother. Fathers with JPC were more involved compared to fathers with other living arrangements, which predicted a higher father-child relationship quality. So, overnight stays may enable fathers to fulfil a more caregiving role and to be more involved with children's everyday lives and routines (Cashmore et al. 2008). This higher level of father involvement also predicts closer father-child bonds. Thus, it is especially important for fathers to stay involved after divorce to ensure a strong father-child relationship. This was true for both father-reported and child-reported father-child relationship quality.

Our third hypothesis about the mediation effect of the co-parental relationship was partly confirmed. Only within the child-reported model, and not within the father-reported model, we found that the co-parental relationship explained the difference we found in father-child relationship quality between children in JPC and children who were living solely with mother. JPC predicted a better co-parental relationship compared to living solely with mother, which subsequently predicted a higher father-child relationship quality perceived by children. This finding is in accordance with previous literature and suggests that parents within a more equally divided living arrangement need to cooperate and make joint decisions which results in a better co-parental relationship (Bauserman 2012; Spruijt and Duindam 2009). While quality of the co-parental relationship was positively related to the quality of the father-child relationship as reported by children, it was not significantly related to the quality of the father-child relationship as reported by fathers. Our result suggests that children, but not fathers, perceive the quality of the father-child relationship to be lower when the quality of the co-parental relationship is low. A possible explanation could be that the co-parental relationship influences parenting practices (Feinberg 2003) which could have a larger effect on how the child rather than the father perceived the quality of the father-child relationship. Future studies are needed to test the plausibility of this explanation.

Next, our hypothesis concerning the moderating effects of loyalty conflicts was not confirmed. Contrary to our expectations, derived from concerns about JPC in the presence of interparental conflicts (Pruett et al. 2014; Smyth et al. 2016), we did not find different effects of living arrangements on the quality of the father-child relationship by the level of loyalty conflicts. This may suggest that a more equally divided living arrangement is beneficial for the father-child relationship irrespectively of the presence of perceived loyalty conflicts (Kruk 2012; Warshak 2014). The level of loyalty conflicts only had a direct negative impact on father-child relationship quality as reported by children. So, as children experience interparental conflicts and feel caught in the middle between their parents, they subsequently perceive the relationship quality with their father weaker. Again, our results suggest that only children, and not fathers, perceive their quality of father-child relationship to be lower in case of many loyalty conflicts. Thus, children's views on the father-child relationship seem to be more strongly affected by the interactions within the interparental subsystem than fathers' views on the father-child relationship. An alternative explanation could be due to sample homogeneity. A large part of the families did not include father reports. Compared to those children of fathers who were not willing to participate, the children in our sample reported a higher father-child relationship quality. As such, and since parents are more likely to provide a more positive picture of parent-child relationships (Aquilino 1999), the variability in the father-reported father-child relationship quality is smaller in our sample than in the general population, which may have inhibited our ability to pick up effects.

Finally, we found a significant interaction effect between children's living arrangements after divorce and child sex on the quality of the father-child relationship as perceived by children, albeit in the opposite direction. The difference found in father-child relationship quality between children in JPC and children who lived solely with mother was stronger for boys than girls. This finding suggests that the quality of the father-son relationship is more easily affected by changes in father-child contact compared to the quality of the father-daughter relationship. According to social learning theory, children learn how to behave through modeling and imitation and parents are their main role models. Bussey and Bandura (1984) have shown that children are more likely to learn from their relationship with the same-sex parent. This may explain why more contact between father and child, has a larger effect on the father-son relationship compared to the father-daughter relationship. Nevertheless, readers should take into account that these findings only pertained to child-reports.

In this chapter, we explored whether results differed depending on who reports on the quality of the father-child relationship. Although we found that the overall picture is very similar, namely that the level of father involvement is an underlying mechanism for the relationship between children's living arrangements after divorce and the quality of the father-child relationship, we found an interesting difference that deserves some attention. The quality of the co-parental relationship explained the difference between living in JPC and living solely with mother in the quality of the father-child relationship as perceived by children, while it was not an underlying mechanism for the quality of the father-child relationship as perceived by fathers. Furthermore, children, and not fathers, experienced weaker father-child relationship quality when children felt caught in the middle. Finally, only in the child-reported model we found a moderating effect of child's sex. These findings highlight the importance of having different perspectives on the impact of divorce on parent-child relationships, as each perspective adds to our understanding of the complex interplay between the different family members involved in a divorce. In addition, these findings also suggest that more research is needed to understand where these differences come from and how they can be explained.

This study has two important limitations. First, the cross-sectional design is limited in its ability to demonstrate causality. Even though we controlled for parents' SES and conflicts before separation, self-selection may still underlie some of the differences in the quality of the father-child relationship found between the three different types of living arrangements. However, in our sample we found strong evidence that the father-child relationship undergoes changes after divorce. Participants in our study were asked whether the father-child relationship at the time of the interview was better or worse compared to the time before the parents started to live separately. Children living solely with their mother reported a more negative change in father-child relationship quality compared to children living mainly with mother and children in JPC. Although we cannot state that self-selection did not play a role, these findings provide suggestive evidence for causal mechanisms. Second, our sample consists of formerly married parents only, which might limit generalizability to families with different family constellations. Also, parents who agreed to participate in the current study were relatively highly educated. This may give a more positive view on father-child relationship quality, since previous research showed that more educated (non-resident) fathers are more likely to maintain frequent contact with their children (Cooksey and Craig 1998; Conger et al. 2010).

Despite these limitations, our study contributed to the existing literature by providing a more comprehensive understanding of linkages between children's living arrangements after divorce and the quality of the father-child relationships, and the mechanisms that underlie this relationship. We made use of a sophisticated SEM model that allowed us to examine multiple complex relationships within the same model. Not only did we take into account the co-parental relationship reported by parents, but we also assessed the loyalty conflicts experienced by children. We also controlled for self-selection effects of parents' SES and interparental conflicts during the year before separation since these characteristics may have been causing families to choose for JPC and also may have an effect on father-child relationship quality. Finally, this was the first study to examine both child reports and father reports on father-child relationship quality within different living arrangements.

Our analyses revealed that the level of father involvement is an important underlying mechanism for the impact of children's living arrangements after divorce on the quality of the father-child relationship. JPC and visitation arrangements for fathers appear to be beneficial to the quality of the father-child relationship, as they allow fathers to remain highly involved in their children's lives. Since having high quality relationships with both parents has short and long-term beneficial consequences for children's mental well-being, it may be suggested that policy makers, lawyers and parents should strive for living arrangements after divorce that allow both parents to remain involved in their children's lives. From the perspective of children, it is also very important to have a positive co-parental relationship. Children who felt caught in the middle between their parents reported weaker father-child relationship quality. Moreover, a strong co-parental relationship (partly) explained the difference between children in JPC and children that lived only with their mother in their self-reported father-child relationship quality. In conclusion, in order to have a strong father-child relationship the current study indicates that it is important to keep fathers involved in children's day-to-day lives and maintain a positive co-parental relationship.

Appendix

Table 6.5 Model fit and test results of model fit comparisons for child-reported father-child relationship quality

Model	χ^2/ $\Delta\chi^2$ (TRd)	*df*/Δ*df*	*p*	scf	CFI/ΔCFI	RMSEA/ΔRMSEA	Added parameter
Model 0	153.43	23	<.001	1.12	0.61	0.13	
Model 1	119.18	22	<.001	1.11	0.71	0.12	
Model 2	94.69	21	<.001	1.13	0.78	0.10	
Model 3	79.28	20	<.001	1.11	0.82	0.10	
Model 4	67.67	19	<.001	1.10	0.85	0.09	
Model 5	36.06	17	.005	1.09	0.94	0.06	
Model 6	29.04	16	.024	1.09	0.96	0.05	
Model 7	22.27	15	.101	1.10	0.98	0.04	
Model 8	16.07	13	.246	1.11	0.99	0.03	
Model 9	11.64	12	.475	1.09	1.00	0.00	
Model 0 vs. 1	31.21	1	<.001	1.25	0.10	0.02	Father involvement regressed on child's age
Model 1 vs. 2	30.03	1	<.001	0.87	0.07	0.01	Co-parental relationship regressed on father-reported conflicts
Model 2 vs. 3	12.63	1	<.001	1.49	0.04	0.01	Father involvement regressed on father's SES
Model 3 vs. 4	10.73	1	.001	1.24	0.03	0.01	Co-parental relationship regressed on mother-reported conflicts
Model 4 vs. 5	29.55	2	<.001	1.19	0.09	0.03	Co-parental relationship regressed on loyalty conflicts
Model 5 vs. 6	7.42	1	.006	1.01	0.02	0.01	Co-parental relationship regressed on re-partnering mother
Model 6 vs. 7	7.00	1	.008	1.05	0.02	0.01	Father involvement regressed on mother-reported conflicts
Model 7 vs. 8	6.53	2	.038	1.01	0.01	0.01	Father involvement regressed on loyalty conflicts
Model 8 vs. 9	3.72	1	.156	1.40	0.01	0.03	Father involvement regressed on re-partnering father

χ^2 chi-square, *TRd* Sattora-Bentler scaled chi-square difference, *df* degrees of freedom, *p* *p*-value, *scf* scaling correction factor, *CFI* Comparative Fit Index, *RMSEA* Root Mean Square Error of Approximation

Table 6.6 Mediation model for child-reported father-child relationship quality

Structural model	Beta (SE)	*B* (SE)	*p*
Father-child relationship regressed on			
Solely living with mother (0 = JPC)	−0.05 (0.16)	−0.05 (0.15)	.751
Mainly living with mother (0 = JPC)	0.20 (0.12)	0.18 (0.11)	.099
Father involvement	0.27 (0.06)	0.32 (0.07)	<.001
Co-parental relationship	0.18 (0.06)	0.15 (0.05)	.003
No loyalty conflicts (0 = no interparental conflicts)	−0.22 (0.11)	−0.21 (0.11)	.052
Loyalty conflicts (0 = no interparental conflicts)	−0.63 (0.15)	−0.58 (0.14)	<.001
Child's sex (0 = boys)	−0.18 (0.10)	−0.17 (0.09)	.060
Father: Interparental conflict	0.01 (0.05)	0.01 (0.05)	.773
Mother: Interparental conflict	−0.12 (0.05)	−0.09 (0.04)	.018
Father: Re-partnering (0 = no partner)	−0.32 (0.11)	−0.30 (0.10)	.003
Mother: Re-partnering (0 = no partner)	0.27 (0.10)	0.25 (0.09)	.007
Father SES	0.14 (0.06)	0.18 (0.07)	.011
Mother SES	−0.11 (0.05)	−0.15 (0.07)	.038
Age child	−0.03 (0.05)	−0.01 (0.02)	.531
Age at separation	−0.03 (0.05)	−0.01 (0.01)	.573
Father involvement regressed on			
Solely living with mother (0 = JPC)	−1.07 (0.09)	−0.85 (0.09)	<.001
Mainly living with mother (0 = JPC)	−0.54 (0.12)	−0.43 (0.09)	<.001
No loyalty conflicts (0 = no interparental conflicts)	−0.18 (0.10)	−0.15 (0.08)	.054
Loyalty conflicts (0 = no interparental conflicts)	0.11 (0.12)	0.08 (0.09)	.370
Age child	−0.27 (0.05)	−0.10 (0.02)	<.001
Father SES	0.21 (0.05)	0.23 (0.05)	<.001
Mother: Interparental conflicts	0.12 (0.05)	0.07 (0.03)	.010
Co-parental relationship regressed on			
Solely living with mother (0 = JPC)	−0.41 (0.13)	−0.43 (0.14)	.002
Mainly living with mother (0 = JPC)	−0.19 (0.11)	−0.20 (0.12)	.085
No loyalty conflicts (0 = no interparental conflicts)	−0.57 (0.12)	−0.60 (0.12)	<.001
Loyalty conflicts (0 = no interparental conflicts)	−0.70 (0.15)	−0.74 (0.16)	<.001
Father: Interparental conflict	−0.13 (0.05)	−0.14 (0.06)	.012
Mother: Interparental conflict	−0.16 (0.06)	−0.13 (0.05)	.006
Mother: Re-partnering (0 = no partner)	0.27 (0.10)	0.29 (0.10)	.006
Indirect effect father involvement			
Solely living with mother (0 = JPC)	−0.29 (0.07)	−0.27 (0.06)	<.001
Indirect effect co-parental relationship			
Solely living with mother (0 = JPC)	−0.07 (0.03)	−0.07 (0.03)	.032

Table 6.7 Moderation model for child-reported father-child relationship quality

Structural model	Beta (SE)	*B* (SE)	*p*
Child-reported father-child relationship regressed on			
Living solely with mother (0 = JPC)	−0.69 (0.21)	−0.64 (0.20)	.001
Living mainly with mother (0 = JPC)	−0.18 (0.20)	−0.16 (0.19)	.384
No loyalty conflicts (0 = no interparental conflicts)	−0.45 (0.17)	−0.41 (0.16)	.010
Loyalty conflicts (0 = no interparental conflicts)	−0.75 (0.21)	−0.70 (0.19)	<.001
Child's sex (0 = boys)	−0.50 (0.15)	−0.47 (0.14)	.001
Father: Interparental conflict	−0.00 (0.05)	−0.00 (0.05)	.956
Mother: Interparental conflict	−0.14 (0.06)	−0.10 (0.04)	.016
Father: Re-partnering (0 = no partner)	−0.47 (0.11)	−0.43 (0.11)	<.001
Mother: Re-partnering (0 = no partner)	0.33 (0.10)	0.31 (0.10)	.001
Father SES	0.20 (0.06)	0.25 (0.07)	.001
Mother SES	−0.12 (0.06)	−0.17 (0.08)	.037
Age child	−0.12 (0.05)	−0.05 (0.02)	.018
Age at separation	−0.01 (0.05)	−0.00 (0.01)	.844
Living solely with mother * No loyalty conflicts	0.22 (0.29)	0.21 (0.27)	.439
Living solely with mother * Loyalty conflicts	−0.11 (0.38)	−0.10 (0.36)	.779
Living mainly with mother * No loyalty conflicts	0.07 (0.24)	0.07 (0.22)	.761
Living mainly with mother * Loyalty conflicts	0.14 (0.29)	0.13 (0.27)	.646
Living solely with mother * Child's sex	0.54 (0.25)	0.50 (0.23)	.030
Living mainly with mother * Child's sex	0.35 (0.21)	0.32 (0.20)	.106

Table 6.8 Model fit and test results of model fit comparisons for father-reported father-child relationship quality

Model	χ^2/ $\Delta\chi^2$ (TRd)	*df*/ Δdf	*p*	scf	CFI/ ΔCFI	RMSEA/ ΔRMSEA	Added parameter
Model 0	153.43	23	<.001	1.12	0.56	0.13	
Model 1	119.18	22	<.001	1.11	0.67	0.12	
Model 2	94.69	21	<.001	1.13	0.75	0.10	
Model 3	79.28	20	<.001	1.11	0.80	0.10	
Model 4	67.67	19	<.001	1.10	0.84	0.09	
Model 5	36.06	17	.005	1.09	0.94	0.06	
Model 6	29.04	16	.024	1.09	0.96	0.05	
Model 7	22.27	15	.101	1.10	0.98	0.04	
Model 8	16.07	13	.246	1.11	0.99	0.03	
Model 9	11.64	12	.475	1.09	1.00	0.00	
Model 0 vs. 1	31.21	1	<.001	1.25	0.11	0.02	Father involvement regressed on age
Model 1 vs. 2	30.03	1	<.001	0.87	0.08	0.01	Co-parental relationship regressed on father-reported conflicts
Model 2 vs. 3	12.63	1	<.001	1.49	0.05	0.01	Father involvement regressed on father's SES
Model 3 vs. 4	10.73	1	.001	1.24	0.04	0.01	Co-parental relationship regressed on mother-reported conflicts
Model 4 vs. 5	29.55	2	<.001	1.19	0.10	0.03	Co-parental relationship regressed on loyalty conflicts
Model 5 vs. 6	7.42	1	.006	1.01	0.02	0.01	Co-parental relationship regressed on re-partnering mother
Model 6 vs. 7	7.00	1	.008	1.05	0.02	0.01	Father involvement regressed on mother-reported conflicts
Model 7 vs. 8	6.53	2	.038	1.01	0.01	0.01	Father involvement regressed on loyalty conflicts
Model 8 vs. 9	3.72	1	.156	1.40	0.01	0.03	Father involvement regressed on re-partnering father

χ^2 chi-square, *TRd* Sattora-Bentler scaled chi-square difference, *df* degrees of freedom, *p* *p*-value, *scf* scaling correction factor, *CFI* Comparative Fit Index, *RMSEA* Root Mean Square Error of Approximation

Table 6.9 Mediation model for father-reported father-child relationship quality

Structural model	Beta (SE)	*B* (SE)	*p*
Father-child relationship regressed on			
Solely living with mother (0 = JPC)	0.03 (0.17)	0.01 (0.09)	.882
Mainly living with mother (0 = JPC)	0.29 (0.15)	0.15 (0.08)	.058
Father involvement	0.31 (0.08)	0.21 (0.05)	<.001
Co-parental relationship	0.03 (0.06)	0.01 (0.03)	.610
No loyalty conflicts (0 = no interparental conflicts)	0.01 (0.12)	0.01 (0.06)	.912
Loyalty conflicts (0 = no interparental conflicts)	−0.52 (0.16)	−0.28 (0.09)	.002
Child's sex (0 = boys)	−0.00 (0.10)	−0.00 (0.05)	.987
Father: Interparental conflict	−0.12 (0.06)	−0.07 (0.03)	.029
Mother: Interparental conflict	0.07 (0.05)	0.03 (0.02)	.196
Father: Re-partnering (0 = no partner)	−0.23 (0.13)	−0.12 (0.07)	.088
Mother: Re-partnering (0 = no partner)	−0.00 (0.11)	−0.00 (0.06)	.975
Father SES	0.08 (0.07)	0.06 (0.05)	.209
Mother SES	0.02 (0.06)	0.02 (0.05)	.700
Age child	−0.07 (0.05)	−0.02 (0.01)	.152
Age at separation	−0.15 (0.05)	−0.02 (0.01)	.008
Father involvement regressed on			
Solely living with mother (0 = JPC)	−1.07 (0.09)	−0.85 (0.09)	<.001
Mainly living with mother (0 = JPC)	−0.54 (0.12)	−0.43 (0.10)	<.001
No loyalty conflicts (0 = no interparental conflicts)	−0.18 (0.10)	−0.15 (0.09)	.054
Loyalty conflicts (0 = no interparental conflicts)	0.11 (0.11)	0.08 (0.09)	.370
Age child	−0.27 (0.05)	−0.10 (0.02)	<.001
Father SES	0.21 (0.05)	0.23 (0.05)	<.001
Mother: Interparental conflicts	0.12 (0.05)	0.07 (0.03)	.010
Co-parental relationship regressed on			
Solely living with mother (0 = JPC)	−0.41 (0.13)	−0.43 (0.14)	.002
Mainly living with mother (0 = JPC)	−0.19 (0.11)	−0.20 (0.12)	.085
No loyalty conflicts (0 = no interparental conflicts)	−0.57 (0.12)	−0.60 (0.12)	<.001
Loyalty conflicts (0 = no interparental conflicts)	−0.70 (0.15)	−0.74 (0.16)	<.001
Father: Interparental conflict	−0.13 (0.05)	−0.14 (0.06)	.012
Mother: Interparental conflict	−0.16 (0.06)	−0.13 (0.05)	.006
Mother: Re-partnering (0 = no partner)	0.27 (0.10)	0.29 (0.10)	.006
Indirect effect father involvement			
Solely living with mother (0 = JPC)	−0.33 (0.09)	−0.18 (0.05)	<.001
Indirect effect co-parental relationship			
Solely living with mother (0 = JPC)	−0.01 (0.02)	−0.01 (0.01)	.617

Table 6.10 Moderation model for father-reported father-child relationship quality

Structural model	Beta (SE)	*B* (SE)	*p*
Father-reported father-child relationship regressed on			
Living solely with mother (0 = JPC)	−0.35 (0.25)	−0.19 (0.13)	.158
Living mainly with mother (0 = JPC)	0.21 (0.26)	0.11 (0.14)	.412
No loyalty conflicts (0 = no interparental conflicts)	0.07 (0.22)	0.04 (0.12)	.756
Loyalty conflicts (0 = no interparental conflicts)	−0.31 (0.26)	−0.17 (0.14)	.221
Child's sex (0 = boys)	−0.22 (0.19)	−0.12 (0.10)	.242
Father: Interparental conflict	−0.12 (0.06)	−0.07 (0.03)	.034
Mother: Interparental conflict	0.09 (0.06)	0.04 (0.02)	.126
Father: Re-partnering (0 = no partner)	−0.30 (0.14)	−0.16 (0.07)	.031
Mother: Re-partnering (0 = no partner)	0.03 (0.11)	0.02 (0.06)	.788
Father SES	0.15 (0.07)	0.11 (0.05)	.033
Mother SES	0.01 (0.06)	0.01 (0.05)	.906
Age child	−0.17 (0.05)	−0.04 (0.01)	.001
Age at separation	−0.12 (0.06)	−0.02 (0.01)	.034
Living solely with mother * No loyalty conflicts	−0.06 (0.28)	−0.03 (0.15)	.817
Living solely with mother * Loyalty conflicts	−0.20 (0.37)	−0.11 (0.20)	.581
Living mainly with mother * No loyalty conflicts	−0.28 (0.28)	−0.15 (0.15)	.319
Living mainly with mother * Loyalty conflicts	−0.46 (0.37)	−0.24 (0.20)	.214
Living solely with mother * Child's sex	0.31 (0.25)	0.17 (0.13)	.208
Living mainly with mother * Child's sex	0.26 (0.26)	0.14 (0.14)	.306

References

Afifi, T. D., & Schrodt, P. (2003). "Feeling caught" as a mediator of adolescents' and young adults' avoidance and satisfaction with their parents in divorced and non-divorced households. *Communication Monographs, 70*, 142–173.

Ahrons, C. R. (1980). Divorce: A crisis of family transition and change. *Family Relations, 29*, 533–540.

Amato, P. R., & Afifi, T. D. (2006). Feeling caught between parents: Adult children's relations with parents and subjective well-being. *Journal of Marriage and Family, 68*, 222–235.

Amato, P. R., & Booth, A. (1996). A prospective study of divorce and parent-child relationships. *Journal of Marriage and Family, 58*, 356–365.

Aquilino, W. S. (1999). Two views of one relationship: Comparing parents' and young adult children's reports of the quality of intergenerational relations. *Journal of Marriage and the Family, 61*, 858–870.

Barnes, H. L., & Olson, D. H. (1985). Parent-adolescent communication and the circumplex model. *Child Development, 56*, 438–447.

Baude, A., Pearson, J., & Drapeau, S. (2016). Child adjustment in joint physical custody versus sole custody: A meta-analytic review. *Journal of Divorce and Remarriage, 57*, 338–360.

Bauserman, R. (2012). A meta-analysis of parental satisfaction, adjustment, and conflict in joint custody and sole custody following divorce. *Journal of Divorce and Remarriage, 53*, 464–488.

Bollen, K. (1989). *Structural equations with latent variables*. New York: Wiley.

Bjarnason, T., & Arnarsson, A. M. (2011). Joint physical custody and communication with parents: A cross-national study of children in 36 western countries. *Journal of Comparative Family Studies, 42*, 871–890.

Braver, S. L., & Votruba, A. M. (2018). Does joint physical custody "cause" children's better outcomes? *Journal of Divorce and Remarriage, 59*, 452–468.

Bussey, K., & Bandura, A. (1984). Influence of gender constancy and social power on sex-linked modeling. *Journal of Personality and Social Psychology, 47*, 1292–1302.

Carlsund, Å., Eriksson, U., & Sellström, E. (2013). Shared physical custody after family split-up: Implications for health and well-being in Swedish schoolchildren. *Acta Paediatrica, 102*, 318–323.

Carroll, J. S., Olson, C. D., & Buckmiller, N. (2007). Family boundary ambiguity: A 30-year review of theory, research, and measurement. *Family Relations, 56*, 210–230.

Cashmore, J., Parkinson, P., & Taylor, A. (2008). Overnight stays and children's relationships with resident and nonresident parents after divorce. *Journal of Family Issues, 29*, 707–733.

Cheadle, J. E., Amato, P. R., & King, V. (2010). Patterns of nonresident father contact. *Demography, 47*, 205–225.

Conger, R. D., Conger, K. J., & Martin, M. J. (2010). Socioeconomic status, family processes, and individual development. *Journal of Marriage and Family, 72*, 685–704.

Cooksey, E. C., & Craig, P. H. (1998). Parenting from a distance: The effects of paternal characteristics on contact between nonresidential fathers and their children. *Demography, 35*, 187–200.

Cox, M. J., & Paley, B. (2003). Understanding families as systems. *Current Directions in Psychological Science, 12*, 193–196.

Dunlop, R., Burns, A., & Bermingham, S. (2001). Parent–child relations and adolescent self-image following divorce: A 10 year study. *Journal of Youth and Adolescence, 30*, 117–134.

Eurostat Statistics Explained. (2016). *Marriage and divorce statistics*. Retrieved from http://ec.europa.eu.eur.idm.oclc.org/eurostat/statistics-explained/index.php/Marriage_and_divorce_statistics#Further_Eurostat_information

Fabricius, W. V., Braver, S. L., Diaz, P., & Velez, C. E. (2010). Custody and parenting time: Links to family relationships and well-being after divorce. In M. E. Lamb (Ed.), *The role of the father in child development* (pp. 201–240). Hoboken: Wiley.

Fabricius, W. V., Sokol, K. R., Diaz, P., & Braver, S. L. (2012). Parenting time, parent conflict, parent-child relationships, and children's physical health. In K. Kuehnle & L. Drozd (Eds.), *Parenting plan evaluations: Applied research for the family court*. Oxford: Oxford University Press.

Fauchier, A., & Margolin, G. (2004). Affection and conflict in marital and parent-child relationships. *Journal of Marital and Family Therapy, 30*, 197–211.

Feinberg, M. E. (2003). The internal structure and ecological context of coparenting: A framework for research and intervention. *Parenting: Science and Practice, 3*, 95–131.

Harach, L. D., & Kuczynski, L. J. (2005). Construction and maintenance of parent–child relationships: Bidirectional contributions from the perspective of parents. *Infant and Child Development: An International Journal of Research and Practice, 14*, 327–343.

Hinde, R. (1976). Interactions, relationships, and social structure. *Man, 11*, 1–17.

Hu, L. T., & Bentler, P. M. (1999). Cutoff criteria for fit indexes in covariance structure analysis: Conventional criteria versus new alternatives. *Structural Equation Modeling, 6*, 1–55.

Kalmijn, M. (2012). Long-term effects of divorce on parent–child relationships: Within-family comparisons of fathers and mothers. *European Sociological Review, 29*, 888–898.

Kalmijn, M. (2015). How childhood circumstances moderate the long-term impact of divorce on father–child relationships. *Journal of Marriage and Family, 77*, 921–938.

Kruk, E. (2012). Arguments for an equal parental responsibility presumption in contested child custody. *The American Journal of Family Therapy, 40*, 33–55.

Låftman, S. B., Bergström, M., Modin, B., & Östberg, V. (2014). Joint physical custody, turning to parents for emotional support, and subjective health: A study of adolescents in Stockholm, Sweden. *Scandinavian Journal of Public Health, 42*, 456–462.

Lamb, M. E. (2000). The history of research on father involvement: An overview. *Marriage and Family Review, 29*, 23–42.

Little, R. J. A. (1988). A test of missing completely at random for multivariate data with missing values. *Journal of the American Statistical Association, 83*, 1198–1202.

Marsiglio, W. (1991). Paternal engagement activities with minor children. *Journal of Marriage and Family, 53*, 973–986.

Mayer, M. (2019). missRanger: fast imputation of missing values. (R package version 2.1.0). https://cran.r-project.org/web/packages/missRanger/index.html

Melli, M. S., & Brown, P. R. (2008). Exploring a new family form–The shared time family. *International Journal of Law, Policy and the Family, 22*, 231–269.

Minuchin, P. (1985). Families and individual development: Provocations from the field of family therapy. *Child Development, 56*, 289–302.

Mortelmans, D., Pasteels, I., Bracke, P., Matthijs, K., Van Bavel, J., & Van Peer, C. (2011). *Scheiding in Vlaanderen*. Leuven: Acco.

MPLUS (Version 8.0). *[Computer Software]*. Los Angeles: CA: Muthén & Muthén.

Nielsen, L. (2011). Divorced fathers and their daughters: A review of recent research. *Journal of Divorce and Remarriage, 52*, 77–93.

Nielsen, L. (2018). Joint versus sole physical custody: Outcomes for children independent of family income or parental conflict. *Journal of Child Custody, 15*, 35–54.

Noël-Miller, C. M. (2013). Repartnering following divorce: Implications for older fathers' relations with their adult children. *Journal of Marriage and Family, 75*, 697–712.

Peters, B., & Ehrenberg, M. F. (2008). The influence of parental separation and divorce on father–child relationships. *Journal of Divorce and Remarriage, 49*, 78–109.

Pruett, M. K., McIntosh, J. E., & Kelly, J. B. (2014). Parental separation and overnight care of young children, part I: Consensus through theoretical and empirical integration. *Family Court Review, 52*, 240–255.

Satorra, A., & Bentler, P. M. (1994). Corrections to test statistics and standard errors in covariance structure analysis. In A. von Eye & C. C. Clogg (Eds.), Latent variables analysis: Applications for developmental research (p. 399–419). Sage Publications, Inc

Shapiro, A., & Lambert, J. D. (1999). Longitudinal effects of divorce on the quality of the father-child relationship and on fathers' psychological well-being. *Journal of Marriage and Family, 61*, 397–408.

Smyth, B., McIntosh, J., Emery, R., & Howarth, S. (2016). Shared time parenting: Evaluating the evidence of risks and benefits for children. In L. Drozd, M. Saini, & J. Olesen (Eds.), *Parenting plan evaluations: Applied research for the family court* (pp. 118–169). New York: Oxford University Press.

Smyth, B., Weston, R., Moloney, L., Richardson, N., & Temple, J. (2008). Changes in patterns of post-separation parenting over time: Recent Australian data. *Journal of Family Studies, 14*, 23–36.

Sobolewski, J. M., & King, V. (2005). The importance of the coparental relationship for nonresident fathers' ties to children. *Journal of Marriage and Family, 67*, 1196–1212.

Sodermans, A., Matthijs, K., & Swicegood, G. (2013). Characteristics of joint physical custody families in Flanders. *Demographic Research, 28*, 821–848.

Sodermans, A. K., Vanassche, S., & Matthijs, K. (2011). Gedeelde kinderen en plusouders: De verblijfsregeling en de gezinssituatie na scheiding. In D. Mortelmans, I. Pasteels, P. Bracke, K. Matthijs, J. Van Bavel, & C. Van Peer (Eds.), *Scheiding in Vlaanderen* (pp. 135–151). Leuven: Acco.

Sodermans, A. K., Vanassche, S., Matthijs, K., & Swicegood, G. (2014). Measuring postdivorce living arrangements: Theoretical and empirical validation of the residential calendar. *Journal of Family Issues, 35*, 125–145.

Spruijt, E., & Duindam, V. (2009). Joint physical custody in the Netherlands and the well-being of children. *Journal of Divorce and Remarriage, 51*, 65–82.

Stafford, M., Kuh, D. L., Gale, C. R., Mishra, G., & Richards, M. (2016). Parent–child relationships and offspring's positive mental wellbeing from adolescence to early older age. *The Journal of Positive Psychology, 11*, 326–337.

Stewart, S. D. (1999). Disneyland dads, Disneyland moms? How nonresident parents spend time with absent children. *Journal of Family Issues, 20*, 539–556.

Tach, L., Mincy, R., & Edin, K. (2010). Parenting as a "package deal": Relationships, fertility, and nonresident father involvement among unmarried parents. *Demography, 47*, 181–204.

Van Egeren, L. A., & Hawkins, D. P. (2004). Coming to terms with coparenting: Implications of definition and measurement. *Journal of Adult Development, 11*, 165–178.

Vanassche, S., Sodermans, A. K., Declerck, C., & Matthijs, K. (2017). Alternating residence for children after parental separation: Recent findings from Belgium. *Family Court Review, 55*, 545–555.

Vanassche, S., Sodermans, A. K., Matthijs, K., & Swicegood, G. (2013). Commuting between two parental households: The association between joint physical custody and adolescent wellbeing following divorce. *Journal of Family Studies, 19*, 139–158.

Warshak, R. A. (2014). Social science and parenting plans for young children: A consensus report. *Psychology, Public Policy, and Law, 20*, 46–67.

Paula Vrolijk is a PhD candidate at the Department of Public Administration and Sociology at the Erasmus University Rotterdam, the Netherlands. Her major research interests include family relationships and adolescents' well-being. In 2017, she graduated from the research master 'Development and Socialisation in Childhood and Adolescence' at Utrecht University. As a junior researcher at Utrecht University her main research focus was on divorced families. Her PhD thesis focuses on the antecedents and consequences of parental autonomy support in adolescence.

Renske Keizer is full professor in Family Sociology at the Erasmus University Rotterdam, the Netherlands. Keizer's primary research interest is the role that families, and in particular fathers, play in strengthening, maintaining or weakening social inequalities. Her research straddles sociology, pedagogical sciences, demography, and developmental psychology. Central to her work is the application of the theory-based life course approach to the behavior and well-being of individuals, and (extended) families. She has a demonstrated track record of significant contributions to multiple fields and to policy debates, through several highly-cited publications in top-tier journals, such as Journal of Marriage and Family, Journal of Family Psychology, Population and Development Review, European Sociological Review, and European Journal of Population. She has received several prestigious grants, amongst which an ERC Starting Grant, a NWO VENI and a NWO VIDI award. In 2016, she was selected as one of the 25 most talented young scholars of all Dutch and Flemish universities. Since 2019 she is member of the Young Academy, the Royal Netherlands Academy of Sciences.

7

Co-Parenting and its Dynamics

Elke Claessens and Dimitri Mortelmans

Abstract Until the end of the twentieth century, child custody arrangements after separation typically continued the gendered pre-separation parenting division, with mothers taking up childcare and fathers paying child support. Recently, there has been a significant rise in co-parenting after separation, reflecting the trend towards more socio-economic, work- and childcare-related gender equality during the relationship. However, it remains unclear to what extent the organization of the pre-separation household dominates over important changes in the lives and labor force participation of parents after separation in choosing to co-parent.

This study uses longitudinal Belgian register data to consider the effect of post-separation dynamics in parents' life course and labor force participation in deciding to co-parent. While certain pre-separation characteristics remain predictive of co-parenting, our results suggest a societal trend towards co-parenting as the parenting norm. Increased time in paid work positively affects co-parenting probabilities, but we find no effect of a post-separation income increase, even though this would imply greater bargaining power to obtain sole custody. As such, the investigated post-separation changes seem to be an indication of parents moving towards supporting and attempting to gain gender equal parenting after separation.

Keywords Shared physical custody · Gender equality · Employment · Income · Re-partnering

7.1 Introduction

When parents separate, child custody arrangements have been found to continue the parental care-giving roles that were present during the relationship. Until the end of the twentieth century this meant that the societally dominant caring roles were

---

E. Claessens (✉) · D. Mortelmans
Centre for Population, Family and Health (CPFH), University of Antwerp, Antwerp, Belgium
e-mail: elke.claessens@uantwerpen.be; dimitri.mortelmans@uantwerpen.be

generally perpetuated in mother-sole custody arrangements. Meanwhile, fathers paid child support to compensate for their unequal share of childcare (DiFonzo 2014; Vanassche et al. 2017). More recently, parents' responsibilities have become less divided. Mothers are now spending more time in the workforce and less time at home caring for children (Bianchi et al. 2012), whereas fathers' active involvement in childcare has extended the father role beyond that of the breadwinner (Meyer et al. 2017; Van Krieken 2005). This increased equality in parental care-giving during the relationship has, in turn, been found to encourage parents to continue to share the care of children after separation (Nielsen 2013a; Trinder 2010). However, in understanding what encourages separating parents to share childcare, research mainly considers characteristics before the separation or at the time of the study (Nielsen 2011, 2013a). This overlooks lifestyle and labor force changes in the turbulent early post-separation years, which may also have an important effect on how parents divide care.

In a recent study on the stability of care arrangements, Poortman and van Gaalen (2017) find that, controlling for the pre-separation situation, post-separation changes in children's needs, father's employment and practical factors can lead parents to stop sharing care within 2 years after separation. Currently, not much is known about the opposite situation, namely what encourages parents to begin sharing care later on. Controlling for important pre-separation characteristics, this chapter investigates the influence of three post-separation dynamics (parents' financial position, labour force participation and re-partnering) on switching to an equally shared physical custody arrangement 2 years after separation. Furthermore, as what facilitates sharing childcare with an ex-partner differs for men and women (Bakker and Mulder 2013; Juby et al. 2005), we also investigate whether post-separation life course and labor force dynamics affect the switch to equally sharing care differently for fathers and mothers. As such, this chapter offers insight both in the largely unexplored role played by post-separation dynamics as in potential gender differences in how parents' post-separation lives affect the division of childcare.

7.2 Theoretical Framework

7.2.1 Sharing Care in Belgium

"Shared physical custody" is a term used for various custody arrangements where parents either equally or unequally, legally and/or physically share the care of their children after separation. In this chapter, we consider it solely as the situation where children live with each parent for an equal amount of time. While not legally mandatory in Belgium, an equal division of physical custody over a child is the primary custody arrangement to be considered by a judge (Vanassche et al. 2017). Embedded in an increasing recognition of the importance of fatherly care, there has been a fourfold increase in the number of children with an alternating residence since the 1990's. Recently, equally shared physical custody has been estimated to represent one fourth of all custody arrangements in Belgium (Mortelmans et al. 2011). Furthermore, children in shared physical custody in Belgium typically spend an (almost) equal amount of time with each parent (e.g. 1 week with the mother, 1 week with the father) (Vanassche et al. 2017).

These considerations make it interesting to study the specific Belgian configuration of fiscal shared physical custody. In this arrangement, parents equally divide the child-related tax benefits, which would otherwise be granted to the parent with whom the child is domiciled. The only requirement is that parents have the child living with them for an equal amount of time, while not paying or receiving child support for that child (FOD Financiën 2018c). Studying fiscal shared physical custody has various advantages. First of all, it exempts us from somewhat arbitrarily deciding the cut-off defining "equally" shared physical custody – a typical challenge in custody research (Bartfeld 2011). Furthermore, the fiscal configuration is open to all separating parents, regardless of their pre-separation union. Therefore, we do not only take into account care agreements of divorcees but also of legally and unregistered cohabitating couples, which are underrepresented groups in custody research (Maldonado 2014). Finally, it is not a restrictive system, in that sense that it does not benefit affluent parents over lower-income groups. As such, while there are specific cases where there are less benefits than when paying tax-deductible child support (e.g. for large families (Gezinsbond 2021)), we can expect minimal selection effects.

7.2.2 Sharing Care, Perpetuating Equality?

Equal shared physical custody is often portrayed as the care arrangement with the best outcomes for all parties. While the benefits of this residency arrangement can be (partially) attributed to it being chosen by less conflicted and better cooperating parents (Fehlberg et al. 2011; Trinder 2010), continued contact with both parents after separation – controlled for the quality of the parental relationship – has been found to have a positive effect on children's academic, psychological, emotional, and social well-being (Bauserman 2002; Nielsen 2013b; Westphal 2015). Children who alternate their residence also generally report a better relationship with their father and an equally good relationship with their mother as children who predominantly live with their mother (Sodermans et al. 2013b). Furthermore, sharing childcare has been found to boost the life-satisfaction of parents (Van der Heijden et al. 2015). Compared to being in a traditional sole custody arrangement, fathers with an equal time share as mothers tend to have a better relationship with their child while not having less time for a social life, whereas mothers have more time to engage in leisure activities and experience more freedom to start a new relationship (Bakker and Karsten 2013; Vanassche et al. 2017). As such, while reflecting equal pre-separation parenting roles (Cancian et al. 2014; Juby et al. 2005), shared physical custody also perpetuates and increases equality after separation.

These benefits can be expected to be more widely applicable with the increasing adoption of shared physical custody as the parenting norm (Nielsen 2014). Nevertheless, in most countries, equally sharing care is not legally mandatory, nor is it the default residency arrangement. An abundance of research therefore looks into which household, parent and child characteristics are predictive of sharing custody after separation. However, most studies – mainly due to data restrictions – consider both these characteristics and choosing to share care as "static", limiting themselves to mapping who has shared physical custody at a certain point in time. We argue that this overlooks the turbulence of the early post-separation years, when shifts in socio-economic position and variability in custody arrangements are common (Feinberg et al. 2007). For example, it is likely that people who do not initially opt for shared physical custody go through various changes (i.e. in terms of resources) that lead them to switch to sharing care later on, while not having the "expected" pre-separation characteristics to do so (Sodermans et al. 2011). In the following sections, we build on existing shared custody research and consider three areas of post-separation dynamics that could affect switching to an equal shared physical custody arrangement 2 years after separation: the financial position, labour force participation and re-partnering. Furthermore, as men and women have been found to have differing post-separation socio-economic trajectories (de Regt et al. 2012; Thielemans and Mortelmans 2019), we also consider whether these dynamics affect the switch to shared care differently for fathers than for mothers.

7.2.3 Labor Force Participation

As mentioned above, equality in caregiving is as much a predictor as it is an outcome of having shared physical custody after separation. During the relationship, this mainly has to do with available time and is therefore strongly connected to the labor force participation of mothers. If a mother spends more time in paid work, she has less time to care for the children and tends to more equally share childrearing responsibilities with the father – which is then more likely to be continued as a shared care arrangement after separation (Meyer et al. 2017; Poortman and van Gaalen 2017). Conversely, mother sole custody is more likely when the mother stayed home (more often than the father) to take care of the children (Cancian et al. 2014). Meanwhile, it remains unclear to what extent changes in labor force participation *after* separation affect the likelihood of parents opting for shared physical custody later on, and whether this differs for mothers and fathers. On the one hand, it is true that many mothers who want to return to the workforce or increase their work volume after separation encounter challenges such as insufficient qualifications or inadequate childcare coverage, trapping them in unemployment or part-time jobs. On the other hand, if a mother were to successfully increase her work volume after the break-up, the new organization of her life may simply be better suited with a shared physical custody arrangement than with sole custody (Meyer et al. 2017). For fathers, we expect different mechanisms to be at play. In this respect it is important to note that greater fatherly involvement in childcare has not led to a notable decrease in Belgian fathers' labor force participation. Also, mothers are still in a stronger position to receive custody (Nielsen 2013a; Sodermans et al. 2011), and having enough resources to care for a child remains a more important consideration for granting custody to fathers than to mothers (Nielsen 2011). This could be especially relevant in the still strongly male-breadwinner oriented Belgian context, where fathers continue to be considered primarily as providers. As such, insofar a father is not yet in full-time employment, it could be expected that a post-separation increase in his work volume may also be of importance in switching to shared physical custody. We therefore formulate the following hypotheses:

H1a: An increase in the mother's work volume after separation increases the likelihood that the ex-partners switch to shared physical custody 2 years after separation.

H1b: An increase in the father's work volume after separation increases the likelihood that the ex-partners switch to shared physical custody 2 years after separation.

It then remains to be seen to what extent the "continuity of care" principle, i.e. that custody outcomes are reflective of the pre-separation care roles (Juby et al. 2005), remains dominant in predicting whether or not parents share care. When investigating the abovementioned hypotheses, we will therefore control for the relative labor force participation of parents – reflecting the division of childcare – prior to separation.

7.2.4 Parental Financial Position

Another important predictor of shared physical custody after separation is the joint parental income. Accommodating a child in each parent's, rather than a joint, household increases the total living and transportation expenses for that child. A shared physical custody arrangement is therefore simply more feasible for couples with more resources (Juby et al. 2005; Kalmijn 2015; Melli and Brown 1994). However, the parental financial situation is not a "fixed" characteristic; job loss, promotion, etc. after separation can induce major shifts in both the joint and relative income position of parents. As having enough resources is an important prerequisite of raising a child in two homes, it seems plausible that an increase in the joint parental income after separation increases the likelihood of switching to shared care later on. The second aspect, relative income, is more complex. Parents' relative financial position is an indicator of bargaining power, and as such also of importance in predicting the custody arrangement (Natalier and Hewitt 2010). When considering the pre- or at-separation household, having shared physical custody is more common among couples who contributed relatively equally to the household finances (Bartfeld 2011). Conversely, and due to mothers still holding a stronger position in gaining custody, a mother's financial advantage over the father makes it more likely to end up with a sole custody arrangement (Cancian and Meyer 1998; Nielsen 2013a). It could therefore be expected that mothers who experience significant financial gains after separation also increase their bargaining power to obtain sole custody, thus making the switch to shared physical custody less likely. Considering the importance of fathers' resources in obtaining custody, a father's financial gains after separation would increase the likelihood of him gaining custody and thus sharing care with his ex-partner. This translates into the following hypotheses:

H2a: An increase in the joint parental income after separation increases the likelihood that the ex-partners switch to shared physical custody 2 years after separation.
H2b: An increase in the mother's income after separation decreases the likelihood that the ex-partners switch to shared physical custody 2 years after separation.
H2c: An increase in the father's income after separation increases the likelihood that the ex-partners switch to shared physical custody 2 years after separation.

We will again control for the joint and relative contribution to the household finances prior to separation in order to consider their lasting importance vis à vis post-separation dynamics.

7.2.5 Re-partnering

The third post-separation change we consider is the parents' partner status. As starting a new family affects parents' available time, having responsibilities towards a new partner and children[1] can increase the benefits of having shared, rather than sole, custody (Cancian et al. 2014). This is especially true for mothers, for whom most studies conclude that the time restrictions and conflicting commitments introduced by having a new partner significantly increase the likelihood of her sharing care, rather than having sole custody (Cancian and Meyer 1998; Juby et al. 2005; Maccoby and Mnookin 1992). The reverse is true for fathers, who tend to experience a decrease in the likelihood of having shared physical custody when entering a new partnership (Cooksey and Craig 1998; Kelly 2007; Smyth 2005). Still, the underlying mechanisms are essentially the same for men and women. As the pattern concerns mothers moving from more mother-oriented arrangements to shared care and fathers from shared care to less frequent visitation, the result of re-partnering is a reduction in custody of children (Bakker and Mulder 2013).

It is important to note, however, that the results for fathers are more ambiguous than for mothers, with certain studies finding no effect at all of men's re-partnering on sharing care (Juby et al. 2005; Smyth and Weston 2004). Furthermore, just as with other characteristics, a parent tends to be considered as "being re-partnered" at

[1]In this chapter we only consider the impact of re-partnering and not of having new children, as we only follow parents up to 2 years after the separation.

the time of separation or the study. It is therefore difficult to put forward causal suggestions concerning the effect of re-partnering on having shared physical custody later on. In a recent longitudinal study on the stability of shared physical custody, Poortman and van Gaalen (2017) found that if a father re-partners after separation, changing from shared to mother sole residence is more likely than staying in shared custody. This is in line with the abovementioned studies and the finding that a new partner decreases the frequency of contact with children for fathers (Bakker and Mulder 2013). Meanwhile, mother's re-partnering was found to have no effect on the stability of the shared care arrangement. A potential explanation is that, when comparing shared and sole custody, mothers who already had shared custody are already at the "minimum" time spent with their children. The time restrictions induced by the new partner may nevertheless still have affected the initial choice for shared custody (Cancian et al. 2014). As such, concerning the likelihood of switching to shared physical custody 2 years after separation, we expect to find similar results for re-partnering as to what has previously been found. We therefore formulate the following hypotheses:

H3a: Mother's re-partnering increases the likelihood that the ex-partners switch to shared physical custody 2 years after separation.
H3b: Father's re-partnering decreases the likelihood that the ex-partners switch to shared physical custody 2 years after separation.

7.2.6 Household and Demographic Characteristics

Not only the socio-economic position and time restraints of parents are important when considering the likelihood of sharing care after separation. Previous research has found that several other socio-demographic and household characteristics are in play. First of all, the age of the child tends to be of great importance. Shared physical custody is less likely for very young children, as infants benefit more from stability in physical care. For older children who have a say in custody proceedings, alternating residences is also found to be less common (Cancian and Meyer 1998; Juby et al. 2005; Sodermans et al. 2013a). Shared custody arrangements have been found to be more likely for boys than for girls, as – from the perspective of increased father involvement when sharing care – fathers generally invest more care in sons than daughters (Spruijt and Duindam 2010). Due to the more extensive care requirements in large families, parents with a greater number of children more frequently opt for a shared custody arrangement (Kalmijn and De Graaf 2000). Finally, while previous research did not find a relationship between the union type and the likelihood of having shared physical custody (Juby et al. 2005; Poortman and van Gaalen 2017), we expect to find some differences in our analyses. As explained in Sect. 2.1, we study a specific Belgian form of fiscal shared physical custody. Choosing for this constellation requires some knowledge of its fiscal implications and insight in the workings of tax returns. Previously married and legally cohabiting parents, for whom tax returns are joint and more complex (Swennen and Mortelmans 2015), could therefore be more likely to opt for fiscal shared physical custody than parents who were informally cohabiting. The age of the youngest child, the gender(s) and number of children and the previous union type of the ex-partners will be included as control variables in the analyses.

As we use administrative records, we cannot account for several important variables related to sharing care. Some examples are parents' education (Cancian et al. 2014), the distance between parents' homes (Bakker and Mulder 2013), mediation and level of conflict between parents (Sodermans et al. 2013a), (mental) health problems (Poortman and van Gaalen 2017) and father's involvement in childcare (Juby et al. 2005). While changes in labor force participation and relationship status could be interacting with some of these factors, we cannot consider them as proxies. Nevertheless, this does not undermine the useful potential of our data in casting a longitudinal lens on the determinants of having shared physical custody.

7.3 Data and Method

7.3.1 Register Data

We make use of register data comprised of information on income, labor and socio-demographics from the Belgian Crossroads Bank for Social Security, linked to fiscal information from individual tax returns. The original sample consists of couples who experienced a divorce or separation either in 2008 or 2011 and were not married or cohabiting 1 year afterwards. The dataset commences 1 year prior to separation and follows each parent, along with their consecutive household(s), up to 2013. We pooled both groups (separated in 2008 or 2011) and selected only those respondents who had at least one minor child 2 years after separation (i.e. in 2010 or 2013). This is an important requirement, as until 2016 fiscal shared physical custody was only possible for children under the age of 18. Because we cannot know to which child the arrangement pertains, we reduce the risk of wrongly attributing it to other children than joint children by omitting couples where one or both parents already have a fiscal shared physical custody, pay child support or have children other than joint children in the household. Same-sex couples are excluded in order to assess gender differences, along with ex-partners who re-partnered with each other within 2 years of separating. Leaving out couples where a partner has missing data on any of the used variables (see Table 7.1), gives us a final subsample of 10,171 couples who were not sharing care after separation, of which 1039 adopted fiscal shared physical custody 2 years after separation.

Table 7.1 Descriptive statistics of categorical predictors and controls

Variables		%
Separation year	2008	48%
	2011	52%
Child gender (ref = mixed)	All boys	36%
	All girls	34%
Number of children (ref = 1)	2	42%
	≥3	12%
Previous union (ref = married)	Legally cohab.	9%
	Informally cohab.	38%
Relative income (ref = mother < father)	Mother = father	27%
	Mother > father	24%
Relative work volume (ref = mother < father)	Mother = father	26%
	Mother > father	18%
Re-partnering (ref = neither)	Only mother	13%
	Only father	14%
	Both	4%

$N = 10{,}171$

7.3.2 *Measures*

The dependent variable in the analysis is switching to fiscal shared physical custody 2 years after separation. The required information was found in each parent's tax return. Three conditions had to be met in order for us to consider the parents to be sharing custody: one of the ex-partners indicated to be doing so and have the children living with them, the other partner indicated to be doing so while the children were domiciled with the other partner and both parents registered the same number of children for whom the arrangement was in place. As the dependent variable in the logistic regression models, fiscal shared physical custody received a binary 0/1 coding, with 1 representing having switched to the arrangement 2 years after separation (i.e. 2010 or 2013). The reference category consists of all parents who did not switch to the arrangement. Regrettably, we do not have information on any other custody arrangements and thus lump together families where the mother has sole custody, the father has sole custody, parents have unequal shared care etc. This can undeniably bias our results, as we are ignoring that previous custody agreements may affect whether or not parents move into shared physical custody (i.e. it may be easier going from unequal to equal shared physical custody than from sole custody). However, this issue does not effectively hinder our research in the sense that our goal is to investigate which parental and household characteristics motivate a switch to fiscal shared physical custody, rather than look at differences between care regimes. This is nevertheless a limitation that should be taken into account and addressed by further research.

The main focus of the analyses is on how post-separation dynamics of parents' post-separation labor force participation, income and partner status affect the likelihood of switching to shared physical custody. Nevertheless, as children's living arrangements are initially decided upon during separation, it is important to also account for the pre-separation household (Juby et al. 2005). We therefore firstly consider the total pre-separation joint income of parents and the relative income situation 1 year prior to separation, where a partner contributed either less than 45%, more than 55% or relatively equally (i.e. 45–55%) to the total income (coded as dummy variables). To assess the effect of post-separation financial shifts on switching to shared physical custody, we calculate an absolute indicator of change in income for both the joint income and each ex-partner's individual income 1 year after separation versus the pre-separation situation. Next we consider work volume, expressed as the total number of full days worked in a year divided by the number of workdays in that year. This provides an indicator of yearly work volume ranging from 0 (unemployed) to 1 (regular full-time work) for each parent. These are added up to obtain the pre-separation joint work volume of parents, ranging from 0 (both parents unemployed) to 2 (both parents in regular full-time employment). For the pre-separation relative labor market participation, we used the same ratio as for income to distinguish between situations where a partner's yearly work volume prior to the separation was smaller, larger or a relatively equal to that of the other partner. Dynamics in labor force participation are calculated as an absolute indicator of change in the work volume for each parent 1 year after separation versus the pre-separation situation. We also distinguish between both parents re-partnering after separation versus only the mother, only the father or neither parent (dummy coding).

Further, we control for the age of the youngest child and whether parents were either legally or informally cohabiting or married prior to separating (coded as dummy variables). Also included are post-separation control variables, lagged by 1 year to explore causal effects on the likelihood of switching to shared physical custody. We consider the number of joint minor children (eligible for fiscal shared physical custody) and whether these children were all boys, all girls or mixed (dummy coding) 1 year prior to (not) switching to shared physical custody (i.e. 1 year after separation). To take into account the possibility that fiscal shared care was becoming more established, we also control for the year of separation (2008 or 2011). The descriptive statistics of all variables used in the analysis are presented in Table 7.1 (see infra).

7.3.3 *Method*

Using SAS 9.4, logistic regression models were applied to the longitudinal register data to test the likelihood that parents switch to shared physical custody 2 years after separation (Table 7.3). First, we estimate a model containing only the fixed pre-, at- and post-separation variables to control for the (lasting) importance of these characteristics in sharing care (Model 1). We then add the longitudinal indicators of change to the model (Model 2). This allows us to determine the effect of post-separation shifts on the likelihood of switching to shared physical custody vis à vis the lasting dominance of pre-separation characteristics.

Table 7.2 Descriptive statistics and bivariate correlations of continuous predictors and controls

Variable	Mean	SD	Q1	Q3
Age youngest child	5	4	2	7
Joint income (gross, €)	57,771	27,285	40,160	70,300
Joint work volume (max = 2)	1.058	0.583	0.663	1.496
Change income mother (gross, €)	5759	8863	2050	9740
Change income father (gross, €)	2336	11,271	−740	5910
Change WV[a] mother (max = 1)	0.03	0.275	−0.01	0.09
Change WV[a] father (max = 1)	−0.04	0.282	−0.08	0.01

Bivariate correlations					
1	2	3	4	5	6
1					
−0.184**	1				
−0.131**	−0.060**	1			
−0.036**	−0.051**	−0.140**	1		
−0.034**	−0.018**	−0.033**	−0.045**	1	
−0.030**	−0.001**	−0.165**	−0.441**	0.020**	1
−0.011**	−0.051**	−0.194**	−0.007**	0.479**	0.014

$N = 10{,}171$
$^{*}p < 0.05$; $^{**}p < 0.01$
[a] *WV* work volume

As we make use of register data, missing data due to non-response or attrition does not pose the same issues as in survey-based longitudinal research (Wallgren and Wallgren 2007). Nevertheless, the integration of several registers into a complete dataset does imply missing information. In our dataset, a missing on a specific variable generally means that someone is not registered with the recording instance. Where we lack information on income or work volume, we are dealing with people who are not part of the regular employee system (e.g. self-employed). As this group makes use of a separate tax return form (which we do not have access to), about 2% of our original sample has largely missing values. On the one hand, this group potentially experiences different post-separation dynamics concerning income and work volume than the rest of the sample. On the other hand, as the fiscal system of shared physical custody may have a significantly different impact on this group, it may be prudent to study them separately anyway. Considering these arguments, and as the sample size remains sufficiently large without these cases, we opt to omit this group completely.

7.4 Results

7.4.1 Descriptive Results

Table 7.1 shows the frequencies of the categorical predictors and control variables included in the analysis. Next, Table 7.2 presents the descriptive statistics of the

Table 7.3 Logistic regression models with pre- at- and post-separation predictors

	Model 1		Model 2	
	Pre-separation/fixed		Post-separation/change	
	Exp (b)	Sig.	Exp (b)	Sig.
Age youngest child at separation	1.151	**	1.156	**
Age youngest child squared	0.988	***	0.988	***
Child gender (ref = mixed)				
All children boys	1.169		1.176	
All children girls	1.195		1.194	
No. of minor children (ref = 1)				
2	1.125		1.108	
≥3	1.286	*	1.305	*
Prev. union (ref = married)				
Legally cohabiting	0.739	*	0.723	**
Informally cohabiting	0.543	***	0.550	***
Joint income (€10.000)	1.464	***	1.445	***
Joint income squared	0.988	***	0.988	**
Relative income[a]				
Mother = father	1.471	***	1.485	***
Mother > father	1.259	*	1.248	*
Joint work volume	1.236	*	1.398	***
Relative work volume[a]				
Mother = father	0.972		0.998	
Mother > father	0.999		0.987	
Separation in 2011 (vs. 2008)	1.169	*	1.149	*
Change income mother			1.044	
Change income mother squared			1.002	
Change income father			1.040	
Change income father squared			1.003	
Change work volume mother			1.585	**
Change work volume mother squared			1.129	
Change work volume father			1.831	**
Change work volume father squared			0.952	
Re-partnering (ref = none)				
Both re-partnered			1.076	
Only mother			1.434	**
Only father			0.842	
−2 LL	6181.925		6113.893	
AIC	6219.925		6173.893	

$N = 10{,}171$
*$p < .050$; **$p < .010$; ***$p < .001$
[a]*Ref = mother < father*

continuous predictors and controls, along with their bivariate correlations. The highest correlations are, not unexpectedly, found between the change of income and change in work volume, both for mothers ($r = 0.44$; $p < 0.01$) as for fathers ($r = 0.48$; $p < 0.01$).

7.4.2 Multivariate Results

Table 7.3 presents the results of the logistic regression models predicting the likelihood of switching to shared physical custody 2 years after separation. Model 1 contains the odds for the pre-separation and fixed controls, while Model 2 adds the effect of post-separation changes in parents' work volume, income and partner status. Overall, pre- and at-separation socio-demographic, economic and household factors remain dominant predictors of sharing care, even 2 years after separation. As expected, the age of the youngest child is non-linear in effect. The likelihood of switching to shared physical custody first increases steeply, peaks at the age of 4 and then consistently decreases again. Next, we find that ex-partners have a higher likelihood of switching to shared care if they have more minor children eligible for the fiscal shared physical custody arrangement, no matter the gender of the children. The previous union of parents also has an effect, though slightly different than expected. Not only informally, but also legally cohabiting significantly reduces the likelihood of switching to shared physical custody, compared to previously having been married. Furthermore, there is no significant difference between the effect of legally and informally cohabiting on switching to shared physical custody.

Model 1 also confirms the importance of joint and relative income for the likelihood of sharing care after separation. First, it is a more likely option for parents who have more resources. However, this effect is non-linear, with a steep initial increase ending in a subtle decrease for the higher-income groups. Second, gender equality is also in play: a relatively equal contribution of mother and father to the joint finances increases the likelihood of switching to a shared physical custody arrangement after separation. Interestingly, this is also the case when mothers earn more than fathers.

While it could be expected that a higher financial capacity places mothers in a stronger bargaining position to gain sole custody, we may very well be seeing a (societally induced) shift towards a personal preference for shared, rather than sole, custody. Furthermore, greater resources are significantly correlated with a higher labor force participation ($r = 0.52, p < .001$), making it more likely (1) that the father took up a significant share of childcare during the relationship and (2) that the mother experiences time restraints that make sharing custody after separation more suitable to her. This may explain why we find no significant effect of parents' relative labor force participation on the likelihood of switching to shared physical custody in Model 1. Finally, the odds of opting for shared physical custody 2 years after separation is greater for who separated in 2011 rather than in 2008, which may again reflect the societal shift towards sharing care.

These results remain quasi unchanged when adding post-separation life course and labor force dynamics to the model (Model 2), which confirms the continuing effect of the pre- and at- separation household, parent and child characteristics on sharing care after separation. A notable difference is the effect of the total pre-separation parental work volume, which is highly significant when including the post-separation dynamics in Model 2. Parents who had a higher work volume prior to separation, are more likely to switch to shared physical custody 2 years afterwards. However, there is no significant difference in the likelihood of sharing care between couples where mothers had an equal or higher, versus lower work volume than fathers. Moving on, Model 2 tests whether post-separation changes in income, labor force participation and partner status affect the likelihood switching to shared physical custody, over and above the pre- and at-separation characteristics. We test for the effect of increases in income by separately adding the change in total joint and individual income to the model. Only individual income changes are included in Model 2, as – against our expectations – an increase in the total joint income after separation did not affect the likelihood of sharing care. In other words, contrary to the pre-separation income, increasing the pooled resources later on does not further encourage parents to switch to shared physical custody. This also holds true for the change in individual income. While the mother's equal or greater contribution to the joint finances during the relationship increases the likelihood of sharing care, neither an increase in her nor the father's income after separation affects switching to a shared physical custody arrangement. Interestingly, labor force participation shows opposite results. In Model 1, work volume (and thus implicit time restraints) of parents had little effect on switching to shared physical custody. Conversely, in Model 2, both the total work volume of parents before separation and an increase in individual work volume after separation significantly increase the likelihood of sharing care. The odds are greater for fathers, supporting the claim that being employed is still a more important consideration for fathers than it is for mothers when deciding on the custody arrangement. An interaction was tested between the effect of mother's and father's change in work volume on opting for shared physical custody, but the result was not significant. Finally, Model 2 considers the effects of mother's and father's re-partnering. As expected, if a mother re-partners, the likelihood of switching to shared physical custody is higher than when both partners remain single. However, this is dependent on father's partner status: if both parents re-partner, the likelihood of sharing care does not differ from when both parents are still single.

7.5 Discussion

Following the societal evolution towards more equality in parenting and household responsibilities, shared physical custody is increasingly becoming the post-separation parenting norm in Western society (DiFonzo 2014). This trend is supported by the increasing body of research stating that post-separation care by both parents is not only beneficial for children, but for parents as well (Van der Heijden et al. 2015; Westphal 2015). Furthermore, while generally not legally imposing it, many countries support shared physical custody by adapting their legal frameworks (Nielsen 2011; Nikolina 2012; Perelli-Harris and Gassen 2012) or by considering it in the calculation of child support (Claessens and Mortelmans 2018; Skinner and Davidson 2009). As a result, shared physical custody after separation has become more common practice and the families choosing this arrangement less distinctive (Meyer et al. 2017), allowing for a wider implementation (of the benefits) of equality in care roles for separated parents. Research nevertheless shows that couples who already experienced more socio-economic, work- and childcare-related equality during their relationship are more likely to share care and that different factors still facilitate and inhibit mothers and fathers to enter a shared physical custody arrangement. However, existing studies are often limited to cross-sectional data, considering only the pre- or at-separation household with respect to the likelihood of sharing care at the time of separation or the study. As such, it remains unclear how the inevitable re-organization in parents' lives after separation affects equality in custody arrangements. Controlling for important pre-separation characteristics, this chapter investigates the influence of three post-separation dynamics (financial position, labour force participation and re-partnering) on switching to an equally shared physical custody arrangement 2 years after separation. Furthermore, we investigate whether post-separation changes that facilitate or inhibit equal caretaking differ for mothers and fathers.

Studies with recent data show that, due to the more general adoption of shared physical custody among a broad variety of families, child, parent and household characteristics have become less predictive of sharing care (Bartfeld 2011). Our results do not entirely support this. First, we do find confirmation that shared physical custody is less likely for very young and for older children (Juby et al. 2005; Maccoby and Mnookin 1992). However, while recent studies found no association with family size (Cancian et al. 2014; Sodermans et al. 2013a), our results do concur with earlier studies showing a positive relationship between a couple's number of eligible children and their likelihood of sharing care (Kalmijn and De Graaf 2000). This could nevertheless be due to the small (10%) number of families with three or more children eligible for fiscal shared physical custody in our sample. Further, the fiscal implications of this arrangement led us to presume that it would be more likely to be chosen by previously married or legally cohabiting couples. However, our results show that previously cohabiting, both legally and informally, reduces the likelihood of switching to fiscal shared physical custody compared to previously married couples. While earlier research explained this relationship as married fathers being more committed to family life and more likely to maintain contact with children than cohabiting fathers (Marcil-Gratton et al. 2000), the increasing acceptance of cohabiting as a suitable parenting union has done away with this disparity (Juby et al. 2005; Swiss and Le Bourdais 2009). As such, we expect that the fiscal shared physical custody arrangement is more likely for married couples in our sample not due to the nature of the union, but due to the still more pervasive legal and fiscal framework surrounding marriage in Belgium (FOD Financiën 2018b).

Although there is evidence that the financial advantage of parents with shared physical custody over parents with a sole custody arrangement is becoming less pervasive (Cancian et al. 2014; Sodermans et al. 2011), we find that the likelihood of sharing care still increases with income. As Melli and Brown (1994) point out, a higher income not only adds to the feasibility of raising a child in two households, but is also positively related to gender equal attitudes on the division of work and childcare, which higher-earning parents can more easily maintain after separation. For the highest income group however, we see a decline in the likelihood of sharing care. An excessive income may point to a more-than-regular work schedule, potentially giving this group less time for childcare and thus leading to a reduced likelihood of switching to shared physical custody. As an indicator of gender equality, a more equal contribution of parents to the joint resources prior to separation increases the likelihood of sharing care later on (Bartfeld 2011). Unexpectedly, this likelihood is also higher in families with higher-earning mothers, while previous research suggests that a mother who contributes more to the total income has more power to influence the custody decision and receive sole custody (Cancian and Meyer 1998). We consider two explanations. On the one hand, our findings support the hypothesis that being in paid employment makes mothers more open to sharing custody (Juby et al. 2005). On the other hand, the societal and normative shift towards sharing care may encourage parents to use their financial "power" to obtain this more (socially) desirable arrangement. This may also explain why the relative work volume during the relationship does not affect the likelihood of switching to shared physical custody in our analysis: no matter the division of labor between couples, it is now expected that both mother and father take up care of the children. If this is true, a better predictor would be the actual contribution to childcare by each parent during the relationship, as this encourages both parents' continued involvement after separation (Poortman and van Gaalen 2017). Unfortunately, we lack information on actual involvement in childrearing. Nevertheless, in the final model we see that the total joint work volume of parents positively affects switching to shared physical custody. Insofar a greater work volume implies greater time restraints for childcare, this finding provide some support for the continuity of care principle (Juby et al. 2005).

Next, we consider the importance of post-separation changes in parents' income, work volume and partner status vis-à-vis the pre- and at-separation situation. In terms of having enough resources to raise a child in two homes, the bargaining power of parents and being in paid work, it could be expected that an increase in mother's, father's and/or the joint parental income increases the likelihood that parents switch to shared physical custody. However, this does not appear to be the case. A possible explanation is that Belgian parents may not be as inclined to reveal increases in their income after separation, as equally sharing care does not exempt parents from having to pay child support if the other partner is in a financially weaker position (Claessens and Mortelmans 2018, in press). As such, the gained bargaining power due to the income increase could be counterbalanced with a potential renegotiation of custody and child support payments, because fiscal shared physical custody cannot be combined with the payment of child support[2] (FOD Financiën 2018a). Conversely, we find that both an increase of mother's and father's work volume increases the likelihood of switching to shared physical custody 2 years after separation. Considering the recent shift from mother sole custody to shared physical custody as the parenting norm and default judicial preference, we suggest the effect of mother's increased labor participation to reflect more experienced time restraints, making sharing care with an ex-partner more preferable than sole custody. For fathers to receive custody, being in paid work and able to provide for the child is still of greater importance than it is for mothers (Nielsen 2013a; Sodermans et al. 2011). Therefore, we are not surprised to find that when a father increases his work volume after separation, parents are more likely to switch to shared physical custody.

The final post-separation change we considered was re-partnering. Existing research provides mixed findings concerning the relationship between having a new partner and shared physical custody, especially for fathers. Furthermore, studies often face the issue of not being able to pinpoint a clear causal relationship (Juby et al. 2005; Kalmijn and De Graaf 2000; Poortman and van Gaalen 2017). Our results show that if a mother re-partners soon after separation, the ex-partners are more likely to switch to shared care. Furthermore, while not refuting that the custody arrangement can influence a parent's decision to re-partner (Bakker and Mulder 2013), the longitudinal nature of our data allows us to posit that a new partner creates time restraints for mothers, making shared physical custody more interesting for her. For fathers, re-partnering does not have a significant effect. This is may be because fathers do not experience significantly less time for a social life when sharing care than when having visitation rights (Bakker and Karsten 2013), suggesting that re-partnering may be perceived as less of a time constraint. However, we find that if both parents are re-partnered, the likelihood of switching to shared physical custody is not significantly different from when neither parent is in a new relationship. This could indicate that the positive effect of mother's re-partnering is neutralized by that of father's re-partnering, meaning that father's re-partnering does – to some extent – have, as hypothesized, a negative effect on the likelihood of switching to shared care. Nevertheless, this relatively unexplored causal relationship between re-partnering and shared physical custody merits further investigation.

7.5.1 Limitations

Despite the usefulness of our longitudinal data, some limitations can be noted. As previously stated, we cannot account for some potentially important variables related to shared physical custody. It would therefore be useful to supplement our administrative data with survey data to obtain more social and subjective measures. We

---

[2]Child support payments cannot be deducted from taxes when having fiscal shared physical custody.

would also benefit from a variable that more accurately reflects time in paid work than our current yearly work volume indicator, for which a score of 0.5 can either indicate working half-time for an entire year or full-time for half a year. A precise measure of time spent in paid work and working hours on a weekly basis would be an undeniably better proxy of time spent with children. Our study of relatively recent separations (2008 and 2011) also limits the amount of time after separation we could consider for both groups. Furthermore, we undeniably miss an important group that shares care outside of the fiscal constellation, which may be a financial consideration. As Vanassche et al. (2017) explain, not opting for fiscal shared physical custody may be a strategic choice of the parent with whom the child is officially domiciled to not share generous child-related benefits and allowances with the other parent. This could imply that parents who have a fiscal shared physical custody arrangement are more prepared to share benefits and are less conflicted. However, as non-fiscal care sharing allows for the payment of child support, the unbalance in received child benefits could easily be corrected. Furthermore, our results match findings where shared physical custody is not a fiscal constellation. As such, we have reason to assume that parents who have fiscal shared physical custody are representative of parents who share care in Belgium at large.

Meanwhile, our data has distinct advantages. First, administrative records provide detailed information over time, with minimal risk of attrition. Furthermore, we have official data on the parenting arrangement and are thus not reliant on parents' own reports, which may be incorrect due to generalizations or recall bias (Sodermans et al. 2014). Of course, we are not certain that if a tax return indicates fiscal shared physical custody this corresponds with parents equally dividing the care of the child. However, this potential discrepancy is an issue faced by all child support research (Juby et al. 2005). Furthermore, it seems unlikely that in the case of fiscal shared physical custody the reality would vary strongly from an equal time share. If one parent did not take up as much care as the other, that last parent could easily claim child support to compensate for the unequal burden of the childcare costs, especially as the non-cooperative parent is claiming half of the child-related tax benefits. Not having to pay (more) child support can therefore be an incentive to respect the equal shared physical custody arrangement. Second, by considering the fiscal arrangement, we are provided with a definition of equally sharing care. This precisely delimited time share shelters our interpretations from difficulties faced by other studies. For example, when defining shared physical custody as "spending at least 33 percent of time with each parent", children who live one-third with their father and two-thirds with their mother are lumped together with children who equally live with both parents, while it is to be expected that these time shares have different implications for e.g. the quality of the parent-child relationship, re-partnering opportunities and the financial burden on parents (Claessens and Mortelmans 2018; Vanassche et al. 2017).

Finally, in terms of adapting to the changing needs of the ever-growing group of separated and complex families, Belgium's fiscal shared physical custody is somewhat of a forerunner. As Meyer et al. (2017) point out, many countries' tax and benefit policies are dependent on family size and/or the number of children in the household, which, due to the increase in shared physical custody, can vary on a regular basis (Hakovirta and Rantalaiho 2011). This highlights the need to reexamine how families are defined in policy and allow for more flexible arrangements between separated parents. In this respect, fiscal shared physical custody sets a good example.

7.6 Conclusions

By looking into the effects of the pre- and at-separation household versus post-separation life course and labor force dynamics on sharing care, this chapter aims to increase the existing knowledge on what facilitates and inhibits an equal division of childcare after separation. Overall, while the analysis shows that certain characteristics remain predictive of sharing care, we also see the impact of the societal trend towards equal shared physical custody as the parenting norm in Belgium. Although bargaining power in terms of income and pre-separation division of work are generally seen as arguments for mothers to obtain sole custody, our results suggest that they no longer significantly work against sharing care with the father. Moreover, the discovered post-separation effects may be an indication of parents supporting and encouraging gender equal parenting, by not using income increases to claim more custody and by reacting to increases in labor force participation by choosing for shared physical custody. Considering the benefits of sharing childcare in terms of gender equality, parental well-being and the parent-child relationship (Van der Heijden et al. 2015; Westphal 2015), further research is warranted into how the post-separation dynamics in lives of parents can affect the likelihood of sharing care. Taking into account the reorganization of parents' lives and potential variability in children's residence during the early years after separation (Poortman and van Gaalen 2017), we suggest to consider a more prolonged post-separation period to further our understanding of not only how parents' custody needs and preferences change after separation, but also which factors (continue to) facilitate gender equal parenting for mothers and fathers.

References

Bakker, W., & Karsten, L. (2013). Balancing paid work, care and leisure in post-separation households: A comparison of single parents with co-parents. *Acta Sociologica, 56*(2), 173–187.

Bakker, W., & Mulder, C. H. (2013). Characteristics of post-separation families in the Netherlands: Shared residence versus resident mother arrangements. *GeoJournal, 78*(5), 851–866.

Bartfeld, J. (2011). *Shared placement: An overview of prevalence, trends, economic implications, and impacts on child well-being*. Report, Institute for Research on Poverty, University of Wisconsin–Madison.

Bauserman, R. (2002). Child adjustment in joint-custody versus sole-custody arrangements: A meta-analytic review. *Journal of Family Psychology, 16*(1), 91.

Bianchi, S. M., Sayer, L. C., Milkie, M. A., & Robinson, J. P. (2012). Housework: Who did, does or will do it, and how much does it matter? *Social Forces, 91*(1), 55–63.

Cancian, M., & Meyer, D. R. (1998). Who gets custody? *Demography, 35*(2), 147–157.

Cancian, M., Meyer, D. R., Brown, P. R., & Cook, S. T. (2014). Who gets custody now? Dramatic changes in children's living arrangements after divorce. *Demography, 51*(4), 1381–1396.

Claessens, E., & Mortelmans, D. (2018). Challenges for child support schemes: Accounting for shared care and complex families. *Journal of European Social Policy, 28*(3), 211–223.

Claessens, E., & Mortelmans, D. (2018, in press). De toegankelijkheid, werkbaarheid en transparantie van de Belgische methoden ter berekening van onderhoudsbijdragen voor kinderen. *Belgisch Tijdschrift voor Sociale Zekerheid.*

Cooksey, E. C., & Craig, P. H. (1998). Parenting from a distance: The effects of paternal characteristics on contact between nonresidential fathers and their children. *Demography, 35*(2), 187–200.

de Regt, S., Mortelmans, D., & Marynissen, T. (2012). Financial consequences of relationship dissolution: A longitudinal comparison of formerly married and unmarried cohabiting men and women. *Sociology, 47*(1), 90–108.

DiFonzo, J. H. (2014). From the rule of one to shared parenting: Custody presumptions in law and policy. *Family Court Review, 52*(2), 213–239.

Fehlberg, B., Smyth, B., Maclean, M., & Roberts, C. (2011). Legislating for shared time parenting after separation: A research review. *International Journal of Law, Policy and the Family, 25*(3), 318–337.

Feinberg, M. E., Kan, M. L., & Hetherington, E. M. (2007). The longitudinal influence of coparenting conflict on parental negativity and adolescent maladjustment. *Journal of Marriage and Family, 69*(3), 687–702.

FOD Financiën. (2018a). *Co-ouderschap en fiscaliteit.* Retrieved from https://financien.belgium.be/nl/particulieren/gezin/gezinssituatie/co-ouderschap

FOD Financiën. (2018b). *Gezinssituatie.* Retrieved from https://financien.belgium.be/nl/particulieren/gezin/gezinssituatie

FOD Financiën. (2018c). *Kinderen ten laste.*. Retrieved from https://financien.belgium.be/nl/particulieren/gezin/personen_ten_laste/kinderen

Gezinsbond. (2021). Kies bewust voor fiscaal co-ouderschap, want dit is niet altijd de beste optie. *Fiscaal Co-ouderschap*, https://www.gezinsbond.be/Gezinspolitiek/onderhoudsgeldcalculator/Paginas/Fiscaal-co_ouderschap.aspx.

Hakovirta, M., & Rantalaiho, M. (2011). Family policy and shared parenting in Nordic countries. *European Journal of Social Security, 13*, 247.

Juby, H., Le Bourdais, C., & Marcil-Gratton, N. (2005). Sharing roles, sharing custody? Couples' characteristics and children's living arrangements at separation. *Journal of Marriage and Family, 67*(1), 157–172.

Kalmijn, M. (2015). Father-child relations after divorce in four European countries: Patterns and determinants. *Comparative Population Studies, 40*(3), 251–276.

Kalmijn, M., & De Graaf, P. (2000). Gescheiden vaders en hun kinderen: een empirische analyse van voogdij en bezoekfrequentie. *Bevolking en Gezin, 29*(2), 59–84.

Kelly, J. B. (2007). Children's living arrangements following separation and divorce: Insights from empirical and clinical research. *Family Process, 46*(1), 35–52.

Maccoby, E. E., & Mnookin, R. H. (1992). *Dividing the child: Social and legal dilemmas of custody*. Cambridge, MA: Harvard University Press.

Maldonado, S. (2014). Shared parenting and never-married families. *Family Court Review, 52*(4), 632–638.

Marcil-Gratton, N., Le Bourdais, C., & Lapierre-Adamcyk, É. (2000). *The implications of parents' conjugal histories for children*. Ottawa: Department of Justice, Research and Statistics Division.

Melli, M., & Brown, P. (1994). The economics of shared custody: Developing an equitable formula for dual residence. *Houston Law Review, 31*, 543.

Meyer, D. R., Cancian, M., & Cook, S. T. (2017). The growth in shared custody in the United States: Patterns and implications. *Family Court Review, 55*(4), 500–512.

Mortelmans, D., Pasteels, I., Bracke, P., Matthijs, K., Van Bavel, J., & Van Peer, C. (2011). *Scheiding in Vlaanderen*. Leuven: Acco.

Natalier, K., & Hewitt, B. (2010). 'It's not just about the money': Non-resident fathers' perspectives on paying child support. *Sociology, 44*(3), 489–505. https://doi.org/10.1177/0038038510362470.

Nielsen, L. (2011). Shared parenting after divorce: A review of shared residential parenting research. *Journal of Divorce & Remarriage, 52*(8), 586–609. https://doi.org/10.1080/10502556.2011.619913.

Nielsen, L. (2013a). Shared residential custody: Review of the research (part I of II). *American Journal of Family Law, 27*(1), 61–71.

Nielsen, L. (2013b). Shared residential custody: Review of the research (part II of II). *American Journal of Family Law, 27*, 123–137.

Nielsen, L. (2014). Shared physical custody: Summary of 40 studies on outcomes for children. *Journal of Divorce & Remarriage, 55*(8), 613–635.

Nikolina, N. (2012). The influence of international law on the issue of co-parenting-emerging trends in international and European instruments. *Utrecht Law Review, 8*, 122.

Perelli-Harris, B., & Gassen, N. S. (2012). How similar are cohabitation and marriage? Legal approaches to cohabitation across Western Europe. *Population and Development Review, 38*(3), 435–467.

Poortman, A. R., & van Gaalen, R. (2017). Shared residence after separation: A review and new findings from the Netherlands. *Family Court Review, 55*(4), 531–544.

Skinner, C., & Davidson, J. (2009). Recent trends in child maintenance schemes in 14 countries. *International Journal of Law, Policy and the Family, 23*(1), 25–52.

Smyth, B. M. (2005). Time to rethink time? The experience of time with children after divorce. *Family Matters, 71*, 4.

Smyth, B. M., & Weston, R. (2004). The attitudes of separated mothers and fathers to 50/50 shared care. *Family Matters, 67*, 8.

Sodermans, A. K., Vanassche, S., & Matthijs, K. (2011). Gedeelde kinderen en plusouders: de verblijfsregeling en de gezinssituatie na scheiding. In D. Mortelmans, I. Pasteels, J. Pacolet, P. Bracke, K. Matthijs, J. Van Bavel, & C. Van Peer (Eds.), *Scheiding in Vlaanderen*. Leuven/Den Haag: Acco.

Sodermans, A. K., Matthijs, K., & Swicegood, G. (2013a). Characteristics of joint physical custody families in Flanders. *Demographic Research, 28*(29), 821–848.

Sodermans, A. K., Vanassche, S., & Matthijs, K. (2013b). Verblijfsregelingen en welbevinden van kinderen: Verschillen naar gezinskenmerken. *Relaties en Nieuwe Gezinnen, 3*(11), 1–29.

Sodermans, A. K., Vanassche, S., Matthijs, K., & Swicegood, G. (2014). Measuring postdivorce living arrangements: Theoretical and empirical validation of the residential calendar. *Journal of Family Issues, 35*(1), 125–145.

Spruijt, E., & Duindam, V. (2010). Joint physical custody in the Netherlands and the well-being of children. *Journal of Divorce & Remarriage, 51*(1), 65–82.

Swennen, F., & Mortelmans, D. (2015). National report: Belgium. In K. Boele-Woelki (Ed.), *European Family Law in Action: Informal Relationships*. Intersentia.

Swiss, L., & Le Bourdais, C. (2009). Father–Child contact after separation: The influence of living arrangements. *Journal of Family Issues, 30*(5), 623–652.

Thielemans, G., & Mortelmans, D. (2019). Female labour force participation after divorce: How employment histories matter. *Journal of Family and Economic Issues, 40*(2), 180–193.

Trinder, L. (2010). Shared residence: A review of recent research evidence. *Child and Family Law Quarterly, 22*, 475.

Van der Heijden, F., Gähler, M., & Härkönen, J. (2015). Are parents with shared residence happier? Children's Postdivorce residence arrangements and parents' life satisfaction. *Stockholm Research Reports in Demography, 17*, 1–35.

Van Krieken, R. (2005). The 'best interests of the child' and parental separation: On the 'civilizing of parents. *The Modern Law Review, 68*(1), 25–48.

Vanassche, S., Sodermans, A. K., Declerck, C., & Matthijs, K. (2017). Alternating residence for children after parental separation: Recent findings from Belgium. *Family Court Review, 55*(4), 545–555.

Wallgren, A., & Wallgren, B. (2007). *Register-based statistics: Administrative data for statistical purposes* (Vol. 553). Chichester: Wiley.

Westphal, S. K. (2015). *Are the kids alright? Essays on postdivorce residence arrangements and children's well-being*. Utrecht: Utrecht University.

Elke Claessens is a post-doc researcher in Sociology within the Centre for Population, Family and Health (CPFH) and a teaching assistant in the Faculty of Political and Social Sciences at the University of Antwerp (Belgium). She teaches Applied Multivariate Statistics to master students in Sociology and Socio-Economical sciences, as well as Research Methods to the third bachelor students of the Faculty of Political and Social Sciences. Her research mainly focusses on the determination and objectification of child support, both in a national and international setting. More recently, her work also includes the investigation of shared physical custody patterns in Belgium.

Dimitri Mortelmans is Full Professor of Sociology at the Faculty of Political and Social Sciences of the University of Antwerp, Belgium. He is head of the Centre for Population, Family, and Health (CPFH). His research concentrates on family sociology and sociology of labour. He has published on divorce, new constituted families, gendered labour careers and work–life balance. He is also the main author of the Step in Statistics book series of which six volumes have been published (in Dutch). On qualitative methodology, he published the Handbook of Qualitative Research Methods and Qualitative Analysis with NVivo. In demography, he (co-)edited Changing Family Dynamics and Demographic Evolution. The Family Kaleidoscope (Edward Elgar), Lone parenthood in the Life Course (Springer) and Divorce in Europe (Springer).

Part III
Shared Physical Custory from the Childrens' Perspective

8

Families after Divorce and Sense of Home in Children

Laura Merla, Jonathan Dedonder, Bérengère Nobels, and Sarah Murru

Abstract This chapter explores the important question of whether, and under which conditions, children alternating between two distinct family dwellings can develop a sense of home that might nourish a sense of belonging to their sometimes, complex family configurations. We first present a theoretical framework to understand the various dimensions that influence children's sense of home in shared custody arrangements, building on Hashemnezhad et al. (2013)'s work. We then show how this framework can be operationalized in quantitative research. For this purpose, we introduce the Sense of Home Instrument (SOHI), a new instrument for measuring the impact of material and behavioral-relational dimensions on teenagers' sense of home at their mothers' and fathers'. We then illustrate its relevance and value with supporting analyses of data collected through a survey conducted with Belgian adolescents aged between 11 and 18. In doing so, we propose new avenues for research on the consequences of divorce and separations for children's identity construction and belonging, where the spatiality of family life is taken into-account.

Keywords Children · Divorce · Shared custody · Home · Family sociology

L. Merla (✉)
UCLouvain, Ottignies-Louvain-la-Neuve, Belgium

University of Western Australia (UWA), Perth, WA, Australia
e-mail: laura.merla@uclouvain.be

J. Dedonder · B. Nobels · S. Murru
UCLouvain, Ottignies-Louvain-la-Neuve, Belgium
e-mail: jonathan.dedonder@uclouvain.be; berengere.nobels@uclouvain.be; sarah.murru@uclouvain.be

8.1 Introduction

The sense of being 'at home' has been largely recognized as a key element to support processes of autonomisation, identity construction and belonging during adolescence. Within the nuclear family model that dominated Western societies until recently, this sense of home has traditionally been conceived in the context of a stable, single reference family dwelling. Post-divorce arrangements where children alternate between two distinct family dwellings challenge this vision, and raise the important question of whether they can develop a sense of home that might nourish a sense of belonging to their sometimes, complex family configurations. In this chapter we explore in particular adolescents' sense of being 'at home' at their mother's and father's in the context of joint physical custody. Drawing on Hashemnezhad et al. (2013), we present a theoretical framework for the analysis of children's sense of home in JPC, and propose a new instrument for measuring the impact of material and behavioral-relational dimensions on teenagers' sense of home, named the Sense of Home Instrument (SOHI). We then illustrate its relevance through supporting analysis of data collected in a survey conducted with Belgian adolescents aged between 11 and 18, and suggest some research hypothesis that could be tested in the future.

8.2 Studying Teenagers' Sense of Home in Post-divorce Families: Relevance and Key Dimensions

8.2.1 Sense of Home and Identity Construction

Living in a stable, single reference dwelling has been considered by some psychologists and lawyers as a necessary condition for children's development, a lack of such "stability" exposing children to the risk of an "identity breakdown" (de Singly and Decup-Pannier 2000: 220). Actually, as Merla (2018) argued elsewhere, living within, and across two households – two 'homes' – challenges the normative model of sedentariness that characterizes Western societies, where the administration of populations has largely relied on the identification of people with one place of residence. This paradigm was reflected in the standard, institutional model of the family, that represents family members as bonded together by physical co-presence and bounded by the confines of the privately-owned land and house that contains them (Morgan 2011).

For social sciences scholars, the family dwelling crystallizes three dimensions of what Bonnin (1999: 23) calls a "house-domus", that is, (a) the localized material capital of the housing, (b) the functionalized, habitable space, as a necessary instrument of domestic practices – which can be daily, festive, repetitive or exceptional, and (c) the symbolic (collective and individual) identity expressions it supports. The second and third dimensions highlight that, through their daily interactions with– and within – the space of the house, people "do" family, that is, engage in practices that define them as family members and nurture their sense of belonging (Morgan 2011). By doing so, they also construct and negotiate their collective and individual identities. This process is particularly important during adolescence, a period defined by sociologists as the moment of autonomy learning (Galland 2010) where teenagers reflexively consider their familial attachments, and distance themselves from the "family-us" to construct their personal identity. By offering teenagers a sense of ontological security and a locus for their socialization with family and peers, the home represents a key resource for their identity building and belonging.

The processes through which teenagers develop a sense of home, and the role this sense plays in identity building, has been mainly studied through a focus on the bedroom, which, according to de Singly (1998) and Poittevin (2005), represents a complex universe supporting processes of autonomization, belonging, and relationships-building with parents, siblings and friends (see also Bovill and Livingstone 2001; Zaffran 2014; Ramos 2018).[1] The bedroom is often considered by adolescents as their "home", a space of intimacy extracted from the common family life, and referring to personal territories (Ramos 2018). They tend to perceive it as a refuge, where they feel safe from an outside world, where they can be themselves, and where they can express their personality and lifestyle. The bedroom is thus a symbolic and meaningful space, where young people can define their identity (Augé 1992 cited by Zaffran 2014: 2). Identity expression manifests itself in the control exercised over space (by closing or not the door, arranging, organizing and decorating it in a certain way), the time and activities that take place in this room, and the persons who are allowed in – or excluded from it – at certain times, including friends (Zaffran 2014). This control appears as an essential condition for the construction of teenagers' identity (Renonciat 2014). According to Amphoux and Mondada (1989), home, symbolized here mainly by the bedroom, is not a place of retreat, totally closed to the other but a "place of the identity of the "I" welcoming the other" (1989: 5). This meeting place allows the young person to welcome other people with whom he or she shares social references. "It then makes it possible to affirm one's belonging and to recognize oneself in those who circulate there" (Zaffran 2014: 2).

Teenagers develop a sense of home not only through the appropriation of a bedroom, but also of other spaces inside or outside the house by using, possessing and surrounding themselves with some objects rather than others, and by occupying and decorating these spaces (de Singly 1998; Poittevin 2005). In this process, they create a space of significant, meaningful symbols that allow them to maintain some form of continuity in their life course and that reflect their own identity (Csikszentmihalyi and Rochberg-Halton 1981; Gyger Gaspoz 2014). Teenagers' sense of being 'at home' under the family roof is thus rooted both in the

[1]It is important to note that the importance of having one's own bedroom is a recent cultural and historical construct, and thus varies through space and time, including in Western Europe (see for instance Wentzel Winther 2017).

time-space of non-family practices (what the teenagers do in their room or on a certain household equipment), where adolescents are in ‘their world’ (de Singly 2007), and the time-spaces of common activities with family members, where what matters is ‘being together’ and/or “being in the presence” of one another (de Singly and Ramos 2010: 12).

But what happens when teenagers have “two” homes? How do they develop a sense of home that positively supports their identity construction and family belonging? This question is particularly crucial, as divorce and subsequent re-compositions blur family boundaries and put feelings of belonging under strain (Zartler 2011). If to date, only a limited number of research has looked into those issues through the lens of children’s home-making, the existing body of work further attests to the importance of feelings of being ‘at home’ in processes of identity construction and belonging. For instance, in their study of how Danish children in large sibling groups relate to bedrooms, Palludan and Winther (2016) put forth that it is by claiming the right to have their own room and belongings at each of their parents’ dwellings – thus making them both ‘their homes’ – that children in joint custody are recognized in their family relations. The “socio-material weight” (Palludan and Winther 2016: 40) they gain through this process determines in turn their status in the household, in particular whether they are considered as hosts, guests, or regular visitors in each house. In their study of joint custody arrangements in Belgium, Merla and Nobels (2019) similarly show that the materiality of space can influence, and be influenced by, the symbolic and physical place that is given to adolescents in the family house and that shapes their sense of being ‘at home’. On the one hand, teenagers leave a spatial imprint of their presence in the home through the personal belongings they permanently leave in the dwelling. These objects help them reaffirm that this house is “their house” each time they return home – thus reflecting the place they occupy in the family configuration. Their (recomposed) family members can also show them that they do belong to the house – and, by extension, the family group – by increasingly giving them a physical place through the materiality of the home’s space. Being assigned a specific, personal drawer in the “children’s” wardrobe or even a wardrobe of one’s own, receiving a personal bed, or a bedroom of one’s own . . . can give them the sense that they are placed on an equal footing with the “permanent” inhabitants of the house. This provides them with a sense of continuity, in spite of their regular absences, as they remain symbolically present for the rest of the family through the marks they leave in each dwelling.

This research is in line with de Singly and Decup-Pannier (2000)‘s claim that the quality of the environment surrounding a relationship, that characterizes each dwelling, plays a key role in shaping teenagers’ sense of home. In addition, these scholars point out that young people in joint custody arrangements do not necessarily put each of their dwellings on an equal footing. Some of them indeed “prioritize one of their two bedrooms, recreating a “habitual” residence” (de Singly and Decup-Pannier 2000: 220). This duality does not necessarily lead to a fragmented sense of home, as teenagers engage in tactics to reinforce the feeling of having only one home, either in one room or in a larger territory“ (de Singly and Decup-Pannier 2000: 227). Also, it is important to note that children who do not have their own room at one, or both of their parents' dwellings, can put in place "homing" strategies, for instance by "delimiting their "corner" by the bed and what is within reach from this bed (personal element of "my corner")" (Ramos 2018: 58).

Repartnering and family re-compositions challenge pre-existing relationships, and raise spatial issues. The re-negotiation of children's and adults' respective position in these new family configurations involves, for instance, competition around the allocation of bedrooms and the delineation between shared and private spaces in the house, as well as other spatial-material strategies and practices that mark the acceptance, or rejection, of the "newcomers" (Marquet and Merla 2015, 2018; Merla and Nobels 2019). Repartnering and family re-compositions thus challenge teenagers' sense of home, reflecting, and participating in, the reconfiguration of their family identity.

By highlighting the agency of teenagers, these works also contribute to the claim that having multiple living spaces can potentially constitute a resource, rather than an impairment, for identity construction. As de Singly and Decup-Pannier note (2000: 220), "sociologists (including Erving Goffman) argue that having multiple living spaces is necessary for the individual. The possibility of independence arises from the multiplicity of spaces (...) Having several addresses is one of the processes implemented by an individual in order not to be reduced to a single identity". Having several places of residence where one feels 'at home', provides access to a heterogeneous repertoire that might thus open up the possibility to construct a single, original self at the intersection of these multiple identities.[2]

8.2.2 Sense of Home: Material and Behavioral Dimensions

The body of research that we mobilized this far highlighted both the materiality of spaces and the importance of relationships in defining adolescents' attachment to place and sense of home. This is in line with the multi-dimensional conceptualization of sense of home and attachment to place proposed by Hashemnezhad and his colleagues (2013), based on an interdisciplinary literature review.

The material dimension refers to the physicality and materiality of a place, including the ways in which a house is decorated, the configuration of the rooms, their number and size, the level of material comfort, smells and temperature, and so on. The walls' colors, the quantity and quality of household equipment and furniture, the number of rooms, their size, their luminosity, the fact that they are lightly – or over – loaded... together influence people's sense of home. This dimension thus refers to the cognitive and formal aspects of places that shape people's spatial perception of their dwelling, which in turn influences how they relate to it.

---

[2]For a discussion of children's socialization in heterogeneous, post-divorce family environments, see for instance Merla (2018).

The behavioral dimension covers the functional aspects of the living environment. This includes the types of activities and practices that are performed in the dwelling and its various spaces, and the relations that take place in those spaces. For instance, teenagers in joint custody arrangements might prefer to spend time in a lively house, where they share several activities with their family members (such as playing, watching tv, cooking, dinning together, etc.) and spend 'quality time' with them, rather than in a house where they feel lonely and isolated because their parents or other family members are less available to spend time with them, or where there is a high level of intra-familial conflict (see for instance Merla and Nobels 2019). This dimension strongly resonates with the relational approach in family sociology, represented by Morgan's notion of 'doing' family, and could therefore be coined as a 'relational' dimension.

The third dimension of Hashemnezhad et al.'s model is the emotional one, and relates to the meaning of, satisfaction with, and attachment to, a given to place (Hashemnezhad et al. 2013: 6). As Merla and Nobels (2019) show in their research, "the positive or negative emotions that are felt [in a place] can influence the child's perception and attachment to a specific space, leading her/him to prefer to remain there, making her/him feeling more comfortable and safe or on the contrary, encouraging her/him to avoid a specific room" (2019: 13). By interpreting the physical setting, children convert a space into a place transforming it in "a center of meaning or field of care that emphasizes human emotions and relationships" (Jorgensen and Stedman 2001: 233). Adolescents thus develop a sense of home that is connected to their emotional links with the material place (e.g. the house) and the social unit that occupies this place (e.g. the family) (Winther 2009: 49).

8.3 The SOHI: A New Instrument for the Study of Children's Sense of Home

In this paper we propose to operationalize this framework through the Sense of Home Instrument (SOHI).[3] We focus here on the material and behavioral-relational dimensions of the sense of home.[4]

This instrument was conceived for surveys with teenagers in secondary schools, usually aged between 11–12 and 18–19. This broad age-range includes children with varied levels of literacy and concentration abilities, and this raises important challenges. Put simply, how participants will read and understand questions may vary greatly, and some of them may tire quickly. This is why we decided to work with a limited number of indicators, which can be measured from a relatively short survey

[3]The SOHI module (including its dimensions, indicators, and sample questions) is provided in the Annex 1.

[4]At this stage, we indeed decided to leave the emotional dimension aside, for as sociologists we felt ill-equipped to approach this aspect through a survey questionnaire.

module. In addition, researchers willing to implement such module in their surveys will need to pay careful attention to the formulation of questions, and run a series of pre-tests to ensure understandability. The questions we are presenting in this section will therefore need to be adapted both to the specific socio-cultural environment and cognitive level of the surveyed populations.

8.3.1 Measuring the Material Dimension

In the SOHI we propose to approach the material dimension through the **level of comfort** that teenagers experience in each of their dwellings, with a particular emphasis on the question of the bedroom (having one's own), and having enough space in the dwelling. Similarly to France and Nordic countries (Winther 2017) having one's own room has become a normative standard in Belgium, leading teenagers to consider it both as a right and a need (de Singly and Decup-Pannier 2000). As we mentioned earlier, being able to "create a material environment that embodies what they consider significant" (Csikszentmihalyi and Rochberg-Halton 1981: 123), where they feel at home, and on which they can have a certain amount of control (Ramos 2018), play a role in adolescents' identity building. In addition, Hashemnezhad et al.'s (2013) model also indicates that factors such as the size and number of rooms, and how much they are loaded are important indicators of the level of comfort afforded by an accommodation.

Here, the perceived level of comfort is evaluated through questions about the physical and material characteristics of the parents' dwellings. These focus, first, on children's perception of their dwelling and second, on teenagers' bedroom more specifically. Concretely, children are first asked to say if the following statements concerning their mothers'/fathers' place are correct (by yes or no): (1) there is enough room for everyone: (2) We are feeling a bit cramped. They are then questioned in a similar way on two statements concerning bedrooms at their mothers'/fathers' place (1) I have a bedroom of my own; (2) I share a bedroom with my siblings and/or other children; (3) I share a bedroom with my parent; (4) I have no bedroom at all. In the Belgian context, having a room of one's own, not sharing a room with one's parent, feeling there is enough space for everyone, and not feeling cramped are indicative of higher levels of comfort.

8.3.2 Behavioral-Relational Dimension

Here we first mobilize factors that have been to date located at the center-stage of scholarship on parent-child relations in post-divorce families, namely the **quality of parent-child relations**, the **level of intra-parental conflict**, and **repartnering**. One of the key entries has resided so far in exploring the link between the type of custody arrangement and the quality of parent-child and intra-parental relationships

(Cashmore et al. 2010; Spruijt and Duindam 2010; Vanassche et al. 2013; Nielsen 2018). Comparing children's wellbeing in shared versus sole custody arrangements, Bauserman for instance (2002) highlights that children in shared custody spend relatively more time with their fathers and express better parental relations. However, Drapeau et al. (2017) argue that, independent from the quantity of time spent with the child, the level of conflict between the parents is a better indicator of the quality of the parent-child relation as the former tends to reflect on the latter. Although the above-mentioned scholarship does not specifically analyze the respective link between, on the one hand, the quality of parent-child relations and levels of intra-parental conflict, and, on the other hand, children's sense of being 'at home' at their parents, they confirm that these two factors both strongly influence, and characterize, the relational context in which adolescents grow up. Finally, studies have also focused on the influence of remarriage/repartnering on parent-child relations but these have emphasized contrasting results leading to positive impacts as well as negative ones (Aquilino 2006). As we highlighted in the theoretical section, repartnering is an important component of children's relational environments.

In the SOHI, the quality of parent-child relations is approached through 10 questions.[5] Children are invited to position themselves on a scale from 1 (not at all) to 5 (at maximum) with regards to the following questions: how good is your relation with your [mother/father]?; does your [mother/father] admire you and respect you?; to what extend do you feel close and have fun with your [mother/father]?; do you share secrets and intimate feelings with your [mother/father]?; how much does your [mother/father] love you?; how much do you love your [mother/father]?; does your [mother/father] appreciate the things you do?; does your [mother/father] find it important to listen to you?; does your [mother/father] think you have good ideas?; does your [mother/father] consider that she can learn a lot from you?[6]

The conflict score between the parents (as perceived by children) is calculated based on the following questions[7]: how often do your parents argue over money?; how often do your parents argue over your education?; how often do your parents argue about the children?; how often do your parents totally disagree with each other?; do your parents sometimes have big conflicts? These questions are asked regarding the relationship between their parents before and after the separation.[8]

Finally, the quality of children's relation with their step-parent is measured through the following question: How is your relation with your [mother/father's] partner? (Very bad/bad/neither good nor bad/good/very good).

---

[5]These questions are drawn from the Leuven Adolescents and Family Survey (LAGO), which were also implemented in the Louvain/Leuven Adolescents Survey (see Sect. 8.4).

[6]In the Lads survey (see Sect. 8.4), these subscales showed a high reliability measurement in the four types of familial configuration (all $\alpha > .85$).

[7]Also drawn from the LAGO questionnaire.

[8]Indices of internal reliability of these questions in the LAdS survey are very good (all $\alpha > .84$), comforting us in the constitution of this score.

The next indicator innovatively and tentatively connects teenagers' sense of home with their **(digital) communication practices**. Indeed, we live in societies marked by the omnipresence of Information and Communication Technologies (ICTs). In this context, relationships among family members are no longer limited to physical, embodied spaces – they go beyond a house's walls via virtual means of co-presence. As Wellman (2018: P. Xix) notes, digital media 'have empowered family members with the ability to go their separate ways while at the same time keeping them more connected'. The development and democratization of ICTs have thus profoundly affected the ways in which family members "stay in touch", offering new forms of "virtual" co-presence that create opportunities to sustain family and social relations across space and time. Through ICT-based frequent and/or ritual contacts, parents and children can create family routines that transcend physical absence and nourish a sense of belonging (Duchêne-Lacroix 2013). Research on non-divorced families with members temporarily away (for professional reasons or in a migratory context) have highlighted the importance of ICTs in maintaining parent-child relations in this context (see for instance Thompson 2005; Yarosh and Abowd 2011; Madianou 2016). But the influence of such contact on the quality of relationships is not clear. For instance, Lee (2009)'s survey among 1300 students aged 12–18 highlights that virtual communication neither weakens nor strengthens the relationship between children and parents. Other studies also point at the potential of constant connectivity for enhancing tensions and conflicts as they offer increased possibilities of surveillance and control (Madianou 2016). Actually, this body of research rather indicates that it is the pre-existing quality of relationships (level of conflicts, stability and strength of ties) that tends to determine the extent to which online communication between parents and children can be satisfying and meaningful, and/or experienced as a form of surveillance and control (Chen et al. 2010; du Preez 2018: 88; Madianou 2016).

ICT affordances can be particularly critical to sustain parent-child relations in post-divorce families where children spend (sometimes long) periods of time without seeing one of their parents (see for instance Gollop and Taylor 2012; Saini et al. 2013; Wolman and Pomerance 2012; Yarosh et al. 2009).[9] Yet, the question of how such practices can feed into children's sense of being 'at home' at each of their parents' remains unexplored. In addition, the question of how continued communication with other household members, such as the parents' new partner, can also contribute to sustaining children's sense of home, remains unexplored.

For this purpose, we propose to measure **the continuity of children's communication with their parents and step-parents** based on two sets of questions. The first set aims at capturing children's everyday uses of communicative platforms and tools with their parents, regardless of their physical location. So, children are asked to indicate, on a 5-Likert scale (1: Never, 2: Several Times a month, 3: Several times per week, 4: Everyday, 5: Several Times a day), how often they use Facebook

[9]For research on divorced parents' uses of ICT for co-parenting, see Dworkin et al. (2016) and Ganong et al. (2012).

Messenger, WhatsApp/Imessage, Skype, Instagram, Snapchat, Twitter, TikTok and online games to communicate with their mother/father. In the second set, we focus more specifically on cross-household communication with a parent/step-parent when the teenager is physically located at the other parents'. Here we try to capture the different forms of co-presence they engage in when interacting with their relatives from a distance (Baldassar et al. 2016; Merla and Papanikolaou Forthcoming). Here, children are asked to indicate on a similar 5-Likert scale, how often they communicate with their mother/father/step-mother/step-father, when staying at the other parent's house, through voice calls (without video, just audio), video calls, messaging (like texting or instant messages), written posts on social networks (like Facebook walls for instance), photo or video posts on social networks (like TikTok or FB or Snapchat) ((e.g. when you stay at your mother's house, how often do you communicate with your father through video calls?) The maximum score on one of these networks could for instance be retained as the "Cross-household digital communication" variable.

8.4 Illustrating the Relevance of This Instrument

The SOHI was initially conceived in the context of a survey conducted in Belgium with teenagers aged 11–18. Although we have subsequently refined some of our indicators, this survey allows us to test the usefulness of our proposed instrument. In this section we briefly contextualize divorce and joint custody in Belgium, then present the LAdS survey itself. We then propose a series of illustrative analysis to underline the relevance of our instrument.

8.4.1 The Context: Divorce and Joint Custody in Belgium

Belgium is an interesting case to study in relation with divorce and joint custody. First, Belgium has historically had a high crude divorce rate, above the EU average. The highest rate was reached in 2010 with a divorce rate of 2.7 (compared with the EU average of 2.0). It has however been slowly decreasing since then (with a rate of 2.2 in 2015) (Eurostat[10]).

Second, Belgium is one of the few EU countries that adopted joint physical custody as a preferential model in case of divorce or separation, as early as 2006. A reform that significantly impacted child custody arrangements. Following the 2006 law, this choice of custody is thus set as the referential type of custody which is examined in priority by the Court in case of parental separation and after the demand of at least one of the parents. In other words, this entails that the parent demanding an

[10]https://ec.europa.eu/eurostat/statistics-explained/index.php/Marriage_and_divorce_statistics

egalitarian joint custody arrangement no longer has to demonstrate the pertinence of this choice. On the other side, if one of the parents opposes this choice of custody, it becomes his/her duty to present a convincing argument supporting a different custodial arrangement (Côté and Gaborean 2015). The adoption of this law comes after the recognition of the legal principal of "conjunct exercise of parental authority" (law of 1995) which is no longer solely held by the parent with whom the child resided, but also follows a societal debate which confronted arguments around parental equality, feasibilities of such custodial arrangements (Marquet 2008), and the best interest of the child (Casman et al. 2010). In parallel, it is also of interest to mention that it seems the 2006 law came as a legal concretization of an adopted social phenomenon, as an increase of the practice of egalitarian joint custody had been observed (without legal support) prior to the adoption of the law (Côté and Gaborean 2015; Van Houcke 2017).

Repercussions of this legal context are a continued increase of the practice of equally sharing custody of children (Van Houcke 2017). More specifically, according to the 2017 Family Barometer of the Belgian Family League (Hosdey-Radoux et al. 2017), as of today, more than four out of ten parents in Brussels and Wallonia experience a divorce or separation, and one out of three separated couples equally share custody of their children. This entails that, in a context where the "classical" nuclear family configuration is still dominating (57% of family configurations), in case of separation, there are roughly as many parents practicing sole custody of their children as there are parents practicing equal joint custody. As sole custody used to be the default mode, this highlights the societal shift towards a preference for egalitarian joint custody.

8.4.2 The Survey

The Leuven/Louvain Adolescents Survey (LAdS) was collaboratively designed in 2017 by researchers from the University of Louvain (UCLouvain)[11] and the University of Leuven (KULeuven), under the supervision of Leen D'Haenens, Koenraad Matthijs and Laura Merla. The survey builds on the KULeuven Adolescents and Families Survey (also known as LAGO) that was created in 2008 and gathered data on the family lives and behaviors of Flemish teenagers aged 12–18.[12] The last, sixth, wave dates from 2014. LAdS was born from a desire to expand the collection of data to the whole country, and enrich the survey with new themes designed collaboratively by the two research teams.[13] Questions in the survey directly related to this

[11] https://uclouvain.be/fr/chercher/cirfase/leuven-louvain-adolescents-survey.html

[12] https://soc.kuleuven.be/ceso/fapos/ongoingprojects/lago

[13] The BWF survey was indeed also designed to provide quantitative data to the ERC Starting Grant project "MobileKids: children in multi-local, post-separation families". This research conducted at the UCLouvain under the supervision of Prof. Laura Merla seeks to understand how children living

chapter concern: (a) adolescents' socio-demographic characteristics; (b) overall quality of their relationships with their parents; (c) family arrangements and relations of adolescents, depending on whether their parents are living together, not living together, or if they only have one parent alive; and (d) adolescents' uses of digital technologies to communicate with their relatives.

In this chapter we build on data collected with French-speaking adolescents in Brussels and Wallonia from November 2017 to March 2018, as data from the Flemish side are not available yet. To ensure a good representativeness, this sample was collected across six provinces (Hainaut, Namur, Luxembourg, Liège, Brabant-Wallon and Région de Bruxelles-Capitale). For each province data was collected from three to five different schools among different educational tracks (general, technical, professional and artistic), with a total of 23 schools. In each school one class was selected per educational degree and type of secondary education, following the school schedule and student's availability. Participants were surveyed in their classrooms at school using a computerized questionnaire presented on a tablet using the SurveyCTO application (www.surveycto.com), with the guidance of Masters student in Sociology from the UCLouvain.

A total of 1678 students answered the survey, but for the purpose of this chapter we focus on the 146 respondents living in joint custody arrangements and aged 11–18 who completed at least 70% of the questionnaire, answered the questions on their relationship with their parents, still had contact with both parents and answered the question on their sense of being at home at each parents'. This sample is varied in terms of gender (52.5% of girls), age (with a relatively even distribution across the age groups 11–13, 14–15 and 16–18, who each represent roughly 1/third of our sample),[14] nationalities (94.3% of the children have the Belgian nationality, and the 5.7% remaining participants come from a variety of countries around the world), and distribution in the Belgian educational system (with 72.2% of respondents in the general education section, 19.6% in the technical section, and 8.2% in the vocational section). The majority of fathers and mothers in our sample have a higher education degree,[15] while it is also important to note that nearly 20% of the children interviewed said they did not know the diploma of one of their parents.

---

in joint custody arrangements in Belgium, France and Italy accommodate to this situation, and places a specific emphasis on how children develop a sense of 'home' and appropriate their own mobility, as well as on their uses of ICT to maintain their family relations. See www.mobilekids.eu. This project has received funding from the *European Research Council (ERC) under the European Union's Horizon 2020 research and innovation program* under grant agreement No 676868. This chapter reflects only the authors' view. The European Commission is not responsible for any use that may be made of the information it contains.

[14]The 11–13 age groups represents 32.9% of our sample (0.6% 11 years, 7.6% 12 years, 24.7% 13 years), the 14–15 age group represents 34.8% of our sample (20.9% 14 years; 13.9% 15 years), and the 16–18 age group represents 32.3% of our sample (11.4% 16 years, 13.9% 17 years and 7.0% 18 years).

[15]Mother primary degree: 7.0%, Father primary degree 2.5%; Mother secondary degree12.0%, Father secondary degree 19.0%; Mother higher education degree 54.4%, Father higher education degree 55.1%; Mother do not know or missing 30.5%, Father do not know or missing 23.4%.

With regards to the different types of post-divorce/separation familial configurations, we distinguished them using a residential calendar (Sodermans et al. 2014). Children who had previously declared that their parents were separated had to fill in a 4 weeks calendar. For each day of the week they were asked to indicate if they resided at their mother's or father's home, making a distinction between day and night. This technique allowed us to compute a percentage of time spent with each parent. This percentage of time was then used to classify children into various family configurations. "Joint Custody" refers to situations where the time of residence with each parent ranges between 30% and 50%.

8.4.3 Empirical Validation of the SOHI

First, it is important to mention that in our sample, teenagers report relatively high levels of feeling at home at their mothers' (*M*: 4.50; *SD*: .98), and at their fathers' (*M*: 4.23; *SD*: 1.20) (over 4 on a 5-levels scale). However, although the difference is small, this sense of home is significantly higher at the mother's place than the father's place ($t(145) = 2.178, p < .05$).

To illustrate the relevance of the SOHI instrument, we explored the correlations between children's sense of home, and four key indicators of our instrument, namely the level of comfort, the quality of parent-child relation, the continuity of communication with the parent, and the quality of relation with the cohabiting step-parent.[16] We also include two variables, namely the age of the child, and parental repartnering (regardless of whether or not the new partner cohabits with the parent). In Table 8.1, the analysis is conducted separately for each parent.

Children's Sense of Home at the Mothers' seems positively correlated with four variables: the quality of relation with the mother, the quality of relation with the cohabiting step-parent, the level of comfort at the mothers' place, and the continuity of communication with the mother. This positive correlation is moderate in the first two cases, and weak in the next two cases. They tend to indicate that a higher sense of home is associated with a higher quality of relations with the mother, a higher quality of relation with her current cohabiting partner, and, to a lesser extent, a higher level of comfort and more continuous communication with the mother. In addition, adolescents' sense of home at the mothers' seems negatively (but weakly) correlated to the age of the children, suggesting that younger teenagers feel more at home at their mothers' than older ones.

Children's Sense of Being at Home at Their Fathers' appears to be correlated with 5 variables. The higher correlation concerns children's sense of home at the father's and the quality of relation with the father. This sense of home is also positively associated with the level of comfort at the father's place, the continuity

[16] A full correlation table between all those variables can be found in Annex 2.

Table 8.1 Correlation between Sense of home at Mother or Father's place and the SOHI indicators

Sense of home		Comfort	Relation with the parent	Continuity of communication	Repartnering	Relation with cohabiting step-parent	Age	Level of conflict
At Mother's	*r*	.237**	.556**	.231**	.123	.479**	−.185*	−.156
	N	146	146	133	144	78	146	129
At Father's	*r*	.377**	.531**	.369**	.230**	.359**	−.103	−.209*
	N	147	147	141	145	90	147	129

*p < .05; **p < .01

of contact with the father, the quality of relation with the cohabiting step-parent, and fathers' repartnering.

We then explored the correlation between mothers' and fathers' variables (Table 8.2).

First, only one correlation between mothers' and fathers' variables is observed in relation with children's sense of home: the sense of home at the mother's is negatively correlated with fathers' repartnering. In other words, it is less good when the father is re-partnered. Second, the quality of relation with the mother is moderately and positively correlated with the quality of relation with the father, and moderately, but negatively, correlated with the fact that the father is re-partnered. Third, we can also observe that the level of comfort at both places is correlated: children who report a good level of comfort at one place, report a similar level of comfort at the other place. And finally, mothers' repartnering is positively associated to fathers' repartnering, reflecting the fact that parents in our survey tend to be in a similar situation.[17]

We then proceeded to a bi-variate analysis of each indicator by children's gender, children's age, and parental repartnering (Table 8.3).

Several effects can be highlighted here. First, children's sense of home at the father's is impacted by children's gender ($t(145) = 3.28, p < .001$) and the father's repartnering ($t(143) = -2.82, p = .05$). More precisely, girls feel more at home at the mother's ($p < .05$) than the father's, while boys report a higher sense of home at the father's place than girls, and the sense of home of both boys and girls is higher when the father is single. Second, girls have more contact with their mother than boys ($t(131) = -2.68, p < .05$), and the 14–15 years old children have more contacts with their mother when they stay at their father's place than the 16–18 years old ($F(2,130) = 2.84$, $p = .062$). Third, the 14–15 years old children have a better relationship with their step-father than the 16–18 years old ($F(2,75) = 3.97$, $p < .05$). And finally, the lowest level of parental conflict is observed when the mother is re-partnered ($t(126) = -2.89, p < .01$).

8.5 Discussion: Research Hypothesis and Directions

The illustrative, empirical validation of the SOHI is based on a small number of surveyed children, and only aimed at highlighting the potential of this instrument. However, based on this exercise, combined with our theoretical framework, we would like to suggest here some interesting hypothesis that might be tested with our instrument. These could be formulated as follows: the higher the level of comfort, the more children will feel at home at their parents'; the better the quality of relation with the parent/cohabiting step-parent, the more the teenager will feel at home at

[17] 60.39% of the parents are in a similar situation, where 31.82% are both solo and 28.57% are both in re-partnered.

Table 8.2 Correlation between variables for the mother and the father

			Father					
			Sense of home	Level of comfort	Quality of the relation	Continuity of communication	Repartnering	Quality of relation with cohabiting step-parent
Mother	Sense of home	*r*	.038	.004	.09	−.036	−.166*	.005
		N	146	146	146	141	144	90
	Level of comfort	*r*	.127	.175*	.056	−.079	−.121	.093
		N	147	158	158	141	154	90
	Quality of the relation	*r*	−.081	−.006	.168*	.035	−.207**	.112
		N	147	158	158	141	154	90
	Continuity of communication	*r*	−.126	−.07	.087	.373**	−.091	.031
		N	133	133	133	130	131	87
	Repartnering	*r*	.012	−.088	−.074	−.064	.222**	−.067
		N	145	154	154	139	154	90
	Quality of relation with cohabiting step-parent	*r*	.116	.131	.15	.164	−.023	−.102
		N	78	78	78	76	78	60

$^*p < .05$; $^{**}p < .01$

Table 8.3 Mean score and Standard deviation (in brackets) for each indicator by gender of the children, their age and parental repartnering

	Sense of home		Continuity of communication		Quality of relation with the cohabitating step-parent		
	Mother	Father	Mother	Father	Mother	Father	Conflict score
Gender							
Girls	4.46 (.93)	3.92 (1.31)	3.38 (1.08)	2.9 (.95)	3.81 *(1.17)*	3.63 *(1.28)*	2.24 *(.93)*
Boys	4.54 (1.03)	4.55 (.97)	2.85 (1.22)	3.16 (1.29)	3.74 *(1.24)*	3.67 *(1.34)*	2.18 *(.91)*
Age							
11–13	4.71 (.74)	4.47 (.92)	3.09 (1.29)	3.02 (1.34)	3.83 *(1.38)*	3.91 *(1.31)*	2.23 *(.90)*
14–15	4.52 (.98)	4.08 (1.34)	3.43 (1.04)	3.20 (1.00)	4.16 *(.88)*	3.56 *(1.31)*	2.14 *(.96)*
16–18	4.26 (1.14)	4.13 (1.28)	2.85 (1.13)	2.84 (1.01)	3.32 *(1.19)*	3.55 *(1.28)*	2.27 *(.90)*
Repartnering							
Solo	4.61 (.82)	4.52 (1.28)	3.15 (1.21)	2.98 (1.09)			2.41 *(.97)*
In couple	4.38 (1.11)	3.96 (1.03)	3.16 (1.10)	3.12 (1.16)			1.94 *(.78)*

his/her place; the higher the current level of conflict between parents, the less likely the teenager will feel at home; the more a teenager maintains continuous online communication with his or her parent, the more that teenager will feel at home at that parent's house. Measuring the relative weight of the material and the relational in shaping children's sense of home might also be done, for instance, through the hypothesis that a better quality of relationship with a parent reduces the negative effect of a low level of perceived comfort on teenager's sense of home at that parent's. As suggested in our tests, children's gender, their age, and parental repartnering might constitute interesting control variables, together with, for instance, the number of years after the divorce, and the age of the child at the time of this divorce. Exploring differences between determinants of children's sense of home at the mother's and the fathers, would be also seem particularly relevant – including in light of each parents' socio-economic situation.

In this paper we decided to propose an instrument with a limited number of indicators, but of course other relevant indicators might be added. Amongst these, we would like to stress the relevance of enriching the behavioral-relational dimension with indicators on children's relationships with their siblings, including half and quasi-siblings. At this stage we did not include this aspect in our instrument, because the complexity of siblings constellations and configurations in post-divorce, recomposed families poses important challenges in terms of survey design, especially in the case of self-administered questionnaires with children from varied ages and levels of cognitive development. However, sibling relationships play a key role in children's lives and there is a crucial need to develop knowledge on this under-researched aspect (Noller 2005; Wentzel Winther et al. 2005).

Finally, we believe it might be worth considering to use/adapt the SOHI instrument, which we have designed for shared custody arrangements, to explore children's sense of home in other post-divorce family configurations.

8.6 Conclusion

In a context of increased mobility, the concept of a single residential dwelling has been increasingly deconstructed with regards to adults, but this is seldom the case about children who are nevertheless experimenting a similar increase in mobility – due among others to parental separation. In particular, this chapter has demonstrated the pertinence and need for increased studies on how the sense of home is constructed by children in the context of multiple-residency. Here, we tried in particular to contribute to debates about the impact of living in two dwellings on adolescents growing in joint physical custody arrangements – a topic that has to date, and to our knowledge, only been studied by scholars mobilizing qualitative methods. Based on Hashemnezhad et al. (2013)'s typology, we did this by proposing a new instrument desgined to explore the material and behavioral-relational dimensions that influence children's sense of being 'at home' at each of their parents'.

One originality of the SOHI lies in the attempt to measure the impact of "classical" indicators studied in the context of joint physical custody (quality of relationship, level of conflict) on the creation (or not) of a sense of home for teenagers. But we also go further by connecting "sense of home" in joint custody arrangements with the online communication practices of teenagers, that allow them to maintain a more continuous relationship with their parents, regardless of where they are physically located.

Our research endeavour has implications for scholarship, both on sense of home and place-attachment, and on children and divorce. Indeed, this chapter helps to design research on sense of home as constructed at the intersection between, and through a combination of, material and behavioral-relational dimensions. Family relations, and the practices ensuring a continuity of these relations across space and time, indeed confer a specific meaning to the material space of the dwelling that teenagers intermittently inhabit, allowing or hindering the possibility to feel 'at home' in those places (Forsberg et al. 2016). Our model brings to the fore the importance of considering the spatiality of the family and of childhood in the study of divorced families, by conceptualising "the home (...) not as a bounded space but as a porous one where children's agency needs to be considered alongside that of adults" (Holloway and Valentine 2000). Living in a divorced family, including in joint custody arrangements, has become increasingly common for children in Belgium, to the point that it has lost its extra-ordinary character (Marquet and Merla 2015), and this edited book confirms this is also happening in other countries. In this context, teenagers engage in daily practices, and develop certain views that give meaning to "their" family configurations. It is important to note in this context, that adolescents in joint custody arrangements who participated in the LAdS survey report relatively high levels of feeling 'at home' at both of their parents. This challenges in itself pre-conceptions about the impossibility to develop a sense of home when one lives within, and across, two post-separation dwellings. But it also shows that, by considering each of their dwelling as their 'home', and by maintaining a rather continuous relationship with their parents beyond the walls of these homes, teenagers demonstrate plasticity and agency in how they deal with, define, and (re)appropriate post-divorce family life.

Qualitative research was, and still is necessary to capture those lived experiences of "home" and "family" in all its complexity and nuances. But our chapter also calls for the development of research drawing on quantitative methods in order to highlight wider trends in the population, and explore the interactions between specific factors, as we have done here. The new research avenues that we have drawn here will need to be further explored in the future, and we hope this chapter will inspire more work on this topic.

Annexes

Annex 1: SOHI Module

Dimension	Indicators	Sample questions
Sense of home	Level of feeling at home at mothers'/fathers'	Do you feel at home when you are at your mothers'/fathers'? Yes, totally; yes, fairly; neither yes nor no; quite not; not at all
Material dimension	Level of comfort:	
	(a) General perception of the dwelling	Tell us if the following statements concerning your mothers'/ fathers' place are correct (by yes or no): (1) there is enough room for everyone: (2) we are feeling a bit cramped.
	(b) Bedroom	Tell us if the following statements concerning bedrooms at their mothers'/fathers' place are correct (1) I have a bedroom of my own; (2) I share a bedroom with my siblings and/or other children; (3) I share a bedroom with my parent; (4) I have no bedroom at all.
Behavioral-relational dimension	Quality of parent-child relations	How good is your relation with your [mother/ father]?; does your [mother/father] admire you and respect you?; to what extend do you feel close and have fun with your [mother/father]?; do you share secrets and intimate feelings with your [mother/father]?; how much does your [mother/father] love you?; how much do you love your [mother/father]?; does your [mother/ father] appreciate the things you do?; does your [mother/father] find it important to listen to you?; does your [mother/father] think you have good ideas?; does your [mother/father] consider that she can learn a lot from you?

(continued)

Dimension	Indicators	Sample questions
	Level of conflict between parents	How often do your parents argue over money?; how often do your parents argue over your education?; how often do your parents argue about the children?; how often do your parents totally disagree with each other?; do your parents sometimes have big conflicts?
	Quality of step-parent-child relations	Does your [mother/father] live with a new partner? If yes, how is your relation with your [mother/father's] partner? Very bad/bad/neither good nor bad/good/very good
	Continuity of communication with parents/step-parents	How often do you use the following items to communicate with your [mother/father]? Facebook Messenger,, WhatsApp/Imessage, Skype, Instagram, Snapchat, TikTok, online games, other (specify)? Never, once a week or less, 2 or 3 times a week, every day, several times a day
		When you stay at your mother's, how often do you have contacts with your father/father's partner? By contact, we mean seeing each other, talking to each from a distance, exchanging messages or online posts, etc. Never, once a week or less, 2 or 3 times a week, every day, several times a day If the answer is often/every day/several times a day: Think about a normal week at your mothers'. How do you usually communicate with your [father/father's partner]? You can choose several proposal: Voice calls (without video, just audio, like a phone call or WhatsAp audio call), video calls, messaging (like texting or instant messages), written posts on social networks (like Facebook walls for instance), photo or video posts on social networks (like TikTok or FB or Snapchat).
		When you stay at your father's, how often do you have contacts with your mother/mothers' partner? By contact, we mean seeing each other, talking to each from a distance, exchanging messages or online posts, etc. (Never, seldom (once a week or less), often (2 or 3 times a week), everyday, several times a day) If the answer is often/every day/several times a day: Think about a normal week at your fathers'. How do you usually communicate with your [mother/mother's partner]? You can choose several proposals: Voice calls (without video, just audio, like a phone call or WhatsAp audio call), video calls, messaging (like texting or instant messages), written posts on social networks (like Facebook walls for instance), photo or video posts on social networks (like TikTok or FB or Snapchat).

Annex 2: Correlation Table

			Mother						Father						Other	
			Sense of home	Comfort	Quality of relation	Communication continuity	Repartnering	Quality of relation with step-parent	Sense of home	Comfort	Quality of relation	Communication continuity	Repartnering	Quality of relation with step-parent	Age	Level of conflict
Mother	Sense of home	r	1	.237**	.556**	.123	.479**	.038	.004	.09	−.166*	.005	−.185*	−.156		
		N	(146)	(146)	(146)	144)	(78)	(146)	(146)	(146) −.036 (141)	(144)	(90)	(146)	(129)		
	Comfort	r		1	.098	.092	−.065	0	.127	.175*	.056	−.079	−.121	.093	−.035	−.037
		N		(158)	(158)	(133)	(154)	(78)	(147)	(158)	(158)	(141)	(154)	(90)	(158)	(129)
	Quality of relation	r			1	.357**	−.026	.334**	−.081	−.006	.168*	.035	−.207**	.112	−.13	−.187*
		N			(158)	(133)	(154)	(78)	(147)	(158)	(158)	(141)	(154)	(90)	(158)	(129)
	Communication continuity	r				1	−.002	.206	−.126	−0.7	.087	.373**	−.091	.031	−.041	−.138
		N				(133)	(131)	(76)	(133)	(133)	(133)	(130)	(131)	(87)	(133)	(125)
	Repartnering	r					1	−.077	.012	−.088	−.074	−.064	.222**	−.067	.005	.249**
		N					(154)	(78)	(145)	(154)	(154)	(139)	(254)	(90)	(154)	(128)
	Quality of relation with step-parent	r						1	.116	.131	.15	.164	−.203	−.102	−.192	−.236*
		N						(78)	(78)	(78)	(78)	(76)	(78)	(60)	(78)	(75)
Father	Sense of home	r							1	.377**	.531**	.369**	.230**	.359**	−.103	−.209*
		N							(147)	(147)	(147)	(141)	(145)	(90)	(147)	(129)
	Comfort	r								1	.210**	.151	.032	.09	−.035	−.153
		N								(158)	(158)	(141)	(154)	(90)	(158)	(129)

(continued)

			Mother						Father						Other	
			Sense of home	Comfort	Quality of relation	Communication continuity	Repartnering	Quality of relation with step-parent	Sense of home	Comfort	Quality of relation	Communication continuity	Repartnering	Quality of relation with step-parent	Age	Level of conflict
	Quality of relation	r									1 (158)	.330** (141)	−.033 (154)	.341** (90)	−.019 (158)	−.310** (129)
	Communication continuity	r N										1 (141)	.14 (139)	.284** (87)	−.126 (141)	−.049 (125)
	Repartnering	r N											1 (154)	0.1 (90)	.007 (154)	−.061 (128)
	Quality of relation with step-parent	r N												1 (90)	−.105 (90)	−.082 (87)
Other	Age	r N													1 (158)	−.028 (129)
	Level of conflict	r N														1 (129)

$^*p < .05$, $^{**}p < .01$

References

Amphoux, P., & Mondada, L. (1989). Le chez-soi dans tous les sens. *Architecture et comportement, 5*(2), 135–150.

Aquilino, W. S. (2006). The noncustodial father? Child relationship from adolescence into young adulthood. *Journal of Marriage and Family, 68*(4), 929–946. https://doi.org/10.1111/j.1741-3737.2006.00305.x

Augé, M. (1992). *Non-lieux. Introduction à une anthropologie de la surmodernité*. Paris: Seuil.

Baldassar, L., Nedelcu, M., Merla, L., & Wilding, R. (2016). ICT-based co-presence in transnational families and communities: Challenging the premise of face-to-face proximity in sustaining relationships. *Global Networks, 16*(2). https://doi.org/10.1111/glob.12108.

Bauserman, R. (2002). Child adjustment in joint-custody versus sole-custody arrangements: A meta-analytic review. *Journal of Family Psychology, 16*(1), 91–102.

Bonnin, P. (1999). La domus éclatée. In P. Bonnin & R. De Villanova (Eds.), *D'une maison à l'autre* (pp. 19–44). Paris: Editions Creaphis.

Bovill, M., & Livingstone, S. (2001). *Bedroom culture and the privatization of media use [online]*. London: LSE Research Online. http://eprints.lse.ac.uk/archive/00000672.

Cashmore, J., Parkinson, P., Weston, R., Patulny, R., Redmond, G., Qu, L., Baxter, J., Rajkovic, M., Sitek, T., & Katz, I. (2010). *Shared care parenting arrangements since the 2006 family law reforms: Report to the Australian government attorney-General's department*. Sydney: Social Policy Research Centre, University of New South Wales.

Casman, M. T., César, A., Waxweiler, C., & Mezabi, D. C. (2010). *Évaluation de l'instauration de l'hébergement égalitaire dans le cadre d'un divorce ou d'une séparation*. Recherche commanditée par le Secrétariat d'État à la Politique des Familles: Université de Liège.

Chen, V., Goh, T., & Li, W. (2010). *Welcome to Facebook: How Facebook influences parent-child relationship*. Paper presented at the Sixth Conference of Taiwan Academy for Information Society, Taiwan.

Côté, D., & Gaborean, F. (2015). Nouvelles normativités de la famille: la garde partagée au Québec, en France et en Belgique. *Canadian Journal of Women and the Law, 27*(1), 22–46.

Csikszentmihalyi, M., & Rochberg-Halton, E. (1981). *The meaning of things. Domestic symbols and the self*. Cambridge: Cambridge University Press.

de Singly, F. (1998). *Habitat et relations familiales*. Paris: Plan Construction et Architecture.

de Singly, F. (2007). *Sociologie de la famille contemporaine*. Paris: Armand Colin.

de Singly, F., & Decup-Pannier, B. (2000). Avoir une chambre chez chacun de ses parents séparés. In F. de Singly (Ed.), *Libres ensemble. L'individualisme dans la vie commune* (pp. 219–236). Paris: Nathan.

de Singly, F., & Ramos, E. (2010). Moments communs en famille. *Ethnologie Française, 40*(1), 11–18.

Drapeau, S., Baude, A., Ouellet, J., Godbout, E., Ivers, H., & Saint-Jacques, M.-C. (2017). Relations between postdivorce custody arrangements, family contexts, and children's adjustment. *Journal of Child Custody, 14*(1), 11–33.

Duchêne-Lacroix, C. (2013). 5ème partie: Caractérisation des situations d'immobilité: réflexions méthodologiques. Éléments pour une typologie des pratiques plurirésidentielles et d'un habiter multilocal. *e-Migrinter*, (11), 151–167. Retrieved from OpenEdition Journals website: http://journals.openedition.org/e-migrinter/323. https://doi.org/10.4000/e-migrinter.323.

Dworkin, J., McCann, E., & McGuire, J. K. (2016). Coparenting in the digital era: Exploring divorced parents' use of technology. In G. Gianesini & S. L. Blair (Eds.), *Divorce, separation, and remarriage: The transformation of family* (Vol. 10, pp. 279–298). Bingley: Emerald Publishing.

Eurostat. (2018, 1 March 2019). *Marriage and divorce statistics*. on https://ec.europa.eu/eurostat/statisticsexplained/index.php/Marriage_and_divorce_statistics. Accessed Apr 2019.

Forsberg, H., Autonen-Vaaraniemi, L., & Kauko, O. (2016). Postdivorce dual residency as narrated childhood experiences. *Journal of Divorce & Remarriage, 57*(7), 433–447.

Galland, O. (2010). Une nouvelle classe d'âge ? *Ethnologie Française, 40*(1), 5–10.

Ganong, L. H., Coleman, M., Feistman, R., Jamison, T., & Markham, M. S. (2012). Communication technology and postdivorce coparenting. *Family Relations, 61*(3), 397–409.

Gollop, M., & Taylor, N. (2012). New Zealand children and young people's perspectives on relocation following parental separation. In M. Freeman (Ed.), *Law and childhood studies: Current legal issues* (Vol. 14, pp. 219–242). Oxford: Oxford University Press.

Gyger Gaspoz, D. (2014). Donner voix à l'espace physique: lorsque la chambre perpétue et écrit l'histoire de l'adolescent au travers d'objets significatifs. Le cas des jeunes en itinérance géographique. *strenae, 7*, 1–13. Retrieved from http://journals.openedition.org website.

Hashemnezhad, H., Heidari, A. A., & Hoseini, P. M. (2013). "Sense of place" and "place attachment". *International Journal of Architecture and Urban Development, 3*(1), 5–12.

Holloway, S., & Valentine, G. (2000). Spatiality and the new social studies of childhood. *Sociology, 34*(4), 763–783.

Hosdey-Radoux, A., Paillet, M., & Woelfle, A. (2017). Le baromètre des parents 2017. *Le Ligueur des parents*, 1–48.

Jorgensen, B., & Stedman, R. (2001). Sense of place as an attitude: Lakeshore owners' attitudes towards their properties. *Journal of Environmental Psychology, 21*, 233–248.

Lee, S. J. (2009). Online communication and adolescent social ties: Who benefits more from Internet use? *Journal of Computer-Mediated Communication, 14*(3), 509–531. https://doi.org/10.1111/j.1083-6101.2009.01451.x

Madianou, M. (2016). Ambient co-presence: Transnational family practices in polymedia environments. *Global Networks*, 1–19. https://doi.org/10.1111/glob.12105.

Marquet, J. (2008). *La famille à l'épreuve de la rupture conjugale*. Bruxelles: Les Cahiers du CEPESS.

Marquet, J., & Merla, L. (2015). *L'intérêt supérieur de l'enfant dans la mosaïque familiale: ce que cela signifie pour les enfants*. Research Report, Louvain-la-Neuve: University of Louvain.

Marquet, J., & Merla, L. (2018). L'espace, un objet central de la sociologie de la famille. In E. Lenel (Ed.), *L'espace des sociologues. Recherches contemporaines en compagnie de Jean Remy* (pp. 141–166). Erès: Toulouse.

Merla, L. (2018). Rethinking the interconnections between family socialization and gender through the lens of multi-local, post-separation families. *Sociologica, 12*(3), 47–57.

Merla, L., & Nobels, B. (2019). Joint physical custody, multi-locality, and lived space: how children from divorced families negotiate a place through space. In L. Murray (Ed.), *Families in motion: spaces, materials and emotions*. Emerald Publishing.

Merla, L., & Papanikolaou, K. (Forthcoming). Doing' and 'displaying' family in polymediatic environments: Conceptual tools for the analysis of children's digital practices. In J. Mikats, S. Kink-Hampersberger, & L. Oates-Indruchová (Eds.), *Creative Families: Gender and Technologies of Everyday Life*. Palgrave McMillan.

Morgan, D. H. G. (2011). *Rethinking family practices*. Basingstoke: Palgrave Macmillan.

Nielsen, L. (2018). Joint versus sole physical custody: Children's outcomes independent of parent–child relationships, income, and conflict in 60 studies. *Journal of Divorce & Remarriage, 59*(4), 247–281.

Noller, P. (2005). Sibling relationships in adolescence: Learning and growing together. *Personal Relationships, 12*(1), 1–22.

Palludan, C., & Winther, I. W. (2016). Having my own room would be really cool: Children's rooms as the social and material organizing of siblings. *Journal of Material Culture*, 1–17. https://doi.org/10.1177/1359183516662675.

Poittevin, A. (2005). Une lecture des espaces pour lire les liens fraternels. *Espaces et sociétés, 1* (120–121), 61–77.

du Preez, A. (2018). Oversharing in the time of selfies: An aesthetics of disappearance? In B. Barbosa Neves, & C. Casimiro (Eds.), *Connecting families? Information and communication technologies, generations, and the life course*. Bristol: Polity Press.

Ramos, E., (2018). La chambre à l'adolescence à l'ère des écrans connectés. Ancrage spatial et mobilité numérique, Les chantiers Leroy Merlin Source, n°24.

Renonciat, A. (2014). La chambre d'enfant: regards croisés. *strenae, 7*, 1–9. Retrieved from http://journals.openedition.org website.

Saini, M., Mishna, F., Barnes, J., & Polak, S. (2013). Parenting online: An exploration of virtual parenting time in the context of separation and divorce. *Journal of Child Custody, 10*(2), 120–140.

Sodermans, A. K., Vanassche, S., Matthijs, K., & Swicegood, G. (2014). Measuring Postdivorce living arrangements: Theoretical and empirical validation of the residential calendar. *Journal of Family Issues, 35*(1), 125–145.

Spruijt, E., & Duindam, V. (2010). Joint physical custody in the Netherlands and the Well-being of children. *Journal of Divorce & Remarriage, 51*, 65–82.

Thompson, B. (2005). Life support: A system of care for military families. *Zero to Three, 25*(6), 49–55.

Van Houcke, F. (2017). Législation sur l'hébergement égalitaire: 10 ans après.... In *CODE – Coordination des ONG pour les droits de l'enfant.*

Vanassche, S., Sodermans, A., & Matthijs, K. (2013). Commuting between two parental households: The association between joint physical custody and adolescent Well-being following divorce. *Journal of Family Studies, 19*(2), 139–158.

Wellman, B. (2018). Foreword: The family has become a network. In B. Barbosa Neves & C. Casimiro (Eds.), *Connecting families? Information and communication technologies, generations, and the life course*. Bristol: Polity Press.

Winther, I. W. (2009). 'Homing oneself' – Home as a practice. *Home and Space, 4*(2), 49–83.

Winther, I. W. (2017). Having my own room would be really cool': Children's rooms as the social and material organizing of siblings. *Journal of Material Culture, 22*(1), 34–51.

Winther, I. W., Palludan, C., Gulløv, E., & Reher, M. M. (2005). *Siblings. Practical and sensitive relations*. Aarhus: Danish School of Education.

Wolman, R., & Pomerance, R. (2012). Telepresence technology in divorce and separation. *Open Access Journal of Forensic Psychology, 4*, 51–68.

Yarosh, S., & Abowd, G. (2011). *Mediated parent–child contact in work-separated families*. Paper presented at the Proceedings of the SIGCHI Conference on Human Factors in Computing Systems (CHI 11), New York.

Yarosh, S., Chew, Y., & Abowd, G. (2009). Supporting parent–child communication in divorced families. *International Journal of Human-Computer Studies, 67*(2), 192–203.

Zaffran, J. (2014). La chambre des adolescent(e)s: espace intermédiaire et temps transitionnel. *strenae, 7*, 1–9. Retrieved from http://journals.openedition.org website.

Zartler, U. (2011). Reassembling families after divorce. In R. Jallinoja & E. Widmer (Eds.), *Families and kinship in contemporary Europe. Rules and practices of relatedness* (pp. 178–191). Basingstoke: Palgrave Macmillan.

Laura Merla is Professor of Sociology at the University of Louvain (UCLouvain, Belgium), and Honorary Research Fellow at the University of Western Australia. Her research has been funded by two Marie Curie Fellowships and an ERC Starting Grant, and focuses on the transformation of family relations in contexts of geographical mobility, through the lenses of migration and family life, and children in post-divorce shared custody arrangements. Her work on families and migration has been widely published in edited books and journals. Her recent publications on children in post-divorce families include a paper on Rethinking the interconnections between family socialization and gender through the lens of multi-local, post-separation families (Sociologica, 2018), a book chapter with Berengère Nobels on Children negotiating their place through space in multi-local, joint physical custody arrangements (in Families in motion edited by Murray et al., 2019), and a book chapter with Jacques Marquet on La parole de l'enfant dans les ruptures et recompositions familiales (in La Parole de l'enfant au bénéfice de ses droits edited by Denéchère, 2019). Laura Merla is a member of the scientific committee of the Journal Enfances, Familles et Générations, of the editorial committee of Recherches sociologiques et anthropologiques, and of the scientific committee of the Caisse nationale des Allocations familiales (CAF, France).

Jonathan Dedonder holds a PhD in Psychology, and is a Research Logistician at the Institute for the Analysis of Change in Contemporary and Historical Societies (IACCHOS) at the University of Louvain (UCLouvain, Belgium). He provides methodological support to academics and other scientists for data collection and analysis of qualitative and quantitative data. He is also an Associate Member of the technological platform Support en Méthodologie et Calcul Statistique (SMCS, UCLouvain), where he provides a variety of training in qualitative, quantitative data analysis and social network analysis (SNA).

Bérengère Nobels is a PhD Student in Sociology at the University of Louvain, Belgium. Her research examines children's lived experiences of multi-locality in the context of joint physical custody arrangements in Belgium, in the larger framework of the ERC Starting Grant Project "MobileKids" (PI: Laura Merla). She recently published with Laura Merla (2019) a chapter entitled "Children negotiating their place through space in multi-local, joint custody arrangements" in the collective volume Families in motion: Ebbing and flowing through space and time (Emerald Publishing, eds Murray L. et al.).

Sarah Murru is a post-doctoral researcher (PhD in Social Sciences, Université libre de Bruxelles). She works at the Interdisciplinary Research Center on Families and Sexualities (CIRFASE) at the University of Louvain (UCLouvain) in Belgium. She is also an Associate Researcher at the Centre for the Study of International Cooperation and Development (CECID), at the Université Libre de Bruxelles (ULB). She has specialized in the conceptualization of resistance, in particular through the study of everyday forms of resistance as well as in the implementation of feminist epistemologies and methodologies. Past research projects include a study of single mothers' resistance in Vietnam. Currently, she is working on children's everyday practices in the context of divorce and shared custody in Italy, within the ERC funded research project "MobileKids" (PI: Laura Merla).

9

Shared Physical Custody and its Socioeconomic Gradient: A Transnational View

Anna Garriga, Jani Turunen, and Laura Bernardi

Abstract This study contributes to the emerging literature on the diffusion of SPC across social strata, by comparing two national contexts, Sweden and Spain, with different prevalence rates of SPC and with diverging social and gender policies in the early XXI century. We draw on the 2006 and 2014 comparative cross-sectional data from the Spanish and Swedish Health Behaviour in School-Aged Children (HBSC), to test two competitive hypotheses (diffusion and diverging destinies hypotheses) on the association of parental socioeconomic status, children's living arrangements in separated families and their relative prevalence in a populaiton. We also examine whether such association is modified by the great increase in SPC in both countries between 2006 and 2014. We present empirical evidence that, independently from the context, SPC arrangements are more frequent among parents with higher socioeconomic status and sole-custody arrangements among other parents; however, social inequality in post-separation arrangements differ in the two countries over time. In Spain, we find evidence in favour of the diffusion hypothesis with increases in the prevalence of SPC going hand in hand with the diffusion of SPC across social strata. By contrast, the Swedish data support the diverging destinies hypothesis with increases in SPC producing no variation in its social stratification over time.

A. Garriga (✉)
Political and Social Department, Universitat Pompeu Fabra, Barcelona, Spain
e-mail: anna.garriga@upf.edu

J. Turunen
Department of Social Work, School of Social Sciences, Södertörn University, Huddinge, Sweden

Stockholm University Demography Unit (SUDA), Stockholm University, Stockholm, Sweden

Centre for Research on Child and Adolescent Mental Health, Karlstad University, Karlstad, Sweden
e-mail: jani.turunen@sh.se

L. Bernardi
LIVES Centre, Swiss Centre of Expertise in Life Course Research and Institute of Social Sciences, University of Lausanne, Lausanne, Switzerland
e-mail: laura.bernardi@unil.ch

Keywords Socioeconomic gradient · Shared physical custody · Diverging destinies · Diffusion hypohtesis · Spain · Sweden

Children's postseparation family arrangements have radically changed due to the increasing legal and social reliance on shared physical custody (SPC) in a great number of Western countries in the last decade. While such changes have been widely debated in the public sphere, particularly because Australia and some European countries have adopted explicit legal regulations about the implementation of SPC (Schweine 2018), only recently have researchers begun to describe their prevalence and examine their consequences.

Most of the research so far reports that the effects of SPC on children's well-being are overall positive, but also that parents in SPC arrangements tend to have a higher socioeconomic status than those in sole-custody arrangements. As a consequence, SPC seems to increase inequalities among children of divorce and separation given that children from better-off parents can partially counterbalance the negative effects of parental separation through SPC, while the latter remains relatively inaccessible for disadvantaged children.

Nevertheless, the contribution of SPC to social inequalities among children depends on whether such a living arrangement remain selective or is spread across social groups, and whether, in the latter case, the positive effects recorded among better off children are also observable among children from different social backgrounds. Research has not yet engaged with the diffusion of SPC across social groups and the consequent disparities among children of different social origin. In this Chapter we contribute to the literature by addressing the question on the evolution of shared physical custody and of its social gradient among children of disrupted family.

As the prevalence of SPC arrangements increases in the population, one scenario is that SPC families become more socially heterogeneous and the initial selectivity of those experiencing SPC gradually disappears as the process of social diffusion goes along (*diffusion hypothesis*). If this is the case, the inequality created by SPC among children of separated families would only be a transitional phenomenon. Children from any background would benefit from the positive effects of SPC over lone parent custody (Sodermans et al. 2013). A second scenario is that the social diffusion of SPC interacts with a parallel increase in the selectivity related to the risk of union break-ups. Recent evidence shows that family instability in most western countries is higher among disadvantaged families and that there has been a reversal of the social gradient of separations (Garriga and Cortina 2017; Härkönen and Dronkers 2006; Kennedy and Thomson 2010). Relatively advantaged parents tend to lead stable and married family lives, while less advantaged ones experience more instances of family dissolution, lone parenthood, and complex family arrangements. In a pivotal work, McLanahan (2004) defined such trends as "diverging destinies". In a context of diverging destinies and class stratification of family developments, the diffusion of SPC among disadvantaged children will not be able to compensate for their increased risk of family disruptions, and social inequality among children of separated families may persist or even increase despite the increase in SPC. The diverging destinies hypothesis offers a theoretical background for a competitive hypothesis to the diffusion of SPC across social strata. As in the case of family stability, better off parents would remain more likely to adopt SPC so that the higher the prevalence of SPC, the higher the inequality among children will be (*diverging destinies hypothesis*).

At present, the few scholars that have examined the diffusion of SPC across social groups have produced mixed evidence in support of both the *diffusion hypothesis* and the *diverging destinies hypothesis* (Brown and Cook 2012; Cancian et al. 2014; Meyer et al. 2017; Sodermans et al. 2013).

The aim of this study is to expand existing research on the diffusion and social selectivity of SPC, with a focus on two country contexts, Spain and Sweden, that had been understudied as far as SPC is concerned. These countries represent compelling contrasting cases for studying social inequalities related to children's living arrangements. While both countries have socially stratified family patterns together with a relatively high percentage of SPC families compared to the European average (Solsona and Spijker 2016), they display different levels of generosity of their welfare states and diverging gender ideologies, characteristics that are related to the patterns of children's postseparation living arrangements (Grunow et al. 2018). Such differences speak in favour of more heterogeneity among SPC families in Sweden than in Spain given that the former context is characterized by a higher level of gender equality. We draw on the 2006 and 2014 comparative cross-sectional data from the Spanish and Swedish Health Behaviour in School-Aged Children (HBSC), to examine whether and to what extent parental socioeconomic status relates to children's living arrangements in separated families as well as whether and the extent to which this association differs between countries and changes between 2006 and 2014, a period in which the prevalence of SPC greatly increases in both.

9.1 Competitive Hypotheses on the Social Stratification of Shared Physical Custody

Low prevalence of SPC is correlated with its concentration among upper-class parents, who adopt alternative custody arrangements after separation or divorce. Pioneer studies on SPC have concluded that the *higher resources averagely available to more advantaged parents* explain social differences in its adoption: higher information levels make them more likely to be aware of the possibility of SPC arrangements when this may be relatively uncommon (Donnelly and Finkelhor 1993); higher financial resources make them able to sustain double residences for their children as well as to engage in the necessary legal procedures to established it under the best conditions; more progressive gender attitudes makes them more likely to have more equal shares of parental responsibilities during union (Sodermans et al.

2013); and higher psychological resources translate into lower levels of interparental conflict which favours adopting SPC (Kitterød and Wiik 2017).

With the *growing support of SPC in family law* (legal presumption for SPC) and with the generalisation of the principle that SPC arrangements have to be considered as the preferred option in cases of separation and divorce debated in tribunals, scholars argue that we should observe a gradual democratisation of SPC across social strata (Sodermans et al. 2013). The trend towards the diffusion of SPC among lower classes would be reinforced by legislative changes favouring SPC, such as granting judges the ability to impose SPC in cases of custodial disagreement, given that low- and middle-class parents tend to have more disagreement on custodial issues than upper-class parents do.

Beside changes in family law, other important social transformations support the *diffusion hypothesis*, that is of a decrease in social inequality in the adoption of SPC rather than solo custody (*Hypothesis 1a*). First, the *growing employment rates of lower class women* (McLanahan 2004), who may now find SPC more attractive than before because of its higher compatibility with paid work. Evidence shows that when the mother is in the labour force rather than inactive during union (Juby et al. 2005), were she to separate from her partner, SPC would be more likely to be chosen. In addition, disadvantaged mothers who had not been working during partnership, have been increasingly incentivised to get into paid employment after separation, by the growing emphasis on activation and welfare to work policies in many European countries as the preferred way to contrast poverty risk among lone parents (Nieuwenhuis 2017). Second, *the diffusion of less traditional gender patterns across social groups* may also have affected the diffusion of SPC. For this reason, increases in SPC prevalence can be partially explained by what Hetherington and Kelly (2002) call "divorce-activated fathers": men who take more active roles in their children's lives after divorce than they did before. Such activation is supported by the results of a qualitative study from Sweden in which mothers in SPC arrangements reported that the fathers had stronger relationships with their children and improved parenting styles after the dissolution of their unions; these mothers also reported that the care obligations had become more gender-neutral (Fransson et al. 2016). Among non-separated parents, recent trends show that *fathers' involvement has also increased in the general population* including in the least advantaged (Dotti Sani and Treas 2016; Sullivan 2010; Sullivan et al. 2014), which may have a positive impact on the increase of SPC among this group. Since, on average, fathers who show little engagement with their children are less likely to engage in SPC after separation than those who are more engaged (Juby et al. 2005; Poortman and van Gaalen 2017; Westphal et al. 2014).

In contrast to the diffusion hypothesis, the competing *diverging destinies hypothesis* would state that the stratification of family break-ups is likely to increase and this increase translates into an unchanged distribution of sole custody over social classes (*Hypothesis 1b*). In support of such a hypothesis are arguments related to the increasing economic and labor market inequality among parents and to the socially stratified father's involvement with their children after separation. First, research in most Western countries has shown that children with lower socioeconomic backgrounds are at a greater risk of living in separated families than other children and this trend has been related to an increase in economic inequality among parents (Cherlin 2018). The arguments go as follows: the increasing polarization between low- and high-paying jobs, especially during the economic recession, and the unfavourable conditions associated to low-paying jobs (precarious jobs, temporary contracts, and unpredictable work schedules) produce ever- growing differences in economic and labour-market conditions between parents of different socioeconomic backgrounds (Smyth et al. 2014). Since financial resources are important to enter a SPC arrangement, economic and labour market inequalities may result in an increasing polarization of post-separation child custody arrangements. Second, since fathers' involvement is an important predictor of SPC, if this is differentially distributed across social groups it may support a diverging destinies hypothesis. There is evidence that the socioeconomic gradient of father's involvement is still present and has even increased in some cases to the advantage of higher status children. (McLanahan 2004; Dotti Sani and Treas 2016; Sullivan 2010; Sullivan et al. 2014). In part this is due to the growing popularity of the intensive parenting ideology among relatively advantaged fathers, sometimes even indicating a class status marker (Kalil 2015; Lareau 2003). Since higher involvement before separation is likely to translate into higher involvement after separation, children having more involved fathers are more likely to have parents (and judges) in favour of post separation SPC arrangements. In addition, regardless of father's level of involvement before separation, fathers with a lower socioeconomic background tend to reduce their involvement after separation (Grätz 2017). Such fathers are more likely than those of higher socioeconomic status to experience additional children with multiple partners after separation and a consequently greater family complexity (Manning et al. 2014; Thomson et al. 2014). Parents' transitions into new partnerships and new parenting roles is generally associated with reduced father involvement with children from previous unions (Berger et al. 2012; Tach et al. 2010). Between the 1980s and the 2000s, the likelihood of bearing children in multiple partnerships and the socioeconomic differences of this demographic behaviour increased in Norway, Sweden, the United States, and Australia (Thomson et al. 2014).

As mentioned above, only a few researchers have focused on the evolution of SPC among socioeconomic groups. These studies' results provide mixed support for both the diffusion and diverging destinies hypotheses. Sodermans et al. (2013) used Flemish data from three cohorts of legally divorced couples from 1971 through 2010 to analyse differences in custody arrangements both before and after two significant legal reforms: the introduction of SPC in 1995 and its adoption as the favoured model in 2006. Sodermans et al. (2013) also showed that among divorced cohorts in which SPC was relatively uncommon, SPC was largely restricted to highly educated parents, and that when SPC became more frequent, it increased significantly among average-educated parents. However, in Flanders, the expansion of SPC remained relatively uncommon among parents with low educational levels. Cancian et al. (2014) analysed court records of divorces in the U.S. state of Wisconsin finalized between 1987 and 2008, showing that in the periods 1993–1998 and 2003–2008, parents with higher total incomes were more likely to have SPC than those with lower incomes. Between 1993 and 1998, the association between SPC and income was particularly strong. Between 2003 and 2008, SPC was still more likely to occur in high-income families but the difference was smaller than in the previous decade. Using the same data, Brown and Cook (2012) found a greater prevalence of SPC in the 2000s than in the 1990s among all income categories except the lowest. Later, Meyer et al. (2017) showed that high-income families were more likely than low-income families to adopt SPC in all time periods and also identified a widening gap in custody outcomes between low- and high-income groups.

All in all, the literature seems to suggest that, on the one hand, there is a tendency towards the diffusion of SPC while on the other, the diffusion process seems to slow down among the most vulnerable families; those with the lowest socioeconomic status. In other words, the diffusion process has positively affected a substantial number of separated families; nonetheless, SPC often remains inaccessible for the least advantaged group.

9.2 Limitations of Existing Research on SPC Social Stratification

Despite the growing relevance of SPC and the open questions about its diffusion across social groups, there are at least three important limitations in the still scant research on SPC social stratification and its development: (a) the focus is on married couples rather than cohabiters; (b) no comparisons between various types of separated families and intact families exist; and (c) the lack of comparative studies hinders identification of the economic and institutional contexts' moderating role in the relationship between custody and children's outcomes.

The lack of consideration for cohabiters is problematic for two reasons. Firstly, excluding children from cohabiting couples excludes a substantial number of children who have experienced parental separation (Meyer et al. 2017; Sodermans et al. 2013). Cohabitation, which is increasing in all Western countries, remains more likely to end in separation than marriage (Kiernan 2004). Secondly, childbearing within cohabitation is more common among parents of low socioeconomic status than among those of high socioeconomic status; consequently, divorced parents tend to have higher socioeconomic status than formerly cohabiting parents (Castro-Martín and Seiz 2014; Garriga et al. 2015; Kennedy and Thomson 2010; Perelli-Harris et al. 2010). For these reasons, excluding cohabiting couples from the analysis results in the exclusion of a disproportionate number of disadvantaged couples, who are the likeliest to cohabit and then separate. Therefore, studying the social diffusion of SPC only among children of divorce while excluding children of separated cohabiters risks creating the misleading perception that SPC is diffused equally across socioeconomic statuses.

The second limitation in the studies on SPC's diffusion across social strata is that their authors have compared the characteristics of couples who have adopted a SPC arrangement to those who have chosen sole custody, without considering couples who do not separate. This lack of a comparison with two-parent families implies not considering important findings from the diverging destinies literature, in which scholars have noted the growing polarization of separation risks and a related worsening of socioeconomic conditions among those who separate irrespective of if they are a lone parent or have SPC. Thus, to understand the dynamics of each type of separated family, it is necessary to compare these groups with intact families.

The third problematic limitation in the SPC literature is its lack of comparative studies across welfare contexts. Regarding parental divorce's effects on children, researchers have explored the extent to which these effects diverge across countries with different levels of generosity towards families with children (Hampden-Thompson 2013; Hampden-Thompson and Pong 2005). However, no scholars have investigated the correlation between the welfare state and the effect of parental socioeconomic status on SPC arrangements.

A welfare state's generosity and ideology can moderate the relationship between parents' socioeconomic status and the probability of shared custody in at least two ways. First, given that parents with SPC must have sufficient resources if they are to accommodate their children in separate households (Melli and Brown 1994), SPC is often more expensive than exclusive custody (in absolute terms). SPC entails double the housing costs and higher related expenditures, including for utilities, household furnishings, play and study spaces, and toys and play equipment. These costs are not significantly reduced when a child spends considerable time with both parents. The economic well-being of mothers with SPC decreases more than that of mothers with sole custody, despite the latter being economically worse off in absolute terms (Bartfeld et al. 2012). In fact, evidence indicates that most fathers in SPC arrangements do not pay child support, which is not the case for noncustodial fathers. For example, in Sweden, 79.7% of sole-custody parents receive child support, as compared to only 10.1% of those who have equal physical custody (Statistics Sweden 2014). Thus, less advantaged mothers may prefer to have sole custody (and receive child support) rather than engage in SPC arrangements. Although a proportion of less advantaged fathers may prefer SPC for purely economic reasons (e.g., to pay less child support), for many of them, the costs of SPC - such as providing extra rooms for children - are greater than the savings in child-support payments due to SPC. This may be why most separated parents, who have relatively few resources adopt sole-custody rather than SPC arrangements. Therefore, it is reasonable to assume that welfare states' generosity can moderate the social gradient of custody arrangements by providing parents of low socioeconomic status with enough resources to maintain separate households that are sufficiently equipped to share child custody. Thus, less advantaged parents in countries with more generous family policies have more chances to engage in SPC than do those in countries where such policies are scarce.

Another possible mechanism behind the welfare state's influence on SPC's diffusion across social strata is the existence and degree of generosity of policies that promote gender equality. Several pieces of evidence support this statement. Firstly, as mentioned, fathers who show little engagement with their children are, on average, less likely to engage in SPC after separation than those who are more engaged (Juby et al. 2005; Poortman and van Gaalen 2017; Westphal et al. 2014) and, among partnered fathers, those with a lower socioeconomic status tend to be less involved in their children's lives than those with a higher status (Dotti Sani and Treas 2016). Secondly, some scholars have found that in countries where family policies encourage both mothers and fathers to engage in paid work and to care for their children, fathers' involvement is more homogeneously spread across the social strata than in countries where such policies do not exist (Gracia and Ghysels 2017; Sayer et al. 2004). A possible explanation of this finding is that less advantaged fathers have less time due to the competing demands of paid work and child-care and, in countries where the state eases external time demands through policies, fathers at all education levels may have more time to spend with their children. In addition to that, the fact that most mothers from all educational levels work in these countries may force fathers to take care of their children. For all of these reasons, if father's involvement is one of the key predictors of SPC and is socially stratified and policies are able to reduce the social gradient of father's involvement, it is reasonable to hypothesize that in countries with generous gender-equality policies, socioeconomic status may have less influence on the SPC arrangement than in countries where such policies are non-existent or scarce.

Overall, in order to overcome the limitations presented here, our study does not only include previously married couples but all children including those from previously cohabiting unions. We compare SPC families not only with lone mother families but also with two –parent families. Moreover, we use a comparative perspective to study the evolution of inequality in SPC, comparing Sweden and Spain.

9.3 Similarities and Differences Between Spain and Sweden as Contexts for SPC

The concurrent evolution of families, separation and SPC in Spain has been very different than in Sweden. The latter is considered as a model of the second demographic transition. Historically, Spain has been regarded as a European country with a particularly great emphasis on the traditional family. Nonetheless, the family situations in these countries are now surprisingly similar, especially concerning the prevalence of divorce, separation, and SPC.

Since the 1960s, Sweden has had one of the highest divorce rates among Western societies. In 1960, the crude divorce rate (the number of divorces per 1000 married women) in Sweden was 1.2 (compared to France, for example, which had a much lower level of 0.7); since the 1980s, the crude divorce rate in Sweden has hovered around 2.4. The trend of less educated couples divorcing more often than relatively highly educated ones also started earlier in Sweden than in most other countries. This tendency emerged around 1980 and became firmly established by 1990 (Hoem 1997). By contrast, Spain was one of the last European countries to enact divorce (in 1981). During the 1980s and 1990s, the number of divorces in Spain was low, as it was in other Mediterranean countries. For example, the 1990 divorce rates in Spain and Italy were 0.5 and 0.6, respectively (Eurostat 2021). However, starting in the 2000s, Spain displayed a unique family development path among Southern European countries, as it moved rapidly from that traditional model to a Nordic family model (Moreno and Marie-Klose 2013). In 2005, Spain's divorce law changed from one of the most restrictive in the world to one of the most liberal (Garriga et al. 2015); by 2014, the divorce rates in Spain and Sweden were far closer, at 2.2 and 2.9, respectively. However, Spanish society has not only witnessed a rapid increase in divorce and lone-parenthood rates; starting in the 2000s, it has also experienced a reversal of the educational gradient for these phenomena from positive to negative (Garriga and Cortina 2017). Traditionally, divorce and sole parenthood were more common among highly educated Spaniards, but today, they are more common among those with low education levels.

Spain and Sweden currently have among the highest rates of SPC within the European context (Solsona and Spijker 2016), even though SPC has evolved very differently in these two countries. Among European countries, Sweden has the highest rate of children in SPC (Bjarnason and Arnarsson 2011). The SPC rate there was 1% in the mid-1980s, increasing to 4% at the beginning of the 1990s; it reached 28% in 2006 and 35% in 2014 (Statistics Sweden 2014)[1]. Swedish legislation has promoted voluntary agreements between parents on custody and contact issues after a union dissolution (Heimer and Palme 2016). Since 1992, a legal presumption of shared custody of children has existed for both cohabiting and married parents; thus, this is the default option unless the parents or a court decide otherwise. In a custody dispute, the courts can decide to apply either shared legal or physical custody against the will of one of the parents as long as the parents do not have severe problems that impede cooperation (Schiratzki 2008). Importantly, however, the Swedish legislation on family issues does not have a presumption of SPC, only legal custody. The legal situation and evolution of SPC in Spain is quite different than in Sweden. Until the divorce reform of 2005 this custody arrangement was only briefly mentioned. However, 5 years later, SPC became the default judicial recommendation in some Spanish autonomous communities and from 2013 the doctrine of the Constitutional Court is that SPC must not be exceptional but normal and even desirable. Following these legal changes, the SPC rate of all custody

[1]The SPC data of Statistics Sweden and of Spanish National Institutes have important differences. Swedish data on SPC from the ULF/SILC surveys have parental reports on the child's living arrangements regardless of previous union status. Spanish data are not self-reports, but the number of sentences of previously married couples with children under 18 where the custody outcome is SPC. In the Spanish legislation it is possible to establish shared custody with different times of stay with parents. The periods may not be equal though they cannot be very decompensated either.

sentences rose from 10% in 2007 to 34% in 2018 (Spanish National Institute of Statistics 2019).

Despite the high rates of SPC in both Spain and Sweden, the existing differences in these welfare states could affect the diffusion of SPC across socioeconomic strata. Firstly, as mentioned, as compared to mothers who have sole custody, mothers with SPC receive less child support from fathers and are therefore more dependent on the labour market and on state financial support. On the one hand, work–family reconciliation policies are necessary for lone mothers to obtain and sustain employment as they have to reconcile work and family without a partner who can share these responsibilities. Sweden's reconciliation policies are more developed than Spain's (Crespi 2007). This could explain why the employment rate among lone mothers is higher in Sweden (74.8%) than in Spain (58.9%; OECD Family Database 2014). Additionally, in Sweden, lone mothers receive more financial support from the state than those in Spain do. For example, in Sweden, the state's contribution to single parents' income, in the form of cash transfers, is around 40%, but in Spain, it is less than 10% (Bradshaw et al. 2018). The differences between the policies of the Swedish and the Spanish Welfare State can be found not only in their generosity but also in their ideology. In Sweden, child custody laws are the result of policymakers' desire to increase gender equality in family life. Since the 1970s, policymakers have worked to implement family policies, such as individual taxation of married couples and gender-neutral parental leave (Schiratzki 2008). These laws and policies are meant to enforce married and cohabiting fathers' care obligations (Bergman and Hobson 2002). In Spain, custody laws have not been accompanied by other family policies oriented towards increasing gender equality. It is therefore reasonable to think that separated families of low socioeconomic status will enjoy better economic conditions and greater father involvement in Sweden than in Spain and therefore that SPC should be more evenly spread across social strata in Sweden than in Spain, despite the increasing SPC rates in both countries (*Hypothesis 2*).

9.4 Data and Methods

We drew on Spanish and Swedish cross-sectional survey data from the 2006 and 2014 HBSC surveys, which the World Health Organization carries out every 4 years (Currie et al. 2008; Inchley et al. 2016). The HSBC includes a sample of adolescents, aged 11–16 years, from more than 40 countries across Europe and North America. Its self-completed questionnaires are administered in schools.

The Swedish sampling relied on a two-step cluster design. First, schools were randomly selected; then, for each chosen school, the students in one class were randomly selected to answer the questionnaire. For the Spanish sample, schools were selected using multistage stratified random sampling, taking into account age, region (i.e., autonomous community), school site (rural or urban), and type of school (public or private). The basic sample unit for the Spanish sample was also a class.

Table 9.1 Descriptive percentages of the Spanish and Swedish 2006 and 2014 samples

Variables	Spain		Sweden	
	2006	2014	2006	2014
Family structure				
Two parents	86.3	83.2	75.4	73.6
Shared physical custody	0.9	5.8	8.2	15.5
Lone mother	12.8	11.02	16.4	10.9
Adolescent gender				
Male	47.9	49.0	49.1	48.4
Female	52.1	51.0	50.1	50.9
Foreign background				
Domestic	85.3	87.1	95.4	89.4
Foreign	14.7	19.8	4.4	9.5
Age				
11–12	34.2	34.2	34.0	34.2
13–14	30.9	33.0	31.3	29.0
15–16	34.9	32.8	34.7	36.0
Family affluence scale				
Low	14.3	13.2	6.2	4.9
Mid	45.8	56.2	36.9	39.1
High	39.9	30.6	56.9	56.0
N	15,559	13,828	4000	6994

The response rates for the Spanish survey were 82%[2] in 2006 (Simões et al. 2012) and 83% in 2014 (Simões et al. 2018); the rates for the Swedish survey were 85% in 2006 (Swedish National Institute of Public Health 2006) and 69.4% in 2014 (Public Health Agency of Sweden 2015). The final Spanish samples comprised 15,559 adolescents in 2006 and 13,828 in 2014; the final Swedish samples comprised 4000 adolescents in 2006 and 6994 in 2014. We included dummy variables for the missing cases of the independent variables.

In the models, we used indicators of family type, parents' socioeconomic status, and control variables; these indicators are shown in Table 9.1 and are described below in more detail.

9.4.1 Family Structure

The family-structure variable groups adolescents into three categories: those in (a) two-parent families, (b) SPC families, or (c) one-parent (lone-mother[3]) families.

[2]The Spanish sample covers adolescents from age 11 or 12 up to age 17 or 18, and its response rates take into account adolescents from ages 11–12 to 17–18.

[3]Children living in a one-parent household with their father are not included. On the one hand, there are too few lone fathers to be analysed separately; on the other hand, they are a very select group.

The questions about family structure on the 2006 and 2014 Swedish surveys and on the 2006 Spanish survey were identical:

- "With whom do you live in the home that you live all or most of the time?" (*mother*, *father*, or *another person*)
- "Do you have another home?" (*yes* or *no*)
- "How often do you stay in the second home?" (*half the time*, *regularly but less than half the time*, *sometimes*, or *almost never*)
- "With whom do you live in the second home?" (*mother*, *father*, or *another person*)

The children who lived with both parents in one household were defined as living in a two-parent family. Those who lived approximately half the time with one parent and half the time with the other parent in separate homes were defined as having an SPC arrangement. Finally, those who lived only or primarily with their mother were defined as having a lone-mother arrangement. The 2014 Spanish survey also includes a question with several descriptions of family situations as part of the family-structure variable. Adolescents who selected the choice *I live with my mother and father* were considered to be in a two-parent family. Those who selected *I live half of the time with my mother and half of the time my father* were classified as being in a SPC family. Those who indicated that *I live with my mother and stay with my father less than half the time* were considered to be in a lone-mother family.

Data on parental occupation can be difficult to collect from young people because they often do not know or are not willing to reveal such information, which results in a high nonresponse rate (Currie et al. 1997, 2008; Molcho et al. 2007; Wardle et al. 2002). Given adolescents' difficulties in answering direct questions about their families' socioeconomic status, we instead measured perceived family affluence by means of the Family Affluence Scale II (FAS-II). The FAS-II[4] includes items that reflect a family's material resources, patterns of consumption, and purchasing power (Currie et al. 2008). The resulting score is based on four items:

1. "Does your family own a car, van, or truck?" (*no* [0]; *yes, one* [1]; or *yes, two or more* [2])
2. "Do you have your own bedroom for yourself?" (*no* [0] or *yes* [1])
3. "During the past twelve months, how many times did you travel away on holiday (vacation) with your family?" (*not at all* [0], *once* [1], *twice* [2], or *more than twice* [3])
4. "How many computers does your family own?" (*none* [0], *one* [1], *two* [2], or *more than two* [3]).

A score of 3 on the third and fourth questions (on vacations and computers) was considered as 2. Therefore, the total FAS-II score has values ranging from 0 to

[4]The 2014 survey used the third version of the survey (FAS-III). However, this version has the same items as the FAS-II (as well as some additional items). For this reason, in 2014, we only used the indicators from the FAS-II, to ensure that our findings from 2006 and 2014 would be comparable.

7. Scores of 0 through 3 are *low*, those of 4 or 5 are *mid*, and those of 6 or 7 are *high* (Due et al. 2009). We merged the *low* and *mid* categories because not enough cases of the former existed among SPC families to perform an analysis. For this reason, we coded the final variable as *low or mid* (1) or *high* (0).

The children's gender was coded as *boy* (0) or *girl* (1). We used two questions ("In which country was your mother born?" and "In which country was your father born?") to measure foreign background, giving the value of 0 if both parents were born in the country of the sample (Spain or Sweden) and 1 if at least one parent was not born in that country[5]. We also controlled for the children's age group (*11–12*, *13–14*, or *15–16*).

We analysed the data using multinomial logistic regressions with three categories of family type (*two-parent household*, *sole custody*, or *SPC*) as the dependent variable. This statistical methodological approach is justified by the choice of a dependent variable with three nominal (unordered) categories. Initially, we analysed each country separately; we then combined the data for both countries to analyse the potential country-interaction effects. To adjust for the sampling design, we weighted the results—with the exception of those comparing Sweden in 2006 and 2014, which we did not weight because the 2006 Swedish sample lacked weights.

To test our hypothesis about the evolution of SPC among socioeconomic groups (Hypothesis 1), we use separated multinomial logistic regression models for Spain and Sweden. For each country, we perform a model for 2006 data and another model for 2014 data in order to observe to what extent the magnitude of the effect of family affluence on custody arrangements has changed over time. Then, to test if the observed change in the coefficients of family affluence is significant or not, we pool data for both survey years and add the main effect of survey year and an interaction term between family affluence and survey year to the model. Finally, to test differences in the relationship between family affluence and custody arrangements between Sweden and Spain (*Hypothesis 2*), we pool 2014 Swedish and Spanish data and perform a multinomial logistic model that includes family affluence, survey year and an interaction term between family affluence and survey year alongside control variables.

9.5 Results

9.5.1 Descriptive Results

Tables 9.2 and 9.3 present the categories of family type according to family affluence for Spain and Sweden, respectively. For Spain in 2006, the prevalence of two-parent

---

[5]We controlled for foreign background because SPC is less common among immigrants (Bergström et al. 2013; Solsona and Spijker 2016) and because immigrants more often have a low socioeconomic status, relative to native-born people (Gotsens et al. 2015; Tinghög et al. 2007).

Table 9.2 Prevalence of family arrangements in Spain by family affluence (percentages)

Family Affluence Scale	2006			2014		
	Two parents	Shared physical custody	Lone mother	Two parents	Shared physical custody	Lone mother
Low	85.14	0.50	14.37	82.15	5.04	12.81
High	87.83	1.52	10.65	87.49	5.59	6.91
Low (separated only)		1.41	98.59		11.16	88.84
High (separated only)		7.60	92.40		14.73	85.27

Table 9.3 Prevalence of family arrangements in Sweden by family affluence (percentages)

Family Affluence Scale	2006			2014		
	Two parents	Shared physical custody	Lone mother	Two parents	Shared physical custody	Lone mother
Low	70.19	6.79	23.02	69.77	9.45	20.79
High	79.51	9.15	11.34	76.99	11.55	11.47
High (separated only)		22.77	77.23		31.24	68.76
Low (separated only)		44.66	55.34		50.18	49.82

families was greater among highly affluent families than among less affluent ones. These differences were larger in 2014. In 2006, among separated families, the most affluent ones had a higher percentage of SPC than the least affluent ones. These differences also existed in 2014, albeit to a lesser extent.

In Sweden, the differences in the prevalence of two-parent families based on family affluence were greater than they were in Spain for both years. Highly affluent families, relative to less affluent families, were more likely to have the two-parent setup. In 2006, the percentage of SPC families was twice as high for very affluent families than for less affluent ones. In 2014, this difference was smaller but was still very large. In 2006 and 2014, among families without two parents, Sweden has a higher proportion of SPC families than Spain did for all levels of family affluence.

Nevertheless, these descriptive results do not rule out the possibility that the differences observed between custody arrangements and family affluence could be explained by differences in socio-demographics. Hence, we performed multinomial logistic regressions to test the effect of family affluence while controlling for these other characteristics.

9.5.2 Associations Between Adolescents' Living Arrangements and Family Affluence in 2014 and 2006

Spain Table 9.4 shows that in 2006, adolescents in less affluent families had a lower probability of living in a SPC family than in a two-parent family (Model 1); however, the effect of family affluence was not significant in 2014 (Model 2). The interaction between year and family affluence was positive and significant (Model

Table 9.4 Multinomial logistic regression of family arrangements in Spain (coefficients)

	Shared physical custody vs. two parents			Lone mother vs. two parents			Lone mother vs. shared physical custody		
	2006	2014	Interaction	2006	2014	Interaction	2006	2014	Interaction
	Model 1	Model 2	Model 3	Model 4	Model 5	Model 6	Model 7	Model 8	Model 9
FAS (ref.: High)									
Low or mid	−1.11***	−0.04	−1.0***	0.27***	0.69***	0.28***	1.39***	0.74***	1.35***
Year (ref.: 2006)			1.28***			−0.54***			−1.82***
Interaction									
Low or mid × 2014			1.04***			0.43**			−0.61*
Gender (ref.: Male)	−0.03	−0.19	−0.16	0.08	0.24*	0.0765	0.12	0.42**	0.31*
Foreign background (ref domestic)	0.36	−0.09	−0.03	0.86***	0.69***	0.719***	0.50	0.79***	0.81***
Age (ref.: 11–12)									
13–14	−0.47	−0.04	−0.12	0.10	0.45***	0.23**	0.57*	0.48***	0.36*
15–16	−0.34	−0.08	−0.16	0.07	0.64***	0.30***	0.41	0.72***	0.45**
Constant	−3.80***	−2.60***	−3.86***	−2.32***	−3.22***	−2.47***	1.49***	−0.61**	1.40***
Log-likelihood	−6587.20	−6577.50	−13,190.36	−6587.20	−6577.50	−12,504.041	−6587.20	−6577.50	−13,190.36

Note. *FAS* Family Affluence Scale. + $p < .10$, *$p < .05$, **$p < .01$, ***$p < .001$

3), indicating a trend towards reduced socioeconomic differences between these family types. By contrast, Models 4 and 5 show that adolescents with *low or mid* family affluence had a higher probability of living in lone-mother families than in two-parent families for both 2006 and 2014. The positive and significant interaction of Model 6 indicates that socioeconomic differences between these family types increased during this period. Models 7 and 8 show that adolescents from less well-off families were more likely to live in lone-mother families than in SPC families for both 2006 and 2014. Last, the effect of family affluence on the probability of living in a lone-mother family (as opposed to in a SPC family) decreased between these years because the interaction between year and FAS-II score was negative and significant (Model 9).

Focusing on the control variables' effects, Models 1 and 2 indicate no significant differences in the probability of living in a SPC family, relative to living in a two-parent family, based on gender, foreign background, or age of the child. However, control variables had notably different effects on the probability of living in a lone-mother family compared to living in a two-parent or SPC family. Adolescents with a foreign background had a higher probability of living in a lone-mother family than in a two-parent family for both years. Some demographic variables had different impacts in each year. In the 2014 data, older adolescents have a higher probability than younger adolescents of living in a lone-mother family than in a two-parent family or SPC. Similarly, girls were more likely to live in a lone-mother family than in a two-parent or SPC family in 2014. The effect of foreign background on the probability of living in a lone-mother family rather than in a SPC family was significant in 2014 but not in 2006.

Sweden The multinomial models from Table 9.5 show that in Sweden, adolescents in SPC families were no more affluent than those in two-parent families in both 2006 and 2014; there were no significant between-year differences in the effects of family affluence (Model 3). Less affluent adolescents, however, had a higher probability of living in a lone-mother family than in a two-parent family in both years (Models 4 and 5). Model 6 shows that the interaction between FAS level and year was insignificant, which indicates that the effect of family affluence is stable over time. Adolescents in low- or mid-FAS families had a higher probability of living in a lone-mother family in both 2014 and 2006 (Models 7 and 8), and the differences between years were not significant (Model 9).

Models 1 and 2 show that in both 2006 and 2014, the probability of living in a SPC family rather than a two-parent family did not differ by gender or age of the child. Adolescents with foreign backgrounds had less risk of living in a SPC family rather than in a two-parent family in 2006, but there was no such difference in 2014. In both years, compared to younger adolescents, older ones had a higher probability of living in a lone-mother family than in a two-parent or SPC family. Girls were more likely than boys to live in a lone-mother family than in a two-parent family in 2014. Adolescents with a foreign background were more likely to live in a lone-

Table 9.5 Multinomial logistic regression of family arrangements in Sweden (coefficients)

	Shared physical custody vs. two parents			Lone mother vs. two parents			Lone mother vs. shared physical custody		
	2006	2014	Interaction	2006	2014	Interaction	2006	2014	Interaction
	Model 1	Model 2	Model 3	Model 4	Model 5	Model 6	Model 7	Model 8	Model 9
FAS (ref.: High)									
Low or mid	−0.14	−0.12	−0.17	0.84***	0.71***	0.85***	0.99***	0.82***	1.03***
Year (ref.: 2006)			0.27**			0.03			−0.24*
Interaction									
Low or mid × 2014			0.06			−0.14			−0.21
Gender (ref.: Male)	−0.12	0.04	−0.01	0.25***	0.19**	0.22***	0.37**	0.16	0.23**
Foreign background (ref: Domestic)	−1.98**	0.00	−0.00	−0.00	0.00	−0.00	1.98**	0.00	0.00
Age (ref.: 11–12)									
13–14	−0.16	0.10	0.01	0.20+	0.39***	0.31***	0.36*	0.29*	0.30**
15–16	−0.22	−0.13	−0.17*	0.48***	0.63***	0.57***	0.70***	0.76***	0.73***
Constant	−1.95***	−1.89***	−2.10***	−2.34***	−2.39***	−2.39	−0.38*	−0.50***	−0.28*
Log-likelihood	−2727.434	−4824.295	−7563.176	−2727.434	−4824.295	−7563.176	−2727.434	−4824.295	−7563.176

Note. *FAS* Family Affluence Scale. + $p < .10$, *$p < .05$, **$p < .01$, ***$p < .001$

Table 9.6 Country-interaction models of multinomial logistic regression for family arrangements in 2014 (coefficients; weighted sample)

	Shared custody vs. two parents (Model 1)	Lone mother vs. two parents (Model 2)	Lone mother vs. shared custody (Model 3)
FAS (ref.: High)			
Low or mid	−0.08	0.72***	0.80***
Country (ref.: Sweden)	0.04***	−0.57***	0.29**
Interaction			
Low or mid × Spain	0.11	−0.07	−0.10
Gender (ref.: Male)	0.07	0.17***	−0.10
Foreign background (ref: Domestic)	0.00	−0.01	−0.00
Age (ref.: 11–12)			
13–14	0.09	0.31**	0.21+
15–16	−0.12***	0.60***	0.72***
Constant	−1.91***	−2.36***	−0.44***
Log-likelihood	−172,857.3	−172,857.3	−172,857.3

Note. FAS Family Affluence Scale. + $p < .10$ *$p < .05$ **$p < .01$, ***$p < .001$

mother family than in a SPC family in 2006, but there were no significant differences by foreign background in 2014.

Comparing Spain and Sweden As shown in Model 1 of Table 9.6,in 2014, the interaction term between family affluence and country is significant which indicates that there were no significant differences by country in the probability of living in a SPC family rather than in a two-parent family (Model 1). Model 2 of Table 9.6 indicates that adolescents of *low or mid* affluence have similar chances of living in a lone-mother family relative to living in a two-parent family in both Sweden and Spain. In addition, Model 3 of Table 9.6 shows that family affluence's effect on the probability of living in a lone-mother family rather than in a SPC family did not differ by country.

9.6 Discussion

This study contributes to the emerging literature on the diffusion of SPC across social strata, by considering children from married and cohabiting unions and by comparing two contexts, Sweden and Spain, with different prevalences of SPC and with diverging social and gender policies. The results suggest that despite the fact that SPC correlates with positive outcomes for children, this effect is unevenly distributed across social strata both in Spain and Sweden. As already demonstrated in the literature, SPC arrangements are more frequent among parents with higher socioeconomic status and sole-custody arrangements among other parents. More original are the results related to the testing of the two competing hypotheses about the evolution of inequality in post-separation childcare arrangements; the *diffusion hypothesis* and the *diverging destinies hypothesis*. Our study clearly shows that the evolution of inequality in post-separation arrangements differ in the two countries. In Spain, we found evidence in favour of the diffusion hypothesis (*Hypothesis 1a*), with increases in the prevalence of SPC going hand in hand with the diffusion of SPC across social strata. By contrast, the Swedish data support the diverging destinies hypothesis (*Hypothesis 1b*), with increases in SPC producing no variation in its social stratification over time. This latter result was surprising as we had expected (*Hypothesis 2*) that SPC would be more widespread across social strata in Sweden than in Spain, given the greater degree of promotion of gender-equal parenting in Sweden and given the greater generosity of the Swedish welfare state towards broken-up families. However welfare state and gender regimes do not seems to make a difference in the association of family affluence and SPC.

How to explain such results? One possibility is to turn towards the countries' legal systems and the way in which it shapes living arrangements opportunities and costs. In Sweden, there is no legal presumption of SPC, and most custody arrangements are decided by the parents outside of the court system and without the advice of a legal counsellor. This leads to the high social selectivity of such arrangements. In a report from Statistics Sweden (2014), only about 4% of respondents said that their decisions were based on "legal advice" (including court decisions and advice from privately hired divorce lawyers). An additional 7% applied advice from social services, whereas over three quarters of parents reported having decided on their own. In Spain, by contrast, some autonomous communities have a legal presumption in favour of SPC while all other cases are decided through a tribunal procedure and the Spanish courts seem much more frequently involved in custodial decisions than the Swedish courts are. The intervention of judges and a legal framework pushing for the implementation of SPC may be more central than the generosity of the welfare state in the accelerated expansion of SPC across social strata.

Another possible explanation of the support for the diverging destinies hypothesis in Sweden and for the diffusion hypothesis in Spain is that our data are capturing different periods of the evolution of SPC in each country. The Spanish HBSC data were collected shortly after the moment in which SPC was included in the legislation, whereas the Swedish data was collected when this living arrangement was already relatively widespread. Since the prevalence of SPC is lower in Spain than in Sweden both in 2006 and 2014, the two contexts are at different stages of the phenomenon. It is well possible that social diffusion is typically related to the first years of strong implantation of the legal framework but it then slows down after having reached a critical threshold. In order to test for such possibility, one shall rather compare Spain in 2006 and 2014, with Sweden in the years in which SPC was at similar levels. Future research may test the diffusion hypothesis in Spain when prevalence rates are higher and similar to Swedish ones nowadays.

This research has limitations that need to be acknowledged in order to correctly interpret the results. First, while the HBSC is the only available data set that allows for comparative research of SPC families, its characteristics limit the analyses in several ways. The first limitation concerns the FAS indicator. Ideally, one would prefer to measure the socioeconomic status of adolescents in SPC by differentiating each parent's household. Such households should be modelled separately because these children are living in at least two households with potentially different levels of resources. However, the FAS questionnaire of the HBSC implicitly assumes that all adolescents can only refer to one household in their responses (e.g., "Does your family own a car, van, or truck?"). This makes it impossible to determine whether the children are referring to one household or are pooling the resources of both. As an example, one of the questions from the FAS-II is: "during the past twelve months, how many times did you travel away on holiday (vacation) with your family?". For adolescents from SPC households, we do not know exactly with whom they travelled: with their mother, their father, or both. For this reason, we cannot rule out the possibility that this study's results would differ if we could have used FAS-II results for each household where the adolescents in SPC arrangements live.

Another limitation of this study's data is the impossibility of distinguishing among the various categories of socioeconomic status; previous researchers have come to different conclusions regarding children at the low and middle income levels. Additionally, this study only has one subjective measure of socioeconomic status. Previous scholars have used objective indicators of parents' socioeconomic status such as education or income, which parents answered. However, we used family affluence as perceived by the adolescent. This single subjective source may not comprehensively capture the socioeconomic conditions of the adolescent's family. The HBSC database offers information on both the father's and the mother's occupation, but it has a high number of missing cases – especially among adolescents who live in lone-mother families – so we had to leave this indicator out. Moreover, despite evidence from the sociological literature that parents' education is one of the most important indicators in terms of both children's well-being and changes related to family structure (e.g., a higher rate of separation among less educated people), the HBSC's international data file does not include questions regarding parents' educational level, with the exception of the Spanish survey in 2014. The database also includes no information about income. Another limitation of the data is that SPC can be defined only as a perfectly equal share between parents (children living half time with each parent). Less restrictive forms of SPC (30–70 shares) may be less costly (economically and practically) for parents and therefore, the diverging results by social strata are rather intensified here. If equal sharing is likely to be more constraining for parents, still some form of sharing is qualitatively different from an arrangement where the child has only visiting rights toward the non-resident parent.

All in all, this study's findings imply a need for more research on the prevalence of SPC across social strata comparing different countries; in addition, they show that cohabiting couples should be included in the sample. Future researchers should overcome this study's acknowledged limitations by using both objective indicators (e.g., income, education, and occupation) and subjective ones to measure parents' socioeconomic status (with responses from both parents and children). Scholars should also consider the differences in socioeconomic status between parents' households for children in SPC arrangements. Furthermore, these future investigations should focus on explaining the differences between countries.

9.7 Conclusion

Despite this study's limitations, its findings raise several important questions regarding the effects of inequality on children's well-being. In Sweden, taking into account the results from both this study and from the diverging destinies literature, we affirm that children from lower socioeconomic strata (as compared to those from higher strata) have a greater probability of parental separation and a lesser probability of living in SPC. In other words, there are two unequal family patterns, both before and after separation. Each pattern may be reinforcing (or helping to create) diverging destinies for children under the second demographic transition.

On the other hand, in the Spanish case, the unequal prevalence of SPC across socioeconomic strata seems to be decreasing. This does not mean, however, that the benefits of SPC are equally diffused to all children. In fact, it means quite the opposite. There are reasons to suspect that SPC may be positive for children of high socioeconomic status but not for those of low socioeconomic status. For less advantaged parents, the conditions of SPC may not be ideal, as it is more expensive than sole custody; these parents also tend to have more conflict in their relationships than more advantaged parents do. The research on SPC's effects on children's well-being, thus far, has only focused on average effects. No researchers have yet checked the differential effects of SPC across socioeconomic strata. Conducting such studies is very important to determine the real effects that the diffusion of SPC has on less advantaged families.

The results of this study indicate that the current debates on the diverging destinies of children and on SPC's diffusion and benefits for children are not separate; rather, they must be analysed together. This research is of crucial importance because several European countries are currently debating the possibility of adopting SPC as a default system.

References

Bartfeld, J., Ahn, H. M., & Ryu, J. H. (2012). *Economic Well-being of divorced mothers with varying child placement arrangements in Wisconsin: Contributions of child support and other income sources*. Madison: Institute for Research on Poverty, University of Wisconsin–Madison.

Berger, L. M., Cancian, M., & Meyer, D. R. (2012). Maternal re-partnering and new-partner fertility: Associations with nonresident father investments in children. *Children and Youth Services Review, 34*(2), 426–436.

Bergman, H., & Hobson, B. (2002). Compulsory fatherhood: The coding of fatherhood in the Swedish welfare state. In B. Hobson (Ed.), *Making men into fathers* (pp. 92–124). Cambridge: Cambridge University Press. https://doi.org/10.1017/CBO9780511489440.005.

Bergström, M. et al. (2013). Living in two homes-a Swedish national survey of wellbeing in 12 and 15 year olds with joint physical custody. *BMC Public Health, 13*, 868.

Bjarnason, T., & Arnarsson, A. M. (2011). Joint physical custody and communication with parents: A cross-national study of children in 36 Western countries. *Journal of Comparative Family Studies, 42*(6), 871–890.

Bradshaw, J., Keung, A., & Chzhen, Y. (2018). Cash benefits and poverty in single-parent families. In R. Nieuwenhuis & L. Maldonado (Eds.), *The triple bind of single-parent families* (1st ed., pp. 337–358). Bristol: Bristol University Press. https://doi.org/10.2307/j.ctt2204rvq.21.

Brown, P., & Cook, S. T. (2012). *Children's placement arrangements in divorce and paternity cases in Wisconsin*. Madison: Institute for Research on Poverty, University of Wisconsin—Madison.

Cancian, M., Meyer, D. R., Brown, P. R., & Cook, S. T. (2014). Who gets custody now? Dramatic changes in children's living arrangements after divorce. *Demography, 51*(4), 1381–1396. https://doi.org/10.1007/s13524-014-0307-.

Castro-Martín, T., & Seiz, M. (2014). *La transformación de las familias en España desde una perspectiva socio-demografica, VII: Informe sobre exclusión y desarrollo social en España 2014* [The transformation of families in Spain from a socio-demographic perspective, VII: Report on exclusion and social development in Spain 2014] (Working Paper 1.1). Madrid: Fundación Fomento de Estudios Sociales y Sociología Aplicad.

Cherlin, A. J. (2018). How inequality drives family formation: The prima facie case. In N. R. Cahn, J. Carbone, L. F. DeRose, & W. B. Wilcox (Eds.), *Unequal family lives: Causes and consequences in Europe and the Americas* (pp. 69–82). Cambridge: Cambridge University Press.

Crespi, I. (2007). *Gender mainstreaming and family policy in Europe: Perspectives, researches and debates* (pp. 13–97). Macerata: Edizioni Università di Macerata.

Currie, C. E., Elton, R. A., Todd, J., & Platt, S. (1997). Indicators of socioeconomic status for adolescents: The WHO health behaviour in school-aged children survey. *Health Education Research, 12*(3), 385–397.

Currie, C., Molcho, M., Boyce, W., Holstein, B., Torsheim, T., & Richter, M. (2008). Researching health inequalities in adolescents: The development of the health behaviour in school-aged children (HBSC) family affluence scale. *Social Science & Medicine, 66*(6), 1429–1436. https://doi.org/10.1016/j.socscimed.2007.11.024.

Donnelly, D., & Finkelhor, D. (1993). Who has joint custody? Class differences in the determination of custody arrangements. *Family Relations*, 57–60.

Dotti Sani, G. M., & Treas, J. (2016). Educational gradients in parents' child-care time across countries, 1965–2012. *Journal of Marriage and Family, 78*(4), 1083–1096.

Due et al. (2009). Socioeconomic Inequality in Exposure to Bullying During Adolescence: A Comparative, Cross-Sectional, Multilevel Study in 35 Countries. *American Journal of Public Health, 99*(5), 907–914.

Eurostat. (2021). *Divorce indicators*. https://appsso.eurostat.ec.europa.eu/nui/show.do?dataset=demo_ndivind&lang=en. Accessed April 13, 2021.

Fransson, E., Sarkadi, A., Hjern, A., & Bergström, M. (2016). Why should they live more with one of us when they are children to us both? Parents' motives for practicing equal joint physical custody for children aged 0–4. *Children and Youth Services Review, 66*, 154–160.

Garriga, A., & Cortina, C. (2017). The change in single mothers' educational gradient over time in Spain. *Demographic Research, 36*, 1859–1888. https://doi.org/10.4054/DemRes.2017.36.61.

Garriga, A., Sarasa, S., & Berta, P. (2015). Mother's educational level and single motherhood: Comparing Spain and Italy. *Demographic Research, 33*, 1165–1210. https://doi.org/10.4054/DemRes.2015.33.42.

Gotsens, M., Malmusi, D., Villarroel, N., Vives-Cases, C., Garcia-Subirats, I., Hernando, C., & Borrell, C. (2015). Health inequality between immigrants and natives in Spain: The loss of the healthy immigrant effect in times of economic crisis. *The European Journal of Public Health, 25*(6), 923–929.

Gracia, P., & Ghysels, J. (2017). Educational inequalities in parental care time: Cross-national evidence from Belgium, Denmark, Spain, and the United Kingdom. *Social Science Research, 63*, 166–180.

Grätz, M. (2017). Does separation really lead fathers and mothers to be less involved in their children's lives? *European Sociological Review, 33*(4), 551–562.

Grunow, D., Begall, K., & Buchler, S. (2018). Gender ideologies in Europe: A multidimensional framework. *Journal of Marriage and Family, 80*(1), 42–60.

Hampden-Thompson, G. (2013). Family policy, family structure, and children's educational achievement. *Social Science Research, 42*(3), 804–817. https://doi.org/10.1016/j.ssresearch.2013.01.005.

Hampden-Thompson, G., & Pong, S. (2005). Does family policy environment moderate the effect of single-parenthood on children's academic achievement? A study of 14 European countries. *Journal of Comparative Family Studies, 36*(2), 227–248.

Härkönen, J., & Dronkers, J. (2006). Stability and change in the educational gradient of divorce. A comparison of seventeen countries. *European Sociological Review, 22*(5), 501–517.

Heimer, M., & Palme, J. (2016). Rethinking child policy post-UN convention on the rights of the child: Vulnerable children's welfare in Sweden. *Journal of Social Policy, 45*(03), 435–452. https://doi.org/10.1017/S0047279415000744.

Hetherington, E. M., & Kelly, J. (2002). *For better or for worse: Divorce reconsidered*. New York: Norton.

Hoem, J. M. (1997). Educational gradients in divorce risks in Sweden in recent decades. *Population Studies, 51*(1), 19–27. https://doi.org/10.1080/0032472031000149696.

Inchley, J., Currie, D., Young, T., Samdal, O., Torsheim, T., & Augustson, L. (Eds.). (2016). *Growing up unequal: Gender and socioeconomic differences in young people's health and Well-being (health behaviour in school-aged children [HBSC] study: International report from the 2013/2014 survey)*. Copenhagen: World Health Organization Regional Office for Europe.

Juby, H., Le Bourdais, C., & Marcil-Gratton, N. (2005). Sharing roles, sharing custody? Couples' characteristics and children's living arrangements at separation. *Journal of Marriage and Family, 67*(1), 157–172.

Kalil, A. (2015). Inequality begins at home: The role of parenting in the diverging destinies of rich and poor children. In P. R. Amato, A. Booth, S. M. McHale, & J. Van Hook (Eds.), *Families in an era of increasing inequality: Diverging destinies* (pp. 63–82). Cham: Springer International.

Kennedy, S., & Thomson, E. (2010). Children's experiences of family disruption in Sweden: Differentials by parent education over three decades. *Demographic Research, 23*(17), 479–508.

Kiernan, K. (2004). Unmarried cohabitation and parenthood in Britain and Europe. *Law & Policy, 26*(1), 33–55.

Kitterød, R. H., & Wiik, K. A. (2017). Shared residence among parents living apart in Norway. *Family Court Review, 55*(4), 556–571.

Lareau, A. (2003). *Unequal childhoods: Class, race, and family life*. Berkeley: University of California Press.

Manning, W. D., Brown, S. L., & Stykes, J. B. (2014). Family complexity among children in the United States. *The Annals of the American Academy of Political and Social Science, 654*(1), 48–65.

Mclanahan, S. (2004). Diverging destinies: How children are faring under the second demographic transition. *Demography, 41*(4), 607–627. https://doi.org/10.1353/dem.2004.0033.

Melli, M., & Brown, P. R. (1994). The economics of shared custody: Developing an equitable formula for dual residence. *Houston Law Review, 31*(2), 543–584.

Meyer, D. R., Cancian, M., & Cook, S. T. (2017). The growth in shared custody in the United States: Patterns and implications. *Family Court Review, 55*(4), 500–512.

Molcho, M., Gabhainn, S. N., & Kelleher, C. C. (2007). Assessing the use of the Family Affluence Scale (FAS) among Irish schoolchildren. *Irish Medical Journal, 100*(8), supplement 37–39.

Moreno, L., & Marí-Klose, P. (2013). Youth, family change and welfare arrangements: Is the South still so different? *European Societies, 15*(4), 493–513. https://doi.org/10.1080/14616696.2013.836400.

Nieuwenhuis, R. (2017). *Peer review on "Single mothers facing poverty: Providing adequate financial, material and social support for sustainable social integration"*. Brussels: European Commission.

Perelli-Harris, B., Sigle-Rushton, W., Kreyenfeld, M., Lappegård, T., Keizer, R., & Berghammer, C. (2010). The educational gradient of childbearing within cohabitation in Europe. *Population and Development Review, 36*(4), 775–801. https://doi.org/10.1111/j.1728-4457.2010.00357.x.

Poortman, A. R., & van Gaalen, R. (2017). Shared residence after separation: A review and new findings from the Netherlands. *Family Court Review, 55*(4), 531–544.

Public Health Agency of Sweden (2015). *Skolbarns hälsovanor i Sverige 2013/14* [Health behaviours in school-aged children in Sweden 2013/14]. Folkhälsomyndigheten: Östersund.

Sayer, L. C., Gauthier, A. H., & Furstenberg, F. F., Jr. (2004). Educational differences in parents' time with children: Cross-national variations. *Journal of Marriage and Family, 66*(5), 1152–1169.

Schiratzki, J. (2008) *Mamma och pappa inför rätta* [Mom and dad in court]. Uppsala: Iustus Förlag.

Schweine, K (2018). Der alternierende Aufenthalt des Kindes bei getrenntlebenden Eltem im Rechtsvergleich (Schweden, Australien und Belgien) [Children alternate residence in comparative law]. In D. Coester-Waltjen, V. Lipp, Eva Schumann, & B. Veit (Eds.), *Das Wechselmodell: Reformbedarf im kindschaftsrecht* [The change model: Reform need in childhood law] (pp. page–page). Göttingen: University of Göttingen Press.

Simões, C., Matos, M. G., Moreno, C., Rivera, F., Batista-Foguet, J. M., & Simons-Morton, B. (2012). Substance use in Portuguese and Spanish adolescents: Highlights from differences, similarities and moderating effects. *The Spanish Journal of Psychology, 15*(3), 1024–1037.

Simões, C., Rivera, F., Moreno, C., & Matos, M. G. (2018). School performance paths: Personal and contextual factors related to top performers and low achievers in Portugal and Spain. The Spanish Journal of Psychology, 21. Retrieved from https://doi.org/10.1017/sjp.2018.37.

Smyth, B., Chisholm, R., Rodgers, B., & Son, V. (2014). Legislating for shared-time parenting after parental separation: Insights from Australia. *Law & Contemporary Problems, 77*, 109.

Sodermans, A. K., Matthijs, K., & Swicegood, G. (2013). Characteristics of joint physical custody families in Flanders. *Demographic Research, 28*, 821–848. https://doi.org/10.4054/DemRes.2013.28.29.

Solsona, M., & Spijker, J. (2016). Effects of the 2010 Civil Code on trends in joint physical custody in Catalonia. A comparison with the rest of Spain. *Population, 71*(2), 297–323.

Statistics Sweden. (2014). *Olika familjer lever på olika sätt—Om barns boende och försörjning efter en separation* [Different families live in different ways—A survey on residence and support of children after a separation]. Örebro, Sweden: Statisktiska Centralbyrån.

Sullivan, O. (2010). Changing differences by educational attainment in fathers' domestic labour and child care. *Sociology, 44*(4), 716–733.

Sullivan, O., Billari, F. C., & Altintas, E. (2014). Fathers' changing contributions to child care and domestic work in very low–fertility countries: The effect of education. *Journal of Family Issues, 35*(8), 1048–1065.

Swedish National Institute of Public Health. (2006). Svenska skolbarns hälsovanor 2005/06 [Health behaviors in Swedish school-children 2005/06]. In *Statens folkhälsoinstitut*. Stockholm: Sweden.

Tach, L., Mincy, R., & Edin, K. (2010). Parenting as a "package deal": Relationships, fertility, and nonresident father involvement among unmarried parents. *Demography, 47*(1), 181–204.

Thomson, E., Lappegård, T., Carlson, M., Evans, A., & Gray, E. (2014). Childbearing across partnerships in Australia, the United States, Norway, and Sweden. *Demography, 51*(2), 485–508.

Tinghög, P., Hemmingsson, T., & Lundberg, I. (2007). To what extent may the association between immigrant status and mental illness be explained by socioeconomic factors? *Social Psychiatry and Psychiatric Epidemiology, 42*(12), 990–996.

Wardle, J., Robb, K., & Johnson, F. (2002). Assessing socioeconomic status in adolescents: The validity of a home affluence scale. *Journal of Epidemiology & Community Health, 56*(8), 595–599. https://doi.org/10.1136/jech.56.8.595.

Westphal, S. K., Poortman, A. R., & Van Der Lippe, T. (2014). Non-resident father–child contact across divorce cohorts: The role of father involvement during marriage. *European Sociological Review, 30*(4), 444–456.

Anna Garriga is a postdoctoral researcher in the Department of Political and Social Science at Pompeu Fabra University. Her research mainly focuses on the causes and consequences of the increasing diversification of family structures in European countries. She has published articles in peer-reviewed journals on the effects of parental separation and post-separation living arrangements on children's well-being and on the determinants of single-motherhood in European countries.

Jani Turunen is Associate Professor and Senior Lecturer of Social Work at Södertörn University, Stockholm, and an affiliate of the Stockholm University Demography Unit. He holds a PhD in Sociological Demography from Stockholm University. His research focuses on different aspects of children's family structure and wellbeing, and on historical change in family structure and kinship. He currently directs a research project on shared physical custody in Sweden.

Laura Bernardi is Full Professor of Life Course Demography and Sociology at the University of Lausanne and co-Editor in Chief of the journal Advances in Life Course Research, co-Editor of the Springer book series Life Course and Social policies, and a member of the Research Council of the Swiss National Research Foundation. Her research interests are in the field of life course sociology and family demography. Her publications range from the cultural determinants of fertility and family behaviours, the role of social influence on fertility and family transitions to spillover and crossover processes in the life course and their effects on wellbeing. She has extensively published in a wide range of peer-reviewed articles in international journals, in the field of demography, sociology and gender, contributed several chapters in collective volumes and has co-edited the books Lone parenthood in the Life Course (Springer); Situating Children of Migrants (Springer); The Demography of Europe (Springer).

10

Parent-Child Contact after Divorce and Impact of Spatial Mobility

Anne-Rigt Poortman

Abstract Shared physical custody, or more generally, frequent contact with both parents is often assumed to benefit children, but having to move back and forth between parents' homes may also be harmful, particularly when parents live far apart. This study examined the role of spatial mobility in the association between frequent parent-child contact and multiple child outcomes. Using the New Families in the Netherlands survey, analyses firstly showed that frequent parent-child contact, on average, was found to be not or modestly associated with better child outcomes. Second, spatial mobility mattered, but in varying ways. Long travel times were negatively associated with children's contact with friends and their psychological well-being, but positively related to educational performance. Furthermore, frequent commutes were negatively associated with how often children saw their friends, but positively associated with child psychological well-being. Third, and most importantly, the impact of parent-child contact and frequent commutes on child outcomes were found to be dependent on traveling time. For child psychological well-being and contact with friends, frequent parent-child contact and/or frequent commutes were found to have positive effects when travel distances were short, but these positive effects disappeared when traveling times increased.

Keywords Divorce · Joint physical custody · Spatial mobility · Child well-being

Shared parenting after divorce has become increasingly popular. Parents more often opt for shared physical custody (i.e., alternating/shared residence) nowadays and nonresident father-child contact has increased over time (Cancian et al. 2014; Poortman and Van Gaalen 2017; Westphal et al. 2014). The rise in shared residence in particular sparked a lively debate about whether such an arrangement is in children's best interests. Three opposing theoretical ideas exist (Westphal 2015). First, continuing contact with both parents is generally assumed to increase

---

A.-R. Poortman (✉)
University of Utrecht, Utrecht, The Netherlands
e-mail: a.poortman@uu.nl

children's access to parental resources (e.g., income, support), and thus, child well-being. Second, shared residence requires children to frequently travel between houses, which may negatively (instead of positively) affect child well-being. Third, children in shared residence may be more exposed to parental conflict or inconsistent parenting, which also decreases their well-being. Similar arguments can be made for nonresident father-child contact – though this literature often relies on the parental resources perspective (Amato 1993).

Most studies examined whether or not shared residence and nonresident father-child contact have positive effects on child well-being (see reviews: Adamsons and Johnson 2013; Nielsen 2018; Steinbach 2018). Only few studies went beyond assessing such overall associations and examined the validity of the different theoretical arguments. This work focused on the role of the parental relationship or, be it less so, on the role of parental resources. Studies examined whether frequent contact with both parents (i.e., shared residence or nonresident father-child contact) is less beneficial for children in case parents have high conflict (Mahrer et al. 2018) or little communication (Sodermans et al. 2013; Vanassche et al. 2013). A handful of studies tap in on the parental resource argument by examining whether frequent parent-child contact is particularly beneficial in case of a good (pre-divorce) parent-child relationship (Poortman 2018; Vanassche et al. 2013; Videon 2002).

Research on the role of having to move frequently between houses is scarce. This argument emphasizes the role of *spatial mobility* that results from having two homes in the association between parent-child contact and child well-being. Although there is some work on how divorce and child residence arrangements are related to moving and the geographical distance between parents (Cooksey and Craig 1998; Feijten and Van Ham 2013; Thomas et al. 2018), few studies relate spatial mobility aspects to child outcomes. Some studies assessed the effect of geographical distance on child outcomes (Jensen 2009; Kalil et al. 2011; Rasmussen and Stratton 2016), but typically use distance as a proxy for parent-child contact because they lack measures for such contact. Other studies focus on the role of both geographical distance and parent-child contact with a particular interest in the potentially stressful effects of traveling over long distances (Schier 2015; Viry 2014). These studies often do not take into account the frequency of commuting. Yet, it is the frequency of commuting that has been argued to negatively affect child well-being and frequent contact is not necessarily the same as this home-switching frequency; e.g., a week to week arrangement involves fewer commutes than an arrangement where a child stays at each parent's house every 3–4 days. It is thus important to consider the associations between parent-child contact, geographical distance and frequency of changing houses and assess their impact on child well-being simultaneously.

This study examines the impact of geographical distance and frequent commutes on child outcomes and their role in the association between parent-child contact and child outcomes. To my knowledge only two larger-scale studies examined the role of frequent commutes on child psychological well-being (Sodermans et al. 2014; Westphal 2015) and only one of these studies took child main residence, distance and frequency of changing houses simultaneously into account (Westphal 2015). The current study extends previous work, and Westphal's study in particular, in three ways. First, I examine multiple child outcomes; not only children's psychological well-being, but also their educational performance and social integration. The latter outcome has rarely been studied (but see Fransson et al. 2018; Prazen et al. 2011), yet the extent to which children are socially integrated, as indicated by their friendships, may in particular be negatively affected by high spatial mobility. Second, the analyses extend measures of parent-child contact beyond child main residence and include nonresident father-child contact, as differences between shared residence and frequent father visitation may only be gradual.

Third, and most importantly, this study examines *the interplay* between parent-child contact, geographical distance and frequent changes between parental homes in their effects on child outcomes. Westphal (2015) and other studies (e.g., Kalil et al. 2011; Sodermans et al. 2014; Viry 2014) explored main effects of parent-child contact and/or distance and/or frequent changes. Yet, arguments about the stress of traveling over long distances is only relevant when children actually travel, that is visit the other parent – implying an interaction between parent-child contact and distance: long distances are particularly problematic when children have frequent parent-child contact with both parents. Or, interpreted the other way around, any positive effects of frequent parent- child contact may weaken or even become negative when children have to commute over long distances. Similarly, and likely even more so given that changing houses is what causes stress rather than contact itself: having to frequently change between parents' homes may be particularly harmful in case parents live far apart. I thus contend that to better understand the role of spatial mobility for the association between parent-child contact and child outcomes, it is more informative to look at interactions. My main argument is that the effects of frequent parent-child contact and frequent changes between homes on child outcomes become less positive or even negative in case of long distances between parental homes.

Using the large-scale survey New Families in the Netherlands – the same data as Westphal (2015) – I first describe the associations between parent-child contact, geographical distance and the frequency of changing between homes. Parent-child contact refers to children's main residence (shared/father/mother) and nonresident father-child contact (if mother residence). Geographical distance is indicated by the time it takes to travel from one parent's house to the other parent's house. Second, I examine the impact of parent-child contact, distance and frequent commutes on three child outcomes: psychological well-being, educational performance and social integration i.e. children's friendships. Third, I study whether the effects of frequent parent-child contact and frequent changes between parental homes on child outcomes depend on how far parents live apart.

10.1 Theoretical Background

After a divorce, parents move to different homes and this often means that children have to commute between two homes – only in rare cases children stay in one home and parents commute. It is this 'circular spatial mobility' (Schier 2015: 206) of children that is argued to negatively affect child outcomes. Children in shared residence or who frequently see the nonresident parent are argued to be worse off because they lack continuity in location and because of the practical difficulties of traveling (Viry 2014; Westphal 2015). This line of reasoning suggests two aspects of spatial mobility to be important: the frequency of commuting and the traveling distance. First, long travels may be stressful for children and imply that children are exposed to different surroundings (Jensen 2009; Viry 2014). When parents live close children likely do not have to travel to another neighborhood or town when visiting the other parent. Short distances thus allow children to continue their social activities (Jensen 2009), which may benefit children. The few findings are mixed: some studies suggest negative effects of long travel distances on child psychological well-being (Jensen 2009; Viry 2014; Westphal 2015) whilst other studies show positive effects on educational outcomes (Kalil et al. 2011; Rasmussen and Stratton 2016).

Second, the frequency of commuting between parental homes is important. When children frequently commute between homes, they lack a stable home and face the organizational difficulties of frequent commutes, such as moving their belongings and informing friends about their whereabouts (Schier 2015; Westphal 2015). Frequent changes may also interrupt daily routines of e.g. doing homework or meeting friends, which may also negatively affect child outcomes. The sparse findings are mixed. Sodermans et al. (2014) find a negative effect of the number of monthly shifts between homes on child psychological well-being, but their analyses include virtually no additional variables. Westphal (2015) includes many controls, including distance and child main residence. She finds a positive effect of frequent commutes on child well-being, which she explains by the more continuous engagement of both parents in children's day-to-day lives in case of frequent changes (Westphal 2015).

In relation to shared residence or more generally, frequent parent-child contact, the second aspect of spatial mobility has typically been emphasized: frequent parent-child contact may be harmful to children because children frequently move between houses and this may outweigh any positive effects of having greater access to both parents' resources (Schier 2015). This line of reasoning does not take into account the distance between parents' homes. The distance argument would lead to an opposing hypothesis. Frequent parent-child contact and frequent changes between houses are often only possible when parents live close to one another, and this shorter distance predicts a positive effect on child well-being. Moreover, as the positive effect of frequent changes on child well-being in Westphal's study (2015) suggests, frequent changes may not necessarily be harmful. I therefore suggest a more nuanced hypothesis. When travel distances are long, frequent commutes may be harmful to child outcomes, especially in terms of social integration. The stress and organizational difficulties of frequent commutes are likely greater in case of longer travels and feelings of lacking a stable home may be much more hard felt when surroundings are spatially far apart. Moreover, daily routines are more likely to be disrupted when children frequently commute over long distances, especially in terms of their social life; it is for example hard to meet with one's friends when a child is often at the other part of town, let alone a different town. A counter argument for social integration may be that, especially in case of long distances, frequent changes between homes allow for maintaining the social contacts and social life attached to the separate homes (e.g., potential step family members, friends at each parent's house). Nonetheless, as most arguments suggest negative effects, I assume that, overall, frequent changes have disruptive effects in case of long distances. These disruptive effects are less likely when parents live close to each other. In that case, frequent changes may even have positive effects. When parents live close, frequent changes may indicate that parents are both equally involved in children's day-to-day activities and routines which may benefit children (Westphal 2015). Furthermore, frequent changes between homes may signal flexibility in that children are free to go to the other parent when they need to. I thus expect that any positive effects of frequent commuting between homes become weaker or turn into negative effects on child outcomes when distances become larger. Because frequent parent-child contact implies frequent changes, a corollary of this reasoning is that frequent parent-child contact is less positively (or even negatively) related to child well-being when travel distances get larger; in that case, the disruptive effects of frequent changes may overshadow any beneficial effects of greater access to parental resources. I furthermore expect that larger travel distances will generally be associated with worse child outcomes. In light of the opposing arguments for the main effects of frequent parent-child contact and commutes and their dependence on travel distance, I refrain from hypotheses about the overall association between child outcomes on the one hand and parent-child contact (i.e., main residence, father visitation) and frequency of changing homes on the other hand.

10.2 Method

I use data from Wave 1 (2012/13) of the New Families in the Netherlands Survey (NFN; Poortman et al. 2014). NFN is an internet survey among nearly 4500 parents who divorced or separated from a cohabiting union in 2010. Statistics Netherlands sampled households with minor children who divorced/separated in that year, and we approached both parents from a former household. In about 30% of households, both parents participated. The response rate was quite similar to earlier Dutch family surveys, amounting to 39% among persons and 58% among former households. Former cohabiters, men (particularly those with young children), younger persons, people of non-Western descent, people on low incomes and those on welfare were underrepresented, whereas men with children officially registered at their address were overrepresented. In the group of former cohabiters, parents from the most urbanized areas and men with one child were also underrepresented.

Questions about children's residence arrangements and child outcomes, were asked about a specific focal child. The focal child was the youngest child in case parents had any children who were ten years or older at the time of the survey, and it was the oldest child in case all children were younger than ten. Given the outcomes studied (see below), I only selected cases in which this child was 4–17 years old. I also excluded cases in which the child's main residence was something other than mother, father or shared residence and cases with missing values on the independent and control variables. These exclusions result in a base sample of $N = 3567$. For the analyses of nonresident father-child contact, only respondents reporting mother residence were selected, resulting in a base sample of $N = 2342$. Note that the number of cases with father residence was low and I therefore do not analyze the role of nonresident mother-child contact. These base samples are used to describe the associations between parent-child contact on the one hand, and travel distance and frequency of changes between houses on the other hand. Also the descriptive statistics of the central independent (i.e., parent-child contact, distance, frequent commutes) and control variables are based on these base samples (see Table 10.1). In the multivariate analyses, the eventual N varies depending on the child outcome studied and the number of missing cases for each outcome (see Tables 10.2 and 10.3).

10.2.1 Measures Dependent Variables

Child psychological well-being. Measured by the Strengths and Difficulties Questionnaire (SDQ; Goodman 1997), developed for children aged 4–17 and consisting of items about child behavior. Example items are "Restless, overactive, cannot stay still for long" or "Gets on better with adults than with other children". Parents indicated how closely items described the focal child's behavior in the past six months or during the current school year (0 = *Not true*, 1 = *Somewhat true*, 2 = *Certainly true*). Following the instructions on the site (www.sdqinfo.org), I summed the scores on the subscales referring to child's hyperactivity, peer problems, conduct problems and emotional symptoms to get the total difficulties score (Cronbach's $\alpha = .84$, based on all the items). The variable was logged as it was skewed to the right.

Child educational performance. If the child was in secondary school, grades were asked for the following courses: mathematics, Dutch and English language. I computed the mean score (range 1–10).

Child friendships. Measured, first, by the number of friends (not on social media) that a child has. This information was originally reported in a discrete way, ranging from 0 = *none* to 7 = *more than 20*, but was recoded to a continuous variable. This variable was logged, because it was skewed to the right. Second, parents were asked to report on how often the child saw their friends (outside school) per month. Also

Table 10.1 Descriptive statistics of the variables used in the analyses

	Total sample		Mother residence	
	Mean	SD	Mean	SD
SDQ (logged)[a]	1.969	.742	2.026	.732
Grade[b]	6.769	.960	6.803	.916
Nr. of friends (logged)[c]	1.676	.596	1.657	.601
Contact friends[d]	11.415	8.211	11.372	8.479
Shared residence	.290			
Mother residence	.657			
Father residence	.053			
Nonresident father visitation (logged)			3.723	1.189
Travel distance (logged)	2.445	.920	2.606	.961
Frequency commutes (logged)	1.901	.755	1.850	.781
Female respondent	.574		.616	
Previous cohabitation	.224		.229	
Age child	10.417	3.535	10.208	3.582
Child is girl	.482		.484	
Mother education	6.309	2.008	6.161	2.015
Father education	6.287	2.183	5.985	2.220
Mother working hours	20.557	12.105	19.286	12.406
Father working hours	37.364	11.798	37.484	12.283
Predivorce conflict	2.357	.807	2.434	.811
Predivorce problems parents	.536	.815	.588	.853
Predivorce household income/10000	2.353	1.281	2.249	1.288
Postdivorce tensions	1.877	.959	1.971	.991
Postdivorce severe conflict	2.963	2.652	3.270	2.697
Postdivorce household income/10000	2.302	1.536	2.182	1.260
Either parent repartnered	.465		.491	
N	3567		2342	

Note. SD not presented for dichotomous variables
[a]N = 3552 (total sample)/N = 2329 (mother residence)
[b]N = 942 (total sample)/N = 571 (mother residence)
[c]N = 3444 (total sample)/N = 2238 (mother residence)
[d]N = 3275 (total sample)/N = 2094 (mother residence)

this information was originally asked for in a discrete way (from 0 = *never* to 7 = *every day*), but recoded to a continuous variable indicating the number of times that a child saw his/her friends per month.

10.2.2 Measures Central Independent Variables

Child main residence. Parents were asked with whom the child lived most of the time: mother, father or about equal. The latter option is coded as shared residence and three dummies were constructed for mother, father and shared residence.

Table 10.2 Multilevel regression analyses of child outcomes on child main residence, geographical distance and frequency of commutes

	Model 1	Model 2	Model 3	Model 4
SDQ[a]				
Shared residence (mother = ref)	−.096**	−.074*	−.232*	
Father residence	.085[b]	.074[b]	−.110	
Distance		.029*	.019	−.029
Freq. commutes		−.053**		−.159**
Shared residence* distance			.071~	
Father residence * distance			.071	
Freq. commutes*distance				.040**
Grades[c]				
Shared residence (mother = ref)	−.024	−.004	.199	
Father residence	−.336*[d]	−.343*[b]	−.045	
Distance		.066~	.094*	.045
Freq. commutes		.018		−.002
Shared residence* distance			−.090	
Father residence * distance			−.112	
Freq. Commutes*distance				.009
Nr. of friends[e]				
Shared residence (mother = ref)	.020	.016	.088	
Father residence	−.026	−.023	−.237	
Distance		−.003	−.005	.017
Freq. commutes		.015		.050
Shared residence* distance			−.035	
Father residence * distance			.077[f]	
Freq. commutes*distance				−.014
Contact friends[g]				
Shared residence (mother = ref)	−.047	−.169	2.412*	
Father residence	.659	.663	.084	
Distance		−.407*	−.159	.388
Freq. commutes		−.490*		.644
Shared residence* distance			−1.240**	
Father residence * distance			.208[f]	
Freq. commutes*distance				−.458*

Note. Models include the control variables and distance is measured by travel time; ~$p < .10$; *$p < .05$; **$p < .01$ (two-sided)

[a]N = 3552 from 2795 households

[b]Difference between father and shared residence significant at $p < .05$ (two-sided)

[c]N = 942 from 761 households

[d]Difference between father and shared residence significant at $p < .10$ (two-sided)

[e]N = 3444 from 2724 households

[f]Difference between father*distance and shared residence*distance significant at $p < .10$ (two-sided)

[g]N = 3275 from 2617 households

Table 10.3 Multilevel regression analyses of child outcomes on nonresident father-child contact, geographical distance and frequency of commutes

	Model 1	Model 2a	Model 2b	Model 3	Model 4
SDQ[a]					
Father-child contact	−.025~	−.023~		−.087**	
Distance		.015	.012	−.070~	−.061~
Freq. commutes			−.044*		−.164**
Father-child contact * distance				.025*	
Freq. commutes * distance					.045**
Grades[b]					
Father-child contact	−.057~	−.050		−.038	
Distance		.084*	.089*	.099	.117~
Freq. commutes			−.021		.029
Father-child contact * distance				−.005	
Freq. commutes*distance					−.019
Nr. of friends[c]					
Father-child contact	.006	.005		.016	
Distance		−.007	−.007	.006	.008
Freq. commutes			.010		.034
Father-child contact * distance				−.004	
Freq. commutes*distance					−.009
Contact friends[d]					
Father-child contact	−.306	−.333~		.267	
Distance		−.237	−.267	.564	.291
Freq. commutes			−.584*		.302
Father-child contact * distance				−.232	
Freq. commutes*distance					−.339

Note. Models include the control variables and distance is measured by travel time; ~$p < .10$; *$p < .05$; **$p < .01$ (two-sided)
[a]N = 2329 from 1915 households
[b]N = 571 from 484 households
[c]N = 2238 from 1856 households
[d]N = 2094 from 1762 households

Nonresident father-child contact. A measure of how many days a year a child had contact with the nonresident father (if the child lived with the mother). This variable was constructed using a crude measure of contact with the father in combination with the information provided in a residential calendar (Sodermans et al. 2014) if they saw each other more than monthly. The crude measure asked how often the nonresident father saw the child: *Never, once or twice a year, several times a year (not monthly)* or *at least once a month*. The first three responses were recoded to yearly contact frequency (1 = 0; 2 = 2; 3 = 7). In case of monthly contact, the residential calendar was filled in indicating with whom the child resided during the day and at night for each day of the 4 weeks in an average month (*"Me"* or *"Ex-partner"*). This information was used to create a more precise measure of yearly contact. The resulting variable was skewed to the right and thus logged to avoid too much leverage by the extremes.

Distance between parental homes. A measure indicating how much time (in minutes) a usual one-way trip takes to the other parent's house. I cut off extreme values at 240 min as 4 h is about the maximum time it takes traveling from North to South in the Netherlands. I also logged the variable, to avoid too much leverage by extreme values. Note that traveling time is a crude measure of geographical distance, especially because the mode of transport was not asked for: a 30-min walk may indicate a smaller distance than a 30-min train ride, though they both take 30 min.

Frequency of commutes. A measure of how often the child moves back and forth between parents' homes on a monthly basis. This variable was constructed using the residential calendar by counting the number of times that there was a change in the place where the child resided (*Me* or *Ex-partner*). This variable was skewed to the right, and hence, logged.

Measures controls. The analyses control for whether the respondent was female (1 = *yes*), and whether the previous union was a cohabitation (1 = *yes*) or marriage (=0). I also control for the following predivorce characteristics (to tackle selection problems) and postdivorce determinants of child outcomes:

Education of parents. Respondents reported their own highest educational level and their ex-partner's (1 = *Less than primary education* to 10 = *Post graduate*). This information was used to construct the mother's and father's educational level.

Predivorce work hours of parents. Respondents reported the number of contractual hours that they and their ex-partner worked per week in the year before divorce. Gender specific measures were constructed to measure the mother's and the father's predivorce work hours. Unemployed parents were assigned zero hours and values higher than 80 h per week were assigned a score of 80.

Predivorce conflict. A scale measuring how often the following things happened in the final year before divorce: "There were tensions or disagreements between you and your ex-partner", "There were heated discussions between you and your ex-partner", "You made serious accusations against each other", "You sometimes stopped talking to each other", and "Arguments got out of hand". Answers ranged from 1 (= *Not at all)* to 4 (= *Often)*. The mean score was taken to create the scale (Cronbach's $\alpha = .87$).

Predivorce household income. Indicates yearly standardized household income referring to a year earlier than the year in which parents separated or divorced officially (if married). These data were obtained from register data from Statistics Netherlands by linking NFN to the registers in a secured environment.

Predivorce parental problems. A count of problems that respondents or their ex-partner experienced during their relationship, i.e.: "Serious physical illness or handicap", "Serious psychological problems", "Violence, drugs or alcohol addiction", and "Contact with the police (excluding traffic offences)".

Child gender. Coded 1 if the focal child is a girl (otherwise 0).

Child age. The focal child's age in years.

Severe postdivorce conflict. A count of the number of the following things that the ex-partner had done since they split up: "Made serious accusations against you",

"Said bad things about you to others", "Called or visited you uninvited", "Turned your children against you", "Wrongly accused you of something", "Spoke ill of your common past", "Scolded, quarreled with you", and "Threatened violence".

Postdivorce tensions. Measures how often the former partners had conflicts or tensions at the time of the survey: 1 "*Never*" to 4 "*Very often*".

Repartnering. Indicates whether either parent cohabited or married with a new partner.

Postdivorce household income. Using register data, a measure of respondents' household income in 2011 (the year before the survey) or in the most recent year before 2011 for which income data were available was constructed.

10.2.3 Analytical Strategy

The analyses consist of three steps. First, I describe the associations between parent-child contact, travel time and the frequency of commutes to get a feel of how spatial mobility aspects are related to parent-child contact. Second, I test for main effects of the central independent variables. In a first model only parent-child contact is included (besides the control variables). This model shows the associations between parent-child contact with multiple outcomes without controlling for spatial mobility. This model is informative from a more general point of view as this study includes child outcomes that have been rarely studied in the literature on postdivorce child residence arrangement i.e. social integration. In a second model, travel time and the frequency of commuting is added to the model, to examine their main effects and how the effect of parent-child contact changes after accounting for spatial mobility. Because the correlation between nonresident father visitation (logged) and the frequency of changes between parents' homes (logged) was too high ($r = 0.73$), only travel time is added to the model, but I also estimate a model in which frequency of commutes and travel time are included. In the third step, interaction models are estimated. In model four, I include an interaction between the measures for parent-child contact and travel time. In Model 4 I replace parent-child contact variables with the measure for frequency of commutes and I estimate interactions between the frequency of commutes and travel time. Because for 30% of households, both parents participated, I conducted multilevel regression analyses. The baseline models that include only the control variables are shown in the Appendix. To save space, the main tables do not include estimates for the controls. In some sensitivity analyses, I checked whether results differed when the number of children was controlled for, but the results did not change. Because peers become more important when children grow older, I also tested whether the effects of parent-child contact and spatial mobility on social integration varied with the age of the child by including interactions between the main independent variables and the child's age for all models. None of these interactions, except for father visitation * child's age on the number of friends – suggesting a negative effect of father visitation at older ages -, were, however, statistically significant.

10.3 Results

Figures 10.1 and 10.2 illustrate how child main residence and father visitation are associated with spatial mobility aspects. Figure 10.1 shows that travel times are considerably shorter in case of shared residence as compared to sole residence. Whereas the average travel time for mother and father residence amount to 22 and 24 min, respectively, and are only marginally significantly different from each other ($p = 0.06$; analyses not shown), the travel time for children in shared residence is significantly less with an average time of about 8 min. These differences are even more pronounced when looking at the distributions of travelling time. Travel times for sole residence range from 0 to 240 min with 75% of children having to travel 25–30 min or less. In contrast, the range is 0 to maximum 75 min in case of shared residence and 75% of children have parents who live within a 10 min travel distance. The association between nonresident father-child contact and travel distance ($r = -.22$) is negative with large distances being associated with fewer visits. The scatterplot suggests a less pronounced association than for child main residence, given the large spread of observations around a fitted regression line.

Figure 10.2 shows that the mean frequency of commutes is lowest for father residence ($m = 6$) and highest for shared residence ($m = 8.5$), with mother residence in between. Though these differences are all significant, they are less pronounced

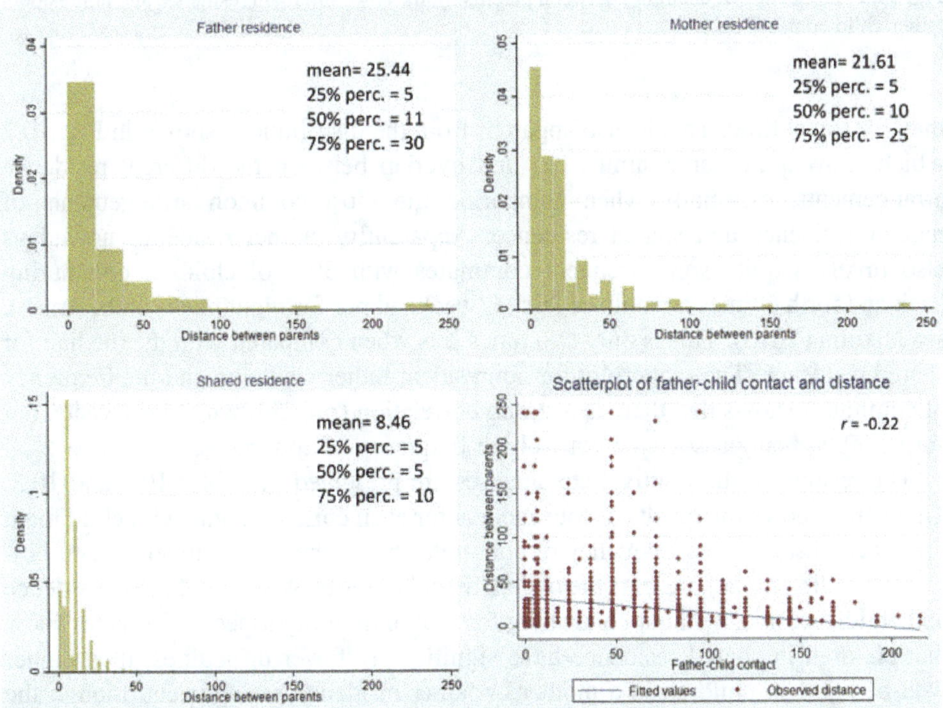

Fig. 10.1 Distance between parents (as measured by travel time) by child's main residence and nonresident father-child contact

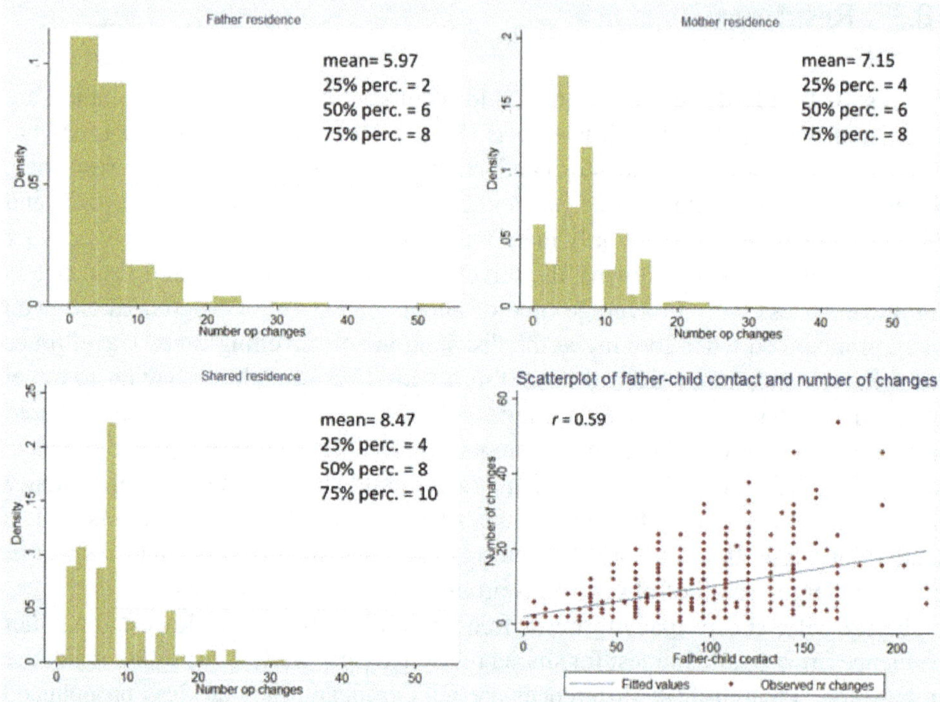

Fig. 10.2 Frequency of changing between parents' homes by child main residence and nonresident father-child contact

than for travel time. This is also apparent from the distributions shown in Fig. 10.2 which show quite some similarities and overlap between the different residence arrangements, especially when comparing the most common arrangements of mother residence and shared residence. Apparently, mother residence nowadays also involves quite some frequent commutes with 50% of children commuting back and forth 6 times a month or less (a 'weekend per fortnight plus'- arrangement, see Nikolina 2015). This is only two times less when compared with the median for shared residence. The scatterplot for nonresident father visitation and the frequency of commutes shows that there is a strong correlation (r = .59) with many visits, not surprisingly, being associated with a high frequency of commutes.

The results for the multivariate analyses are presented in Tables 10.2 and 10.3. Table 10.2 shows the results of four models for each child outcome with child main residence, distance and frequency of commutes being the central independent variables. The first model presents the overall associations between child main residence and child outcomes without controlling for spatial mobility aspects. Estimates show that children in shared residence have significantly fewer difficulties, thus higher well-being, than children in a mother or father residence arrangement, though the effect sizes are modest (.096/SD of .74 = .13 and (.096 + .085)/SD of .74 = .24).

Furthermore, although children in shared residence do not stand out, either positively or negatively, for the other outcomes, children in father residence have significantly lower grades than those in mother or shared residence. Effect sizes are somewhat bigger than for SDQ but still modest (.35 and .33). Child main residence bears no association with the measures for social integration.

In model 2 distance and the frequency of commutes are added to model 1. These spatial mobility aspects affect two out of the four child outcomes: child psychological well-being and the amount of monthly contact with friends. As expected, when travel times are longer children have more social and psychological difficulties (hence, lower child psychological well-being). In addition, the longer it takes to travel from one parent to the other, the less contact that children have with their friends. Note that traveling distance does not affect the number of friends. Further, frequent commutes are associated with less contact with friends but also higher (rather than lower) child psychological well-being – the latter finding being in line with Westphal's study using the same data (Westphal 2015). As shared residence is associated with less travel time and more frequent changes, the main effect of shared residence on SDQ becomes somewhat smaller in model 2, but is still significant.

A more nuanced picture emerges in models 3 and 4, where interaction terms between distance and main residence (model 3) and distance and frequency of commutes (model 4) are included. Although the interaction term is marginally significant ($p = .076$), shared residence leads to fewer child difficulties than mother residence in case travel times are minimal but this beneficial effect becomes weaker the longer it takes to travel to the other parent's house. When the frequency of commutes is considered in model 4, findings are more convincing. When traveling distance is minimal, frequent changes between parents' houses lead to fewer child difficulties, but this beneficial effect becomes smaller the longer children have to travel (interaction term = .040, $p = .005$). Panel A in Fig. 10.3 shows a graphical representation of the results in model 4 by plotting the predicted SDQ (logged) for different combinations of travel distance (logged) and number of commutes (logged; for three values: minimum of 0, medium of 2 and maximum of 4). The figure clearly shows that frequent commutes are particularly beneficial when travel times are minimal. At the maximum possible travel time of 5.5, the effect of frequently changing houses is reversed but not statistically significant ($p = .154$; analyses not shown).

Also for contact with friends, models 3 and 4 show significant interactions. Children in shared residence more often see their friends than children in mother residence when travel distance is minimal, but this advantage becomes less the longer the travel time (interaction term = −1.24; $p = .002$ in model 3, Table 10.2). Panel B in Fig. 10.3 illustrates this finding showing that shared residence has opposing effects when comparing the minimum and maximum travel distance. When parents live zero minutes apart (e.g., a few houses apart), children in a shared residence arrangement see their friends more often, but when parents live

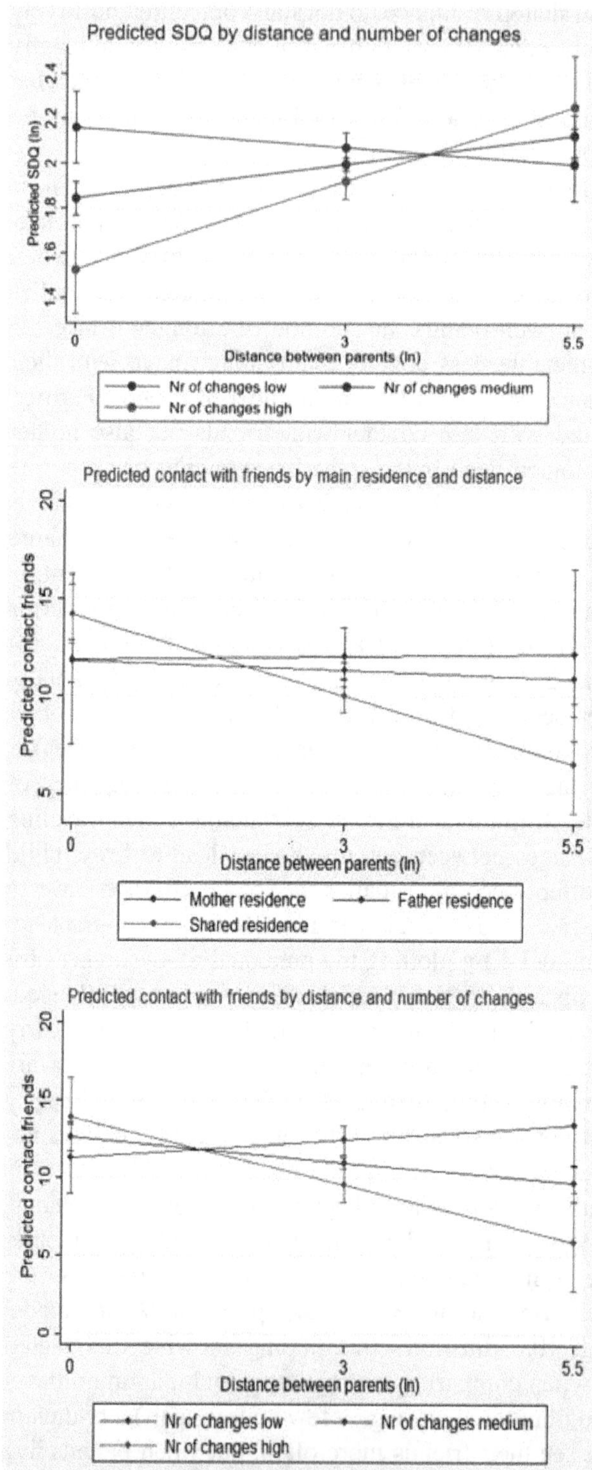

Panel A: Interaction between frequency of commutes and travel distance in their effect on SDQ.

Panel B: Interaction between child main residence and travel distance in their effect on the frequency of contact with friends.

Panel C: Interaction between frequency of changing between parents' homes and travel distance in their effect on the frequency of contact with friends.

Fig. 10.3 Graphical illustrations of the statistically significant interactions in Table 10.2

far apart (maximum of 4 h i.e., ln(distance) = 5.5) children in shared residence see their friends less often than children in sole residence and this difference is statistically significant (results not shown). A more realistic maximum distance for children in shared residence is 60 minutes (see Fig. 10.1). At this travel distance children also see their friends (statistically) significantly less than their counterparts in sole residence (not shown). Also the interaction between frequency of commutes and travel distance is statistically significant (interaction term = −.458; p = .031). As the graphical representation in Panel C of Fig. 10.3 shows, the frequency of commutes has no effect on how often children see their friends when travel distances are minimal, but at the maximum possible travel distance frequent commutes imply statistically significant less contact with friends (b = −1.876; p = .005; results not shown). Note that no significant interactions are found for the other child outcomes.

Table 10.3 presents the results of similar models but now when parent-child contact is measured by nonresident father-child contact (in case children live with the mother). Model 1 shows the overall associations between father visitation and child outcomes suggesting that father visitation has little to no effect on child outcomes. None of the estimates is statistically significant at the conventional level of 5%. In models 2a and 2b spatial mobility aspects are added. Because the correlation between father-child contact (logged) and the frequency of commutes (logged) was too high (r = .73) to include both these variables in the models, model 2a includes father visitation and distance whereas model 2b includes distance and frequency of commutes. Results show that spatial aspects matter for all outcomes except the number of friends. Distance matters for children's grade, but in an unexpected way. The longer it takes to travel from one parent to the other parent, the higher the grade. Frequent commutes are important for child psychological well-being and the amount of contact with friends. Children who travel more frequently, have fewer difficulties (thus higher well-being) than those travelling less frequently. And frequent commutes negatively affect the amount of contact with friends.

In models 3 and 4, the interaction terms between distance and father visitation (model 3) and distance and frequent commutes (model 4) are added. Only for child SDQ there are significant interactions and these are illustrated in Fig. 10.4. The pattern is similar regardless of whether one looks at father-child contact or the frequency of changing between parents' homes, which is not surprising given the high correlation between these variables. Frequent father-child contact or frequent commutes lead to fewer social and psychological difficulties when parents live close to each other, but no longer so when travel distances are large. In case of a maximum travel time, frequent visitation or frequent changes have no statistically significant association with child difficulties at the 5% significance level (although the number of changes is marginally significant; b = .085; p = .091 – results not shown).

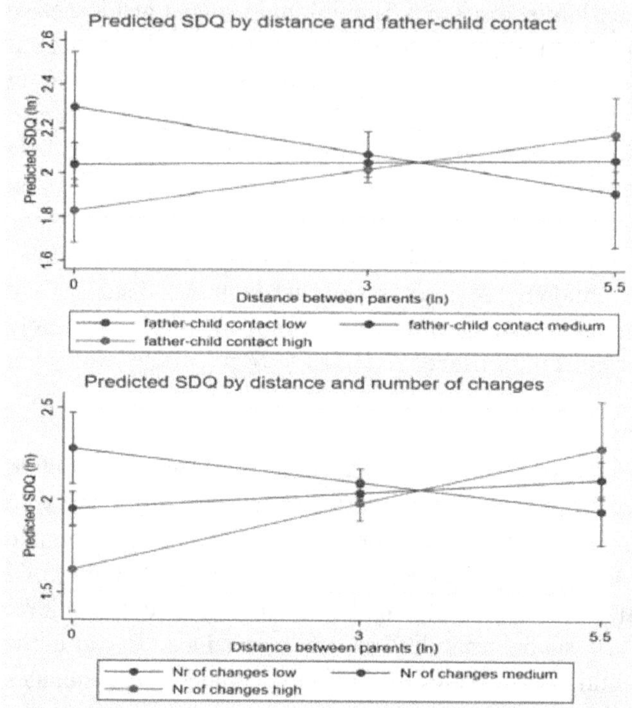

Panel A: Interaction between father-child contact and travel distance in their effect on SDQ.

Panel B: Interaction between frequency of commutes and travel distance in their effect on SDQ.

Fig. 10.4 Graphical illustrations of the statistically significant interactions in Table 10.3

10.4 Conclusion

The recent increase in shared residence fueled a debate about whether such an arrangement serves the interests of children. Although it is typically assumed that shared residence or, more generally, frequent contact with both parents benefits children, some scholars have argued that having to move back and forth between parents' homes may be harmful (Westphal 2015). This study examined the validity of this argument by looking at spatial mobility and its role in the association between frequent parent-child contact and child outcomes. The study's main contributions were its focus on multiple child outcomes and its examination of the interplay between distance, frequency of commutes and parent-child contact.

First, frequent parent-child contact, on average, was not or modestly associated with child outcomes. Although the role of spatial mobility was central, the main associations between parent-child contact and child outcomes are worth mentioning here as this study was one of the first to include multiple child outcomes. In line with previous studies, father visitation was associated with none of the studied child outcomes. Only child psychological well-being was significantly better for children in shared residence as compared to those in sole residence, but effect sizes were modest. For other outcomes, no positive (or negative) effects were found of shared residence. Only children who resided with the father were found to perform worse at school, but this group is small and may be selective (e.g., mother ill).

Second, spatial mobility matters for child outcomes, but not always in ways as would be expected. When it comes to children's social integration, longer travel times and having to frequently move back and forth between houses led children to see their friends less often. These findings are as one would expect given that frequent commutes and longer distances make it more difficult to meet with friends. Note that these findings suggest opposing implications for how frequent parent-child contact impacts on a child's friendships: frequent contact (i.e., shared residence or father visitation) was associated with frequent changes suggesting a negative impact, but also with lower travel times which rather predicts positive effects on contact with friends. Also noteworthy is that spatial mobility affects children's (physical) contact with friends, but not the number of friends. Perhaps digital contact via social media is used to maintain friendships in case of long distances or frequent commutes (Viry 2014). Longer travel times were also found to affect child psychological well-being negatively, which is in line with previous findings (Viry 2014) and corroborates the argument that traveling and different surroundings may be stressful (Jensen 2009; Schier 2015).

In contrast, educational performance was positively associated with longer distances when traveling to visit a nonresident father. This finding is in line with previous findings (Kalil et al. 2011; Rasmussen and Stratton 2016). Previous work attributed this positive effect to the greater contact and thus possibly greater exposure to conflict in case of short distances or to the fewer moves between parents' households in case of long distances (ibid.), but this study controlled for parent-child contact, conflict and frequent commutes. Selectivity and reversed causation may play a role here: when a child performs well at school, parents may be more inclined to live further apart as they are not worried about any disruptive effects of long travels on performance vis-a-vis parents whose child performs less well. Another reason may be that long travel distances may interfere little with daily routines such as doing homework or attending extra classes because long commutes are planned at different times in the week than short ones: long travels are likely planned in weekends rather than during weekdays. Another unexpected finding is that frequent commutes overall have a positive influence on child psychological well-being (as was already shown by Westphal 2015, but see Sodermans et al. 2014). Frequent shifts between parents' houses may benefit children because parents are both equally involved in their child's daily life (Westphal 2015) and frequent moves may signal flexibility in that children are free to go to the other parent as often as they want or need. Spatial mobility thus suggests little harm for children in shared residence:

travel distances are shorter in case of shared residence which positively affects child psychological well-being and the greater frequency of changing houses does not seem to negatively affect child psychological well-being.

Third, and most importantly, the impact of parent-child contact and frequent commutes on child outcomes were found to be dependent on traveling time. Frequent parent-child contact (be it in the form of shared residence or father visitation) was found to be positively associated with child psychological well-being when travel distances were short, but this positive effect disappeared when travel distance increased. The pattern was more pronounced for the frequency of commutes: when parents lived close to each other frequent changes between parents' homes were associated with higher child psychological well-being, but this was no longer the case when parents lived far apart. Further, children in shared residence met their friends more often than children in sole residence when parents lived close, but when parents lived far apart they met their friends less often. Also frequent commutes were associated with less contact with friends in case of long travels. No such interactions were however found when looking at nonresident father visitation. Frequent father-child contact mattered little for children's contact with friends, regardless of travel distance. This inconsistency may be explained by temporal aspects of spatial mobility. Children in shared residence may be more likely to change houses during weekdays whereas visits to nonresident fathers may more often take place in weekends, which may interfere less with children's social activities and their contacts with friends.

These findings call for a more nuanced interpretation of the possibly disruptive role of moving back and forth between parent's homes in case children frequently see both their parents. The stress of being exposed to different locations and the practical difficulties of changing houses seem to only be important when parents live far apart. When parents live close, frequent parent-child contact has positive effects in terms of having access to both parents' resources, parents' continuous engagement in children's lives and the possibility to freely move between parents' houses. But when parents live far apart, these positive effects are counteracted by the stress of long travels and of having to adjust to new surroundings and by the disruptive effects on daily routines when it comes to children's social lives. The findings also call for a more optimistic view on the role of frequent parent-child contact for child outcomes. Although this study corroborates earlier findings suggesting no or modest *overall* positive effects of shared residence and father visitation (Adamsons and Johnson 2013; Nielsen 2018), frequent parent-child contact has stronger positive associations with child outcomes when parents live close - and for shared residence this is often the case as most parents live within 10 min travel distance.

This study also has some limitations, which call for further research. The cross-sectional design of the study does not allow for strong causal inferences. Selectivity and reversed causation may explain some of the observed associations, as was for instance suggested when discussing the positive association between travel distance and educational performance. Ideally, future research should use panel data to address these issues, though large-scale panel data containing a sufficient number of divorced people are difficult to find. Another limitation concerns the used measure for distance. NFN only includes information about travel time, and lacks information about the geographical distance between parents in kilometers or more specific information about the mode of traveling. Whether children travel by foot, bike, car or public transportation may also be important as some traveling modes e.g. imply greater organizational and practical difficulties of traveling than others or may feel more stressful. Future research may want to use less crude measures to capture geographical distance or examine the mode of travel. A related suggestion for future research is to have a closer look at the temporal organization of multi-locality: at which days in the week do children go to the other parent, week or weekend days? As speculated above, it may be that moves during weekdays may be more disruptive to children's daily routines such as meeting with friends or doing homework, than moves during weekends. Finally, NFN surveyed parents quite shortly after divorce and separation. Given the sampling design parents were, on average, divorced/separated for only 2 years. It may well be that traveling may become increasingly tedious for children after a while. Future research may examine the effects of spatial mobility in the longer term.

All in all, this study suggests that the spatial mobility arising from traveling between two homes is not necessarily a bad thing. When parents live close, frequent parent-child contact and frequent moves between parental homes appear to be beneficial for children. It is only when children have to travel over long distances that these benefits disappear. Because parents with a shared residence arrangement typically live close to each, concerns about the greater spatial mobility of children in shared residence find little empirical support overall in this study.

Appendix: Baseline Models

Table A Multilevel analyses of multiple child outcomes on control variables: total sample and mother residence only

	SDQ	Grade	Nr. of friends	Contact friends
Total sample	N = 3552	N = 942	N = 3444	N = 3275
Female respondent	−.069**	.041	.033	−.536~
Previous cohabitation	−.012	.113	.034	−.283
Age child	−.006	−.112**	.015**	.363**
Child is girl	−.173**	.290**	.081**	−.182
Mother education	−.030**	018	.006	−.269**
Father education	−.024**	.012	−.006	−.240**
Mother working hours	−.001	−.003	.003**	.015
Father working hours	−.002~	.001	.000	.000
Predivorce conflict	.022	.012	−.005	−.016
Predivorce problems parents	.072**	.033	−.009	.228
Predivorce household income/10000	−.009	−.024	.013~	−.126
Postdivorce tensions	.082**	−.069*	−.029*	−.391*
Postdivorce severe conflict	.034**	−.006	−.005	.113
Postdivorce household income/10000	−.027**	.002	.020**	.219*
Either parent repartnered	−.047~	.043	.029	.377
Mother residence only	N = 2329	N = 571	N = 2238	N = 2094
Female respondent	−.128**	.096	.054~	−1.252**
Previous cohabitation	−.012	.170	.033	−.687
Age child	−.008~	−.085**	.014**	.320**
Child is girl	−.173**	.217**	.081**	−.402
Mother education	−.030**	.004	.007	−.247*
Father education	−.020**	.033	−.012~	−.313**
Mother working hours	−.001	−.005	.003*	.009
Father working hours	−.002~	−.000	−.000	−.002
Predivorce conflict	.022	−.053	−.025	−.029
Predivorce problems parents	.072**	.045	−.018	.109
Predivorce household income/10000	−.013	.006	.012	−.131
Postdivorce tensions	.095**	−.092*	−.030~	−.487*
Postdivorce severe conflict	.027**	.018	.004	.180*
Postdivorce household income/10000	−.032*	−.024	.023*	.183
Either parent repartnered	−.065*	.147	.049~	.596

~p < .10; *p < .05; **p < .01 (two-sided)

References

Adamsons, K., & Johnson, S. K. (2013). An updated and expanded meta-analysis of nonresident fathering and child well-being. *Journal of Family Psychology, 27*, 589.

Amato, P. R. (1993). Children's adjustment to divorce: Theories, hypotheses, and empirical support. *Journal of Marriage and the Family, 55*, 23–38.

Cancian, M., Meyer, D. R., Brown, P. R., & Cook, S. T. (2014). Who gets custody now? Dramatic changes in children's living arrangements after divorce. *Demography, 51*, 1381–1396.

Cooksey, E. C., & Craig, P. H. (1998). Parenting from a distance: The effects of paternal characteristics on contact between nonresidential fathers and their children. *Demography, 35*, 187–200.

Feijten, P., & Van Ham, M. (2013). The consequences of divorce and splitting up for spatial mobility in the UK. *Comparative Population Studies, 3*, 405–432.

Fransson, E., Låftman, S. B., Östberg, V., Hjern, A., & Bergström, M. (2018). The living conditions of children with shared residence–the Swedish example. *Child Indicators Research, 11*, 861–883.

Goodman, R. (1997). The strengths and difficulties questionnaire: A research note. *Journal of Child Psychology and Psychiatry, 38*, 581–586.

Kalil, A., Mogstad, M., Rege, M., & Votruba, M. (2011). Divorced fathers' proximity and children's long-run outcomes: Evidence from Norwegian registry data. *Demography, 48*, 1005–1027.

Jensen, A. M. (2009). Mobile children: Small captives of large structures? *Children & Society, 23*, 123–135.

Mahrer, N. E., O'Hara, K. L., Sandler, I. N., & Wolchik, S. A. (2018). Does shared parenting help or hurt children in high-conflict divorced families? *Journal of Divorce & Remarriage, 59*, 324–347.

Nielsen, L. (2018). Joint versus sole physical custody: Outcomes for children independent of family income or parental conflict. *Journal of Child Custody, 15*, 35–54.

Nikolina, N. V. (2015). *Divided parents, shared children: Legal aspects of (residential) co-parenting in England, the Netherlands and Belgium* [Dissertation]. Utrecht: Utrecht University.

Poortman, A. (2018). Postdivorce parent–child contact and child well-being: The importance of predivorce parental involvement. *Journal of Marriage and Family, 80*, 671–683.

Poortman, A., & Van Gaalen, R. (2017). Shared residence after separation: A review and new findings from the Netherlands. *Family Court Review, 55*, 531–544.

Poortman, A., Van der Lippe, T., & Boele-Woelki, K. (2014). *Codebook of the survey New Families in the Netherlands (NFN). First wave*. Utrecht: Utrecht University.

Prazen, A., Wolfinger, N. H., Cahill, C., & Kowaleski-Jones, L. (2011). Joint physical custody and neighborhood friendships in middle childhood. *Sociological Inquiry, 81*, 247–259.

Rasmussen, A. W., & Stratton, L. S. (2016). How distance to a non-resident parent relates to child outcomes. *Review of Economics of the Household, 14*, 829–857.

Schier, M. (2015). Post-separation families: Spatial mobilities and the need to manage multi-local everyday life. In C. M. Aybek, J. Huinink, & R. Muttarak (Eds.), *Spatial mobility, migration, and living arrangements* (pp. 205–224). Cham: Springer.

Sodermans, A., Vanassche, S., & Matthijs, K. (2013). Verblijfsregelingen en welbevinden van kinderen: verschillen naar gezinskenmerken. *Relaties en Nieuwe Gezinnen, 3*, 1–29.

Sodermans, A. K., Vanassche, S., Matthijs, K., & Swicegood, G. (2014). Measuring postdivorce living arrangements: Theoretical and empirical validation of the residential calendar. *Journal of Family Issues, 35*, 125–145.

Steinbach, A. (2018). Children's and parents' well-being in joint physical custody: A literature review. *Online publication ahead of print in Family process*. https://doi.org/10.1111/famp.12372.

Thomas, M. J., Mulder, C. H., & Cooke, T. J. (2018). Geographical distances between separated parents: A longitudinal analysis. *European Journal of Population, 34*, 63–489.

Vanassche, S., Sodermans, A. K., Matthijs, K., & Swicegood, G. (2013). Commuting between two parental households: The association between joint physical custody and adolescent wellbeing following divorce. *Journal of Family Studies, 19*, 139–158.

Videon, T. M. (2002). The effects of parent-adolescent relationships and parental separation on adolescent well-being. *Journal of Marriage and Family, 64*, 489–503.

Viry, G. (2014). Coparenting and children's adjustment to divorce: The role of geographical distance from fathers. *Journal of Divorce & Remarriage, 55*, 503–526.

Westphal, S. (2015). Chapter three from *Are the kids alright. Essays on postdivorce residence arrangements and children's wellbeing* (Dissertation). Utrecht: Universiteit Utrecht.

Westphal, S. K., Poortman, A., & Van der Lippe, T. (2014). Non-resident father–child contact across divorce cohorts: The role of father involvement during marriage. *European Sociological Review, 30*, 444–456.

Anne-Rigt Poortman is Professor at the Department of Sociology, Utrecht University (Chair: 'Family Diversity and Life Course Outcomes'). She has specialized in family sociology and social demography. She is particularly interested in divorce and separation, new relationship types and legal aspects of partner relationships. Currently she is the program leader of a large data collection and related research program about how and why outcomes for parents and children vary across different postdivorce family types.

Part IV
Shared Physical Custody: A Dynamic Perspective

11

SPC and its Varied Methods of Implementation

Benoit Hachet

Abstract Drawing on quantitative contextual data, this largely qualitative study comprehensively explores the different ways of obtaining shared physical custody (SPC) in France. I show that the choice of SPC depends on the historical context in which the marital separation occurred. I distinguish three ways of entering into SPC: situations of parental disagreement settled by law, situations in which a third party intervened in the decision, and situations of parental agreement. In this final category, I discuss the category of agreement itself, showing that behind seemingly obvious, though far from explicit, ways of reasoning lie processes of influence and negotiation occurring between separated mothers and fathers.

Keywords Shared physical custody · Parental agreement · Parental disagreement · Parental negotiation

Drawing on quantitative contextual data, this largely qualitative study comprehensively explores the different ways of obtaining shared physical custody (SPC) in France. I show that the choice of SPC depends on the historical context in which the marital separation occurred. I distinguish three ways of entering into SPC: situations of parental disagreement settled by law, situations in which a third party intervened in the decision, and situations of parental agreement. In this final category, I discuss the category of agreement itself, showing that behind seemingly obvious, though far from explicit, ways of reasoning lie processes of influence and negotiation occurring between separated mothers and fathers.

B. Hachet (✉)
EHESS (School of Advanced Studies in the Social Sciences), Paris, France
e-mail: Benoit.hachet@ehess.fr

11.1 Theoretical Framework

While the psychologically oriented question of the well-being of children prevails in research on SPC (see the Robert E. Emery's chapter in this volume), there are other perspectives which must not be neglected. Demographic research on conjugal separation categorizes its target population according to the place of residence of the child; which is to say, according to whether the child lives with the mother, the father or with both parents. Studies carried out on an international scale (Bjarnason and Arnarsson 2011), at a national level (Sodermans et al. 2013), as well statistical approaches towards court judgements relating to divorce settlements (Cancian and Meyer 1998), all converge around the observation that SPC constitutes a minority of cases, that the parents who adopt this arrangement post-separation belong to more advantaged social strata; and that, on the other hand, it is beginning to spread more widely across society (Cancian et al. 2014). In Belgium, for example, "a more heterogenous social group is now likely to share responsibility for children after divorce, generalizations made on the basis of previous studies are no longer valid" (Sodermans et al. 2013). In effect, SPC has undergone democratisation.

Regardless of the objectives of the studies conducted, the countries studied, and the quantitative methodology used, the research on the determinants of SPC are in accordance with the following points.

It is more commonly adopted when the duration of separation is shorter, when the parents are on good terms with each other, when the father is more invested in the children before the separation and is recognized as such by the mother, and when the children are between 5 and 10 years old (Juby et al. 2005; Berger et al. 2008; Melli and Brown 2008; Spruijt and Duindam 2009; Kitterod and Lyngstad 2012; Nielsen 2013; Sodermans et al. 2013; Biland and Schütz 2015; Sodermans et al. 2015).

"Although increasing numbers of parents share custody of their children, we still know little about how divorced parents negotiate this process" (Stafford Markham and Coleman 2012, 587). My principle objective here is to address this lacuna. To be clear, the objective is not to consider how the popularity of SPC, relative to other forms of custody, varies from one cross-section of the population to the next; I am interested rather in how the process which leads towards SPC unfolds; and an emphasis is placed on how the parents themselves reconstruct this process. By engaging with parent's testimonies, we arrive a typology of modes of entry into SPC ordered according to a sliding scale: on one end, those cases where parents arrive at SPC without need for intervention of a third party, on the other those cases which required a high level of intervention. We arrive thereby at an updated understanding of the dynamics of negotiation involved (Strauss 1978), both formal and informal. I draw on the results of a two-pronged quantitative and qualitative field study, whose protocol I will outline after providing an overview of the French context.

11.2 The Choice of Shared Physical Custody (SPC) in France

The case of France is interesting: the participation rate of women in the labour force is high (85% of 25–49 years olds), as is the number of unmarried parents (6 out of 10 children are born out of wedlock). In addition, while SPC may not be a legal presumption in this country, for a little under two decades legal provision for equal custody has existed. The law authorizing SPC in France dates back to 2002. It was implemented around the same time as in other European countries, after the Scandinavian nations but before countries in southern and eastern Europe. Although the possibility of SPC is mentioned first in the body of the 2002 law, even before that of establishing residency with one or the other parent, this does not mean that it is the default option, as is the case in Belgium for example. According to the most recent data available, compiled by the Insee (The National Institute of Statistics and Economic Studies) using tax returns, children in shared physical custody number 400,000, accounting for 2.7% of children under the age of eighteen in France (Algava et al. 2019). Another estimate based on social data about beneficiaries of the Cnaf (National Fund for Family Allowances) who share family benefits because they share custody of their children,[1] indicates that 239,000 children were part of an SPC arrangement in 2017—versus 33,000 in 2007 (Céroux and Hachet 2019). Though it remains a small-scale phenomenon, SPC has increased significantly in France in recent years.

A 2012 survey by the French Ministry of Justice estimated that SPC was the result of 17% of all judges' rulings on divorces and separations involving children[2] (Guillonneau and Moreau 2013). Following this survey, in 2014, a sample of parents who divorced in 2012 were asked questions about the choice of living arrangements for their children after separation (Belmokhtar and Cretin 2015). The authors note that regardless of the chosen living arrangement, "the choice of living arrangement is a given [i.e., an obvious choice] for eight parents in ten" (Belmokhtar and Cretin 2015, 2). For parents sharing custody of children, 77% of women and 91% of men answered that the choice "was from the beginning *a given*,[3]" while only 13% of women and 4% of men responded that the choice was made after lengthy reflection" (Belmokhtar and Cretin 2015, 2). This data is consistent with results obtained in Sweden, a country in which SPC is much more widespread than in France. The question used by Swedish researchers as the title of their article—"Why should they live more with one of us when they are children to us both?" (Fransson et al. 2016)—

[1]Since 2007, parents with children in SPC in France have been able to share family benefits. Neither parents with a single child in SPC nor those who do not share benefits are included in this data.

[2]Primary residency with the mother represented 71% of decisions and primary residency with the father, 12% (Guillonneau and Moreau 2013). This data does not take into account non-adjudicated SPC.

[3]My emphasis.

eloquently shows that the choice of SPC is linked to the question of parenting style and parenting equality.

11.3 Data and Methods

This study draws on research data from a wider research project carried out within the framework of a doctoral thesis addressing the question of the temporal dimension to the experience of parents within an SPC arrangement. In collecting and analyzing the findings of this study, two distinct angles of approach towards the process of entering into such an arrangement were adopted. In the first place, we carried out semi-directive interviews with parents who shared equal custody. This allowed us to build categories which were in turn incorporated into a questionnaire targeting a wider population. Our research strategy consisted in sequentially collecting qualitative and quantitative data with a view to heightening the "complementarity" and enhancing the "development" of methods (Bryman 2006).

Between 2011 and 2017, I conducted 55 interviews with 42 parents in situations of equally split SPC of their children following a separation. Because this number of parents included seven former couples, my interview corpus was actually composed of 35 SPC situations in total. Recruitment took place via several channels, snowballing from family member to family member or friend, at family mediation centers, or at public institutions that offer support to parents. When constructing my sample, I took particular care to make sure my participants had diverse profiles in terms of age, gender, number of children, levels of income and education, former marital status, their use of the legal system, blended families, and length of separation. I interviewed an equal number of mothers and fathers, and the average age of parents was 41.5 years old (ranging from 32 to 54 years old), while the average age of children was 9.6 years old (from 1 to 16 years old). The average length of separation was 4.4 years (from 2 months to 12 years), and a third of recruited parents did not go through the legal system. In seven cases, a single child was impacted by SPC; in 24 cases, two children; three children in three cases; and four children in one case. A part of the interview guide was devoted to the subject of the process of entry into SPC addressing how the decision was taken, whether the parents were in agreement or, if not, who had directed them towards SPC, whether or not they had consulted psychologists, appealed to family mediation or lawyers from the start, and whether or not parents had initiated legal proceedings. Through a thematic analysis of interviews, involving a comparison of parental narratives, allowed for the construction of categories related to the process of entry into shared custody: whether it was the product of agreement, disagreement or an intermediary state. These categories were then further used as an item in the construction of a questionnaire distributed to parents abiding by an SPC arrangement.

France's RA-CAF-2016 survey is based on a questionnaire given to 20,000 parents (from a population of more than 100,000 individuals) who receive child benefits from the state's National Fund for Family Allowances and who share the money that they receive because they have SPC arrangements or because they have reported to their local office that their children alternate between homes. Published on line in June 2016, this questionnaire was elaborated with the oversight and collaboration of the Cnaf (National Funds for Family Allowance), and contributed to the completion of my doctorate. 5103 parents completed the questionnaire, a response rate of 25,5%. Within this group, 87% of SPC parents indicated that their children live « as much time with one parent as with the other». This result confirmed the pertinence of our decision to define SPC as an arrangement involving equal custody, a decision based on further research into equal parenting responsibility after divorce.

For the presentation of the results, I use quantitative data to assist in locating in-depth interviews within the larger sample of SPC cases. This work is based above all on the comprehensive analysis of each of the categories which thereby were brought into focus. The methodological pivoting back and forth of our approach proved to be effective in advancing our comprehension of parental reasons for entering into SPC. For example, as will become clear, the category of 'parental agreement' as endpoint was the product of diverse modalities of negotiation as intermediary step.

11.4 Results

I will first present the data obtained from the quantitative study, which I only use here to provide statistical context, before turning to the impact that the time period had on decision-making, and then proposing a comprehensive approach to each way of entering into SPC.

11.4.1 Three Ways of Entering into SPC

In the questionnaire-based RA-CAF-2016 survey, the first question was about the ways of entering into SPC. Parents were asked how SPC was implemented, with six possible responses (Table 11.1).

I will start by noting that that there are no discrepancies between the answers provided by mothers and fathers when it comes to reconstructing the process which led them towards SPC. The majority of parent respondents (70%) stated that SPC was implemented with mutual agreement. 16% responded that it was the result of a legal ruling following a parental disagreement—in the overwhelming majority of cases, it was the father who wanted SPC, while the mother was against it. In order to avoid a binary opposition between agreement and disagreement, I have introduced a third category of SPC situations, which are the result of intervention by a third party. This category of intermediary situations, which accounts for 14% of parental

Table 11.1 Implementation of SPC

Typology of entering into SPC	Share of answers
Mutual agreement	**70%**
Disagreement settled in court	**16%**
Father requested it	14%
Mother requested it	2%
Third party intervention	**14%**
Children's request	9%
Judge's suggestion	3%
Family mediation	2%
N = 5103	100%

RA-CAF-2016, Parents with children in SPC in the French National Fund for Family Allowances

responses, primarily reflects demands by children (9%) and to a lesser degree, a judge's proposal (3%) or a decision made during family mediation (2%).

The level of intervention required varies somewhat depending on parental experience. Parental accord is higher (74%) among those who had shared custody on equal terms for more than 10 years, compared to those who had done so for less than 2 years (62%). Instances of disaccord decrease in step with the duration of SPC (20% to 14%), and with the greater prominence accorded to the voice of children in the decision-making process (12% to 6%). We may deduce from these findings that joint custody arrangements which began earlier are more often the result of a mutual agreement between parents; more recent cases, attesting to a greater diversity of social backgrounds, are more likely to involve decisions where the demands of the father were heeded against the advice of the mother, and the voice of children taken into consideration. We shall now take a retrospective look at how parental arrangements were implemented before law of 2002.

11.4.2 The Choice of SPC Prior to the 2002 Law

The decision to implement SPC has different meanings depending on the time period in which a marital separation occurred. Here, I will refer to the experiences of two mothers who divorced in 1982 and 1984, and who implemented SPC of their children, and that of two fathers who went through several separations or divorces, without SPC when they occurred prior to 2002, and with SPC after.

Two Pioneers

Geneviève, a teacher in a Parisian suburb, divorced in 1982, when her children were 6 and 3 years old:

> We undoubtedly wouldn't have had the idea on our own because when we got a divorce, we didn't even know it existed. It was the very beginning of divorce by mutual agreement [1975] but it was the lawyer—we got just one lawyer for the divorce—and it was the lawyer who told us, "Look, I don't understand. You're going to go before the family affairs judge for custody of the children when since you get along so well why not opt for a system of shared physical custody?" We didn't know, because it was still the good ol' system when we had to choose which one of us would get the children. (Geneviève, 65, retired teacher, D37, S34, SPC15, Paris suburbs, 2013) [4]

The "*good ol' system*" of choosing the parent who would get custody colored their perception of what had to be done after a divorce at the time. The lawyer who enabled them to consider this type of custody drew upon the fact that they got along well, which, before the 2002 law, was a vital condition for implementing SPC, as one parent could not request it without the other's agreement. The reasons given by Geneviève relate to the necessity for gender equality:

> I'm the one who left, who decided to leave my husband because I no longer wanted to live with him, I couldn't see myself anymore . . . there it is, I felt like we no longer had enough things in common. But for me, from the beginning, it struck me as absurd to deprive him of his children when from the very start he had been a, well, I don't like this word, but a perfect father. Meaning he took care of them all the time, he knew how to change diapers, he knew how to give them their bottle, he got up at night, he took them to the doctor . . . and I didn't see what right I had, just because I was the female in the couple, to claim the right to keep the children. So since we had the same mindset—politically at least—, it all happened rather quickly after that. (Geneviève, 65, retired teacher, D37, S34, SPC15, Paris suburbs, 2013)

Monique, a physician in a small town in the *département* of Vendée, separated from her husband in 1984, when their three children were 14, 11, and 6 years old. Unlike in Geneviève's case, Monique's husband was not involved in child rearing tasks:

> I was the one who took care of the children. I'm the one who carried them, I'm the one who managed everything, even though [my husband] did some things, he did them when it suited him. I organized my work schedule to do this . . . it struck me as logical that his position as the father be maintained, that's how it seemed to me, clear. I didn't think that depriving the children of their father was a solution. I wouldn't say this was a radical opinion, but almost. (Monique, 67, retired physician, D40, D37, S32, SPC16, village in the west of France, 2011)

Despite their unequal involvement in bringing up their children, Monique tried to convince her husband to take a greater role in raising their children because she wanted to "*maintain his position as the father*," following the same logic as Geneviève. In the two configurations described, the mothers could have logically requested and obtained sole custody of their children, but not doing so was for them a "radical" act.

[4] In this article, the following information is provided for all the interviewed parents: their anonymized first name, their age, their occupation, the genders and ages of their children, how long (in years) they have been in an SPC arrangement, where they live, and the date of the interview.

Two Fathers Who Divorced Both Before and After 2002

Claude is a stock-keeper and lives in a village in the south of France. In 1988, he divorced for the first time, from a wife with whom he had two sons aged five and two; in 1994, he separated from the mother of his third son, who was 1 year old at the time; and in 2013, he separated from the mother of his fourth son and his first daughter, when they were 15 and 10 years old. During the first two separations, the primary residence was established at the mothers' homes, with the agreement of Claude, who had visitation and physical custody rights every other weekend and half of vacations. The idea of implementing SPC did not occur to him because "*It wasn't the done thing. It was impossible. No information about this arrangement had trickled down to us*" (Claude, 54, stock-keeper, S15, D10, SPC2, village in the south of France, 2015).

Christian, a retired serviceman who lives in a village in the *département* of Saône-et-Loire, has been divorced twice: the first time in 1997 when his first children were 12, 7, and 4 years old; and the second time in 2009 when the children from his second marriage were 7 and 4 years old. In 1997, he did not request SPC because "*it didn't really exist back then, it was very rare, and also, I was still in the military at the time and I couldn't stop working*" (Christian, 54, retired serviceman, D13, S10, SPC4, village in the east of France, 2015).

Since SPC's enshrinement in law in March 2002, it has "*trickled down*" to the entire population, and not only those with the highest social standing. Lawmakers' recognition of SPC has democratized access to this arrangement. As a result, during their last separations, in 2011 for Christian and 2013 for Claude, the same fathers who had not envisaged SPC of their children a few years earlier, implemented it at this time. The law changed the universe of possibilities for them, and their past experiences reinforced their choices.

In 2013, Claude separated from his third wife, with no conflict surrounding the separation. He justifies the choice of SPC, comparing it to other types of arrangements:

> Because in reality, when a parent has their child every other weekend and for half of vacations, they aren't raising them, the children are there on vacation, and from experience I saw that they had lost their bearings, and it was only by chance that they all came back to me. But my entire generation—I'm talking about 1961 here—they all separated, and everyone did every other weekend, and everyone had problems with it. [. . .] It's the best balance for the kids. With shared physical custody, you get to raise your kids more or less properly. (Claude, 54, stock- keeper, S15, D10, SPC2, village in the south of France, 2015)

In 2011, during his second divorce, Christian also chose to implement SPC. The legislative context allowed him to envisage it as a way to avoid reliving the painful experience of his first separation, in 1997:

> We got a traditional divorce—every two weeks and half of vacations. It went badly in the sense that after a while I wasn't seeing my kids anymore, and now that they're adults, and after I fought for years to have them, they indirectly hold it against me for having abandoned them. [. . .] For me, it was out of the question to do the same thing I did during my first

> divorce. That was too painful. After six years of legal battles, I stopped. It's too masochistic. (Christian, 54, retired serviceman, D13, S10, SPC4, village in the east of France, 2015)

The arguments made by Christian to justify the choice of SPC do not stem, as is the case with Claude, from this kind of arrangement being better for children's well-being. His motivation was to avoid making the same mistake as during his previous divorce. He did not want to become distanced from his children as he did from those from his first marriage. The legal existence of SPC offered him the possibility of not doing the same thing again.

Although all the mothers and fathers cited here lacked information about SPC in the 1980s and 1990s, the playing field was not level when it came to their social and cultural resources. Aspirations for post-divorce gender equality were much more widespread at the time in higher social groups (Geneviève was a teacher and Monique a physician) than in working-class milieus (Claude and Christian were, respectively, a stock-keeper and a serviceman). The former opted for egalitarian choices at the risk of transgressing the dominant norms—and their ex-husbands followed them—while the latter did not consider doing so (nor did their ex-spouses) before the law was voted on and became widely known.

11.4.3 The Choice of SPC Following the 2002 Law

I will now move on to explore the major categories presented in Table 11.1. I will first examine cases of disagreements settled in court, before turning to situations in which a third party successfully intervened, before concluding with the category of mutual agreements between parents.

Disagreements Settled in Court

The RA-CAF-2016 survey reveals that in 16% of cases, SPC was implemented against the wishes of one of the two parents following a legal ruling (Table 11.1). In 90% of cases, it was the father who wanted SPC contrary to the mother's wishes (Table 11.1). Among the participants in the interview-based survey, I met two fathers, Jérôme and Laurent, who wanted SPC of their children, while the mothers opposed it. I did not encounter any situations in which mothers requested SPC in court while the fathers were against it. I will therefore only present these paternal situations, as explained by the fathers themselves.

Jérôme, a researcher, was the father of three children aged ten, five, and one when his wife left him in 2010:

> The breakup was pretty sudden—it happened in all of five minutes. I asked her if she had someone else, if she loved him, if she planned on living with him. I got three affirmative answers so then it was settled ... Anyway, we knew then that we would separate immediately. [...] We talked about the kids right away and then ... Thing is ... She wanted custody ... But I said, "I want shared physical custody, you have somebody, you have a family, but I

> won't have anything left otherwise." So . . . It was both a question of personal equilibrium . . . A little bit of honor too . . . (Jérôme, 39, researcher, D11, S7, S3, SPC1, Paris, 2011)

Jérôme expresses his desire for "*shared physical custody*" in relation to the suddenness of the breakup, which left him completely bereft. He wanted to continue to be part of a family with his children, to avoid being alone. He was driven less by the fact that continuing co-parenting was the obvious option than by a burst of pride, of "*honor*," after being stripped of his identity. His request for SPC stems from a reasoning that is more family-based than paternal. One can imagine that his wife was not expecting this request, because, as he mentions, he was not that involved with bringing up the children:

> For the division of labor, it was still . . . Even if I wasn't the most macho guy, she handled lots more things when it came to cleaning, she prepared the meals. [. . .] On Wednesdays, it was always her who watched the kids . . . During trips, she took care of them at night . . . I took them to school or daycare in the morning, but pretty often she was the one who took care of them.

Laurent, an oncologist in Marseille, and later Paris, separated from the mother of his 4-year-old son in 2006:

> We were living in Marseilles and at the end of 2006, I requested shared physical custody, which was refused. I had my son every other weekend and two days a week on the weeks when I didn't have weekends. We were slowly moving toward shared physical custody. In 2009, his mother moved to Paris in the middle of the year. The courts didn't like that much and they gave me full custody with the argument that you don't make [children] leave school in the middle of the year. In September, his mother regained full custody and I had every other weekend. This custody arrangement didn't suit me, so I decided to change job and move to Paris. Once I was settled in Paris in September 2010, I again requested shared physical custody, which was refused, with a family investigation, psychologists and everything, even though there hadn't been one before. It was only in March 2011 that the courts ruled in favor of true shared physical custody, which began in September 2011 when my son was ten years old. (Laurent, 50, oncologist, S11, SPC2, Paris, 2013)

Laurent waited 5 years before being able to implement SPC due to parental disagreements about this arrangement. The courts ultimately granted him his wish, at the cost, for him, of a move and a job change. Unlike Jérôme, Laurent specifies that he "*had always been a 'mom-dad,'*" meaning a father actively involved in raising his son. Regardless of their level of involvement in child rearing tasks, these two fathers requested and obtained SPC.[5]

SPC Requested by Children

While SPC proposals made by judges to non-petitioning parents (3%) and the development of the arrangement during family mediation (2%) were rare in 2016,

[5]The survey protocol I used excluded situations in which one parent requested SPC and did not obtain it.

requests by children accounted for 9% of responses about how SPC was implemented (Table 11.1).

According to the RA-CAF-2016 survey, 9% of SPC arrangements were established "at the children's request" (Table 11.1). In the interview-based survey, I encountered two cases that fall within this category. Ludovic, who separated from his wife in 2009, with children aged five and three, did not immediately request SPC, mainly "*because the children were little, and everything that I read about shared physical custody said that it wasn't good for little kids*" (Ludovic, 41, videographer, D9, S6, (S1), SPC1, Paris suburbs, 2013, 2016). Though he did not directly consult "child specialists," Ludovic read oft-circulated negative opinions about SPC of young children. For 4 years, he and his ex-wife adopted a unique arrangement of split parental time. His children lived with their mother, and every morning, he went to the home of his ex-wife, who worked very early hours. He woke up his children, dressed them, made their breakfasts, and took them to school. During this period, he also spent every other weekend and half of vacations with his children. His paternal investment did not transform into a request for SPC until his children suggested the idea:

> In fact, they're the ones who asked for it. One day, they came home from school and the older one said, "Why don't we do one week one week, like my friends at school?" I discussed it with their mother, who agreed.

During those 4 years, Ludovic did not request SPC because he felt guilty for having left, and because he believed his children were too young to live in a situation of SPC. It was therefore their request that allowed him to imagine the possibility of SPC and discuss it with their mother. At the time, his children were 9 and 6 years old, and no longer 5 and 2 years old, and—an important factor—his wife had found a boyfriend. The fact that the mother of his children was no longer alone undoubtedly favored the request by the children, that of their father, and their mother's acceptance. Thus, more generally, post-separation configurations must be taken into consideration to understand a parent's motivation for or resistance to entering into SPC.

What Lies Behind Parental Agreement?

In my quantitative survey, 70% of parents stated that the implementation of SPC had been decided on in agreement with the other parent (Table 11.1). While situations of parental disagreement or those resulting from intervention by a third party are easily understood, the same is not true for the agreement category, which appears to reflect that SPC was an obvious choice, a given. Nonetheless, this "given," or "obviousness," awakens the sociologist's curiosity and calls for more in-depth explanations.

Discourse About Shared "Obviousness"

Though not all the SPC parents encountered use the term "obvious" to explain what drove them to adopt SPC, many of them do nonetheless use this vocabulary, or terms such as "natural" or "normal" that express the same idea. What does the obviousness of SPC mean to the parents who chose it? Sandrine is the only mother encountered who explains that the choice of SPC had been decided well before the separation:

> Shared physical custody . . . We had already talked about it when we got married, before having kids, because there were people around us already divorcing and trying to figure out the issue of custody . . . we had already talked about shared physical custody, we felt like it was a good compromise, one week with Dad, one week with Mom. So that was it, after that we lived our life . . . and then, bad luck, we were getting a divorce, and it came about naturally that my husband and I did fifty fifty, meaning every other week, there you have it. (Sandrine, 36, nurse, S9, D6, SPC2 months, Paris suburbs, 2011)

In order for this decision, made 10 years earlier, to be respected in 2011 when the separation occurred, other conditions had to be present. One main condition for the parents to be able to discuss SPC as the obvious solution was the father's involvement in parenting and domestic responsibilities. Later in the interview, Sandrine explains:

> My husband always took care of the children while I was working. So it was natural for me that it should continue, even after the divorce.

For Sandrine, SPC was the continuation of parental responsibility in another form. Marie-Pierre expresses this maternal discourse recognizing the father's capacities in the same way, with nearly the same words:

> It was natural because in our parenting couple we were already taking care of the children in an equal way, he took care of them a lot, and so did I. (Marie-Pierre, 37, nurse, D12, D 9, SPC7, Paris suburbs, 2011)

Her ex-husband confirms these comments:

> The decision to go for shared physical custody was spontaneous and natural. We didn't discuss it, not at all [. . .]. It was obvious. I was involved in my daughters' upbringing, we can say it was obvious. There wasn't any discussion (Bojan, 38, teacher, D12, D9, SPC7, Paris suburbs, 2011).

The "natural," "obvious," or "spontaneous" nature of implementing SPC means that parents did not need to force their ex-spouses to change their habits in order to split physical custody of their children after the marital separation. The two parents both felt competent in caring for their children, and felt the other parent was equally competent.

A Paternal Initiative Accepted by the Mother

The following cases recount situations in which fathers initiated SPC and were able to convince mothers to implement this arrangement. These are therefore situations of parental agreement whose protagonists identified the father as the initiator.[6] In this category, we see fathers invested in their children and, generally, marital breakups initiated by the mother. Stéphane states:

---

[6] These situations should not be confused with cases of disagreements over SPC of children that are settled by law.

> I couldn't imagine any arrangement other than shared physical custody at the very least. She had no choice. I was involved. I took partial parental leave when my second daughter was born. I have always been there. Traditional custody was unthinkable. (Stéphane, 34, optician, D8, D6, SPC4, city in the east of France, 2014)

Later in the interview, we learn that his marriage ended after he discovered that his wife was having an extra-marital affair: *"She had someone else, she denied it for a long time. Once I had proof, the breakup was immediate."* The story of the separation sheds new light on the fact that Stéphane's ex-wife did not have a *"choice."* Not only were they sharing parental responsibilities but his ex-wife, being the cause of the breakup, could not refuse Stéphane what he considered to be the *"minimum,"* meaning shared physical custody of their daughters. Some women can therefore be prompted to accept implementation of SPC because they feel responsible for the breakup. "It is a matter of guilt or restitution for 'causing' the divorce" (Stafford Markham and Coleman 2012, 597). Whoever causes the breakup carries a feeling of guilt[7] that drives him or her to limit his demands. Conversely, Ludovic, who left his wife after finding a new girlfriend, did not see himself requesting SPC right away:

> I was the one who left her, I wasn't going to take away her kids too by asking for shared physical custody. (Ludovic,41, videographer, D9, S6, (S1), SPC1, Paris suburbs, 2013)

Not every situation of father-initiated SPC is implemented due to the mother who has caused the breakup feeling guilty. Claude and Muriel separated by mutual agreement. Claude thought that SPC was the most stabilizing solution for the children. Muriel would have preferred *"traditional custody"* but she accepted a joint arrangement *"for the children"*:

> I would have preferred traditional custody. But it was easier for the children in a difficult separation. The children come first. My husband didn't want a "once every two weeks" arrangement. What's important is that the children come first. They wanted shared physical custody, and so did my ex-husband. (Muriel, 42, unemployed, S15, D10, SPC2, village in the south west of France, 2015)

Muriel accepted SPC not only because Claude requested it, but because her children did too. After discussing the arrangement with them, she conformed to their wishes.

A Maternal Initiative Accepted by the Father

Cases of SPC initiated by the mother appear to be very rare, if we rely on the quantitative data concerning parental disagreements. In the RA-CAF-2016 survey, the cases in which "the mother requested it against the father's wishes" account for 2% of responses on the implementation of SPC.[8] This data gives the impression that there are many more fathers than mothers who want to share physical custody of their children. But these results only concern legal proceedings in which the parents'

[7] Or *may* carry a feeling of guilt . . .

[8] According to data from the Ministry of Justice, when one parent requests shared physical custody and the other primary custody, the request for shared physical custody comes from the mother in only 13 percent of cases (Guillonneau and Moreau 2013).

requests differed. Yet the interview-based survey reveals that some jointly agreed-upon SPC arrangements were initiated by the mother. Rachid left his partner in 2003, when their son was 3 years old. In this interview excerpt, he explains how SPC was implemented:

> In 2003, I was depressed, really, really down, and personally I wouldn't have felt myself capable of taking care of [him]. So it was his mom who took charge. Because of the circumstances, because I was . . . at rock bottom. So she told me, "Okay, for [our son] it would be best"—well I don't know if it was for her or for [our son]—"that we share." Honestly there's one thing that's for sure, it's that I didn't feel capable of doing it. I was more in the traditional dad mindset, I'm not going to be able to take care of [him], I'll have him every other weekend, something like that. To be completely frank at the beginning I had that mentality in my head . . . very quickly, raising my son, well that became the only certainty in my life. (Rachid, 45, city hall employee, S15, SPC12, city in the west of France, 2015)

Unlike in the previously mentioned cases, although Rachid initiated the breakup, his spouse, and not him, requested SPC. Without the intervention of the mother of his son, it is clear that he would not have SPC of his child. It was the mother's initiative that allowed him to find a place as a father, and looking after his son provided him with an element of certainty in what was a difficult situation.

Louise and Arnaud separated in 2004, when they had a 5-year-old daughter and a 2-year-old son. They agree that SPC was implemented at the mother's initiative:

> At the time . . . Arnaud didn't feel . . . Well . . . Their father didn't necessarily feel like he could completely handle . . . Dealing with two pretty young kids, and so that's why we went for the idea of the splitting the week in two. (Louise, 43, architect, D15, S11, SPC10, Paris, 2014)

> She had to struggle within her own progressive mindset—because I was lucky to have someone very progressive—against her idea of taking the children. But she had it from the beginning, as part of her humanist side, this idea of equality, which is very present. (Arnaud, 42, architect, D15, S11, SPC10, Paris, 2014)

Louise underlines limited competency and limited paternal motivation to take care of young children, whereas Arnaud underlines the "*luck*" he had to be with someone "*progressive*" and "*humanist.*" The mother's argument centers on the concrete possibility of the father being able to care for the children, and the necessary adaptations to be made to enable SPC. Later in the interview, Louise explains that splitting the week in half allowed her to continue to handle everything, especially the laundry, as "*they went to their father's home with clean clothes, and came back with dirty clothes.*" The father's argument is completely detached from material considerations and relates to a world of conceptual justification. For the father, Louise's progressivism explains why she was able to combat the norm of maternal physical custody and allow him to be a father in daily life, albeit exempted, in this case, from a certain number of domestic responsibilities. The opportunity to implement SPC, as well as the terms of the arrangement, depends on the age of the children (Hachet 2017).

Julie, who separated in 2008 from the father of her daughter, 1 year old at the time, mentions the importance of her own experiences as a child:

> At first I was so angry that it crossed my mind more than once, I'm not saying I wasn't thinking it would be simpler if he just wasn't there . . . But, well, at the same time, I had a father who was gone all the time and I know what it's like not to have a father. So yeah, I didn't want to put my daughter through that. I took it on myself for her, you know, but now honestly things are better. (Julie, 43, piano teacher, D6, SPC4, city in the west of France, 2013)

Julie resists the "*simpler*" possibility of getting rid of the father of her daughter because of her memories of her own father's absence. She wages an inner battle, like Louise does with the norm, to give her ex-partner a place. In both cases, the breakups were sudden, and initiated by the woman. In both cases, the mothers took the initiative to involve their spouses in some degree of family mediation, which resulted, in addition to discussions of concrete arrangements, in committing the fathers to their roles.

11.5 Discussion and Limitations

My results are consistent with research that indicates that implementation of SPC is primarily the result of parents who agree on this type of arrangement. They also confirm the results of Alexander Masardo, which show the importance of historical context in the choices made by parents: "It is reasonable to suppose that the more widely accepted the practice of shared residence becomes, the more likely it is to be taken up as a serious option when parents separate" (2011, 133). This historical context is also a legal context. Thus, a change in the Catalan civil code in favor of "custodia compartida" largely contributed to the spread of this practice among the population (Solsona and Spijker 2016).

My study also allows for an expansion of the ways of entering into SPC beyond a binary opposition between spontaneous agreements, legal or otherwise, and parental disagreements settled in court. I have shown that on one hand, there is an intermediary category in which a third party intervened in the decision, and on the other, that the category of "parental agreement" can itself be split into several different modes. In France, direct proposals made by judges during hearings are few, as are decisions for SPC made during family mediation. In contrast, for nearly 10% of parents with SPC, the request for SPC by children was decisive and brought about the parents' agreement, particularly when the children were older. Children had a role in implementing SPC, as they did in how it subsequently functioned: "Children's narratives reveal how most of them engaged in different kinds of decision-making practices on a regular basis" (Berman 2018, 111).

The category of parental agreements is most often considered as "a given" (Fransson et al. 2016) and as a result is little examined. I have shown that parental agreements on SPC, brought to court or not, hide decision-making processes that can be lengthy and in which one of the two parents is able to influence the other to accept his or her choice. I have also shown that SPC results not only from pressure from fathers to have access to their children, but also from initiatives by mothers to ensure their children have an invested father. "These mothers believed that sharing custody was the right thing to do for their children" (Stafford Markham and Coleman 2012, 593).

The study's limitations reside in the lack of systematic questioning of the two parents sharing physical custody of their children, which would have allowed for a subtler understanding of the types of negotiation at work. They also stem from the selection of subjects questioned, meaning parents in situations of SPC. I was consequently unable to gain access to parents who would have liked to implement SPC but who did not do so. The parametres of my research also prevented me from taking into consideration situations in which parents had ended an SPC arrangement, even in cases where it had been the choice of both parents - who subsequently were unable to maintain it. Finally, another limitation is that I collected these parental statements sometimes several years after a separation, which may have generated bias in reconstruction of the past (Bourdieu 1986).

11.6 Conclusion and Perspectives

In the relevant literature, analysis of the reasons that parents implement SPC after a separation or divorce is often limited to brief commentary about legal rulings. All the research on this subject concurs that in the vast majority of cases, SPC is the result of parental agreement. However, the way in which agreement is reached between parents is rarely examined. By focusing on this question of parental agreements, I have shown that they take form well before a legal ruling, and at times entirely outside of the court system. Here are the primary results:

The background circumstances which lead to conjugal separation exerted an influence on the macro level in determining whether and in what form SPC would be possible or practical. Before the law of 2002 parents coming from less advantaged social strata, and fathers in particular, often did not consider requesting SPC. Once the law had authorized it, the new norm spread across society to the point of impacting upon the decision-making process of individuals from social groups who would otherwise have been least open to equality in parenting. In short, parents henceforth made their decision as individuals in response to the particularities of their situation.

The ages of the children matter. With the youngest, parents most often agree that it is best for them to live with their mother. Decisions to implement SPC can thus be delayed until a time when the fathers, in particular, feel more capable of taking on parental responsibility. Older children intervene in the choice of the kind of living arrangement.

Gender matters. The guilt felt by the individual who decides to end a relationship has different impacts on the choice of custody arrangement depending on the gender of the individual who leaves. If the woman leaves, she will more readily accept a request for SPC by her former spouse, to make up for her departure. If the man leaves, he is less likely to request SPC, feeling like he is not allowed to go beyond what the dominant norm attributes to fathers, meaning every other weekend and half of vacations.

Repartnering matters. Our findings did not allow us to measure precisely the impact of new relationships on custody arrangements, or for that matter on the delayed implementing of SPC. The effect of re-pairing is never unequivocal: the configurations which it produces vary according to whether or not the new partner has children, the age of the children concerned, and the arrangement in place prior to family recomposition.

SPC may be considered the obvious choice for parents already sharing parental tasks before a separation. It can also result from the preference of one parent who was able to convince the other, outside of court. This can therefore serve to distinguish between paternally-initiated SPC and maternally-initiated SPC. We find ourselves confronted with a more complex reality than that captured by the often employed, yet overly static, category of 'parental agreement'. This chapter has identified some of the dynamics of negotiation which are often instrumental in driving the delicate process of transition towards such an arrangement. To expand on this study, it would be useful to conduct quantitative surveys specific to the implementation of SPC, in France as well as in comparable countries. The results would allow the influence of SPC as "a given," (i.e., as a seemingly obvious choice) to be measured, as well as the impacts of legislation, social policies, and national cultures on post-divorce co-parenting.

References

Algava, E., Penant, S., & Yankan, L. (2019). En 2016, 400 000 enfants alternent entre les deux domiciles de leurs parents séparés. *Insee Première*, n°1728, janvier.

Belmokhtar, Z., & Cretin, L. (2015). Le regard des divorcés sur la résidence de leurs enfants. *Infostat Justice*, 139, décembre.

Berger, L. M., Brown, R., Joung, E., Melli, M. S., & Wimer, L. (2008). The stability of child physical placements following divorce: Descriptive evidence from Wisconsin. *Journal of Mariage and Family, 70*, 273–283.

Berman, R. (2018). Children's influence on dual residence arrangements: Exploring decision-making practices. *Children and Youth Services Review, 91*, 105–114.

Biland, É., & Schütz, G. (2015). Physical custody of children in the province of québec: A quantitative analysis of court records. *Que savons-nous? 5*,

Bjarnason, T., & Arnarsson, A. M. (2011). Joint physical custody and communication with parents: A cross-national study of children in 36 western countries. *Journal of Comparative Family Studies, 42*(6), 871–890.

Bourdieu, P. (1986). L'illusion biographique. *Actes de la Recherche en Sciences Sociales, 62–63*, 69–72.

Bryman, A. (2006). Integrating quantitative and qualitative research: How is it done ? *Qualitative Research, 6*(1), 97–113.

Cancian, M., & Meyer, D. R. (1998). Who gets custody? *Demography, 35*(2), 147–157.

Cancian, M., Meyer, D. R., Brown, P. R., & Cook, S. T. (2014). Who gets custody now? Dramatic changes in children's living arrangements after divorce. *Demography, 51*, 1381–1396.

Céroux, B., & Hachet, B. (2019). Dix ans de partage des allocations familiales dans le cadre de la residence alternée (2007–2017). *L'E-ssentiel*, n°184, mars.

Fransson, E., Sarkadi, A., Hjern, A., & Bergström, M. (2016). Why should they live more with one of us when they are children to us both. Parents' motives for practicing equal joint physical custody for children aged 0-4. *Children and Youth Services Review, 66*, 154–160.

Guillonneau, M., & Moreau, C. (2013). La résidence des enfants de parents séparés. De la demande des parents à la décision du juge. Exploitation des décisions définitives rendues par les juges aux affaires familiales au cours de la période comprise entre le 4 juin et le 15 juin 2012. Rapport du ministère de la Justice, Direction des affaires civiles et du sceau.

Hachet, B. (2017). L'alternance et ses moments: Âge, genre et temporalités de la résidence alternée. *Enfances, Familles, Générations, 27.*

Juby, H., Le Bourdais, C., & Marcil Gratton, N. (2005). Sharing roles, sharing custody? Couples' characteritics and children's living. *Journal of Marriage and Family Relations, 67*(1), 157–172.

Kitterod, R. H., & Lyngstad, J. (2012). Untraditional caring arrangements among parents living apart: The case of Norway. *Demographic Research, 27*(5), 121–152.

Masardo, A. (2011). Negotiating shared residence: The experience of separated fathers in Britain and France. In J. Bridgeman, H. Keating, & C. Lind (Eds.), *Regulating family responsabilities* (pp. 119–136). Aldershot: Ashgate.

Melli, M. S., & Brown, P. (2008). Exploring a new family form- the shared time family. *International Journal of Law, Policy and Family, 22*, 231–269.

Nielsen, L. (2013). Shared residential custody: Review of the research (part I of II). *American Journal of Family Law, 26*, 61–71.

Sodermans, A. K., Matthijs, K., & Swicegood, G. (2013). Characteristics of joint physical custody families in Flanders. *Demographic Research, 28*, 821–848.

Sodermans, A. K., Botterman, S., Havermans, N., & Matthijs, K. (2015). Involved fathers, liberated mothers? Joint physical custody and the subjective well-being of divorced parents. *Social Indicators Research, 122*(1), 257–277.

Solsona, M., & Spijker, J. (2016). Influence du Code civil catalan (2010) sur les décisions de garde partagée. Comparaisons entre la Catalogne et le reste de l'Espagne. *Population, 71*(2), 313–341.

Spruijt, E., & Duindam, V. (2009). Joint physical custody in the Netherlands and the well-being of children. *Journal of Divorce and Remarriage, 51*, 65–82.

Stafford, M. M., & Coleman, M. (2012). The good, the bad and the ugly: Divorced mothers' experiences with coparenting. *Family Relations, 61*(4), 586–600.

Strauss, A. (1978). *Negotiations: Varieties, contexts, processes, and social order.* San Francisco: Jossey-Bass Inc Pub.

Benoit Hachet is an associate professor of sociology at EHESS (School of Advanced Studies in the Social Sciences) in Paris. He defended a thesis in 2018 on the temporal experience of parents with children in Shared Physical Custody. He works on marital separations, parenthood and contemporary family temporalities.

12

Shared Physical Custody: Challenges and Opportunities of Coparenting

Joëlle Darwiche, Cindy Eira Nunes, Nahema El Ghaziri, Camille Imesch, and Séverine Bessero

Abstract This chapter focuses on the issue of shared physical custody (SPC) in the broader context of coparenting interventions. To identify if and how these interventions address the issue of SPC, we provide a systematic overview of the currently available types of coparenting interventions after marital dissolution. To be selected, the interventions had to be published in peer-reviewed journals, target separated or divorced parents, integrate work on coparenting, and include a custody focus within the intervention curriculum or as a targeted outcome. Finally, they had to be subject to empirical evaluation.

As a second step, using a case study, we investigate how the issue of SPC may be addressed before divorce, during couple therapy. We describe the therapy sessions to highlight the factors that may protect or undermine the development of a cooperative coparenting relationship while separating, and eventually create a positive shared-custody scenario after divorce. We also analyse the couple's progress regarding individual symptomatology and coparenting satisfaction based on self-reported questionnaires and on the quality of their observed coparenting interactions.

From a therapeutic perspective, this chapter aims to deepen our understanding of the challenges and opportunities of coparenting during and after separation and its intertwinement with the issue of SPC.

Keywords Coparenting · Shared physical custody · Intervention · Couple therapy

---

J. Darwiche (✉) · C. E. Nunes · C. Imesch
Family and Development Research Center, Institute of Psychology, University of Lausanne, Lausanne, Switzerland
e-mail: joelle.darwiche@unil.ch; cindy.eiranunes@unil.ch

N. El Ghaziri
Center for Primary Care and Public Health (Unisanté), University of Lausanne, Lausanne, Switzerland
e-mail: Nahema.El-Ghaziri@unisante.ch

S. Bessero
Couples and Families Therapeutic Consultation, Geneva University Hospitals, Geneva, Switzerland
e-mail: Severine.Bessero@hcuge.ch

12.1 Introduction

In this chapter, we discuss the issue of Shared Physical Custody (SPC) from the perspective of therapeutic coparenting interventions. Coparenting interventions offer therapeutic work focused on the coparenting relationship, meaning the way parents support or undermine each other in relation to their parental duties (McHale and Irace 2011). When separated or divorced couples discuss and plan a SPC scenario, the partners endorse their coparental role. Therefore, we aim to investigate whether and in which way post-separation or divorce coparenting interventions address the issue of custody, and of SPC, in their treatment plan. To answer this question, we provide a systematic overview of the currently available types of coparenting interventions that specifically address the issue of custody and/or that include the issue of custody in their outcomes, while being subject to empirical evaluation. The selected studies define SPC as time that children spent in each home varying from one-third (70%/30%) to an equal share (50%).

Moreover, we investigate if, ahead of the separation process, the issue of SPC (whether it is an asymmetrical or a split arrangement) is also present during couple therapy. How can separating partners be engaged as coparents, and how does their coparenting dynamic impact the decision process of SPC? To answer this second question, we provide a case study of a distressed couple that has decided to separate during couple therapy. This case study will enable an examination of the possible improvements or setbacks faced by couples in their coparenting relationship during the process of separation. It will also enable reflection on how the matter of custody affects this process and its possible intertwinement with the coparenting relationship.

This work represents a novelty in the field, as the approaches for handling the SPC issue by different coparenting interventions have not yet been explored. Furthermore, it explores via a case study how one can intervene on the coparenting relationship, as well as the role of SPC-related issues, in the couple's trajectory from marriage to divorce. This last aspect could be of interest to professionals involved in either marriage or post-separation counselling.

12.2 Theoretical and Empirical Framework

Coparenting is a specific psychological and relational dynamic between the adults in charge of a child or children (Favez 2017). Accordingly, in the context of family developmental psychology, it refers to the emotional experience of being a coparent. It relates to the way parents share leadership, work together to resolve disagreements, and support—or undermine—each other concerning their parental duties (Kamp Dush et al. 2011; McHale and Irace 2011). Several dimensions of coparenting have been identified (Favez 2017): (1) cooperation and support between parents, (2) conflict or competition between parents, (3) effective division of parenting tasks, (4) commitment to parenting, (5) agreement on issues related to childrearing, and (6) triangulation (for example, one parent recruiting the child into a coalition against the other). Effective coparenting is motivated by the well-being of the child or children and may change according to the child's developmental needs. Noticeably, the positive impact of coparenting alliance and the deleterious effect of coparenting conflict have been shown to remain relevant throughout the family lifecycle (e.g. Choi et al. 2019; Martin et al. 2017; Murphy et al. 2016).

Coparenting is one of the most important processes being discussed in contemporary studies on relationships and parenting (McHale and Lindahl 2011; Morril et al. 2010). Child developmental studies have shown that coparenting functioning is a pivotal factor in the intrafamilial dynamic, exerting significant impact on a child's psychological adjustment (e.g. Teubert and Pinquart 2010). Studies concerning intact families (for a review, see Mangelsdorf et al. 2011) as well as those concerning post-divorce families (e.g. Ahrons 2007; Adamsons and Pasley 2006; Pruett et al. 2007) have shown that coparenting quality predicts important developmental processes, such as children's conflictual peer relations, as well as externalising and internalising behavioural problems (Choi et al. 2019; McHale and Lindahl 2011).

Because coparenting is a key aspect of the parents' functioning—for both intact families and separated or divorced families—existing research assumes that it represents a major aspect of the decision-making process concerning shared physical custody evaluations and court decisions (Nielsen 2017). Particularly, when there is a highly conflictual coparenting relationship, SPC is generally not considered the best solution for the children (Wallerstein et al. 2000). However, some authors have warned against placing too much emphasis on coparenting quality in this context, as we do not have the empirical justification to conclude that coparents in conflict should not choose SPC or would not have a successful SPC arrangement (Leclair et al. 2018; Nielsen 2017). While a conflictual coparenting relationship might complicate the experience of SPC or even be deleterious in cases of violence or abuse, the presence of conflict in itself should not be considered as hindering the possibility of a SPC arrangement. Many different factors play a role in realizing a positive SPC experience, such as socio-economic factors as well as relational and psychological factors (Steinbach 2018). SPC promotes the preservation of the parent–child relationship, with research indicating that it is a positive factor in children's adjustment and well-being, even if there are occasional tensions and difficulties in the relationship between their parents (Braver 2014). For that reason, one should not forgo this option without a solid rationale.

Nevertheless—and given the extensive empirical literature showing that coparenting affects a child's outcomes before (e.g. McHale and Lindahl 2011) and after separation or divorce (e.g. Adamsons and Pasley 2006; Lamela and Figueiredo 2016)—interventions supporting the coparenting relationship may be necessary at different stages of transition from marriage to separation or divorce (Pruett and Donsky 2011). During the separation process, the coparenting relationship may be significantly challenged. Parents may experience difficulties due to the spillover effects between marital distress and coparenting disagreements (Stroud et al. 2015). Indeed, as highlighted by the family systems theory, each subsystem (e.g. the romantic relationship) has the potential to affect the other subsystems (e.g. the coparenting relationship; Cox and Paley 1997). Regarding the parental couple, some authors suggest that the romantic relationship should be considered a predictor, as it chronologically comes first and represents the basis of trust and support on which the coparental relationship will develop. Substantial studies have found that mothers' and fathers' perceptions of the romantic relationship will not only affect their own coparental behaviour but also the behaviour of their partner (Christopher et al. 2015; Le et al. 2016). More importantly, an experimental study by Kitzmann (2000) revealed that romantic conflict altered the quality of later coparental interactions. Accordingly, one could expect that marital distress associated with separation or divorce may complicate the coparental interactions. However, the opposite may also be true. Feeling undermined in one's parental role or witnessing the other parent disrespecting the rules that were set for the child's education may generate anger and disillusion about the partner, therefore affecting the parents' romantic relationship, as it was shown in intact families (Schoppe-Sullivan et al. 2004). In the context of divorce and separation, spillover effects from romantic distress onto coparenting may first emerge. However, as tensions between parents increase, spillovers could also travel in the opposite direction, from the coparenting subsystem to the romantic one, eventually complicating and/or extending the separation process. This hypothesis highlights the importance of providing interventions that consider these spillover effects from one subsystem to another at the different stages of separation or divorce.

Concerning the question of custody arrangements—and more specifically, the question of SPC—supportive coparenting may have a facilitating role in the agreement process (Sullivan 2008). We may ask the following question: is coparenting a continuous process before, during, and after separation? If this were the case, it would imply that pre-separation cooperative coparenting might be a protective factor in custody arrangements, whereas conflictual coparenting prior to separation might represent a risk factor for any agreement regarding custody. If coparenting is instead a discontinuous process, a separation might affect the previous coparenting relationship either negatively or positively. In the former case, the partners may experience so much marital distress that it prevents coparenting cooperation during the transition to separation and divorce. In the latter case, on the contrary, parents may even improve their coparenting relationship once the decision to separate has been taken. Some data have shown, for example, that the dissolution of marriages with high coparental conflict had less negative effects, or even had positive effects on children, compared to the dissolution of marriages with low interparental conflict (Booth and Amato 2001).

Given the role of coparenting for the family well-being and especially for the child's outcomes, a number of interventions targeting the coparenting relationship have been developed for post-divorce parents. Through our systematic literature review, we aim to identify the programs that included SPC as a topic of discussion and/or as an outcome, to better evaluate the importance that was given to SPC in these treatment programs.

We then take a step back to document, through the case study, how and when the issue of SPC emerged during the therapy of a separating couple. We will explore two hypotheses to get insights on the issue of continuity and/or discontinuity of the coparenting relationship pre- and post-divorce: (a) coparenting is a continuous process; cooperative coparenting would be a protective factor whereas conflictual coparenting before separation would be a risk factor for agreement regarding custody; (b) coparenting is a discontinuous process as the decision to separate will noticeably modify the coparenting dynamic, either in a positive or a negative way.

12.3 Review of Post-separation and/or Divorce Coparenting-Based Programs

This systematic literature review was carried out to identify the available coparenting-based programs intended for separated and/or divorced parents and to select those that explicitly include the issue of custody as a target of intervention and/or as an outcome.

Previous papers reviewed interventions following separation or divorce (for example, Lee et al. 1994; Pruett and Donsky 2011). However, those reviews either did not focus on coparenting interventions per se or did not specifically target how interventions included custody-related aspects. These reviews showed that numerous resources are available to parents after divorce and that they either draw from the traditional litigation approach (e.g. court-connected services; court-based system-wide interventions) or from the alternative dispute resolution approach (e.g. mediation outside of the court process; parent education programs; Pruett et al. 2011). Depending on the approach, the focus of these programs varies: (1) it can be to reach legal and practical agreements, reduce litigated custody cases, and help parents to implement and comply with their parenting plans (e.g. mediation; parenting coordination); (2) and/or it can be to inform couples about the repercussions of divorce, promote the inclusion of both parents, strengthen the quality of the parent-child relationship and the coparenting relationship, and help the parents to refrain from arguments in the best interest of their children (Pruett and Donsky 2011). It may not be easy for parents, or for mental health professionals, to find their way through the multitude of methods available (see Emery 2012, for a conceptual system of dispute resolution alternatives). In this review, we focus on coparenting-based programs, whatever their setting, to identify the existing interventions targeting the coparenting relationship after separation or divorce. We detail the objectives of these programs and analyse if and how aspects of custody are present as a target of the intervention.

12.3.1 Method

Inclusion Criteria Studies were included in the review based on five criteria: (1) in-press or published articles in peer-reviewed journals; (2) programs targeting separated or divorced parents (or those in the process); (3) programs with a coparenting focus (e.g. improvement of coparenting support, reduction of coparenting conflict, children caught in the middle), as one of the main aims of the intervention or as a secondary aim; (4) programs including a custody focus within the intervention curriculum or as a targeted outcome; and (5) availability of the program's empirical validation (qualitative and/or quantitative).

This review follows the Cochrane guidelines for conducting a systematic review of interventions (Higgins and Green 2008). The review was carried out by the first three authors, and the final decision regarding the summarized data (see Table 12.1) was reached by consensus.

Literature Search For the purpose of this review, three electronic databases were systematically searched: Pubmed, Web of Science, and APA PsycNET (which combines the databases of PsycINFO, PsycARTICLES, PsycCRITIQUES, and APA Books). The searches were conducted between December 2018 and January 2019. The following keywords were entered into the three search engines: (co-parent* OR interparent*) AND (therapy OR treatment OR intervention OR program) AND (divorce OR separation).

Selection Procedure The search identified 710 references in the different databases (see Fig. 12.1. Flow chart of the selection process). All resulting references were imported into a citation manager (Zotero 5.0), which removed the duplicates automatically. In addition, some duplicates were removed manually, leaving 573 records. Irrelevant records were removed from screening via title and abstract (screening 1), and then via full-text (screening 2), leaving 48 references and 33 different coparenting-based programs. Then, we identified 16 references and 13 coparenting-based programs specially focusing on custody issues through their program protocol (screening 3); 5 of these 13 programs also included the issue of custody as an outcome. The 13 programs are presented in Table 12.1. Regarding outcomes, only those related to custody are reported.

12.3.2 Results

Global Description of the Programs Only a minority of programs are manualised (N = 5), i.e. a handbook was used to guide the intervention, which is recognized as a condition to ensure fidelity for both clinical work and research purposes. A total of 6 programs are mandated programs, at least for a portion of the participants, and the rest are voluntary. The settings vary and include a self-study handbook (N = 1), a mix of individual and joint parent sessions (N = 2), joint parent sessions (N = 2), online interventions (N = 3), and group sessions (N = 5). A total of 2 programs also include sessions with the child or children. The number of sessions ranges from 1 to a maximum of 20, or 40 h.

Table 12.1 Coparenting-based programs with a custody focus

Program	Articles	Manual	Setting	Purpose	Coparenting-based	Custody	Evaluation	Population	Outcomes
1. Child-focused mediation (CF) & Children in focus (CI)	Ballard et al. (2013) Rudd et al. (2015)	No (CI: Handbook provided to parents) Not specified (CF)	Individual intake sessions and up to 6 joint sessions + (CI) 1 session with child followed by a discussion (mediator, child specialist and parents)	Increase awareness on impact of divorce on child Child-focused (CF + CI)	**High**: Psychoeducation on the importance of coparenting for the child, work on coparenting cooperation and conflict	Intervention: Making of developmentally sensitive parenting plans (CF + CI); adjustment of parenting plans to child's developmental needs Outcome: Rate of agreement, parenting time, provisions	RCT with follow-up, 3 groups: Child-focused mediation (CF), child-inclusive mediation (CI) and mediation-as-usual (MAU)	N = 69 parents mediating initial divorces or separations	Rates of agreement higher compared to MAU More parent-child time compared to MAU More likely to include provisions for coparental communication compared to MAU
2. Co-parenting for successful kids program	Choi et al. (2017)	No	Online	Improve coparenting in case of custody disputes Protect children from interparental conflict	**High**: Strengthen communication skills with the other parent and maintain children out of conflict	Intervention: Strategies for developing a child-centered co-parenting plan Outcome: Knowledge on parenting plan	Retrospective evaluation of program	N = 2662 separating parents	Improved parents' knowledge and ability to develop a parenting plan More effective on parents of a toddler

(continued)

Table 12.1 (continued)

Program	Articles	Manual	Setting	Purpose	Coparenting-based	Custody	Evaluation	Population	Outcomes
3. Mediation	Emery et al. (1991, 1994, 2001)	Yes	6 joint sessions	Empower parents to make own decisions about custody Negotiate agreements Engage parents in children's interest Child-focused	**High**: Identification of interparental agreement and disagreement, resolution of interparental conflict, enhancement of team work within mediation	Intervention: Develop and test out parenting plan Outcome: Settlement, satisfaction with settlement (parenting plan), non-residential parent-child time	RCT with 12-year follow-up: Mediation and litigation	N = 85 parents contesting child custody	More settlement in the mediation group compared to litigation group More satisfaction regarding settlement for fathers in the mediation group than in the litigation group (long-term) Mothers were more satisfied than fathers, but no differences between groups for mothers Increased non-residential parent-child contact compared to litigation group (long-term)

4. Online parenting programs	Bowers et al. (2014)	No	Online	Enhance interparental cooperative communication and management of conflict Enhance adequate communication with children	**High**: Increase awareness of the effects of coparenting on family dynamics; improvement of parents skills and confidence regarding cooperative conflict management	Intervention: Encourage parents to develop a parenting plan Outcome: No	Post-intervention evaluation	N = 1543 divorcing parents Mandated or not	
5. PACT program	Brown et al. (2009)	No	4 joint sessions +2 individual sessions	Reduce interparental conflict Comply with parenting plan and court orders Support responsivity to child's needs Increase child Well-being	**Medium**: Interparental conflict resolution and impact of interparental conflict on children	Intervention: Decision for a parenting plan and discussion on how the agreement will be put into action Outcome: No	Pre-post evaluation with 1-year follow-up	N = 22 divorcing couples with custody issues Mandated	
6. Pais por inteiro (Papi)	Lamela et al. (2010)	Yes	8 group sessions	Work on the parenting plan Improve quality of coparenting relationship Enhance parents' adjustment to transition	**Medium**: Interparental conflict resolution, coparenting negociation, skills on conflict management and coparental coordination	Intervention: Work on parenting plan Outcome: No	Pilot RCT: Pais por Intero and no intervention	N = 16 divorced parents	

(continued)

Table 12.1 (continued)

Program	Articles	Manual	Setting	Purpose	Coparenting-based	Custody	Evaluation	Population	Outcomes
7. Parenting apart: Effective co-parenting	LaGraff et al. (2015)	Yes	1 group session	Education about impact of separation and conflict on children Concrete actions to take to help children (skill learning) Parenting plan	**Medium**: Discussion of topics such as risk of triangulation, parents' use of putdowns, risk of putting child in the middle of conflict, cooperative versus parallel parenting	Intervention: Development of a parenting plan in the best interest of children; discussion of strategies to ease the transitions between homes for children Outcome: No	Retrospective evaluation of the program +2-month follow-up survey	N = 139 divorcing parents Mandated	
8. Parenting coordination	Quigley & Cyr (2017)	No	Joint sessions (40 h), including some sessions with children	Implement parenting plans Child-focused	**High:** Assess coparenting impasses; education on impacts of conflict on children; communication techniques; conflict management; decision making	Intervention: Decision making regarding the parenting plan Outcome: No	Pre-post evaluation	N = 6 high conflict families after separation with history of litigation Mandated	
9. Parenting together	Stolz et al. (2017)	Yes	3 group sessions	Psychoeducation and practice on custody agreements, judicial process,	**High**: Discussion and instruction related to challenges in coparenting,	Intervention: Psychoeducation and practice on custody agreements and	Retrospective evaluation of the program	N = 55 never-married parents, in court for child	

				coparenting, healthy communication and parenting plan	coparenting roles; skills for problem solving, strategies to communicate and reduce conflict; encouragement to remove children from coparenting conflict	writing a parenting plan; discussion of legal issues (e.g. rights of fathers) Outcome: No		custody or payment issues	
10. PEACE program (Parents' Education About Children's Emotions)	McKenry et al. (1999)	No (handbook provided to parents)	2 group sessions	Enhance children post-divorce adjustment Increase awareness of impact of divorce on child Communication skills	**Low**: Coparenting communication skills;	Intervention: Psychoeducation on parenting arrangements; role of the residential and non-residential parent; legal aspects of divorce (e.g. types of parenting arrangements); importance of both parents Outcome: Custody (satisfaction, formal and informal changes), attitude	Post evaluation: PEACE program and no program	N = 236 divorcing parents, attended after filing divorce Mandated	No program effect on custody related outcomes (satisfaction, changes nor attitude towards the non-residential parent role)

(continued)

Table 12.1 (continued)

Program	Articles	Manual	Setting	Purpose	Coparenting-based	Custody	Evaluation	Population	Outcomes
						towards the non-residential parent role			
11. Proud to parent	Rudd et al. (2017)	No	Online	Reduce interparental conflict Increase decision-making as a parenting team Maintain both parents' presence in children's life	**High**: Psychoeducation and exercise to improve coparenting, reduce interparental conflict, triangulation and children's exposure to conflict; working on making parenting decisions as a team	Intervention: Importance of both parents' presence Outcome: Reaching agreement and resolving custody issues	RCT with 1-year follow-up, 4 groups: Intervention with/without waiting period and control group with/without waiting period	N = 182 unmarried parents having filled out for paternity establishment	Less agreement and resolution of custody issues in proud to parent group compared to the no program group (overall for the intervention group with a waiting period)
12. What about the children: A guide for divorced and divorcing parents	Arbuthnot et al. (1996)	No (handbook provided to parents)	Self-study handbook	Sensitize parents to effects of divorce on children Work on practical suggestions to minimize negative effects	**Low**: Psychoeducation on interparental conflict	Intervention: Forms of parenting plans; importance of non-residential parent; effects of father absence; dealing with the legal system;	RCT with 1-year follow-up (self-study vs waiting-list)	N = 358 divorcing parents	

						benefits of alternate dispute resolution Outcome: No			
13. Working together program	Owen & Rhoades (2012)	Yes	3 group sessions	Target aspects of conflictual coparenting	**High:** Psychoeducation on children's needs in coparenting; coparenting dynamics; decrease negative interparental communication; develop strategies for effective cooperation	Intervention: Work on expectations regarding decisions, agreements and parenting plans Outcome: No	Pre-post evaluation +2-month follow-up	N = 20 divorce parents with high conflict Mandated	

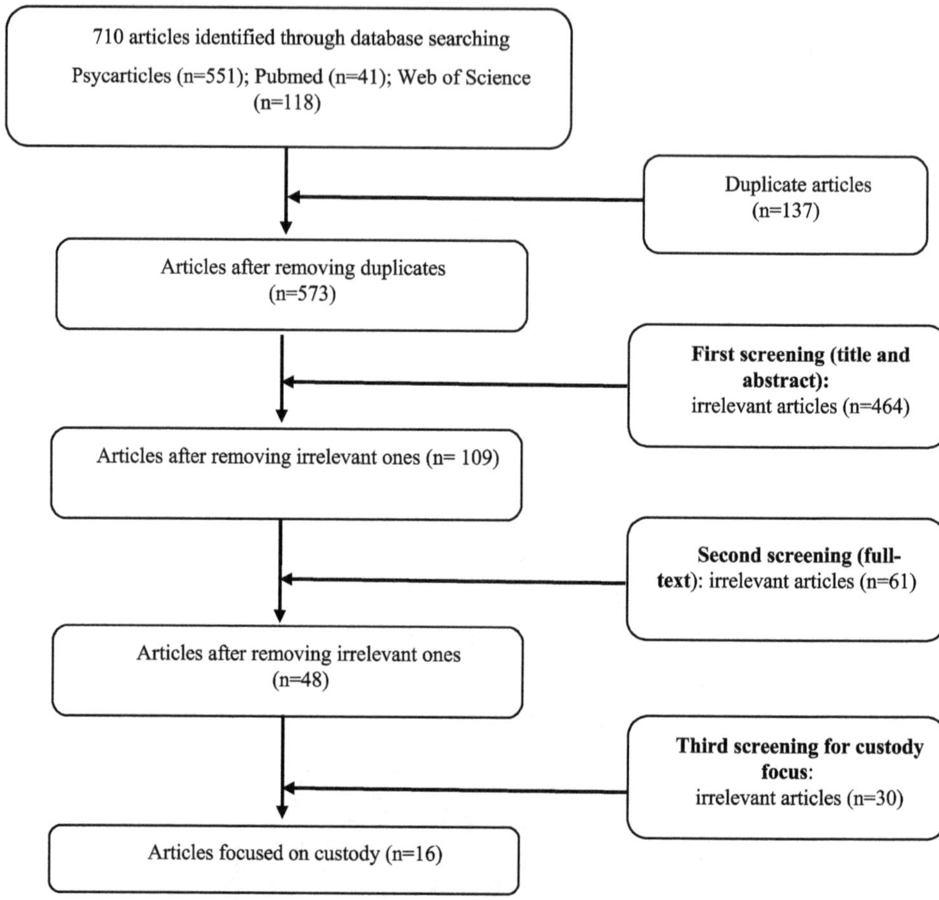

Fig. 12.1 Flow chart of the selection process

The main aims of these programs are presented by the authors as follows, with some programs having up to 4 different aims:

1. Work on the coparenting relationship, such as improving cooperation and managing of coparental conflict (Programs 2, 4, 5, 6, 9, 11, and 13);
2. Work on the implementation of, and compliance with, parenting plans or decisions related to custody, and empowering parents to make their own decisions about custody (Programs 3, 5, 6, 7, 8, 9, and 11);
3. Increase the awareness of the repercussions of divorce on children (Programs 1, 7, 8, 10, and 12);
4. Work on global communication skills and psychoeducation (Programs 5, 6, 9, and 10)
5. Work on communication skills to increase the child's well-being or adjustment (Programs 3, 4, 5, and 7); and
6. Enhance each parents' adjustment to the transition (Program 6).

As the programs were selected based on their coparenting and custody foci, these aims are naturally the most represented in the main goal of the programs.

We also note that only one program (*Pais por inteiro,* Lamela et al. 2010) presented the parents' adjustment to the transition to divorce as a main goal. The 12 other programs' main goals rather concerned the children or the coparental coordination.

Work on the Coparenting Relationship The proportion of coparenting work differed according to the programs. We rated as *high* the programs that included clearly more than 50% of coparenting content in their intervention, *medium* those including about 50%, and *low* those including clearly less than 50%. The majority of programs were rated as high in coparenting focus (N = 8), while a minority was rated as medium (N = 3) or low (N = 2). The main targeted coparenting aspects were the strengthening of skills to increase supportive coparenting and decrease conflictual coparenting, with some programs working more specifically to help keep the child out of conflict (Programs 2, 7, 9, 11, and 13) or including information about the importance of good coparenting for the child (Programs 1, 4, 5, 8, and 9).

Custody as a Target and/or as an Outcome For all the programs, work on the development, adjustment, and/or implementation of parenting plans was present. It is noteworthy that some of them also explicitly included more specific targets such as the discussion of legal issues (Programs 9, 10, and 12), the role of the residential and non-residential parent and the effects of father's absence on child outcome (Programs 10, 11, and 12), and strategies to ease the transitions between homes for children (Program 7).

A total of 5/13 programs also included the issue of custody as an outcome. These programs assessed their impact on reaching agreement (Programs 1, 3, and 11), satisfaction with or knowledge of the parenting plan (Programs 2, 3, and 10), improvement of the distribution of parenting time or provisions for coparental communication (Programs 1 and 3), and attitude towards the non-residential parent's role (Program 10). As the type of empirical validation was heterogeneous (RCT, pre-post measures, post-test measures only), as well as the sample sizes (less than 20 parents to about 2500 parents), the global picture of the outcomes obtained must be taken very cautiously.

Regarding the reaching of an agreement, the results were conflicted, with 2 programs having a positive impact (Programs 1 and 3) and one having a negative impact (Program 11) on reaching agreement. A total of 2 programs had a positive impact (Programs 2 and 3) and one had no impact (Program 10) on the satisfaction with the development of the parenting plan. Furthermore, a positive impact was observed in Programs 1 and 3 for the improvement of the distribution of parenting time or provisions for coparental communication, with some long-lasting effects 12 years after the intervention (Program 6); and no effect was observed for Program 10 regarding a change in attitude towards the non-residential parent role.

Conclusion This section allowed the identification of 13 post-divorce coparenting interventions that included the issue of SPC as a target of intervention and, for some of them, also as an outcome. These programs allow therapeutic work on the coparenting relationship with one of the aims being to facilitate the building of a parenting plan and/or to reduce the conflicts related to it. These programs are indeed offered to parents who are at different moments of the separation process, with some parents still in the process of discussing custody, and others more advanced in the process, e.g., parents who have already chosen a custody arrangement and are in court for payment issues.

However, how can we intervene on the coparenting relationship when the couple is still on the verge of separation? Will marital dissolution affect the coparenting dynamic or will the partners maintain a stable coparenting relationship despite separation? Will the issue of custody emerge at this stage, and how? In order to answer these questions, a case study is provided. It illustrates the trajectory of a distressed couple who entered couple therapy then decided to separate around the third therapy session. A clinical analysis of the case is provided and is combined with information gathered from independent assessment of the couple's progress, as they took part in a randomized controlled trial (RCT) in the context of their therapy. In the following section, we first describe the RCT and the methodology that was used to analyse the case (Pragmatic case study method; Fishman 2017), then present the results of the case analysis.

12.4 Case Study: Coparenting While Separating

12.4.1 Method

Through the case studies within RCT methodology (Fishman 2017), we may deepen our knowledge of how a treatment model is implemented, which contributes to our practical and theoretical knowledge of couple therapy with parents. The RCT in which Linda and Paul were involved aimed to assess the efficacy of a brief intervention for parents in intact families. In this trial, parents of a child (or stepchild) aged 16 years or younger and living in the same household participated in either a brief as-usual couple therapy or in an integrative brief systemic intervention (IBSI; Darwiche et al. 2017a, b) combining therapeutic work on romantic and coparenting relationships. Treatments were comparable in length and number of sessions. The brief as-usual couple therapy and the IBSI were both conducted by expert therapists trained in systemic psychotherapy. Couples were recruited from various therapy centres in the French-speaking part of Switzerland. The randomization allocated Linda and Paul to IBSI.

The aim of our case study analysis within this trial is not to assess the efficiency of IBSI but rather to illustrate the therapeutic process of a separating couple. The objective is to collect observations on a specific coparenting trajectory and on how custody-related issues were integrated within this trajectory.

The case study analysis was carried out using the pragmatic case study method (Fishman 2017), a small-scale research methodology that allows for the exploration of the processes and outcomes of an intervention. Following this method, the case of Linda and Paul was analysed with a detailed, session-by-session, qualitative approach based on the videotaped session material and on the therapist's feedback on the process. The clinical case analysis was then articulated by using the outcomes obtained through self-reported questionnaires and observational tasks. A synthesis of the pragmatic case study is proposed in this chapter.

Integrative Brief Systemic Intervention This manualised intervention is organized into six sessions spanning 6 months. In Session 1, the marital and/or coparenting difficulties are explored in order to get the partners involved as a marital dyad and as coparents. Sessions 2 to 5 represent the intervention phase during which work is conducted on the marital and coparenting vulnerabilities and on the resources that the partners can rely on. The therapist works on the spillover effects of one relationship on the other (e.g. negative emotions provoked by marital conflict transferring directly to coparenting interactions; Bonds and Gondoli 2007). With highly conflictual couples, a therapeutic lever is to raise the partners' awareness of the potentially harmful effects of their conflicts on their children. It is assumed to motivate the partners to work together for the sake of their children. Once more insightful of their children's needs, the parents may be better able to confront conflictual and deeply rooted couple problems (Oppenheim and Koren-Karie 2013). Session 6 is dedicated to reflecting on the intervention, its effects, and on possible follow-up sessions to the therapy. At each session, the clients' feedback is sought concerning their experience during the therapeutic process and the therapeutic relationship to maximize the mobilizing effect of the limited therapeutic timeframe.

IBSI was developed for couples in a romantic relationship; therefore, the manual does not directly include custody-related issues. However, as custody issues are directly linked to the role of coparent—a key target in IBSI—it is covered with couples such as Linda and Paul, who decide to separate during the intervention.

Therapist Linda and Paul's therapist is a psychologist who had completed a 5-year post-master's systemic psychotherapy program and who had 1 year of clinical experience with IBSI. She also attended supervision sessions throughout the study facilitated by the IBSI expert trainers.

Measures As research participants in the RCT, Linda and Paul completed several validated questionnaires and participated in videotaped discussions prior to the first and after the last IBSI session. The results of their three self-reported questionnaires measuring their individual symptomatology (Outcome Questionnaire 10; OQ®10.2; Lambert et al. 2005), coparenting alliance (Parenting Alliance Measure; PAM; Abidin and Konold 1999), and coparenting conflict and triangulation (2 subscales of the Coparenting Inventory for Parents and Adolescents; CI-PA; Teubert and Pinquart 2011) are presented below. The OQ®10.2 is a 10-item measure on a 5-point Likert scale (range 0–4) for a maximum score of 40, designed for the measurement of client functioning in relation to therapy. Higher scores indicate more distress, and a score of 17 is considered a conservative clinical cut-off (Rothballer Seelert et al. 2015). The PAM is a 20-item measure on a 5-point Likert scale (range 1–5) for a maximum score of 100, assessing the dimension of coparenting support; higher scores indicate more coparenting support. The 2 x 8-item subscales of the CI-PA assess the presence of coparenting conflict and triangulation of the child. Items are scored on a 5-point Likert scale (range 1–5) for an average score between 1 and 5. The mean of the two subscales is computed to indicate negative coparenting. A higher score indicates more negative coparenting.

During the videotaped discussions, Linda and Paul were invited to talk about topics they agreed and disagreed on regarding their coparenting relationship (2 × 5-min discussions). Their interactions were assessed using a coding system (Darwiche et al. 2017a, b) assessing the following items: Shared emotion/enjoyment of child, Agreement or Accommodation, Competition, Endorsement, Triangulation, Mutual investment, Positive « we-ness » as parents, Problem solving, Defensiveness, and Pressure for change. Coding of the tasks was done by the 4th author of this chapter, who is an expert trainer in the coding system.

This study received ethical approval from the Ethical Committee of the University of Lausanne in 2015. The personal data of Linda and Paul were anonymised.

12.4.2 Results

Clinical Case Analysis

Linda and Paul attended six IBSI therapy sessions with intervals of 3 weeks to 1 month between sessions. Both are in their forties and are employed in social work. They met at work 15 years ago and married 4 years later. They have two boys aged 10 and 8 and one 5-year-old daughter.

A Couple in High Marital and Coparenting Distress The first two sessions focused on each partner's personal background and on analysing each partner's request for couple therapy. The couple decided to enter psychotherapy after Paul cheated on Linda. Linda explains that there were several issues in the relationship and that she accepted her husband's habit of going out frequently. However, she feels that his unfaithfulness crossed a boundary. She is now expecting him to be more involved at home and with the children and to go out less often. She also threatens to leave him if he spends another night out. Paul feels that he has absolutely no space for decision-making at home and is dissatisfied with his wife's control over him.

The couple has been distressed for 5 years, since the birth of their last child. At the time, Paul was suffering from depression due to professional difficulties. Since then, Linda has taken it upon herself to help her husband overcome his depression. She considers that she has been taking care of everything related to the home and the children, leading her to feeling burned out. At this point of the session, Linda dominates the conversation, helping Paul finish his sentences, even though he speaks clearly. Linda seems to be the one in control, whereas Paul stays in the background.

Both describe important coparenting conflicts: Linda is unsatisfied with Paul's lack of involvement at home, and Paul feels similarly about Linda's lack of recognition of said involvement. The children are impacted by these difficulties, as they sometimes witness their parents' conflicts and express their fear of them disappearing, dying, or leaving them to be cared for by other people. Linda adds that they also worry about their father's health.

Events that Led to the Separation Decision and Active Support from the Therapist to Protect the Children The third session is requested ahead of schedule after Linda's discovery of an expensive hotel bill. She is very upset and demands an explanation. Paul confesses to having been unfaithful again. Linda is clearly lost and rattled. Following this discovery, she is certain that she wants a separation and wants to immediately break the news to the children. Paul prefers to announce it after their family holiday. During this session, the therapist helps the couple determine an appropriate time and manner of explaining the decision to their children, and the parents agree that it will be shared after the holiday.

During this session, the atmosphere quickly becomes tense and reproaches are thrown left and right, in particular regarding the coparenting relationship: Linda does not trust in Paul's capacity to be alone with the children. Paul blames Linda for involving the kids in their conflicts and for pushing her fears on them. During this session, the therapist almost systematically interrupts Linda and Paul as soon as a marital dispute arises in the conversation to help them focus on the concrete ways in which they could protect their children from their personal issues. The therapist invites the parents to formally commit to avoid arguing in front of the children during the holiday. This step is not an easy one to take as they both have a lot of anger towards the other, as a parent and not only as a partner: Paul explains that his wife insinuates to the kids that he is a bad father; Linda angrily replies that the kids do not have a present father and that they can feel it. At that moment, the therapist tries to work towards better cooperative coparenting by underlining the risks of having children caught in the middle of a contentious separation. Furthermore, due to the risks of spillover from the marital conflict on the other family relationships, the therapist helps the parents remember the importance of the bond the other parent has with the children.

Organization of the Separation and Custody-Related Questions: Strengthening the Coparenting Relationship The fourth session focuses on the organizational aspects of the separation process. The parents were able to protect their children from their conflicts during the holiday and to discuss it calmly during the session. They succeeded in planning Paul's departure from the house and his future shared time with the kids, as well as the creation of separate bank accounts. The parents have decided to announce the separation to the kids the next day, and Paul asks the therapist for advice on how to share this decision with them. The idea of implementing SPC is also raised by Paul. Linda is preoccupied because of the psychological state of her husband, but both agree that this needs to be discussed again later, when the concrete changes linked to the separation will have been put in place (for example, Paul's new home). The therapist comments positively on the fact that the parents have been able to put things into perspective.

Linda and Paul realise that they are able to discuss the situation in a constructive way, even if tensions are still present. They hesitate between making the transition towards separation gradually (for example, by spending the weekends all together) and changing their habits more radically. In any case, they realise that taking the decision to separate has made them feel at peace. Paul hopes that they will still be bonded together: 'I would like the kids to feel that they have the love and attention of both their parents'. Both of them are willing to go on with therapy: 'It is now that we need your help, notably to discuss the custody issues'. For the first time since the beginning of the sessions, and now that the decision to separate is made, the therapist feels that they are able to set a clearer goal for the therapy: she suggests supporting Linda and Paul during the separation process, first as coparents, and later, as partners. That way they might be able to understand more deeply what happened in their romantic relationship and preserve the positive elements of their story.

Distress Due to the Ambiguity in Communication and Boundaries: Acknowledging the Marital Suffering, Supporting the Parenting and Coparenting Relationships By the fifth session, Paul has moved out and lives temporarily in a hotel. He prefers to wait and see how his health will evolve as well as his professional situation before moving into an apartment. He still comes often to the family home. This creates tensions regarding boundaries and personal space. The children reacted rather calmly to the separation, without expressing strong emotions, and were able to ask their parents many questions later.

Linda feels that she needs to look back to understand what happened to their romantic relationship. She blames Paul for not having been able to share his discontent towards her sooner. Paul believes that he tried but that she was not able to listen: during his first burnout for example, she refused to accept taking additional help with the kids and pressured Paul to help her instead. He feels that it is very difficult for him to forgive her for this episode. The therapist encourages them to give themselves time before revisiting these aspects of their relationship because their emotions are still too strong, and it is difficult for each of them to acknowledge the other's suffering. She also stresses that Linda and Paul were able to preserve the parent-child bond and that they even increased the trust they have for one another as parents.

Moving Forward as Parents and Coparents, Despite Conflicts and Individual Suffering The sixth session allows for further clarification of each parent's personal space. The geographical space is now better implemented. They report that they argued about one of their children in front of them, and that the children asked them to stop. However, they felt in this situation that they were more able to handle the conflicts in a cooperative way.

Paul is facing new professional difficulties, and he is feeling worse psychologically. However, this time, they have decided to get the help of an au pair. It seems that the separation has helped them in making these decisions, and this is a relief for both of them. Paul explains that it is worth learning how to better cooperate even though they were not able to do this during their marriage. Both want to go on with therapy after this last session.

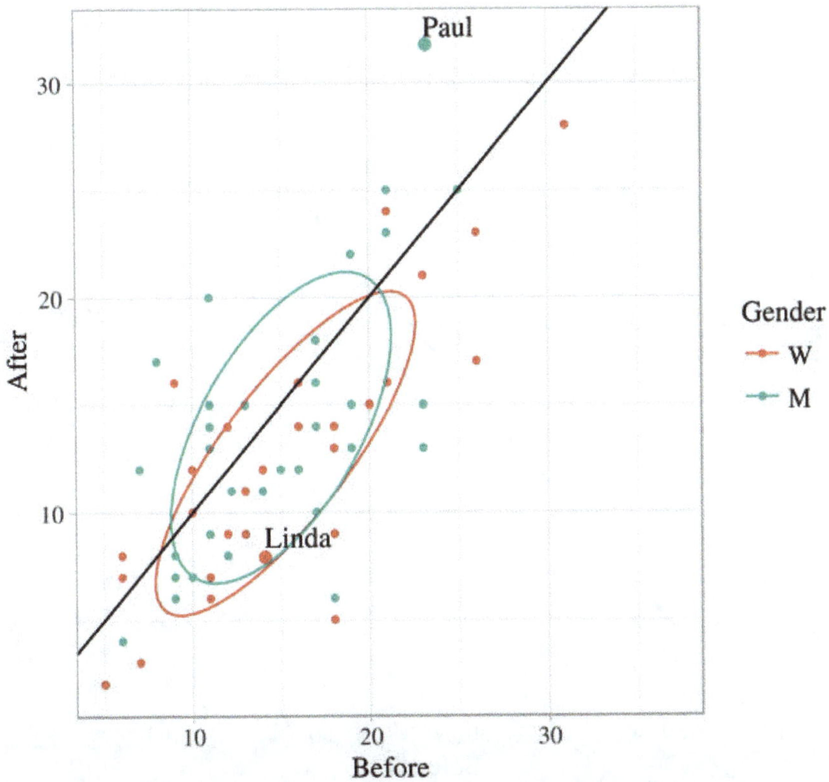

Fig. 12.2 Scores of Symptomatology (OQ). Note. Ranging from 0 to 40. Clinical cut-off = 17

Pre-post Data for Questionnaires and Observational Tasks

The pre-post therapeutic evolution for individual symptomatology, coparenting alliance, negative coparenting, as well as the quality of coparenting interactions is presented in graphs. Scatter plots were used to graphically illustrate the pre-post intervention scores of Linda and Paul, amongst the whole sample of the RCT (N = 35 couples having completed an IBSI). The results are illustrated for individual symptomatology (Fig. 12.2), coparenting alliance (Fig. 12.3), and negative coparenting (Fig. 12.4). The trend line represents the absence of change; scores indicating progress in coparenting alliance are located above this line, and scores indicating a decrease in individual symptomatology and in negative coparenting are located below this line. The confidence ellipses visually show the area that contains 50% of the individuals.

Individual Symptomatology Paul scored above the clinical cut-off of 17 (Rothballer Seelert et al. 2015) before therapy, and his individual level of distress then increased from before to after the sixth session (23 to 32). Paul's scores were exceptionally high compared to 50% of the group (Cf. Figure 12.2). Linda, on the other hand, scored below the clinical cut-off before therapy, and her level of symptomatology decreased during the course of therapy (14 to 8); her scores were similar to 50% of

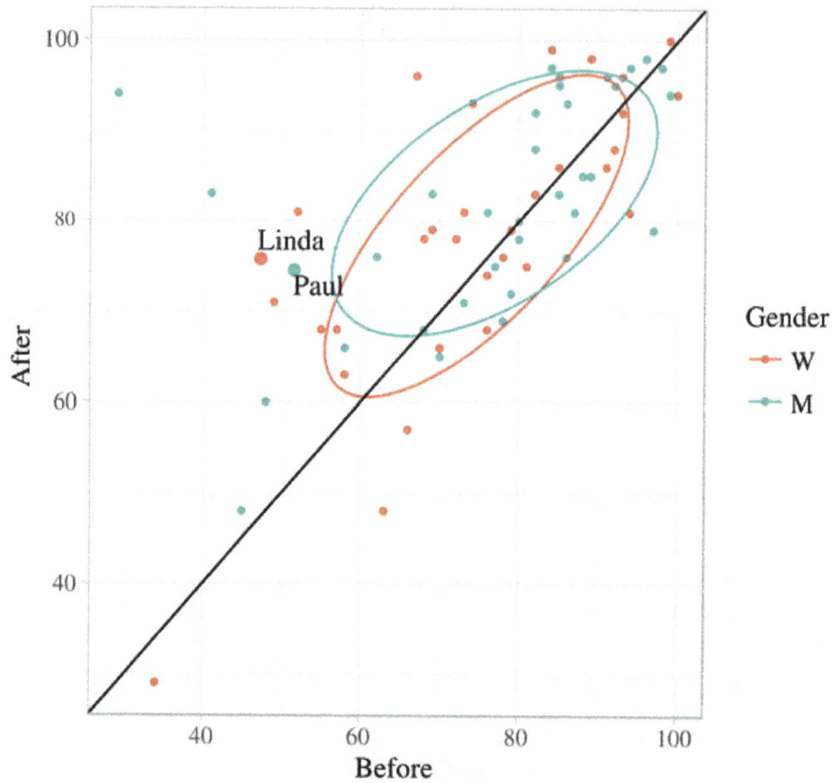

Fig. 12.3 Scores of Coparenting Alliance (PAM). Note. Ranging from 20 to 100

the group (Cf. Figure 12.2). These results are in line with what Paul expressed during therapy: he felt severe personal distress, particularly towards the end of therapy as he was facing professional difficulties and may have been suffering also from having left the family home. Linda's low level of symptomatology before therapy may be related to the fact that she was trying to manage the whole family and had to rely on all her personal energy: 'I cannot allow myself to be overloaded while my husband is in distress'.

Coparenting Alliance Both parents' perception of their coparenting alliance significantly improved during the course of therapy in spite of the separation (51 to 75 for Paul, and 47 to 76 for Linda). In comparison with 50% of the participants (Cf. Fig. 12.3), their scores were lower before therapy but improved remarkably (e.g. for items such as 'I believe the other parent is a good parent' or 'I feel good about my child's other parent's judgment about what is right for our child'). Paul and Linda's evaluation, therefore, confirmed the clinical analysis that showed strengthened cooperative coparenting at the end of the six sessions: Paul got more involved with the kids, and Linda recognised his efforts.

Negative Coparenting The data show a slight increase in negative coparenting for Linda (0.4 to 0.9); her scores however remain close to 50% of the participants

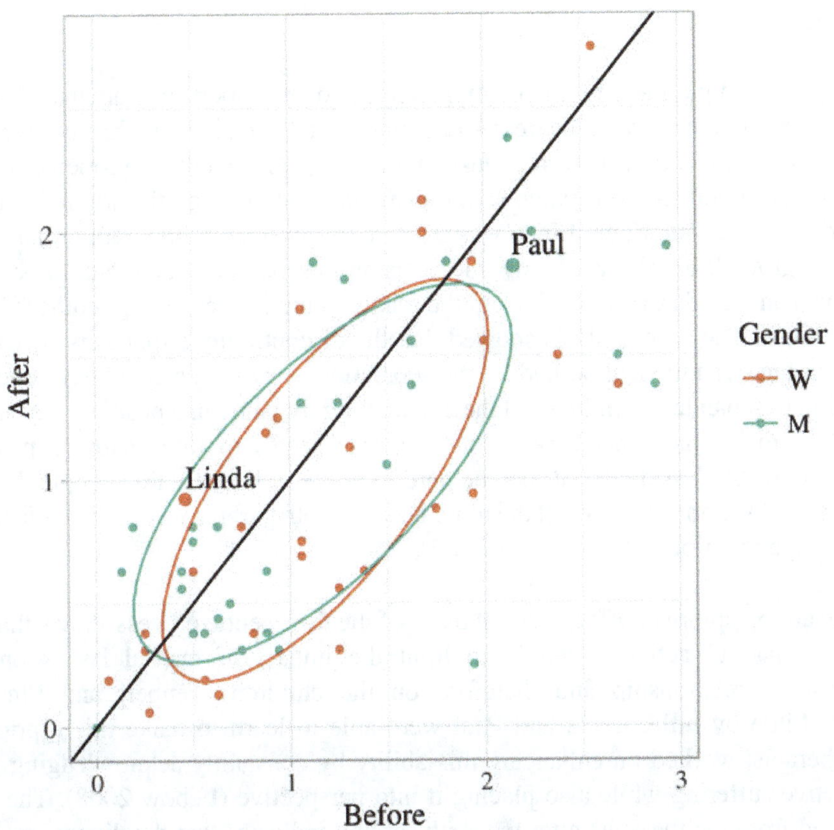

Fig. 12.4 Scores of Negative Coparenting (CIPA). Note. Ranging from 0 to 5

(Cf. Figure 12.4). Paul's scores were higher than 50% of the group but a slight decrease in his perception of negative coparenting was observed (2.1 to 1.9). This result may be related to the higher level of conflict and risk of triangulation of the child that Linda and Paul experience due to the separation process, but which does not prevent them from coparenting improvement (increase of coparenting alliance and, for Paul, decrease of negative coparenting).

Quality of Coparenting Interactions Coding from the observational tasks showed a higher rate of shared emotion, validation, and involvement (agreement task); and a higher rate of agreement, validation, and problem resolution as well as a decrease in defensiveness (disagreement task), when comparing pre-and post-results. The other items remained stable, and a decrease of shared emotion was observed during the disagreement task. These results are in line with the clinical analysis: despite the high number of difficulties, Linda and Paul's coparenting interactions improved during the course of therapy.

Discussion

During this couple therapy, the therapist appeared to support the parents, allowing Paul—who was in personal distress—to maintain and even increase his involvement as a father and a coparent (Kamp Dush et al. 2011). This can be considered to be a positive evolution for these parents, as they functioned in a significantly imbalanced way during their marriage; Linda was the family manager, while Paul remained in the background. In this case study, the decision to separate helped Paul to be more involved and Linda to step back from the risk of being a gatekeeping mother (Pruett et al. 2007). The case analysis showed that the discontinuity hypothesis (when the coparenting dynamic is modified by the separation) may be the conclusive one: the decision to separate has influenced the coparenting dynamic in a positive way and in turn, the more functional coparenting dynamic seems to foreshadow a positive outcome for SPC. Although it may be hard to prove, it is likely that couple therapy facilitated this improvement, all the more because both parents were fully engaged in the therapeutic process.

Regarding spillover effects, the analysis of the therapeutic process shows that the therapist had to actively step in to limit the impact of marital issues on the coparenting relationship and therefore on the children (Teubert and Pinquart 2010). Little by little, Linda and Paul were able to learn to make this a priority. The therapist worked on enhancing this ability by constantly acknowledging their respective suffering while also placing it into perspective (Lebow 2008). The data gathered from the therapist after the sixth session indicates that the divorce process and the SPC are running their course. Changes were also observed in the children, as reported by the parents (Amato and Afifi 2006). The youngest child—who was very agitated before the separation—is now calmer, whereas the oldest child—who was taking on too many adult responsibilities—is now more able to disclose his emotions and the difficulties he is facing. The therapist also pointed out that the parents became more aware of their children's behaviors; for example, Linda realized after the sixth session that before this stage, she did not notice how worried the children were for their parents because she was too wrapped up in her marital distress. This observation clearly illustrates the presence of spillover effects and highlights the importance of untangling these effects during therapy to minimize the negative fallouts of marital distress, both before and after separation.

To conclude, this couple therapy case study illustrates the high risks of spillover from feelings of anger, resentment, and humiliation experienced in the marital relationship for the other family relationships. However, Linda and Paul had the necessary resources to keep their children's well-being at the center of their concern, even with the additional weight of the father's depression. It can be expected that the discussions regarding SPC will benefit from this more positive atmosphere between them and that the goal of SPC will contribute to reinforcing this new dynamic, within the secure context of therapy.

12.5 Discussion and Conclusion

This chapter aimed to address the question of SPC from the perspective of coparenting and, more specifically, from the prism of coparenting-based interventions, as coparenting is considered a central factor of family dynamics, before and after separation or divorce (Pruett and Donsky 2011; McHale and Irace 2011).

The literature review of existing coparenting-based programs targeting custody-related issues showed that parents have a choice of several types of help, from a self-study handbook to more intensive parent groups sessions, or a mix of individual, joint, and child-inclusive sessions. These interventions may assist them in strengthening their coparenting relationship, better managing their interparental conflicts, and being more aware of the risks of their children being caught in the middle of their conflicts. The help sessions may also help parents to develop a parenting plan, adjust it to their children's developmental needs, and discuss legal issues or work toward an agreement in the case of custody disputes. However, research on the impact of these programs on custody-related aspects is scarce and the results vary. More studies are needed to assess these programs using rigorous methods—such as randomized control trials—to confirm findings. An effort should also be made to consistently include custody-related aspects in the curriculum of these programs and in the outcomes, which would contribute toward increasing our knowledge of the impact of the programs on these specific aspects. More research is also needed to identify specific therapeutic strategies and skills required to help distressed couples work together toward reaching a custody agreement.

The case study allowed us to explore more thoroughly the therapeutic process of a separating couple, to gain insight into how a cooperative coparenting relationship can develop, and how custody-related issues may be discussed, despite the difficulties associated with separation. The clinical case analysis, as well as the results obtained regarding the parents' individual symptomatology, coparenting alliance, and negative coparenting, highlighted the fact that it is possible for severe personal distress and acute suffering within the marital relationship to coexist with the development of effective coparenting. However, the case analysis also showed that there is a fine line between succeeding and failing, as a cooperative coparenting team could be overwhelmed by feelings of sadness and hostility due to the dissolution of their marriage. In this situation, Paul and Linda certainly benefited from being in couple therapy; they wanted to continue to engage in such therapy to help them face the many changes they needed to adapt to and to be able to discuss the opportunities offered by SPC in a trusting environment. In Linda and Paul's situation, some discontinuity was observed in the experience of being a coparenting team. The decision to separate appears to have positively impacted their coparenting relationship, rebalancing Linda and Paul's roles as parents and coparents and clarifying their personal space. This supports the discontinuity hypothesis.

We can assume that the positive evolution of Linda and Paul's coparenting relationship may be an asset for implementing SPC; in turn, the opportunity of a SPC scenario may be a powerful way of giving both parents the opportunity to be involved with their children and to cooperate with one another. The SPC scenario may also reinforce parents' commitment to work as a coparenting team, thereby providing a protective factor from the distancing and disengagement of vulnerable parents (those in similar situations to Paul in the case study).

Limitations This work has the following limitations. The first limitation is that only published and available information was retrieved for our review. The authors of the reviewed material were not contacted for further information, which may have been relevant regarding incomplete information (e.g. manual). The next limitation involves generalizing from a case study. This could be a sensitive process, as Linda and Paul's experience of the transition from marriage to separation and divorce was obviously unique. One cannot completely exclude the possibility that the observed changes in Linda and Paul may be due to other processes, rather than the intervention itself. Nevertheless, as mentioned in the method section, pragmatic case studies are increasingly recognized as contributing to the building of evidence for intervention practice and theory (McLeod and Elliott 2011). Case studies provide research that is practitioner-friendly by showing how an intervention applies to a specific case (Fishman 2017). However, a future step should be to accumulate more cases such as that of Linda and Paul, followed within different types of interventions, to increase the generalizability of our observations. These observations also need to be combined with the quantitative data from RCTs to increase our understanding of the creation of a SPC scenario during the transition from marriage to divorce.

Conclusion Any effort to ease the transition of care between mental health professionals who specialize in therapy for married couples and those who specialize in post-divorce mediation could certainly be beneficial for the couples and shape their emotional experience of coparenting during marriage, the separation process, and after a divorce. This could be achieved through more suitable training of couples and family therapists regarding the specific information and/or required skills to address legal decisions and child-custody arrangements. These benefits may also be achieved by improved coordination between therapists of divorced couples and therapists of married couples. This is of great importance as custody challenges, including SPC, are inextricably linked to how parents raise their children.

References

Abidin, R. R., & Konold, T. R. (1999). *Parenting alliance measure professional manual.* Odessa: Psychological Assessment Resources.

Adamsons, K., & Pasley, K. (2006). Coparenting following divorce and relationship dissolution. In M. A. Fine & J. H. Harvey (Eds.), *Handbook of divorce and relationship dissolution* (pp. 241–261). Mahwah: Lawrence Erlbaum Associates Publishers.

Ahrons, C. R. (2007). Family ties after divorce: Long-term implications for children. *Family Process, 46*(1), 53–65.

Amato, P. R., & Afifi, T. D. (2006). Feeling caught between parents: Adult children's relations with parents and subjective well-being. *Journal of Marriage and Family, 68*, 222–235. https://doi.org/10.1111/j.1741-3737.2006.00243.x.

Arbuthnot, J., Poole, C. J., & Gordon, D. A. (1996). Use of educational materials to modify stressful behaviors in post-divorce parenting. *Journal of Divorce & Remarriage, 25*(1–2), 117–137. https://doi.org/10.1300/J087v25n01_08.

Ballard, R. H., Holtzworth-Munroe, A., Applegate, A. G., D'Onofrio, B. M., & Bates, J. E. (2013). A randomized controlled trial of child-informed mediation. *Psychology, Public Policy, and Law, 19*(3), 271–281. https://doi.org/10.1037/a0033274.

Bonds, D. D., & Gondoli, D. M. (2007). Examining the process by which marital adjustment affects maternal warmth: The role of coparenting support as a mediator. *Journal of Family Psychology, 21*(2), 288–296. https://doi.org/10.1037/0893-3200.21.2.288.

Booth, A., & Amato, P. R. (2001). Parental predivorce relations and offspring postdivorce well-being. *Journal of Marriage and the Family, 63*, 197–212.

Bowers, J. R., Ogolsky, B. G., Hughes, R., Jr., & Kanter, J. B. (2014). Coparenting through divorce or separation: A review of an online program. *Journal of Divorce & Remarriage, 55*(6), 464–484. https://doi.org/10.1080/10502556.2014.931760.

Braver, S. (2014). The costs and pitfalls of individualizing decisions and incentivizing conflict: A comment on Afcc's think tank report on shared parenting. *Family Court Review, 52*(2), 175–180.

Brown, J. H., Bledsoe, L., Yankeelov, P., Christensen, D., Rowan, N. L., & Cambron, M. L. (2009). PACT: A collaborative team model for treating high conflict families in family court. *Juvenile and Family Court Journal, 60*(2), 49–67. https://doi.org/10.1111/j.1755-6988.2009.01026.x.

Choi, J.-K., Hatton-Bowers, H., Brand, G., Poppe, L. M., & Foged, J. (2017). Co-parenting for successful kids: Impacts and implications. *Journal of Extension, 55*(6), UNSP 6RIB1.

Choi, J.-K., Parra, G., & Jiang, Q. (2019). The longitudinal and bidirectional relationships between cooperative coparenting and child behavioral problems in low-income, unmarried families. *Journal of Family Psychology, 33*, 203–214. https://doi.org/10.1037/fam0000498.

Christopher, C., Umemura, T., Mann, T., Jacobvitz, D., & Hazen, N. (2015). Marital quality over the transition to parenthood as a predictor of coparenting. *Journal of Child and Family Studies, 24*, 3636–3651. https://doi.org/10.1007/s10826-015-0172-0.

Cox, M. J., & Paley, B. (1997). Families as systems. *Annual Review of Psychology, 48*, 243–267. https://doi.org/10.1146/annurev.psych.48.1.243.

Darwiche, J., Imesch, C., & Eira Nunes, C. (2017a). *Système de codage des interactions conjugales et coparentales. Manuscrit inédit, Institut de psychologie*. Lausanne: Université de Lausanne.

Darwiche, J., Carneiro, C., Vaudan, C., Imesch, C., Eira Nunes, C., Favez, N., & de Roten, Y. (2017b). *Parents in couple therapy: An intervention targeting the romantic and the coparental relationships*. Manuscrit in revision.

Emery, R. E. (2012). *Renegociating family relationships*. New York/London: The Guildford Press.

Emery, R. E., Matthews, S. G., & Wyer, M. M. (1991). Child custody mediation and litigation: Further evidence on the differing views of mothers and fathers. *Journal of Consulting, 59*(3), 410–418. https://doi.org/10.1037/0022-006X.59.3.410.

Emery, R. E., Matthews, S. G., & Kitzmann, K. M. (1994). Child custody mediation and litigation: Parents' satisfaction and functioning one year after settlement. *Journal of Consulting, 62*(1), 124–129.

Emery, R. E., Laumann-Billings, L., Waldron, M. C., Sbarra, D. A., & Dillon, P. (2001). Child custody mediation and litigation: Custody, contact, and coparenting 12 years after initial dispute resolution. *Journal of Consulting, 69*(2), 323–332.

Favez, N. (2017). *Psychologie de la coparentalité*. Paris: Dunod.

Fishman, D. B. (2017). The pragmatic case study in psychotherapy: A mixed methods approach informed by psychology's striving for methodological quality. *Clinical Social Work Journal, 45* (3), 238–252.

Higgins, J. P. T., & Green, S. (2008). *Cochrane handbook for systematic reviews of interventions*. Chichester: Wiley.

Kamp Dush, C. M., Kotila, L. E., & Schoppe-Sullivan, S. J. (2011). Predictors of supportive coparenting after relationship dissolution among at-risk parents. *Journal of Family Psychology, 25*(3), 356–365.

Kitzmann, K. M. (2000). Effects of marital conflict on subsequent triadic family interactions and parenting. *Developmental Psychology, 36*, 3–13. https://doi.org/10.1037//0012-1649.36.1.3.

LaGraff, M. R., Stolz, H. E., & Brandon, D. J. (2015). Longitudinal program evaluation of « Parenting Apart: Effective Co-Parenting. ». *Journal of Divorce & Remarriage, 56*(2), 117–136. https://doi.org/10.1080/10502556.2014.996044.

Lambert, M. J., Finch, A. M., Okiishi, J., & Burlingame, G. (2005). *Administration and scoring manual for the OQ10.2*. Salt Lake City: OQ Measures LLC.

Lamela, D., & Figueiredo, B. (2016). Coparenting after marital dissolution and children's mental health: A systematic review. *Jornal de Pediatria, 92*(4), 331–342.

Lamela, D., Castro, M., & Figueiredo, B. (2010). Pais por inteiro: Avaliação preliminar da eficácia de uma intervenção em grupo para pais divorciados. [Preliminary efficacy evaluation of a group intervention program for divorced parents.]. *Psicologia: Reflexão e Crítica, 23*(2), 334–344. https://doi.org/10.1590/S0102-79722010000200016.

Le, Y., McDaniel, B. T., Leavitt, C. E., & Feinberg, M. E. (2016). Longitudinal associations between relationship quality and coparenting across the transition to parenthood: A dyadic perspective. *Journal of Family Psychology, 30*, 918–926. https://doi.org/10.1037/fam0000217.

Lebow, J. (2008). Separation and divorce issues in couple therapy. In A. Gurman (Ed.), *Clinical handbook of couple therapy* (pp. 459–477). New York: Guilford.

Leclair, V., St-Amand, A., & Bussières, E.-L. (2018). Association between child custody and postseparation coparenting: A meta-analysis. *Canadian Psychology/Psychologie Canadienne, 60*(2), 90–101. https://doi.org/10.1037/cap0000140.

Lee, C. M., Picard, M., & Blain, M. D. (1994). A methodological and substantive review of intervention outcome studies for families undergoing divorce. *Journal of Family Psychology, 8*(1), 3.

Mangelsdorf, S. C., Laxman, D. J., & Jessee, A. (2011). Coparenting in two-parent nuclear families. In J. P. McHale (Ed.), *Coparenting: A conceptual and clinical examination of family systems* (pp. 39–59). Washington, DC: American Psychological Association.

Martin, M. J., Sturge-Apple, M. L., Davies, P. T., Romero, C. V., & Buckholz, A. (2017). A process model of the implications of spillover from coparenting conflicts into the parent-child attachment relationship in adolescence. *Development and Psychopathology, 29*, 417–431. https://doi.org/10.1017/S0954579417000086.

McHale, J. P., & Irace, K. (2011). Coparenting in diverse family systems. In J. P. McHale & K. M. Lindahl (Eds.), *Coparenting: A conceptual and clinical examination of family systems* (pp. 15–37). Washington, DC: American Psychological Association.

McHale, J. P., & Lindahl, K. M. (2011). *Coparenting: A conceptual and clinical examination of family systems*. Washington, DC: American Psychological Association.

McKenry, P. C., Clark, K. A., & Stone, G. (1999). Evaluation of a parent education program for divorcing parents. *Family Relations: An Interdisciplinary Journal of Applied Family Studies, 48*, 129–137. https://doi.org/10.2307/585076.

McLeod, J., & Elliott, R. (2011). Systematic case study research: A practice-oriented introduction to building an evidence base for counselling and psychotherapy. *Counselling and Psychotherapy Research, 11*(1), 1–10.

Morril, M., Hines, D. A., Mahmood, S., & Cordova, J. V. (2010). Pathways between marriage and parenting for wives and husbands: The role of coparenting. *Family Process, 49*, 59–73. https://doi.org/10.1111/j.1545-5300.2010.01308.x.

Murphy, S. E., Jacobvitz, D. B., & Hazen, N. L. (2016). What's so bad about competitive coparenting? Family-level predictors of children's externalizing symptoms. *Journal of Child and Family Studies, 25*(5), 1684–1690. https://doi.org/10.1007/s10826-015-0321-5.

Nielsen, L. (2017). Re-examining the research on parental conflict, coparenting, and custody arrangements. *Psychology, Public Policy, and Law, 23*(2), 211.

Oppenheim, D., & Koren-Karie, N. (2013). The insightfulness assessment: Measuring the internal processes underlying maternal sensitivity. *Attachment and Human Development, 15*(5–6), 545–561. https://doi.org/10.1080/14616734.2013.820901.

Owen, J., & Rhoades, G. K. (2012). Reducing interparental conflict among parents in contentious child custody disputes: An initial investigation of the working together program. *Journal of Marital and Family Therapy, 38*(3), 542–555. https://doi.org/10.1111/j.1752-0606.2010.00215.x.

Pruett, M. K., & Donsky, T. (2011). Coparenting after divorce: Paving pathways for parental cooperation, conflict resolution, and redefined family roles. In J. P. McHale & K. M. Lindahl (Eds.), *Coparenting: Theory, research, and clinical applications* (pp. 231–250). Washington, DC: American Psychological Association.

Pruett, M. K., Arthur, L. A., & Ebling, R. (2007). The hand that rocks the cradle: Maternal gatekeeping after divorce. *Pace Law Review, 27*(4), 709–739.

Pruett, M. K., Ebling, R., & Cowan, P. A. (2011). Pathways from a US co-parenting intervention to legal outcomes. *International Journal of Law, Policy and the Family, 25*(1), 24–45.

Quigley, C., & Cyr, F. (2017). Children's perspectives on parenting coordination: Insights from the Montreal parenting coordination pilot project. *Journal of Child Custody: Research, Issues, and Practices, 14*(2–3), 151–174. https://doi.org/10.1080/15379418.2017.1371093.

Rothballer Seelert, K., Hill, R. D., Rigdon, M. A., & Schwenzfeier, E. (2015). Measuring patient distress in primary care. *Clinical Research and Methods, 31*(7), 483–487.

Rudd, B. N., Ogle, R. K., Holtzworth-Munroe, A., Applegate, A. G., & D'Onofrio, B. M. (2015). Child-informed mediation study follow-up: comparing the frequency of relitigation following different types of family mediation. *Psychology Public Policy and Law, 21*, 452–457. https://doi.org/10.1037/law0000046.

Rudd, B. N., Poladian, A. R., Holtzworth-Munroe, A., Applegate, A. G., & D'Onofrio, B. M. (2017). Randomized control trial follow-up: Online program and waiting period for unmarried parents in title IV-D court. *Journal of Family Psychology, 31*, 381–386. https://doi.org/10.1037/fam0000255.

Schoppe-Sullivan, S. J., Mangelsdorf, S. C., Frosch, C. A., & McHale, J. L. (2004). Associations between coparenting and marital behavior from infancy to the preschool years. *Journal of Family Psychology, 18*, 194–207. https://doi.org/10.1037/0893-3200.18.1.194.

Steinbach, A. (2018). Children's and parents' well-being in joint physical custody: A literature review. *Family Process, 58*(2), 353–369. https://doi.org/10.1111/famp.12372.

Stolz, H. E., Sizemore, K. M., Shideler, M. J., LaGraff, M. R., & Moran, H. B. (2017). Parenting together: Evaluation of a parenting program for never-married parents. *Journal of Divorce & Remarriage, 58*, 358–370. https://doi.org/10.1080/10502556.2017.1322855.

Stroud, C. B., Meyers, K. M., Wilson, S., & Durbin, C. E. (2015). Marital quality spillover and young children's adjustment: Evidence for dyadic and triadic parenting as mechanisms. *Journal of Clinical Child & Adolescent Psychology, 44*, 800–813. https://doi.org/10.1080/15374416.2014.900720.

Sullivan, M. J. (2008). Coparenting and the parenting coordination process. *Journal of Child Custody, 5*. https://doi.org/10.1080/15379410802070351.

Teubert, D., & Pinquart, M. (2010). The association between coparenting and child adjustment: A meta-analysis. *Parenting: Science and Practice, 10*(4), 286–307.

Teubert, D., & Pinquart, M. (2011). The Coparenting Inventory for Parents and Adolescents (CI-PA): Reliability and validity. *European Journal of Psychological Assessment, 27*(3), 206–215.

Wallerstein, J. S., Lewis, J., Blakeslee, S., & McIntire, K. (2000). *The unexpected legacy of divorce: A 25 year landmark study* (Vol. 77). New York: Hyperion.

Joëlle Darwiche is an associate professor of couple and family psychology at the Institute of Psychology of the University of Lausanne. She is the director of the Family and Development research center (FADO) of the University of Lausanne, a research lab that promote research in family and developmental psychology and encourage dialogue between researchers and practitioners. She is also a certified couple and family psychotherapist and director of the Master of Advanced Studies in systemic psychotherapy at the University of Lausanne. Her research mainly focuses on couple and family dynamics and on the evaluation of clinical interventions. She has published on transition to parenthood, couple therapy, and family interactions, assessed in various types of families and at different stages of life.

Cindy Eira Nunes is a SNSF (Swiss National Science Foundation) doctoral student at the Institute of Psychology and a member of the FAmily and DevelOpment research center (FADO) at the University of Lausanne, Switzerland. Her research focuses on couple psychotherapy and, more specifically, on the analysis of coparenting improvement during couple therapy for parents. She has published a meta-analysis and systematic review on the efficacy of programs integrating coparenting work for couples and families.

Nahema El Ghaziri is a research fellow at the migrant care unit of the University Center for Primary Care and Public Health of Lausanne, Switzerland. Her research interests are in the field of family dynamics. Her PhD focused on self-esteem and the quality of the parental couple relationships. She currently works on understanding the effects of forced migration on the family unit.

Camille Imesch M.Sc., is an SNSF (Swiss National Science Foundation) junior researcher at the Institute of Psychology and a member of the Family and Development Research Center (FADO) at the University of Lausanne, Switzerland. She also has a Master of Advances Studies in systemic psychotherapy and works in private practice as couple and family therapist.

Séverine Bessero M.Sc., has a Master of Advances Studies in systemic psychotherapy. She practices as a clinical psychologist and psychotherapist with fifteen years' therapeutic experience with couples and families. She is currently working in the Specialized Programme for Family and Couple Therapy of the Geneva University Hospitals, Geneva, Switzerland.

Part V
Child Support and the Legal Structure

13

Separation of Parents and SPC in Germany

Sabine Walper, Christine Entleitner-Phleps, and Alexandra N. Langmeyer

Abstract Multilocal, dual residence or shared parenting arrangements after parental separation are increasingly discussed in many countries because they seem best suited to allow for more equally shared parental roles and children's equal access to both (biological) parents. So far, there is little information about shared physical custody in Germany. The present research uses the second wave from a large German survey "Growing up in Germany" (2013–2015) to investigate the prevalence, preconditions, as well as possible outcomes of shared physical custody after separation. The sample comprises 1042 children (below age 18) with separated parents (maternal report). Measured by children's overnight stays with each parent, less than 5% of these children lived in a dual residence arrangement (50:50 up to 60:40% of time with either parent). Shared physical custody was more likely if maternal and paternal residence were in close proximity, and if the mother had higher levels of education. As expected, shared physical custody was more likely if the parents had a positive cooperative (co-parenting) relationship while co-parenting problems did not seem to have independent effects. The findings are discussed with respect to other research addressing issues of self-selection into different parenting arrangements and the still limited role of shared physical custody in Germany in facilitating more equal gender roles.

Keywords Shared Physical Custody · Legal Custody · Contact to Non-Resident Parent · Coparenting

---

S. Walper (✉) · C. Entleitner-Phleps · A. N. Langmeyer
German Youth Institute (DJI), Munich, Germany
e-mail: walper@dji.de; entleitner-phleps@dji.de; langmeyer@dji.de

13.1 Introduction

During the past decades, most Western countries have seen considerable changes in family and gender roles, which are reflected not only in rising employment rates among mothers, but also in fathers‘ increasing involvement in child rearing (e.g., Hall 2005). This trend towards more engaged fathering has been pointed out for nuclear families but is also evident in separated and divorced families, indicated by an increase in non-resident fathers' contact to their children (Amato et al. 2009; Westphal et al. 2014). Fathers' overall higher involvement is likely to affect parents' decisions about the division of parenting time and children's physical custody after separation or divorce. In fact, parenting arrangements in separated families, as well as statutory rules in family law, are changing. In many countries, an increasing share of separated parents tends to choose a parenting arrangement with (almost) equal time and responsibility for children, and some countries even favor this solution in the legal system (Fehlberg et al. 2011).

Such dual-residence shared parenting or shared physical custody is strongly discussed in Germany, too. Its proponents view it as a better solution for separated parents and their children than the traditional preference for children's residence with one parent – typically the mother – who holds sole physical custody. In particular, shared physical custody has been proposed to provide a broad range of advantages, not only for the father-child relationship (Bjarnason and Arnarsson 2011), but also for separated mothers' employment opportunities (cf. Sünderhauf 2013), and particularly for children's well-being (e.g., Nielsen 2018b). However, there is also concern about the increased demands and potential stress placed on parents and children in organizing children's moves between households and making sure that the children feel at home in both households instead of feeling home in none (e.g., Kinderrechtekommission des Deutschen Familiengerichtstags e.V. 2014).

So far, the current family law in Germany is not yet adapted to this parenting arrangement. While joint legal custody has become the most common arrangement for divorced parents, decisions of the family court about physical custody strongly favor sole physical custody. Furthermore, rules for child alimony payments similarly reflect the traditional preference for children's residence with one parent holding sole physical custody (Schumann 2018). According to the German family law, child alimony is only reduced in cases with strictly equally shared physical custody time while asymmetrical types of shared physical custody are not considered in legal decisions about alimony payments. This issue clearly fuels public debates. While there is some agreement that adaptations in the complex legal system of German family and tax law are necessary, there is also a controversy about the appropriate scope of these changes. While some demand that shared physical custody should be the new norm for separated families, others favor a more cautious approach, which is sensitive to case-specific conditions and children's best interest when deciding about their physical custody (Kinderrechtekommission des Deutschen Familiengerichtstags e.V. 2014).

The situation of separated families in Germany is far from clear. Official statistics do not inform about post-separation parenting arrangements, and only very few survey data provide highly limited insight into shared physical custody (Bjarnason and Arnarsson 2011; Institut für Demoskopie Allensbach 2017; Kalmijn 2015). The present paper seeks to fill this gap. We present data on the distribution of different parenting arrangements among separated families with minor children in Germany and identify correlates which may reflect likely predictors. In the following, we discuss findings on shared physical custody as evident in international research and provide background information about separated families in Germany.

13.2 Shared Physical Custody in Separated Families: International Evidence

Shared physical custody among separated parents has become a major issue not only in family law but also in social science research in many countries (Fehlberg et al. 2011). Given the intensive debate about pros and cons of shared care, the large number of investigations focuses on outcomes of shared compared to sole physical custody, particularly children's well-being (Bauserman 2002; Bergström et al. 2015; Nielsen 2018a; Steinbach 2018). In comparison, the number of studies which address issues of selective access to and use of shared physical custody is more limited (e.g., Poortman and van Gaalen 2017; Sodermans et al. 2013). However, both lines of research are similarly important and in fact interdependent, even more so since questions about the role of physical custody for children's well-being cannot be properly addressed without paying attention to the selective use of these different parenting arrangements (Fehlberg et al. 2011).

13.2.1 Issues Related to the Definition and Changing Prevalence of Shared Physical Custody

Since national or state-specific family law varies in how shared parenting is defined, it is no surprise that related studies use different criteria with different cut-off points distinguishing shared and sole physical custody. The major focus is on children's overnight stays with each parent, since overnight stays are regarded as the key element of children's residence with parents (Baude et al. 2016). In contrast, seeing a parent only during daytime is viewed as visitation of the non-custodial parent, even if a child spends considerable number of hours with this parent. Definitions of shared physical custody mostly range between time splits of 50:50 (strictly equal shares of overnight stays) to more asymmetrical distributions of overnight stays between parents up to 70:30 (Baude et al. 2016; Sünderhauf 2013).

These variations make it difficult to compare rates, predictors, and outcomes of shared physical custody across countries and studies. Furthermore, comparisons of findings are complicated by variations in target populations and samples used in empirical research. While some studies consider only children from divorced families, others also include children of unmarried separated parents, and parents who never cohabited. Not the least, variations in the social and legal context have to be considered.

Comparative data suggests that shared physical custody is particularly prevalent in Sweden, which strongly supports egalitarian roles in the family system and allows family courts to order shared physical custody in cases of post-separation legal conflict. According to survey data from 2011, about 42% of all children between 4 and 18 years, who did not live in a nuclear family, were raised in shared physical custody (Hakovirta and Rantalaiho 2011). Reforms in family law in Australia (Fehlberg et al. 2011) and Belgium (Sodermans et al. 2013) in the first decade of the new millennium have also strengthened shared physical custody as the legal norm. This has contributed to an increase of shared physical custody, as well as changes in the conditions under which separated families realize shared physical custody. For example, while earlier divorce cohorts in Belgium more selectively chose shared physical custody under conditions of low conflict between parents, this advantage has vanished in more recent divorce cohorts (Sodermans et al. 2013).

However, the trend of shared physical custody is not always upwards. In the Netherlands, shared care increased prior to and shortly after a reform of family law in 2009 which strengthened shared physical custody. Starting from a low level of 5% in the 1980s and 1990s, shared physical custody increased among recently divorced couples to 20% in 2008 (prior to the reform) and up to 28% in 2010 (post reform), but decreased in the following years to 22% in 2013 (Poortman and van Gaalen 2017). Although the reasons for this change in trend are far from clear, it seems likely that parents' experiences in practicing shared physical custody may have revealed its challenges and demands which could have cautioned later divorcing parents to opt for shared care. In this context, it is interesting to note that shared physical custody appeared to be less stable across time than sole physical custody. About 20% of the children who were in shared care when their parents divorced changed to sole physical custody, mostly with the mother, while only 2% of those who started in maternal custody changed to shared physical custody. This likely reflects the challenges involved in shared physical custody for parents and children (Poortman and van Gaalen 2017).

13.2.2 Conditions Affecting the Choice of Shared Physical Custody

Even if parents and children evaluate shared physical custody as their best option, managing its logistics is likely to be demanding. Available evidence suggests that separated parents' choice of parenting arrangement is linked to resources and barriers at the individual, family, and contextual level.

Conditions at the Individual Level: Age, Socio-Economic Condition and Level of Education

Many findings show that the *age of children* matters. Whereas parents of infants and toddlers are less likely to choose shared physical custody (Hyest and About 2007; Juby et al. 2005), this arrangement is most commonly used with children aged 3 to 12 years (Juby et al. 2005; Sodermans et al. 2013), especially in the primary-school age. For infants and toddlers, sole maternal custody may be preferred to allow for maternal breastfeeding and to meet very young children's higher need for stability in context. Furthermore, fathers may feel less competent and comfortable in taking care of infants, but become increasingly involved during the preschool and primary school age. In adolescence, the rate of children in shared physical custody declines (Spruijt and Duindam 2009), most likely because peer relations become more important. As young people like to spend more time with their friends, navigating between both parents' homes may be seen as hindrance to self-determined leisure time planning. However, age at parental separation may also matter with somewhat different effects. Evidence from Canada suggests that a divorce during children's adolescence is more likely to be followed by shared care, perhaps to preserve closeness to both parents in the direct aftermath of a divorce (Juby et al. 2005). This may indicate that the time since parental divorce plays an additional role. Young people may be more likely to opt out of shared physical custody after having practiced this arrangement for a while.

Across studies and countries, *parents' higher socio-economic resources*—education and income—have been found to increase the likelihood of shared physical custody (Juby et al. 2005; Spruijt and Duindam 2009; Kaspiew et al. 2009). This is likely to reflect the higher financial demands of shared physical custody which requires appropriate housing conditions and child-related equipment in both homes. At the same time, shared physical custody might not only depend on higher financial resources, but could also allow for higher earnings as it should be easier for mothers to combine family responsibilities and gainful employment. Better chances for maternal employment and financial independence are seen as core benefits of shared physical custody. However, similar to issues raised about income, the links between shared physical custody and maternal employment are far from clear. While shared physical custody could facilitate mothers' employment, it could also be more strongly favoured by working mothers when facing separation or divorce.

In this context, data about pre-divorce family conditions are of particular interest. A prospective study from the Netherlands found that only parents' level of education, but not their pre-divorce income was relevant for the choice of shared physical custody (Poortman and van Gaalen 2017). In addition, shared physical custody was more likely to be chosen if the mother worked more hours prior to the divorce, and if the father had a shorter way to work. Prospective data from Canada, however, confirmed an independent effect of pre-divorce income with higher rates of shared physical custody among families with higher pre-divorce income (Juby et al. 2005). Interestingly, this latter study found higher rates of shared physical custody not only among parents with university education, but also among those without a high school diploma. Perhaps, these latter families used shared physical custody to compensate for difficulties in alimony payments. Furthermore, shared physical custody was more common if the father had higher educational resources than the mother compared to families with equal educational resources or higher maternal education. Employment conditions were also found to matter, independent of parental education and income. Poortman and van Galen (2017) reported higher rates of shared care among families with higher maternal working hours prior to parental separation. Other data similarly suggest that shared physical custody was more likely if the mother worked at least part-time prior to parental divorce and if the father did not work in the evenings or at weekends (Juby et al. 2005). In sum, parents' education and pre-divorce employment conditions seem to affect the choice of shared physical custody more consistently while findings on income differ.

Conditions at the Family Level

A *new partnership* also seems to change conditions for parenting arrangements. Data from Canada suggest that if the mother moves in with a new partner, shared physical custody is more likely than sole maternal care (Juby et al. 2005). Australian findings similarly support that shared physical custody is twice as prevalent if the mother lives with a new partner compared to mothers who live alone (Kaspiew et al. 2009). Exclusive time with the new partner may be seen as an advantage of shared physical custody, thus making it a more attractive option for repartnered mothers. However, data from Germany do not support this effect of maternal repartnering. In particular, previous analyses of the data used here did not show different rates of shared physical custody when comparing single and repartnered mothers (Walper 2016).

Some evidence points to the salience of *fathers' pre-divorce involvement in family work*. Juby et al. (2005) found that shared physical custody was more likely if the father's principal activity prior to divorce included caring for the family. Other data also indicate that fathers' pre-separation involvement in daily childcare is a particularly relevant factor (Fehlberg et al. 2011; Poortman and van Gaalen 2017). This continuity of fathers' involvement in the parenting role, even when the partnership ends, is quite in contrast to findings from earlier decades. In the past, fathers' active contribution to parenting more strongly depended on its framing by the partnership with the mother – as indicated by the notion of a "package deal" between paternal involvement and partnership (Amato et al. 2009).

Parents' willingness and ability to cooperate is of special interest, as it suggests itself that shared physical custody needs more parental coordination than sole physical custody. In line with this expectation, prospective findings from the Netherlands show that pre-divorce interparental conflict, as well as conflict during the divorce procedure, had negative effects on the choice for shared physical custody

(Poortman and van Gaalen 2017). Other studies also indicate that separated parents with shared care report less conflict, especially about parenting issues, than parents with children in sole physical custody (Cashmore et al. 2010).

However, findings regarding the link between interparental conflict and shared parenting are not consistent (Nielsen 2013) and parental communication is not guaranteed in shared care. According to data from Australia, the great majority of parents with shared physical custody reported at least weekly contact, but a minority of parents who practiced shared parenting communicated less than once a month or never (Kaspiew et al. 2009, p. 160). About one fifth of the parents with shared parenting reported that the relationship with the other parent was conflictual or even threatening.

Conditions at the Contextual Level

Contextual conditions shape options and preferences for parenting arrangements. For example, given the higher demands on balancing family tasks and employment for both parents, flexible and family friendly work conditions facilitate shared physical custody (Nielsen 2013). Furthermore, as mentioned above, changing legal conditions seem to affect who opts for shared physical custody. In Belgium, the court has to consider shared physical custody if parents disagree about their post-divorce parenting arrangement. When this was introduced in family law, the earlier advantages of lower conflict among parents with shared care faded (Sodermans et al. 2013). Australian researchers similarly warn that shared physical custody may increasingly become the compromise solution for highly conflicted parents who cannot settle the issue of physical custody (Fehlberg et al. 2011). Interestingly, a qualitative study from Sweden shows that parents with toddlers consider shared physical custody as beneficial for children's well-being, even if their relationship is conflicted (Fransson et al. 2016). This suggests that shared physical custody has become normative irrespective of the quality of the interparental relationships. Conditions in Germany, however, are likely to differ since shared physical custody is less widespread and less anchored in family law.

Finally, the *distance between both parents' homes* is likely to affect the logistics of shared care. A larger distance makes it more difficult to maintain shared physical custody and ensure that the child is involved in regular childcare, manages his or her way to school, and sees his/her friends when staying at either parents' home. Several studies show that shared physical custody is more likely if parents' homes are in close proximity (Kaspiew et al. 2009). Data from the first wave of the German survey „Growing Up In Germany" (AID:A) conducted in 2009 are in line with these findings, although they address the frequency of contact and not overnight stays. Frequent (at least weekly) contact to the non-residential father was considerably more likely if the child and the father lived in the same town or village while long distances were linked to a lack of contact (Schier and Hubert 2015).

13.3 Separated Families in Germany

13.3.1 Changing Family Forms and Labor Division

As many other European countries, Germany faces considerable instability of couple relationships. Every third marriage is estimated to end in divorce, and every second divorce involves children (Statistisches Bundesamt 2018c). In 2017, at least 124.000 minors experienced parental divorce. Although divorce rates are slightly declining, this trend does not indicate a higher stability of unions in general. Cohabitation has become increasingly common, not only among childless couples, but also among parents. In 2017, every third child (34.7%) was born to unmarried parents (Statistisches Bundesamt 2018b). The large majority of unmarried parents cohabits when a child is born (about 80%), but these unions are more likely to separate than married parents (Langmeyer 2015; Schnor 2012). In 2017, 11% of all households with minors were headed by two unmarried parents (Baumann et al. 2018, p. 59). Additional 19% were single parent households, mostly headed by the mother (88%; Baumann et al. 2018, p. 67). While stepfamilies cannot be identified by official statistics, survey data allow estimates ranging between 7 and 13% of all families (Bundesministerium für Familie Senioren Frauen und Jugend 2013).

Since 1998, joint legal custody is the default case when married parents get divorced. Most unmarried couples officially establish joint legal custody at the birth of their child, and as legal default this continues when they separate. Although custody can be changed by the family court, most separated parents hold joint legal custody. Physical custody, however, differs substantially from legal custody. Although the German family law does not preclude shared physical custody, sole physical custody held by one parent–typically the mother–was (and still is) viewed as the preferred arrangement because it seemed best suited to meet children's needs for continuity. In this line, the Commission on Children's Rights of the German Family Court Council cautioned: "Continuity of contact to both parents only comes at the expense of discontinuity in the child's living environment" (Kinderrechtekommission des Deutschen Familiengerichtstags e.V. 2014). Quite importantly, as indicated by the high share of single mothers compared to single fathers, sole physical custody (of the mother) is also most in line with traditional family roles with mothers taking the main responsibility for family work and child rearing.

Looking at the division of labour in families, the male-breadwinner-model and its modernized form are still widespread in Germany. Although 74% of all mothers were employed in 2016 (Statistisches Bundesamt 2017b), the majority of them works only part-time (69% in 2017), even more so, if they live in a partnership (Statistisches Bundesamt 2017a). In couple households with minors, 71% of the mothers were part-time employed, compared to only 6% of the fathers. This gender difference is only slightly lower in single-parent families, about 58% of all single mothers, but only 12% of the single fathers, were part-time employed (Statistisches Bundesamt 2017a). Looking at family work, women with partners still manage the majority of family tasks including household choirs and childcare (Nitsche and Grunow 2016). Sharing household, child rearing duties, and gainful employment equally is still a rare exception. With regard to other European countries, Germany has the highest gender gap in employment hours (Organisation for Economic Co-operation and Development (OECD) 2017). Only 1.2% of the parents are dual-earner couples who both work nearly full-time and share family and work duties almost equally. Although egalitarian gender role attitudes are wide-spread (Blohm and Walter 2018) and fathers strive try to be an active part of their children's life (Zerle-Elsäßer and Li 2017), family roles in Germany are far from egalitarian.

The more traditional division of labour as well as tax benefits for married couples make lone parenthood a major risk factor for poverty. German data from EU-SILC 2016 indicates that 32.6% of the single parent households were at risk of poverty (having less than 60% of the needs-weighted median income of the population), compared to only 11% of couples with children (Statistisches Bundesamt 2018a). Only every second non-resident parent seems to provide any financial child support and only one out of four pays more than the minimum (Lenze 2014). While some fathers may not be able to provide, this also indicates a wide-spread lack of commitment to the child among separated fathers in Germany.

13.3.2 Shared Physical Custody in Germany

The findings reported so far do not suggest beneficial conditions for shared physical custody in Germany. This is also reflected in data on post-divorce parenting arrangements. Kalmijn (2015) used data from CILS4EU (2010/2011) to compare 14-years old students' post-divorce contact and relationship with their father in Germany, the Netherlands, England, and Sweden. The findings revealed the highest rate of youth without contact to their father in Germany (20.7%). Conversely, the rate of shared physical custody was lowest in Germany (9.8%), followed by England (10.9%), while Sweden had the highest rate (36%). The relationship quality to their father, however, was quite good among German youth in separated families, 51.6% reported a "very good" relationship. Controlling for country differences, shared physical custody was more common among non-immigrants, families with higher SES, if the mother was employed, and for male children.

Further comparative data are available from the HBSC study (2005/06) which included more than 200,000 school-aged children (age 11, 13 and 15 year) from 36 western countries (Bjarnason and Arnarsson 2011). The aim of this study was to examine parenting arrangements in different countries, as well as parent-child communication patterns. Germany was found to belong to the countries with low rates of shared physical custody. Among youth from non-nuclear families in Germany, only 4.2% were raised in shared physical custody (own calculation). At the same time, German youth in shared physical custody seemed more advantaged in terms of communication with their father than the average of all children. In Germany, only 15% of the children in shared physical custody, but 35% of those in nuclear families found it difficult to talk to their father about things that really bothered them. On average across countries, this difference was much less pronounced (29% vs. 32%). Interestingly, a similar advantage of shared physical custody was found for communication with the mother in Germany, while overall, there was no difference between nuclear families and those with shared physical custody. It is not clear whether these findings reflect positive effects of shared physical custody in Germany or a particularly selective use of this arrangement by well-functioning separated families.

A recent study tried to shed more light on shared physical custody in Germany (Institut für Demoskopie Allensbach 2017). Of 603 separated mothers and fathers, only two thirds knew or had ever heard of shared physical custody. But different from the numbers reported so far, 22% of the separated parents indicated that they shared parenting almost equally. Even 41% reported almost equal shares of parenting prior to their separation. However, more specific questions about each parents' contribution revealed that only 15% confirmed shared physical custody ("Wechselmodell") and only half of these (7%) actually met the standard criteria of overnight stays in shared physical custody. This is more in line with expectable findings and data from the German family panel *pairfam* which revealed less than 5% of separated families with shared physical custody (Walper 2016).

Although parents' estimates of shared physical custody are obviously no objective criteria, further findings of this study suggest that parental cooperation facilitates shared care (Institut für Demoskopie Allensbach 2017). Compared to the average of all separated parents, those who indicated almost equal shares of childcare reported twice as often to have a good or very good relationship with their child's other parent. Well working mutual agreements–indicating cooperative co-parenting–were substantially more prevalent among parents who shared childcare. The large majority of parents who shared child-related responsibilities explained that they wanted to give the child the opportunity to have both parents around. About half agreed that sharing childcare makes it easier for parents to work or have time for themselves. Only 11% saw shared physical custody as a chance to pay less child support to the former partner. Satisfaction with the current parenting arrangement was substantially higher among those parents who were involved in at least half of the child rearing tasks than among those who participated less. About 51% viewed an almost equal sharing of parenting tasks as ideal.

13.3.3 Research Questions

Despite these few findings, there is a clear lack of data on shared physical custody in Germany. Available evidence suggests that shared physical custody is still rare. In order to pay attention to the expectable heterogeneity of families without shared physical custody, we sought to also consider variations in contact to the non-residential parent (see e.g., Spruijt and Duindam 2009). Our analyses address the following research questions:

1. How many separated families in Germany use shared physical custody and how does their share compare to families with sole physical custody, but varying degrees of contact to the non-resident parent? We were interested in the distribution of four parenting arrangements: (1) shared physical custody, (2) sole physical custody with frequent contact to the non-resident parent, (3) sole physical custody with rare contact to non-resident parent, and (4) sole physical custody without contact to the non-resident parent.
2. Which factors are linked to separated parents' choice of shared physical custody? Considering the available international evidence, we expected that characteristics of the child (age and gender) and the mothers (level of education, employment status, new partnership), as well as the distance between both parents' homes are relevant factors. For separated parents who are still in contact, we expected that cooperative co-parenting is linked to higher rates of shared parenting while co-parenting conflict might impede shared parenting. Given the lack of legal institutionalization of shared physical custody in Germany, we assumed that less conflicted parents are more likely to opt for shared care, similar to earlier findings, e.g. for Belgium (Sodermans et al. 2013).

13.4 Method

13.4.1 Data and Sample

Our analyses are based on data from the second wave of a large representative German survey on children and youth ("Growing up in Germany"; AID:A, 2013–2015; Walper et al. 2015) with over 25,000 target subjects in the age range between birth and 32 years. The sample was drawn from nation-wide register data, and the participants were contacted and interviewed by professional interviewers. All interviews were conducted by telephone. In addition to the target participants who were interviewed from age nine onward, one parent – in most cases the mother – provided additional information on the minor children including socio-demographic and structural data. In this study we only focused on the parent's view in order to maximize the sample and include information on all minor children. The AID:A survey covers a broad range of information about the lives of children, teenagers, and young adults, including stressors and strains, family life, child care, schooling, occupational training and work, leisure time activities, socioeconomic conditions, and well-being.

In line with our research questions, we restricted the sample to target children up to age 17 with separated or divorced parents. Parents' marital status prior to separation was no selection criterion. Hence, the sample comprises previously married as well as unmarried parents. Based on these criteria, a subsample of 1090 target children could be identified which comprised 8% of all minors in the AID:A II sample. In the large majority of cases, the mother participated and provided information about family conditions and the child. In only 47 cases, household information was provided by the father. These latter cases had to be excluded since our focus was on maternal conditions (reported by mothers). The final sample consisted of 1042 minor children with separated parents, including 53.4% boys and 46.6% girls. The children had an average age of 10.54 years (SD = 4.97). 20.2% of the children were below school age, 24.8% were elementary school age (6 to 10 years old), while more than half of the children were 11 to 17 years old (55.1%).

With respect to marital status, 31.8% of the mothers were never married, 38.3% were divorced, 16.4% were still married but permanently separated, and 13.5% were remarried. In two thirds of the cases (65.8%), the mother reported having joint legal custody with the father. Every fourth mother (25.7%) lived in a new partnership.

13.4.2 Indicators

The indicators used in our analyses rely on information provided by the target child's mother.

Shared Physical Custody was defined by children's overnight stays with each parent, allowing for minor asymmetries in the distribution of overnight stays (60:40). We chose to use this strict criterion since current German family law considers a share of overnight stays of 70:30 as sole physical custody with extended contact. However, it should be mentioned that our findings are quite robust, even when using the less strict criterion of overnight stays (up to 70:30, see discussion). Shared physical custody was coded (as 1), if the child or adolescent slept at least 12 nights (40%) at one parent's home and not more than 19 nights (60%) per month at the other parent's home. In sole physical custody (coded 0), the child slept more than 19 nights (>60%) at one parent's house and less than 12 nights (<40%) per month at the other parent's house. In the unweighted data, only 4.3% of the children were in shared physical custody.

For cases of sole physical custody, three *levels of children's contact with the non-residential parent* were distinguished. Contact between the non-resident parent and the child included personal contact, telephone calls, or other ways of contact (letters, mail, emails etc.). Given the many ways of contact with the child addressed by the related item, the frequency of children's contact with the non-resident parent as reported by mothers was quite high. Accordingly, we distinguished children with at least weekly contact to the father (frequent contact), those with less frequent contact, and those without contact to the non-resident father. More than half of the children had at least weekly contact to their non-resident father (unweighted data: 53.2%). Only one out of four children had less frequent contact (once or twice a month or even less: 25.0%). Finally, 17.5% of all children with separated parents had no contact to the father (unweighted data).

The *distance between both parental homes* was assessed by mothers' estimates using five categories: 1 = in the same house, in the same neighbourhood", 2 = in the same town or village, but more than 15 minutes away, 3 = in a different village, but less than 1 h away, 4 = further away but in Germany, 5 = further away, in another country. Our analyses use this indicator as continuous variable.

Both biological parents' *legal custody* for the child was assessed by maternal self report (1 = no, 2 = yes). A *new maternal partnership* was taken into account if the new partner lived in the same household as mother and child (1 = no partner in the household, 2 = new partner in the household). Mothers also reported on *child age* and *gender*. The *region of maternal residence* (East- vs. West Germany) was coded from information provided by the interviewer. Region was included since considerably higher rates of children are born to unmarried parents in East than in West Germany suggesting less involvement among separated fathers in the East.

Mothers provided detailed information about household composition, net family income, their education, and employment situation. *Poverty risk* was based on the net per capita income weighted by household needs (indexed by household composition according to the new OECD scale). The threshold value for poverty risk was set by the EU, at 60% of the median needs-adjusted equivalence income, dividing the sample into two groups (0 = above poverty threshold, 1 = below poverty threshold). *Maternal employment* status was used as dichotomous indicator (1 = mother is not employed, including unemployment, being in school/university/further education, housewife, maternity protection/parental leave, or retirement, 2 = mother is employed). We classified *mother's level of education* by using the Comparative Analysis of Social Mobility in Industrial Nations (CASMIN) (Brauns et al. 2003), which takes in account the level of general school education as well as the occupational/academic training. Due to small sample sizes in some categories, we combined categories as follows: 1 = basic education (no school leaving certificate/school leaving certificate awarded after successful completion of eighth respective ninth grade and other school leaving certificates with and without job training); 2 = intermediate education (school leaving certificate awarded after 10 years of schooling (roughly comparable with US high school diploma) with and without job training); 3 = general qualification for university entrance (final exam at the end of secondary education, i.e. after 12 or 13 years of schooling with and without job training), 4 = higher tertiary education (vocational university or university degree). In a second step we reduced these four categories to two, defined by general qualification for university entrance (1 = no, 2 = yes). We also added *child gender* (1 = male, 2 = female). *Age of the child* was split in three age groups: 1 = 0–5 years, 2 = 6–10, 3 = 11–17 years) in order to test non-linear effects, expecting higher prevalence of shared physical custody in elementary school age.

Questions about the quality of separated parents' *co-parenting* were restricted to cases of contact between both parents, since the respective indicators require a minimum of contact and exchange between both parents. The items used in the AID:A survey were adapted from the German version of the Parent Problem Checklist (Dadds and Powell 1991). Two dimensions of co-parenting were measured: cooperation (2 item-scale, Cronbach's alpha = .81 e.g. "We are a good team as parents") and negative co-parenting (conflict, triangulation and differences, 7 item-scale, Cronbach's alpha = .87, e.g. "We have generally different views about parenting"). Both subscales were negatively correlated ($r = -.31$, $p < .001$).

For the present analysis, we dichotomized them by median-split because of the small group size of respondents who were practicing shared physical custody.

13.4.3 Analytic Strategy

We first present information about the distribution of shared parenting arrangements and father-child contact, using weighted data to compensate for the relatively small proportion of respondents with low education. Descriptive and multivariate analysis were calculated with unweighted data. We analysed bivariate links between parenting arrangements and the predictor variables (Chi^2- Tests) and inspected standardized residuals to identify local deviations between the observed and the expected cell frequencies. It is noted if the standardized residual value reached a minimum of 2.0 (or − 2.0 and lower), which indicates that the observed value differs more than two standard deviations from the expected value (Haberman 1973).

Secondly, we used logistic regressions to control for the mutual interdependence of the predictors and test their unique links to parenting arrangements. These analyses distinguish between shared and sole physical custody, but disregard variations in father-child contact. Three models were tested: (1) In order to provide information about factors relevant for the large sample, we initially restricted the analyses to predictors which were available for all cases, addressing child-related factors, socio-economic and regional factors, residential distance, and mothers' household structure (stepfamily formation). These analyses exclude co-parenting quality as predictor, since information on co-parenting quality was only available for cases with interparental contact. Adding this predictor would have excluded families without contact between parents. (2) Next, we restricted the same analysis to families with parents' joint legal custody. These analyses are of particular interest in the context of the current debate about how to regulate shared parenting legally, since it has been argued that a consistent legal reform would best construe shared parenting as arrangement based on and restricted to shared legal custody (Wissenschaftliche Dienste 2018). (3) Thc final analysis was restricted to families with contact between parents and included co-parenting quality as predictor. Note that even the latter two analyses cannot easily be compared since the sample size was reduced when focusing families with joint legal custody *and* contact between parents.

13.5 Results

13.5.1 Descriptive Results

As suggested above, only few families practiced shared physical custody. This is even more evident when using the weighted data: Only 3.3% of all children with separated parents lived in shared physical custody (60:40). Slightly less than half of the children had at least weekly contact to their non-resident father (weighted data: 48.0%), while 27.4% had infrequent contact to the non-resident father and 21.3% had no contact.

Our first set of analyses addressed bivariate links between these parenting arrangements and their correlates considered as likely predictors. Table 13.1 shows these results. As expected, shared physical custody was significantly more likely if the father lived at short distance, but frequent contact also increased with shorter distance ($\chi^2 = 147.19$, df = 12, $p < .001$). If the father lived in the same house or in the same neighbourhood, shared physical custody was twice as likely (13.1%) than if he lived in the same town or village but more than 15 minutes away (7%). At a distance of more than 1 h, shared physical custody was not realized at all. As indicated by high positive standardized residuals in the case of highest proximity, the observed data for shared physical custody and frequent contact to the non-resident father exceeded the expected values significantly. In contrast, the standardized residuals for rare or no contact to father were negative, showing that these arrangements are unlikely in the case of high proximity. If the father lived more than 1 h away (in Germany or in another country), the child was significantly more likely to live with the mother and to have just infrequent or no contact to the non-residential father.

Legal and physical custody were also strongly linked ($\chi^2 = 194.948$, df = 3, $p < .001$). Shared physical custody as well as frequent contact to the non-residential father were both strongly associated with joint legal custody, whereas sole legal custody was more prevalent in families without contact to the non-residential father. With regard to socio-economic factors, maternal education ($\chi^2 = 50.15$, df = 9, $p < .001$), her employment status ($\chi^2 = 23.66$, df = 3, $p < .001$), and poverty risk ($\chi^2 = 8.74$, df = 3, $p < .05$) were also linked to the child's parenting arrangement. Children of mothers with basic education were significantly more likely to have no contact to the father. In contrast, the chances of shared physical custody were much higher if the mother had tertiary education. Interestingly, the chances of shared parenting were not affected by poverty and unemployment, while having no contact to the father was particularly more likely in cases of maternal unemployment and living in poverty risk.

Children's age also mattered for the choice of parenting arrangements ($\chi^2 = 21.59$, df = 6, $p < .001$). Shared physical custody was most likely during the elementary school years, while having no contact was significantly more prevalent among children below age six.

Finally, the quality of parents' co-parenting was also significantly associated with their parenting arrangement. If parental cooperation was high, shared physical custody, and frequent contact to the non-residential father were substantially more likely than at a low level of cooperation ($\chi^2 = 110.31$, df = 3, $p < .001$). Negative co-parenting, child gender, the region (East- vs. West-Germany), and mothers' co-residence with a new partner were not linked to the parenting arrangement.

Table 13.1 Bivariate links between predictor variables and arrangements of parental care in separated families

	Shared physical custody	Maternal residence, frequent contact to non-resident father	Maternal residence, infrequent contact to non-resident father	Maternal residence, no contact to non-resident father	Total
Distance to the non-resident father (N = 1022, Chi² = 147.19, df = 12, p < .001)					
Same house/ same neighbourhood	13.1%[a]	72.3% [a]	11.7%[a]	2.9%[a]	100% (n = 137)
Same village, but >15 min away	7.0%	60.7%	21.8%	10.5%[a]	100% (n = 229)
Another village, <1 h away	2.5%	55.3%	27.4%	14.7%	100% (n = 441)
Further away but in Germany	0.0%[a]	33.9%[a]	35.2%[a]	30.9%[a]	100% (n = 165)
Further away, in another country	0.0%	30.0%[a]	30.0%	40.0%[a]	100% (n = 50)
Legal custody (N = 1021; Chi² = 194.948, df = 3, p < .001)					
Sole legal custody	0.6%[a]	32.4%[a]	28.9%	38.1%[a]	100% (n = 349)
Joint legal custody	6.0%[a]	64.3%[a]	23.2%	6.5%[a]	100% (n = 672)
Maternal education (N = 1041; Chi² = 50.15, df = 9, p < .001)					
Basic education	1.5%	41.2%	25.7%	31.6%[a]	100% (n = 136)
Intermediate education	2.1%[a]	50.4%	28.8%	18.7%	100% (n = 379)
Qualification for university entrance	5.2%	56.3%	23.1%	15.4%	100% (n = 229)
Higher tertiary education	7.7%[a]	59.9%	21.2%	11.1%[a]	100% (n = 297)
Employment status (N = 1041; Chi² = 23.66, df = 3; p < .001)					
Mother is employed	4.6%	56.2%	24.2%	15.0%	100% (n = 833)
Mother is not employed	3.4%	40.9%[a]	28.4%	27.4%[a]	100% (n = 208)
Poverty risk (N = 1024; Chi² = 8.74, df = 3, p < .05)					
Above poverty threshold	4.7%	54.9%	24.5%	15.9%	100% (n = 774)
Below poverty threshold	3.6%	46.8%	26.4%	23.2%[a]	100% (n = 250)

(continued)

Table 13.1 (continued)

	Shared physical custody	Maternal residence, frequent contact to non-resident father	Maternal residence, infrequent contact to non-resident father	Maternal residence, no contact to non-resident father	Total
*Child age (N = **1042; Chi^2 = 21.59; df = 6, p < .001)***					
0–5 years	2.4%	50.5%	22.4%	24.8%[a]	100% (n = 210)
6–10 years	8.1%[a]	52.7%	24.0%	15.1%	100% (n = 258)
11–17 years	3.3%	54.4%	26.5%	15.9%	100% (n = 574)
*Co-parenting: Cooperation (N = **714; Chi^2 = 110.31, df = 3, p < .001)***					
Low cooperation	2.2%[a]	56.3%[a]	35.9%[a]	5.6%[a]	100% (n = 359)
High cooperation	10.1%[a]	79.2%[a]	10.7%[a]	0.0%[a]	100% (n = 355)
*Co-parenting: Negative co-parenting (N = **708; Chi^2 = 1.29, df = 3, n.s.)***					
Low negative co-parenting	5.6%	67.8%	23.4%	3.1%	100% (n = 354)
High negative co-parenting	6.8%	68.4%	22.9%	2.0%	100% (n = 354)
*Child gender (N = **1042; Chi^2 = 1.00; df = 3, n.s.)***					
Male	4,9%	53,4%	24,5%	17,3%	100% (n = 556)
Female	3,7%	52,9%	25,7%	17,7%	100% (n = 486)
*Region (N = **1042; Chi^2 = 0.60; df = 3, n.s.)***					
West-Germany	4,5%	53,3%	24,9%	17,3%	100% (n = 840)
East-Germany	3,5%	52,5%	25,7%	18,3%	100% (n = 202)
*New partnership (N = **1038, Chi^2 = 6.041, df = 3, n.s.)***					
No partner in the household	4.5%	55.4%	23.9%	16.2%	100% (n = 771)
New partner in the household	3.7%	47.6%	28.8%	19.9%	100% (n = 267)

Note: [a]Standardized residuum SR < −2.0 or > +2.0

13.5.2 Multivariate Results

In a second step, we tested which factors proved more important if considered in the context of the other factors. We used logistic regression models with a dichotomous depended variable (1 = shared physical custody vs. 0 = all other forms) and nine predictors. The first logistic regression model integrates most factors from the descriptive results (see Table 13.1), except shared legal custody and poverty risk. We excluded shared legal custody because it is a legal pre-condition for shared parenting and may mediate–or in this case obscure–other effects which we are interested in. Poverty risk was excluded since it might not only affect the choice of parenting arrangement but could also be affected by it (e.g., via maternal employment). Hence, it seemed less clear whether poverty should be considered as predictor or outcome variable.

Table 13.2 Predictors of shared physical custody[a]: Findings from logistic regression analyses

		Odds ratio (OR)		
		(1)	(2)	(3)
Child age	6–10 years (ref.)			
	0–5 years	0.33*	0.37*	0.38
	11–17 years	0.46*	0.30**	0.33**
Child gender (female vs. male)		0.66	0.64	0.77
Maternal education (qualification for university entrance vs. basic/intermediate education)		3.31**	3.23**	3.19**
Mother employed		0.69	0.73	0.65
Distance to nonresident father		0.38***	0.44***	0.52**
New partner in household		1.31	1.74	1.85
Region (East vs. West-Germany)		0.74	0.94	0.81
Positive cooperation		–	–	4.92**
Negative co-parenting		–	–	2.01
N		1.017	666	521
Nagelkerke's R^2		.18	.18	.21

* p < .05; ** p < .01, *** p < .001

[a]1 = shared physical custody, 0 = all other arrangements; Model (1): all separated families included; Model (2): separated with joint legal custody of both parents; Model (3): separated families with joint legal custody and contact between both parents

As shown in Table 13.2, Model 1 yielded three significant predictors of shared physical custody: maternal education, distance to the non-resident father, and child age. In line with many findings, high maternal education was found to facilitate shared physical custody (OR = 3.31, $p < .01$). Furthermore, a long distance in commuting to the father reduced the likelihood of shared parenting (OR = 0.38, $p < .001$). Similar to bivariate findings for child age, shared physical custody was less likely for young children (below age 6: OR = 0.33, $p < .050$) and for older children (age 11 and older: OR = 0.46, $p < .050$) compared to elementary school age children (6–10 years old). Compared to bivariate descriptive findings, maternal employment was no longer linked to shared physical custody. Model 2, which was restricted to families with joint legal custody, revealed the same robust results as Model 1 (see Table 13.2).

The third logistic regression model was based on a further reduced sample of families with joint legal custody and contact between parents (see Column 3 in Table 13.2). It adds both dimensions of co-parenting (positive cooperation and negative co-parenting) to the picture. As expected, co-parenting quality matters because the chances of shared physical custody were almost five times higher if separated parents cooperated well in child rearing tasks. In addition, negative co-parenting had an unexpected marginally positive effect. Parents with above-average negative co-parenting tended to have a higher likelihood of shared physical custody than those with little negative co-parenting ($p = .07$). Young children (below age 6) were no longer less likely to experience shared physical custody, most likely because the substantial share of young children without contact to their father was not included in these analyses. Independent of co-parenting quality, older children (11–17 years old) were less likely to live in shared physical custody than elementary school age children. Maternal education and distance to the father's home remained significantly linked to shared physical custody.

13.6 Discussion

The findings reported here provide important insight into shared physical custody and its predictors in Germany. Compared to findings which were based on a less thorough counting of children's overnight stays with each parent (Institut für Demoskopie Allensbach 2017; Kalmijn 2015), we found considerably lower rates of shared physical custody. However, our data are well in line with findings from the German family panel *pairfam* which revealed less than 5% of separated families with shared physical custody (Walper 2016). Hence, we are led to conclude that shared physical custody is still the rare exception in Germany. Although a less restrictive criterion of overnight shares up to 70:30 doubles the rate of shared physical custody, its relative frequency is still very low (Walper, Langmeyer & Entleitner-Phleps in prep.).

This may not come as surprise given the rather traditional division of labor among couples in nuclear families. Since fathers' involvement in childcare prior to the separation has been pointed out as important predictor of shared physical custody, the little chances for such involvement could explain the low prevalence of shared physical custody. Unfortunately, the data used here do not provide information about fathers' pre-separation involvement in parenting and thus do not allow testing its predictive role in parents' choice of post-separation parenting arrangement. Future research should address these links between pre- and post-separation paternal involvement in Germany.

Overall, the descriptive results on bivariate links between parenting arrangements and their correlates, as well as the regression models, are in line with international findings. Parental socio-economic resources, particularly parental education, have consistently proven to be highly important (Fehlberg et al. 2011; Juby et al. 2005; Poortman and van Gaalen 2017). This is supported by the strong positive link between maternal education and shared physical custody in our data. Our analyses were restricted to educational resources, although finances have been hypothesized to also play a role because shared physical custody involves higher expenses. However, maternal income may not only affect the choice of shared physical custody but is also likely to be affected by it, thus obscuring the interpretation of findings. To some extent, this also holds true for maternal employment, since better chances for separated mothers to be gainfully employed should be a major important advantage of shared physical custody. However, prospective findings have shown that maternal employment prior to separation affects the choice of parenting model (Poortman and van Gaalen 2017). In our data, neither bivariate links nor the regression models suggest a significant link between shared physical custody and maternal employment. Although maternal employment and parenting arrangement are significantly linked at a bivariate level, this is not due to higher employment rates in shared physical custody, but rather to high unemployment rates among mothers who have no contact to the child's father. Future research should monitor whether shared physical custody in Germany can eventually pave the way for single mothers' better chances on the labor market.

Residential proximity between both parents was a more important and robust factor in shared physical custody. In fact, short distances of up to 15 min seemed particularly suitable for shared physical custody. However, causal interpretations could be misled since separating parents might choose residential proximity if they plan to establish shared physical custody with the child. Prospective research would be most informative in this respect.

Finally, our analyses showed that co-parenting quality is an important factor in establishing shared parenting in Germany. Successful and reliable cooperation clearly increases the chances of shared physical custody. At the same time, however, there was an unexpected inverse link indicating (marginally) more co-parenting problems among parents with shared physical custody. Although this effect was only marginally significant and should not be overestimated unless replicated, it seems relevant to consider its interpretations. Conflicted parents could be prone to choose shared physical custody in order to minimize conflict by dividing the child most evenly. Alternatively, shared physical custody could also trigger more conflict because it demands more communication. Such issues need to be addressed in longitudinal research.

Overall, our findings seem highly robust against changing definitions of shared physical custody. Additional analyses (Walper et al. in prep.) indicate only very few minor changes in effects, e.g. increasing the significance of co-parenting problems as more prevalent in shared physical custody arrangements and decreasing age differences in the first decade of life. This suggests that the differences between parents who practice more or less symmetrical forms of shared parenting seem to be very limited. Nevertheless, specific comparisons would seem helpful in guiding lawmakers' decisions about when to advice which form of shared physical custody.

There are further factors which could not be explored in this paper. For example, migration background was not included in our analyses for several reasons. The share of (first and second generation) migrants in the sample was lower than expected by official statistics since participation in the interviews required mastery of the German language. The majority of migrants included in our sample has European background, so issues of cultural diversity would have to be neglected. Further studies, however, should address this factor in more detail.

We hope that these findings provide a starting point for more in-depth research on shared physical custody in Germany. In guiding the necessary legal reform, it will be important to provide further insight–particularly with respect to children's well-being, which should be the most important criterion for parents' choice of post-separation parenting arrangement.

References

Amato, P. R., Meyers, C. E., & Emery, R. E. (2009). Changes in nonresident father-child contact from 1976 to 2002. *Family Relations, 58*(1), 41–53.

Baude, A., Pearson, J., & Drapeau, S. (2016). Child adjustment in joint physical custody versus sole custody: A meta-analytic review. *Journal of Divorce & Remarriage, 57*(5), 338–360.

Baumann, T., Hochgürtel, T., & Sommer, B. (2018). Familie, Lebensformen & Kinder. In Statistisches Bundesamt & Wissenschaftszentrum Berlin für Sozialforschung (Hrsg.), *Datenreport 2018: Ein Sozialbericht für die Bundesrepublik Deutschland* (S. 50–101).

Bauserman, R. (2002). Child adjustment in joint-custody versus sole-custody arrangements: A meta-analytic review. *Journal of Family Psychology, 16*(1), 91–102.

Bergström, M., Fransson, E., Modin, B., Berlin, M., Gustafsson, P. A., & Hjern, A. (2015). Fifty moves a year: Is there an association between joint physical custody and psychosomatic problems in children? *Journal of Epidemiology and Community Health, 69*(8), 769–774.

Bjarnason, T., & Arnarsson, A. M. (2011). Joint physical custody and communication with parents: A cross-national study of children in 36 Western countries. *Journal of Comparative Family Studies, 42*(6), 871–890.

Blohm, M., & Walter, J. (2018). Einstellungen zur Rolle der Frau und der des Mannes. In Statistisches Bundesamt & Wissenschaftszentrum Berlin für Sozialforschung (Hrsg.), *Datenreport 2018: Ein Sozialbericht für die Bundesrepublik Deutschland* (S. 397–S. 402).

Brauns, H., Scherer, S., & Steinmann, S. (2003). The CASMIN educational classification in international comparative research. In J. H. P. Hoffmeyer-Zlotnik & C. Wolf (Eds.), *Advances in cross-national comparison: A European working book for demographic and socio-economic variables* (pp. 196–221). New York, Boston, Dordrecht, London, Moscow: Kluwer Academic/ Plenum Publishers.

Bundesministerium für Familie Senioren Frauen und Jugend. (2013). *Stief- und Patchworkfamilien in Deutschland.: Monitor Familienforschung 31*. Berlin.

Cashmore, J., Parkinson, P., Weston, R., Patulny, R., Redmond, G., Qu, L., et al. (2010). *Shared care parenting arrangements since the 2006 family law reforms: Report to the Australian government attorney-general's department*. University of New South Wales: Social Policy Research Centre.

Dadds, M. R., & Powell, M. B. (1991). The relationship of interparental conflict and global marital adjustment to aggression, anxiety, and immaturity in aggressive and nonclinic children. *Journal of Abnormal Child Psychology, 19*(5), 553–567.

Fehlberg, B., Smyth, B., Maclean, M., & Roberts, C. (2011). Legislating for shared time parenting after separation: A research review. *International Journal of Law, Policy and the Family, 25*(3), 318–337.

Fransson, E., Sarkadi, A., Hjern, A., & Bergström, M. (2016). Why should they live more with one of us when they are children to us both? Parents' motives for practicing equal joint physical custody for children aged 0–4. *Children and Youth Services Review, 66*, 154–160.

Haberman, S. J. (1973). The analysis of residuals in cross-classified tables. *Biometrics, 29*(1), 205–220.

Hakovirta, M., & Rantalaiho, M. (2011). Family policy and shared parenting in Nordic countries. *European Journal of Social Security, 13*(2), 247–266.

Hall, S. S. (2005). Change in paternal involvement from 1977 to 1997: A cohort analysis. *Family and Consumer Sciences Research Journal, 34*(2), 127–139.

Hyest, J.-J., & About, N. (2007). *Rapport d' information No. 349 sur la résidence alternée.*

Institut für Demoskopie Allensbach (2017). *Getrennt gemeinsam erziehen: Befragung von Trennungseltern im Auftrag des BMFSFJ. Untersuchungsbericht*. Allensbach. https://www.ifd-allensbach.de/uploads/tx_studies/Abach_Trennungseltern_Bericht.pdf

Juby, H., Le Bourdais, C., & Marcil-Gratton, N. (2005). Sharing roles, sharing custody? Couples' characteristics and children's living arrangements at separation. *Journal of Marriage and Family, 67*(1), 157–172.

Kalmijn, M. (2015). Father-child relations after divorce in four European countries: Patterns and determinants. *Comparative Population Studies, 40*(3), 251–276.

Kaspiew, R., Gray, M., Weston, R., Moloney, L., Hand, K., Qu, L., et al. (2009). *Executive summary: Evaluation of the 2006 family law reforms*. Melbourne: Australien Institute of Family Studies.

Kinderrechtekommission des Deutschen Familiengerichtstags e.V. (2014). Das Wechselmodell im deutschen Familienrecht. *FamRZ, 14*, 1157–1166.

Langmeyer, A. (2015). *Sorgerecht, Coparenting und Kindeswohl: Eltern Sein in nichtehelichen Lebensgemeinschaften*. Wiesbaden: Springer.

Lenze, A. (2014). *Alleinerziehende unter Druck. Rechtliche Rahmenbedingungen, finanzielle Lage und Reformbedarf*. Bertelsmann Stiftung: Gütersloh.

Nielsen, L. (2013). Shared residential custody: Review of the research (part I of II). *American Journal of Family Law, 27*(1), 61–71.

Nielsen, L. (2018a). Joint versus sole physical custody: Outcomes for children independent of family income or parental conflict. *Journal of Child Custody, 15*(1), 35–54.

Nielsen, L. (2018b). Joint versus sole physical custody: Children's outcomes independent of parent–child relationships, income, and conflict in 60 studies. *Journal of Divorce & Remarriage, 59*(4), 247–281.

Nitsche, N., & Grunow, D. (2016). Housework over the course of relationships: Gender ideology, resources, and the division of housework from a growth curve perspective. *Advances in Life Course Research, 29*, 80–94.

OECD. (2017). *Dare to Share – Deutschlands Weg zur Partnerschaftlichkeit in Familie und Beruf*. Paris: OECD Publishing. http://dx.doi.org/10.1787/9789264263420-de

Poortman, A.-R., & van Gaalen, R. (2017). Shared residence after separation: A review and new findings from the Netherlands. *Family Court Review, 55*(4), 531–544.

Schier, M., & Hubert, S. (2015). Alles eine Frage der Opportunität, oder nicht? Multilokalität und Wohnentfernung nach Trennung und Scheidung. *Zeitschrift für Familienforschung, 1*, 3–31.

Schnor, C. (2012). Trennungsrisiko von Paaren mit Kindern: Der Einfluss der Religion in West- und Ostdeutschland. In J. Huinink, M. Kreyenfeld, & H. Trappe (Hrsg.), *Familie und Partnerschaft in Ost- und Westdeutschland: Ähnlich und doch immer noch anders* (S. 229–255). Leverkusen: Verlag Barbara Budrich.

Schumann, E. (2018). *Gemeinsam getragene Elternverantwortung nach Trennung und Scheidung – Reformbedarf im Sorge-, Umgangs- und Unterhaltsrecht? Gutachten B zum 72. Deutschen Juristentag*. München: Verlag C.H. Beck.

Sodermans, A. K., Matthijs, K., & Swicegood, G. (2013). Characteristics of joint physical custody families in Flanders. *Demographic Research, 28*, 821–848.

Spruijt, E., & Duindam, V. (2009). Joint physical custody in the Netherlands and the well-being of children. *Journal of Divorce & Remarriage, 51*(1), 65–82.

Statistisches Bundesamt. (2017a). *69% der Mütter und 6% der Väter sind in Teilzeit tätig. Pressemitteilung Nr. 345*. Wiesbaden.

Statistisches Bundesamt. (2017b). *Erwerbstätigkeit von Müttern: Deutschland über EU-Durchschnitt*. Wiesbaden.

Statistisches Bundesamt. (2018a). *Alleinerziehende in Deutschland 2017*. Begleitmaterial zur Pressekonferenz am 2. August 2018. Wiesbaden.

Statistisches Bundesamt. (2018b). *Bevölkerung: Eheschließungen, Geborene und Gestorbene 2017 nach Kreisen*. https://www.destatis.de/DE/Themen/Gesellschaft-Umwelt/Bevoelkerung/Eheschliessungen-Ehescheidungen-Lebenspartnerschaften/Publikationen/Downloads-Eheschliessungen/eheschliessungen-geborene-gestorbene-5126001177004.pdf?__blob=publicationFile&v=5

Statistisches Bundesamt. (2018c). *Deutlich weniger Ehescheidungen im Jahr 2017: Pressemitteilung Nr. 251 vom 10.07.2018*. Wiesbaden.

Steinbach, A. (2018). Children's and parents' Well-being in joint physical custody: A literature review. *Family Process, 58*(2), 353–369.

Sünderhauf, H. (2013). *Wechselmodell: Psychologie – Recht – Praxis: Abwechselnde Kinderbetreuung durch Eltern nach Trennung und Scheidung*. Wiesbaden: Springer Fachmedien.

Walper, S. (2016). Arrangements elterlicher Fürsorge nach Trennung und Scheidung: Das Wechselmodell im Licht neuer Daten aus Deutschland. In Deutscher Familiengerichtstag e.v. (Hrsg.), *Brühler Schriften zum Familienrecht: 21. Deutscher Familiengerichtstag* (S. 99–143). Bielefeld: Gieseking Verlag.

Walper, S., Bien, W., & Rauschenbach, T. (Hrsg.) (2015). *Aufwachsen in Deutschland heute: Erste Befunde aus dem AID:A-Survey 2015*. München: Deutsches Jugendinstitut.

Walper, S., Langmeyer, A., & Entleitner-Phleps, C. (in prep.). Shared physical custody among separated families in Germany: The role of gender attitudes.

Westphal, S. K., Poortman, A.-R., & van der Lippe, T. (2014). Non-resident father-child contact across divorce cohorts: The role of father involvement during marriage. *European Sociological Review, 30*(4), 444–456.

Wissenschaftliche Dienste. (2018). *Sachstand Fragen zum Wechselmodell*. Aktenzeichen WD 7–3000 – 056/18. Berlin.

Zerle-Elsäßer, C., & Li, X. (2017). Väter im Familienalltag – Determinanten einer aktiven Vaterschaft. *Zeitschrift für Familienforschung, 29*(1), 11–31.

Sabine Walper is Research Director at the German Youth Institute and Professor of Education and Youth Research at Ludwig-Maximilians University in Munich, Germany. Her main field of research addresses issues of family diversity, family relationships, parenting, and children's and adolescents' development in different family contexts, focusing families in poverty and families with separated and repartnered parents. Trained as psychologist and psychological therapist, she developed and evaluated parenting programs. She is Co-Principle Investigator of the German Family Panel pairfam and supervises the large-scale national assessments "Growing up in Germany – Everday contexts" and the monitoring of the national program Early Prevention (Frühe Hilfen) conducted at the Germany Youth Institute. She is strongly involved in political consulting and currently chairs the expert committee of the Ninth National Report on Families in Germany.

Christine Entleitner-Phleps works in the team of Research Director Prof. Dr. Sabine Walper at the German Youth Institute (DJI) in Munich. She studied Education and Sociology at the University of Innsbruck and completed her Doctoral thesis at the Ludwig-Maximilians-Universität München. Her main research interest follows quantitative family research with a special focus on complex family structures after divorce/separation and their everyday family life practices.

Alexandra N. Langmeyer is head of the working group "Living Situation and Developmental Contexts of Children" at the German Youth Institute (DJI) in Munich. She studied education, psychology and law at the Ludwig-Maximilians-Universität München and received there her doctoral degree. Her doctoral thesis was about coparenting and physical custody in cohabiting families. Her quantitative research focuses practices of everyday life, development and well-being of children. This especially in the context of family and divorce research.

14

Post Separation Family Arrangements and Child Maintenance Policies

Mia Hakovirta and Christine Skinner

Abstract This book chapter provides new insights to the question of how child maintenance policies have responded to changing post separation family arrangements and most specifically shared physical custody (SPC). We analyse how SPC is implemented and how it operates in child maintenance policies in 13 countries: Australia, Belgium, Denmark, Estonia, Finland, France, Iceland, New Zealand, Norway, Spain, Sweden, the UK and the U.S. The comparative analysis is based on vignette questionnaire collected in 2017. There are differences in how countries have acknowledged and recognized shared physical custody in their child maintenance policies. It varies from complete annulment of obligations, to some countries making finer grained adjustments to reduce child maintenance obligations and yet others' making no changes as a result of shared physical custody, with the paying parent still having to provide the full amount of child maintenance. It seems there is no standard practice and nor do the different arrangements map easily onto child maintenance scheme typology. The latter is surprising, as it might have been expected that similarly structured child maintenance schemes would treat shared physical custody in similar ways. This variability demonstrates a lack of coherence across child maintenance policies on how to deal with this phenomenon of greater gender equality in post-separation parenting arrangements.

Keywords Child maintenance · Child support · Shared care · Joint physical custody · Shared physical custody · Comparative research · Vignette

---

M. Hakovirta (✉)
Department of Social Research, University of Turku, Turku, Finland
e-mail: miahak@utu.fi

C. Skinner
Department of Social Policy and Social Work, University of York, York, UK
e-mail: christine.skinner@york.ac.uk

14.1 Introduction

Most western countries have a variety of policies designed to secure incomes after parental separation, including setting child maintenance obligations, which is the financial contribution to be paid by a non-resident parent to a resident parent for supporting children post separation (International Network of Child Support Scholars 2019). In the vast majority of cases worldwide, and irrespective of welfare regime, these payments are made from a minority care-time non-resident father to a majority care-time, resident mother. In some countries, if parents are unable or unwilling to pay, the state may provide guaranteed or advanced maintenance (Corden 1999; Skinner et al. 2007, 2012).

In the face of rising rates of family breakdown, through divorce or separation, more families become subject to child maintenance policies, making this an increasingly important policy aspect of modern family life. Also, as we have seen throughout this book, shared physical custody has become more common in separated families. Certainly, a growing number of separated parents jointly share the care of their child(ren) either equally, or at least 30% of care by each parent (Fehlberg et al. 2011; Trinder 2010; Smyth 2017; Hakovirta and Eydal 2020). Multiple terms are used for this phenomenon, including shared care, shared residence or joint physical custody.[1] For the purposes of standardisation we use shared physical custody (SPC) throughout this chapter. It means that the child spends equal time living with both parents and both parents physically care for the child. Shared physical custody arrangements however, also signify a greater ambiguity in family roles and responsibilities as well as more fluidity in living arrangements as children live with both their parents separately and move across their parents' households (Cancian et al. 2014; Carlson and Meyer 2014).

In turn, this creates more family complexity presenting substantial operating challenges for child maintenance policies; that is if they pay any regard to care arrangements at all. Certainly, the traditional breadwinning father is no longer the norm in many countries, because more mothers stay in employment post childbirth and dual earner families are more common. Child maintenance policies are of interest because they have to deal with this fluidity and complexity in care arrangements and this has direct consequences for the economic well-being of children and their parents. Such policies also embody a set of values regarding parental responsibility post-separation (Skinner et al. 2007). Yet, we know little about how countries deal with this challenge of accounting for the sharing of care between parents, especially what happens when that share is nearly equal. Nor do we know about

[1]There are a number of terms used to describe this arrangement. Shared residence is used in Norway (Haugen 2010), and alternating residence in Sweden (Singer 2008) and shared care in the UK (Haux et al. 2017) and shared care in Australia (Smyth 2017). In the U.S., shared care is described as 'shared physical custody', 'dual residence', 'alternating residence' and 'shared placement' (Fehlberg et al. 2011).

the policy principles that might guide operations, or the policy adaptions, or how they might differ across countries, or what these differences might signify.

This chapter intends to fill some of that gap in knowledge. It will provide answers to the questions of how child maintenance policies deal with the sharing of responsibility between separated parents and whether the guidelines in child maintenance policies take account of the degree to which the other parent engages in care. We take a comparative approach across 13 countries in total: Australia, Belgium, Denmark, Estonia, Finland, France, Iceland, New Zealand, Norway, Spain, Sweden, the UK and the U.S.[2] These countries represent different child maintenance schemes (Skinner and Davidson 2009) which we describe in more detail in the next section.

The analysis here updates and extends the work of Skinner et al. (2007) who produced one of the first comparative studies that considered shared physical custody arrangements in child maintenance policies across 14 countries, albeit briefly. Also, it extends the work of Skinner et al. 2012, who looked more in–depth across five countries (Finland, Iceland, Netherlands, UK and U.S). The study reported here adapts Skinner et al.'s (2007) original model families approach to look in more detail at shared physical custody arrangements and child maintenance rules and formulae as well as across a different set of countries (which now includes Spain, Estonia and Iceland). In the model family method used in this 2017 study, national experts are presented with fictitious families in a range of different circumstances and are asked to provide information on policy responses relating to those circumstances. This exposes how policy can operate through the application of decisions, rules and guidelines in a set of proscribed circumstances to produce different outcomes (in this case child maintenance amounts). By adapting this method we work out what the child maintenance amounts might be for different shared physical custody arrangements and therefore the research reported here extends the documentary policy analysis of child maintenance schemes provided by Claessens and Mortelmans (2018) in eight countries (Canada, Denmark, Finland, France, Germany, Netherlands, Sweden and UK).

This chapter will add to this emerging body of comparative evidence by providing new insights into how countries deal with (or fail to deal with) family complexity as socicty and policies adapt to new post-separation parenting arrangements. Too little is known about the intersection of these two issues despite; a growing policy interest in some countries, a large amount of research exploring the changing nature of family and gender relationships and a growing number of studies on child maintenance policies.

14.2 Typologies of Child Maintenance Schemes

The reorganisation of parental relations after separation or divorce assumes the right of the child to receive maintenance from both parents. From the parental point of view, it is the legal responsibility of both parents to take charge of the child's care, education and maintenance in accordance with their abilities, regardless of whether the child is in the care of one or both parents (Wikeley 2009). Parental obligations after separation or divorce differ substantially between countries in terms of their underlying philosophy, structures, rules and organisation and in particular produce very different outcomes.

Notably, there have been a few attempts to provide comparative analysis of child maintenance schemes including the early pioneering work of Millar and Warman (1996) and Corden (1999). Millar and Warman studied family obligations across nine European countries and explored whether there were common trends towards new definitions of family obligations in the context of changing family structures and relationships. They did not construct a typology but their main conclusion was that agreements about financial arrangements post separation relied mainly on private agreements between parents and in some countries these were ratified by the courts. Some countries relied on standard rules or guidelines while in others, cases were dealt with individually on a discretionary basis. Six of the nine countries they compared had some form of guaranteed maintenance scheme.

Corden (1999) compared child maintenance regimes in ten European countries: Austria, Belgium, Denmark, Finland, France, Germany, the Netherlands, Norway, Sweden and the UK. She found each regime developed from a different legal and historical background, but the general pattern was towards equal treatment for all children in respect of child maintenance, irrespective of the marital status of their parents. Each country had different structural and administrative arrangements and decisions about whether to pay and how much child maintenance to pay, were made variously by parents themselves (with or without help), by court judges or officials, or by administrative staff in social security or welfare offices. The UK and the Netherlands at that time were the only countries which had no specific scheme to advance child maintenance, apart from general social assistance benefits.

As previously mentioned, Skinner et al. (2007) undertook a large cross-national analysis of child maintenance schemes in 14 countries. They considered the logics of formal decision making, the determination of child maintenance obligations and the enforcement and penalty provisions used in the event of non-compliance. They clustered countries according to the weight given to the court and/or agency in setting child maintenance orders using the data they collected in 2006. Three maintenance schemes emerged and were identified as operating a court, agency or hybrid scheme. In Austria, Belgium, Canada, France, Germany and Sweden, courts had the main responsibility for the determination of formal child maintenance obligations. In Australia, Denmark, New Zealand, Norway and the UK, an administrative agency was responsible for assessment, collection and transfer of child maintenance payments. These countries represent the agency model. In Finland, the

Netherlands and the U.S., responsibility for the determination of child maintenance obligations lay with several institutions, for example with the municipal welfare board and/or the court. Generally, Skinner et al. (2007) found that court based schemes operated on a more discretionary basis and cases were treated individually, whereas agency and hybrid schemes tended to take more standardised approaches and applied formulae and rules in the decision-making process.

For the purposes of comparison, we clustered our countries according to the typology developed by Skinner et al. (2007) based on the different institutional loci of decision-making. Thus, Australia, Denmark, New Zealand, Norway and the UK were categorized as agency schemes, the same as before. Belgium, Estonia, Spain, Sweden and France were categorized as court based schemes, as courts had the main responsibility for the determination of formal child maintenance obligations. Finland, Iceland and the U.S., were considered as hybrid schemes because they locate their decisions regarding child maintenance in several institutions which are an amalgamation of courts and agencies.

We used this typology as it is reasonable to expect that the different institutional settings might have a bearing on how the sharing of care time is accounted for in calculating child maintenance obligations. Whilst our research study is exploratory and descriptive, it is possible to consider that court based systems are more discretionary and are more likely to recognise shared physical custody arrangements as they tend to treat cases on an individual basis and in that regard will follow changing social norms. Whereas, agencies generally apply more fixed rules and formulae and may be less likely to respond to changing social norms and rising trends in shared physical custody arrangements, because to do so may require legislative changes to operational procedures and this could inhibit responsiveness and adaptation. However, where agency schemes do recognise shared physical custody, it might be they take a more standardised approach producing similar outcomes across countries compared to court based schemes.

14.3 Prior Research on Shared Physical Custody and Child Maintenance

In many countries a major legal premise in family law is that children should share time with both parents after separation (CRC 1989). However, sharing care of children, beyond traditional gendered and more limited visitation arrangements, is more complex than present guidelines in child maintenance policies recognize (Melli and Brown 1994; Beld and Biernat 2002; Bartfeld 2011; Claessens and Mortelmans 2018).

Claessens and Mortelmans' (2018) documentary analysis of eight countries revealed that the shared physical custody arrangements are accounted for in child maintenance policies in various ways, some of which can be highly accommodating and others disadvantageous for the modern post-divorce family. They suggested that policy concerning gender equality in shared physical custody arrangements does not consistently translate into child maintenance policies. In the U.S. almost all states explicitly address shared physical custody in their child maintenance guidelines and typically produce orders that are lower than would be the case under other time sharing arrangements (Brown and Brito 2007). Other research in the child maintenance context suggests that shared physical custody does not necessarily lead to fathers providing financial support for their children (i.e. in the form of child maintenance to the other parent) and the obligation can be annulled in some cases (Singer 2008; Hakovirta and Rantalaiho 2011). Yet, qualitative evidence suggests that mothers often carry more of the responsibility than their former partners for management of children's daily lives, including paying school-related expenses, medical, and dental costs (Cashmore et al. 2010; Lacroix 2006). In Australia Lodge and Alexander (2010) found that everyday expenses were usually paid by the parent they lived with for most of the time. In the case of equal time parenting, the 'vast majority' of adolescents said that both parents made a contribution to their everyday expenses.

Less is known however, about how child maintenance policy works in practice within and across countries and what the levels of child maintenance payments are if children are in shared physical custody arrangements. Skinner et al. (2007) compared maintenance awards under shared physical custody for two children in £ppp[3] per month in 2006. They reported that the highest maintenance award in those countries where maintenance was expected to be paid was in Canada and the U.S. In Australia, France, Norway, New Zealand and the UK obligations were lower, but the parent who had higher income still paid maintenance. In Belgium, Denmark Finland, Netherlands and Sweden the child maintenance obligations were annulled. The other study by Skinner et al. (2012) compared the effect of shared care on child maintenance amounts. In comparison to the situation where children had two weekend visits, in shared physical custody situations, the amount was substantially reduced in the U.S., only reduced a little in Finland, whereas in the UK the obligation to pay was eliminated completely. In Iceland shared physical custody had no effect on maintenance awards. Proponents that argue for a shared physical custody presumption being embedded in family law and family policies hope it will benefit children by promoting both parents' continued involvement and encouraging them to share more equal responsibility for raising their children. The evidence to date shows how more equal care arrangements may produce different financial impacts and we aim to investigate this further with a deeper systematic comparative analysis with new research data collected in 2017.

14.4 Methods

The aim of this section is to explore whether shared physical custody arrangements are taken into account in child maintenance policies and if so, in what ways does this happen and how does it vary across countries?

We use a model family approach in which national informants complete a detailed standardised questionnaire providing information on their policy. They were asked to describe their child maintenance policy and to calculate the amount of child maintenance in the prescribed hypothetical model families according to their own country's policies and legal guidelines. This method has been used successfully to make comparisons of the tax/benefit package for families (e.g. Bradshaw and Finch 2002; see Bradshaw 2009 for an overview). As part of the model families approach we generated a number of vignettes that are short stories of fictitious families that provide fixed details of family situations (see Soydan and Stål 1994; Barter and Renold 1999). Vignettes are the component part of the model family approach and have been used successfully in many comparative studies on child maintenance policies (e.g. Corden 1999; Skinner et al. 2007, 2012, 2017; Meyer et al. 2011; Meyer and Skinner 2016; Hakovirta and Eydal 2020). Vignettes represent real-life situations in meaningful social circumstances, and the national informants (who are our respondents) could then offer their observations and interpretations from within their own policy contexts, but for standardised family types. This ensures that as far as possible, like is being compared with like and standardized comparison across countries is reliable as the stimuli is held constant for national informants across the countries.

Data was collected at the end of 2017. We recruited national informants through professional contacts in the research community. Mostly there was one informant from each country. Many of the national informants were academics who had earlier experience in similar studies either as informants, or were involved in collecting or analysing vignette data in previous child maintenance studies or based on their earlier contribution to the field. As each informant was an expert in the field of enquiry in their own country, it eased the task of data collection and validation and thereby helped provide a deeper and insider's interpretation of the policy framework and the operational rules and processes.

National informants completed a detailed standardised questionnaire providing information on shared physical custody and child maintenance policy. They were also asked to calculate the amount of child maintenance the law required the parent to pay in the prescribed model families according to their own county's policies and legal guidelines. Note that the calculated child maintenance amounts they produced were related to the model family and their current circumstances, which were fixed at a certain point in time.

Vignette method has some limitations. First limitation, which is typical to this type of research, is that the data are from only one policy expert in each country; including multiple experts within a country could lead to more confidence in the policy descriptions. Second, we do not have information from court experts who deal with the issues in child maintenance cases. Finally, we focus here only on the level of obligation, and this amount may or may not be paid. The data therefore highlight how policy works in these particular model family situations.

In the vignette we first provided a basic situation (Base Case 'A') which included information for national informants to describe how their policy works and all necessary information to calculate the child maintenance obligation. Our vignette story was as follows:

> Mary and Paul are getting a divorce after ten years of marriage. They have two children. Emily, aged seven, and Sophia, aged ten. Both children attend a local school and there are no school fees. After the divorce, Mary and the children will continue to live in the rented apartment Mary and Paul shared during marriage so that the children can stay in their home. Paul will rent a new apartment in the same suburb nearby. The number of bedrooms, rent and other housing costs of both apartments are averages that are typical in your country. Paul is employed and earns median monthly male full-time earnings for your country. Mary is also working, earning median monthly female full-time earnings for your country. Mary and Paul have agreed that they will have 'joint legal custody' of the children, sharing the major decisions affecting the children. In terms of living arrangements, Emily and Sophia will have two overnight stays from Friday afternoon until Sunday afternoon at their father's home every other weekend.

In the base case both parents were working full time and had median incomes that were typical (median monthly earnings) in their country. In that way the parents are presented as being on a level playing field in that both are earning typical wages for full-time employees, except of course commonly there is a gender pay gap which will vary across countries. These gender inequalities are automatically reproduced here as we use gender specific median income amounts in the vignettes. We then asked the informants to calculate the outcome in terms of whether there would be a formal child maintenance arrangement, and if so, the monthly amount that would be awarded in these circumstances. In the next scenario of the same vignette, the situation is otherwise exactly the same as in base case 'A', but Mary and Paul had a shared physical custody arrangement in which the children spend exactly an equal amount of time with both parents. Every other week is spent with Mary and every other week with Paul. We asked the experts to explain how the outcomes would differ now that the parents had an equal shared physical custody arrangement. This equal care scenario would represent an ideal of equality with a presumption of 50:50 care-time and one that is perfectly and consistently exercised by parents. In that regard model family approaches cannot take account of the messy reality of families' lives in which arrangements may vary frequently. That is both the strength of the model family approach (standardisation) and its potential weakness as it can only give an approximation of reality.

We conducted the analysis in three main ways: First, we provide the country context and present reported prevalence rates and definitions of shared physical custody (Table 14.1). Second, we analyse the answers to the questions on child maintenance policy and shared physical custody exploring how it was acknowledged in child maintenance policy, highlighting variations in approaches (Table 14.2). Third, we are using the informants' calculations of the amounts of child maintenance liabilities when the children in the model family had two

Table 14.1 The prevalence rates of shared physical custody with the source of data and national informants reports' on the different thresholds used to define shared physical custody and the time thresholds used in child maintenance schemes to define shared physical custody

Country	Reported prevalence rates of shared physical custody, %	Source and year for prevalence rates	Time thresholds used for determining prevalence rates of shared physical custody, %	Time thresholds used within child maintenance schemes to determine shared physical custody, %
Agency based child maintenance scheme				
Australia	20	The longitudinal study of separated families Australia	35–65	35–65
Denmark	22–40	Survey children and young people in Denmark	43–50	36–50
New Zealand	5	Child support files	40	48–52
Norway	25	Survey on contact and residential arrangements	50	50
UK	3–17	Understanding society survey and ONS omnibus	50	50
Court based child maintenance scheme				
Belgium	37	Divorce in Flanders survey	33–66	33–66
Estonia	N/A	N/A	N/A	Not regulated
France	17	A survey of divorced parents	Judges discretion	50
Spain (Catalonia)	8–40	Spanish national statistics	Parenting plan, discretion	No specific threshold
Sweden	35	Children and their families	Approx. 50	50
Hybrid based child maintenance scheme				
Finland	15	Child maintenance and custody statistics	Approx. 50, parents' discretion	43–50
Iceland	24	Interaction of parents and children after divorce survey	50	50

(continued)

Table 14.1 (continued)

Country	Reported prevalence rates of shared physical custody, %	Source and year for prevalence rates	Time thresholds used for determining prevalence rates of shared physical custody, %	Time thresholds used within child maintenance schemes to determine shared physical custody, %
U.S. (Wisconsin)	35–50	Court records in Wisconsin	50	25

Source: Column 1 and 2 are based on relevant national surveys or statistics as reported by national informants in each country (cited in text) and column 3 depends on information collected from the respondents numbers are not fully comparable as the information comes from different sources in each country (official statistics, administrative records or surveys). *N/A* not available

Table 14.2 Accounting for shared physical custody (50/50) in child maintenance schemes as reported by national informants in each country, in 2017

	Whether both parents' incomes are counted if there is 50/50 timeshare	Whether there is an obligation set to pay child maintenance if there is 50/50 timeshare	Reduction or annulment of child maintenance if there is 50/50 timeshare
Agency scheme			
Australia	Yes	Yes	Yes, reduction
Denmark	No	No	Annulled
New Zealand	Yes	Yes	Yes, reduction
Norway	Yes	Yes	Yes, reduction
UK	No	No	Annulled
Court scheme			
Belgium	Yes	Yes	Yes, reduction
Estonia	Yes	Yes	No
France	Yes	Yes	Annulled[a]
Spain (Catalonia)	Yes	Yes	Yes, reduction
Sweden	Yes	Yes	Annulled[a]
Hybrid scheme			
Finland	Yes	Yes	Yes, reduction
Iceland	No	Yes	No
U.S. (Wisconsin)	Yes	Yes	Yes, reduction

[a]Child maintenance might be annulled if the income levels of parents are equal

overnight stays with their non-resident parent every other weekend and compared that to when there was equal shared physical custody (keeping parental incomes the same as in the base case). We calculate the financial outcomes by modelling child maintenance amounts in pppUS$ across countries, facilitating a meaningful cross country comparison of policy outcomes (Fig. 14.1). The analysis is therefore

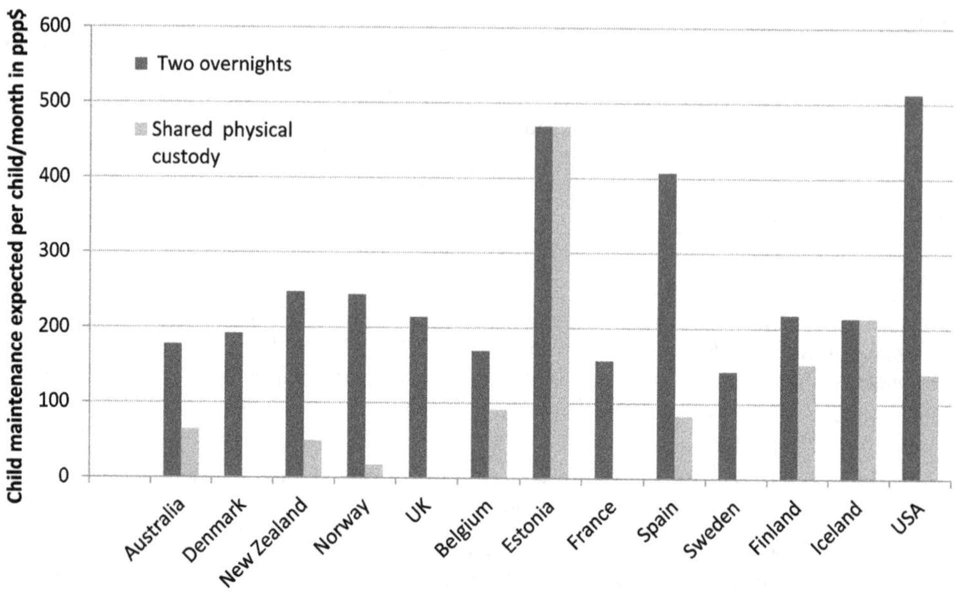

Fig. 14.1 The amount of child maintenance (per child) expected to be paid in a model family when a child stays with one parent two nights every other weekend versus the situation that parents have shared physical custody

descriptive and the data is based on model families and is not based on real live cases using representative samples.

14.5 Findings

14.5.1 Prevalence of Shared Physical Custody

We start the analysis by presenting the 'care context' and the information provided by national informants on what they know about the prevalence of shared physical custody. Defining shared physical custody is difficult as the definition is broad and can be used to cover a range of care arrangements. Very often comparative work on shared physical custody arrangements is bedevilled by different terms, definitions, time thresholds, measures, and units of analysis which means that cross-national comparisons and research translation present formidable challenges. In general, it refers to a sharing of care time of children between parents, but the care-time can range from 25% to 50% spent with each parent (see Fehlberg et al. 2011; Smyth 2017; Trinder 2010). Also the source of information on prevalence matters – whether the information comes from official statistics, administrative records or surveys. For example, many studies are reliant on divorce records to estimate the incidence of shared physical custody arrangements. To some extent, these may underestimate the prevalence of shared physical custody as divorce records ignore the separations from co-habitant relationships. In addition, some countries may have no readily available information.

Keeping these challenges in mind, Table 14.1 presents the prevalence rates of shared physical custody arrangements (column 1) and the various different time thresholds that these were based on (column 2) as reported by national informants. Informants' reports refer to a range of different sources (official records, surveys) and are therefore highly variable. Even so, to our knowledge they represent the most recent sources of information in each country and are the best available. On a cautionary note therefore, the variations in the ways shared physical custody is defined is important as it affects the prevalence rates presented. For example, prevalence may be higher if it is defined as each parent having care for at least 30% of the time rather than a 50/50 split.

So far only a few countries have adopted a legal presumption of 50/50 joint custody; for most countries there is no clear definition and it is only mentioned as an arrangement where children live an equal amount of time with both parents. It is better to think of the numbers in Table 14.1 therefore, as descriptive information and not data per se, as the latter term implies some sort of standardisation, which clearly it is not. We give more detail on sources from each country when reporting the analysis of the table. In relation to the last column 3 of Table 14.1, we also show the time thresholds used for shared physical custody, but taken from within each country's child maintenance scheme. Again, this is as reported by national informants, based on their knowledge of administrative rules and how legal institutions and judicial decision-making might work in practice. For the purposes of comparison, we have grouped countries in Table 14.1 by the type of maintenance scheme to see if there appears to be any common pattern between the reported prevalence rates (column 1) and official time thresholds used in different child maintenance schemes (column 3).

The results in Table 14.1 show that the reported rates vary markedly and there is no easily discernible pattern; which is not surprising given the range of information sources (Estonia had no data). However, what is of interest is that shared physical custody remains a minority arrangement for real separated families across all countries, with only one region of Spain having a high reported rate of 40%. Next we report the prevalence rates according to the child maintenance regimes even though the rates do not easily follow the maintenance typology.

In the agency regime with relatively lower prevalence rates are the UK and New Zealand. In the UK, reports from a number of different survey sources show that prevalence ranges from 3% to 17% depending on the source. Notably however, some accounts from resident parents suggest that 50–50 time arrangements could be as low as 1% (resource quoted as Haux et al. 2017). In New Zealand no robust information is available. Under the pre-2013 Child Support formula approximately 5% of cases were shared physical custody cases (i.e. each carer had at least 40% of care-time) but this does not include private arrangement cases which are not part of the formal child support system. Five percent can be seen as a lower bound, but it is unlikely that the true figure is many times that because shared physical custody in private agreements between parents may be defined more loosely as more-or-less equal care.

In the other countries among *agency regimes* about 20–25% have shared care arrangements. In Australia 20% of children under 18 years of age had shared physical custody arrangements, as reported by the one parent survey in 2012 (Qu et al. 2014). In Denmark, shared physical custody arrangements are not registered in administrative data and therefore are only accessible in surveys. The incidence of shared physical custody arrangements are recorded by the age of children. The proportion of all children of divorced parents reported to have shared physical custody in 2013 was 22% of 3-years-olds, 40% of 11-years-olds and 32% of 15-years-olds (Ottosen et al. 2014). In Norway when mothers' and fathers' responses are considered together (i.e. where both agree the child has shared physical custody) it accounted for 25% of children of separated parents according to survey data in 2012 (Kitterød and Wiik 2017).

In court based regimes the countries had the highest rates among all countries studied, expect in France. In France, shared care is considered when children spend roughly an equal amount of time with each parent. In 2012, 16.9% of children of divorced parents and children born out of wedlock are reported as having shared physical custody arrangements. Percentages are based on a survey of the decisions issued by Family Justice Judges (resource quoted as Belmokhtar 2014). Spain could also be considered as belonging to this lower group, but simultaneously also to the higher group, depending on the region. In Spain, the care arrangements post-separation are based on parenting plans which parents must submit to court and include the commitments they make regarding the custody, care and education of their children. Therefore, there is no precise definition and no specific threshold used to define shared physical custody. The figures are based on the number of divorce orders judges consider shared physical custody. There are striking regional disparities with proportions ranging from higher than 40% in Catalonia as opposed 8% in Extremadura in 2015. The average however, is 24.6% of the total number of divorces involving children where care is shared by parents (Flaquer et al. 2017) and this would put Spain in the higher group. In Belgium studies suggest that shared physical custody (defined as spending between 33% and 66% of the time with each parent) has become more popular in recent decades. Specifically, less than 10% of the children whose parents separated between 1990 and 1995 were in shared physical custody. By 2006 or later, 37% of children were reported to be in the care of each parent for at least 33% of the time (Vanassche et al. 2017). In Sweden, the Supreme Court has stipulated that arrangements with a less-than-equal split must generally be regarded as contact unless there are special factors pointing in the opposite direction (Newnham 2010). Shared physical custody therefore occurs for 35% of children of separated parents in Sweden in 2012/13 (SCB 2014).

In hybrid regimes, only in the U.S., Wisconsin, shared care has become popular post separation living arrangement of children. In the U.S. there is no national data. The national informant notes that the most recent data on divorce comes from court records in Wisconsin. Meyer et al. (2017) report that in divorces in 2010, 35–50% had shared physical custody, the lower percentage referring to 50/50 timeshare and higher percentage to 25% time share. In Finland, the reported prevalence rate is approximately 15% of children have shared physical custody. This is based on records from parents who have confirmed the child's residence agreement with the Social Welfare Board as having a shared physical custody arrangement (Child custody and maintenance 2017). However, not all parents in Finland confirm their child residence agreements with the Social Welfare Board and the extent to which this data reflects actual arrangements remains unclear. In Iceland, according to survey data, among divorced parents, 24% of children lived in shared physical custody (defined as 50/50 time share) (Júlíusdóttir 2009).

Time thresholds used to calculate the prevalence of shared physical custody in surveys and court records (shown in column 2 of Table 14.1) is not always the same as that used for determining child maintenance obligations. Therefore, it is important to see how within child maintenance schemes the measures might differ for recognising shared physical custody from that used in surveys or administrative records, and we report that in Table 14.1 column 3.

We can see in Table 14.1 that in five countries an equal time threshold of 50% is reportedly used to determine shared physical custody for child maintenance purposes (Norway, UK, France, Sweden and Iceland). This matches well with the idea of a gender equal split of parental responsibilities post-separation. In another five counties however, a range of time is used to determine the threshold for shared physical custody with most having a lower, more generous level than a 50% time share. So Australia, Denmark, and Belgium use a lower bound of about a third of time (35%, 36% and 33% respectively), whereas in NZ and Finland it was a bit higher (48% and 43% respectively). The U.S. (Wisconsin) child maintenance system appears to give the most generous recognition, setting its threshold at 25% of care time. In some countries (Spain and Estonia) it is numerically impossible to define as there is no standard threshold, or no regulations setting care time in child maintenance schemes.

Surprisingly perhaps, there are no clear similarities in the thresholds used by the type of child maintenance institutional arrangement. For example, it cannot be said that court based systems (which are generally more discretionary) were more likely to operate a more generous lower level for recognising shared physical custody than agencies (which generally apply more fixed rules and formulae). Given the discretionary nature of court based systems, it would have been reasonable to assume they would be quicker at responding to changes in social norms (such as rising trends in shared physical custody arrangements) than would be the case for administrative type child maintenance systems and therefore more likely to set lower thresholds for recognising joint physical custody. However, there is no evidence of that here using this data and this methodology of national informants. Moreover, when comparing the prevalence rates reported in column one of Table 14.1 with the thresholds used in child maintenance schemes in column three there are also no obvious patterns. This is also interesting, because it might have been expected that in countries which report higher prevalence rates of shared physical custody, the child maintenance schemes would have operated more generous lower time thresholds in recognition of this trend, but there is no evidence here of that either. There does seem to be some relationship between column two (thresholds used in reports to identify shared physical custody) and column three (thresholds used in child maintenance schemes). In 6 of the 13 countries, they correspond directly (Australia, New Zealand, UK, Belgium, Sweden and Iceland). This might suggest that maintenance schemes may have referred to available reports to set thresholds, but we do not know if this is the case. Suffice to say for now; there seems no obvious relationship between reported prevalence rates of shared physical custody and the reported time thresholds used for child maintenance purposes.

In the next section we consider in more detail how child maintenance schemes operate in taking account of shared physical custody and what potential effect this might have, such as whether the amounts of child maintenance is reduced for the shared physical custody scenario.

14.5.2 Accounting for Shared Physical Custody in Child Maintenance Policies

First, we begin our detailed analysis of child maintenance schemes by considering whether they treat parents equally in terms of assessing both their incomes for the purposes of determining how much maintenance should be paid. In recent years, counting both parents incomes to assess child maintenance liabilities has grown in popularity, what is called an 'incomes shares' approach. The income shares approach is considered to be more flexible and therefore more equipped to accommodate changing family realities and are sometimes cited as better able to accommodate shifts in shared physical custody (Cancian and Costanzo 2019). In Table 14.2 column 1, we indeed show that for families who are deemed to have shared physical custody arrangements, counting both parents' incomes is common practice. Nine of the thirteen countries adopt an income shares approach, with only three countries (Denmark, UK and Iceland) determining child maintenance liabilities based on the non-resident parent's income only. In the U.S. (Wisconsin) both parents' incomes are counted only in shared physical custody cases, not in sole physical custody cases where only the non-resident parent's income is assessed.

At face value, when considering an incomes shares approach, it seems there is a greater recognition of gender equality in parental obligations post-separation when determining child maintenance amounts; at least that is when there is shared physical custody. However, we also need to consider whether the obligation to pay still exists. A system can theoretically use an incomes share assessment approach – but at the same time decide that there is no longer an obligation for either parent to pay child maintenance when it is deemed they have shared physical custody. Effectively, parents are considered to be taking equal responsibility, regardless of any disparities in their incomes. We explore that next in columns 2 and 3 of Table 14.2 where we show three possible outcomes: (a) that automatically no child maintenance is set because there is deemed to be shared physical custody (the child maintenance obligation is effectively annulled), (b) there is still an order made for child maintenance, but amounts may be adjusted/reduced, or (c) child maintenance is still required and no adjustments are made, meaning having shared physical custody makes no difference and parents pay the same amounts regardless.

Looking across columns 2 and 3 of Table 14.2, the results show that if there is equal time share only two countries (Denmark and the UK) deem there to be no obligation and therefore child maintenance is annulled. In France and Sweden it is annulled only if parents have equal incomes. Appositely, only in Estonia and Iceland do child maintenance guidelines not recognize the division of care as a factor that can modify child maintenance obligations: thus the child maintenance obligation is unchanged even in cases of shared physical custody. For the majority of countries however, an obligation to pay remains where there is equal time share and for most, the amounts are reduced/adjusted by varying degrees depending on the rules applied (Australia, NZ, Norway, Belgium, France, Spain (Catalonia), Sweden, Finland and U.S. (Wisconsin)).

In some of those countries however, there is a complex interrelationship between assessing care time and assessing the incomes of both parents in determining what the level of child maintenance should be. So it is not always the case that shared physical custody on its own reduces child maintenance, but rather an income discrepancy between parents may mean the richer parent still has to pay, despite having shared physical custody. We think that an income effect is operating in Australia, New Zealand, Norway, Belgium and U.S. (Wisconsin) (we discuss that further in the next section). In France and Sweden, we have recorded in column 3, Table 14.2 that child maintenance may be still be paid according to the rules, but it is unlikely this would happen in practice (even if parents have slightly different income levels) because very few of those who have shared physical custody received or paid child maintenance in France and Sweden, at least that was in 2004 and 2014 (Moreau et al. 2004; SCB 2014). Table 14.2 therefore only shows whether there is likely to be an effect as a result of shared physical custody, but not the actual child maintenance monetary outcomes that are produced. However, we can measure the strength of that effect when we examine the actual amounts of child maintenance calculated using the model families in the next section.

14.5.3 Levels of Child Maintenance

In this section we analyse the child maintenance schemes to show how much they would determine as being the formal child maintenance obligation in two different care-time scenarios. We calculate the amount the liable parent is obliged to pay per child in our fictitious model family (Fig. 14.1). We first show how much child maintenance would be set in each country for the base case which shows the first care time scenario; that is where children have two overnight stays every other weekend with one parent. In the next care time scenario, we analyse what happens when the children have shared physical custody arrangements (applying the 50/50 time threshold in each country). In all scenarios, we use the male and female median incomes for full-time earners and hold them constant. The amounts of child maintenance produced for the model family are reported in Fig. 14.1 and it assumes that it is always paid (of course in a real family this might not always be the case).

The first set of bars present the child maintenance amounts due in the first care-time scenario of two overnight stays per fortnight, and both parents have median incomes. In this situation, in all countries, the non-resident parent (the one who has the children to stay two nights per fortnight) is expected to pay child maintenance. The maintenance awards are clearly lowest in Sweden, followed by France and Belgium (less than 200 ppp$/month), while U.S. (Wisconsin), Estonia and Spain[4] (Catalonia), require the highest amounts (over 400ppp$/month).

The next set of bars show child maintenance liabilities when the model family moves from a situation of regular contact to one of shared physical custody (care-time scenario two: 50/50). Shared physical custody as tested in our model family has a greater impact on what the other parent is expected to pay. We cluster countries into three groups accordingly. In group 1, full reduction is taken of shared physical custody and a zero amount of child maintenance is set (full reduction). In group 2 a partial reduction is available and the maintenance amount is reduced to a greater or lesser extent across countries (partial reduction): in group 3, no account is taken of shared physical custody and therefore no reduction in child maintenance is made.

In the *full reduction group* 1, are four countries, Denmark, UK, France and Sweden and the child maintenance obligation would be set at zero. This reflects the assumption that if parents share care of their child equally (and for France and Sweden if the parents' incomes' are also roughly similar) then the cost of rearing the child must be met equally between them.

In the *partial reduction group* 2 are Australia, New Zealand, Norway, Spain (Catalonia) Belgium, Finland and the U.S. (Wisconsin). The policy and practice guidelines in these countries make more fine grained calculations of how much child maintenance should be paid in shared physical custody situations. When comparing the amounts calculated for our model family from having two overnight stays to having shared physical custody, then the level of reduction varies. Child maintenance amounts are reduced by at least a half if not more in Australia, New Zealand, Norway, Spain (Catalonia) and U.S. (Wisconsin), but reduced by less than a half in Belgium and Finland.

In the *no reduction group* 3, are Estonia and Iceland. In our model family, the other parent is still expected to pay the full amount of child maintenance even where there is shared physical custody and both parents work full-time. In those two countries the liable parent always pays the minimum payment, which seems to be a relatively high amount compared to the other countries, according to our calculations based on this model family using pppUS$.

---

[4]In Spain, the non-resident parent would also be expected to contribute to the children's housing costs, which we do not include in the analysis.

Overall, again we see no obvious relationship between the type of child maintenance scheme and the three groups, other than to say that the only two counties that give a full reduction of maintenance irrespective of the parents' income are agency schemes Denmark and UK. That is because neither country uses an incomes shares approach to calculate obligations, also for the UK at least, the reason is to keep the administrative system simple.

14.6 Concluding Discussion

In this chapter, using new evidence from a comparative study we have filled the gaps in knowledge about how child maintenance schemes across different countries take account of shared physical custody arrangements. We have analysed data from 13 countries exploring this phenomena and have applied a model family approach that presents an idealised situation in which the parents in our model separated family are gender equal in terms of their work and care-time commitments.

We have found a very high degree of variation across countries and there is no obvious pattern in the approach adopted that relates to the type of child maintenance scheme in countries – whether they are agency based, court based or a hybrid of the two. So neither the administrative rules nor judicial decision making in relation to different child maintenance schemes and their calculations show any clear consistency either within or across the scheme types. Still, it is somewhat surprising that we can find no relationship in our data as we have standardised our approach using model families. However, it is important to note that institutional and administrative arrangements do not fully explain the differences in child maintenance outcomes (Meyer and Skinner 2016). Even so, our findings in this regard could signify that internationally there is no communication about or consensus emerging on what the child maintenance obligations should be in the light of this phenomenon of more equal care arrangements being made between separated parents. Certainly, whilst the prevalence rates of joint physical custody may be growing (or are at least are believed to be growing) they are still not the common arrangement. That is according to our data provided by national informants' examination of the available administrative and survey evidence in their countries. An examination of the possible factors that might affect prevalence rates themselves (such as the availability of free childcare within countries) is beyond the scope of the research reported in this chapter.

What we have found however, is that most commonly, countries provide a partial reduction in child maintenance amounts in cases of shared physical custody compared to when the parents in the model family had the more typical arrangements whereby children spend two nights every other weekend living in one parent's household. Arguably, this more fine-grained approach could be considered better than the other two approaches (see below) as some account is taken of the gender pay gap, as this is what shows up in our model family where we use male and female median earnings. Of course this may not be an explicit policy intention underpinning child maintenance policies, but may simply reflect the application of operational procedures and judicial decision making based on judgments about each parents' capacity to pay. Even so, the outcome potentially creates a redistributive effect as the richer parent pays child maintenance to the poorer parent for the upkeep of the children.

Less commonly four countries provided a full reduction in child maintenance amounts when there was equal shared care. Thereby, assuming, that the situation between the parents in our model family was equal and therefore neither owed any child maintenance to the other. This approach has previously been criticized for two main reasons (see Melli and Brown 1994). First, it assumes that parents have similar incomes, which even in our idealised model family, is not the case given the gender pay gap in median earnings. In real life cases the picture is bound to be worse. Certainly, statistics show that mothers' total income decreases immediately after parental separation and very often is much lower than fathers' incomes. Indeed, fathers' incomes can even show a rise post separation (e.g. Andress et al. 2006; Mortelmans and Defever 2017). Second, this approach of providing a full reduction in child maintenance assumes that expenses are borne equally by both parents. However, not all costs relate to the time children spend living with parents as some of the childrearing costs may be paid disproportionally by one of the parents, irrespective of sharing care time. In reality, mothers often carry most of the responsibility for management of children's daily lives, including paying school-related expenses and health care costs (Cashmore et al. 2010). So whilst some country's child maintenance policies might be attempting to deliver equal treatment to both parents with similar time care and employment circumstances, the impact on outcomes might be anything but equal. Cook and Skinner (2018) point out that economically, for truly gender equal outcomes to be produced in separated families, equity based solutions might be needed that favour the more economically disadvantaged parent, which in societal terms are usually mothers. So in relation to our analysis, an equity solution would best fit with the fine grained partial reduction approach. However, regardless of which policy assumptions are in place, it is certainly a quicker and easier operational process to assume equality in family circumstances where there is shared physical custody, thereby avoiding calculating reductions in child maintenance amounts.

Finally, we found it was unusual to make no reductions in child maintenance amounts when there was shared physical custody (at least that is for our model family), It only happened in 2 of the 13 countries, Estonia and Iceland. Conceivably, the underlying operational assumptions in these countries could be based on a strong male breadwinner model in which the father is not excused from his economic obligation to pay full maintenance regardless of sharing care time.

Overall, it seems there is no standard practice in dealing with shared physical custody in child maintenance policies. The three different approaches that we found of making full reductions, partial reductions or no reductions in child maintenance amounts when there was equal care arrangements did not map easily onto the child maintenance typology, which highlighted different institutional settings. The latter is surprising, as it might have been expected that similar child maintenance schemes would treat shared physical custody in similar ways, or that one type of setting – be it court or agency – would show signs of being more responsive to perceived changes in social norms of shared physical custody as measured by the prevalence rates in countries. We found no evidence of institutional settings or prevalence rates having a key influence on child maintenance outcomes in our model family.

Many questions remain about recognising the sharing of care responsibilities between parents in separated families. There is patchy information on its prevalence and many interpretations of what it is and how to measure it across countries. This makes it not only very difficult to measure, but also difficult to consider a range of factors relating to other family policies (such as childcare provision) that might cast some light on the reasons for variations in rates across countries. More specifically, within child maintenance systems, it would be helpful to know more about the justifications underlying the different formulae used to measure shared care and the rationales of whether and how to make any adjustments/reductions in the amounts expected. Perhaps those institutions are the best places to investigate this phenomenon as they generally have to respond to separated parents' changing family practices and are therefore closest to understanding what is going on regarding shifting social norms around care arrangements.

References

Andress, H.-J., Borgloh, B., Bröckel, M., Giesselmann, M., & Hummelstein, D. (2006). The economic consequences of partnership dissolution – A comparative analysis of panel studies from Belgium, Germany, Great Britain, Italy, and Sweden. *European Sociological Review, 22*(5), 533–560.

Barter, C. & Renold, E. (1999). The use of vignettes in qualitative research, University of Surrey, Social Research Update 25–25. https://sru.soc.surrey.ac.uk/SRU25.html, Accessed 17 Feb 2021.

Bartfeld, J. (2011). *Shared placement: An overview of prevalence, trends, economic implications, and impacts on child well-being*. Madison: University of Wisconsin–Madison: Institute for Research on Poverty.

Beld, J. M., & Biernat, L. (2002). Federal intent for state child support guidelines: Income shares, cost shares and the realities of shared parenting. *Family Law quarterly, 37*(2), 1165–2002.

Belmokhtar, Z. (2014). Une pensionn alimentaire fixée par les juges pour deux tiers des enfants de parents séparés. Infostat Justice numero 128. http://www.justice.gouv.fr/art_pix/INFOSTAT%20128.pdf. Accessed 1 Mar 2019.

Bradshaw, J. (2009). An international perspective on child benefit packages. In S. Kamerman, S. Phipps, & A. Ben-Arieh (Eds.), *From child welfare to child well-being: An international perspective on knowledge in the service of policy making* (pp. 293–308). Dordrecht: Springer.

Bradshaw, J., & Finch, N. (2002). Child benefit packages in 22 countries. *A comparison of child benefit packages in 22 countries*. Leeds: Department for Work and Pensions Research Report No. 174, Corporate Document Services.

Brown, P., & Brito, T. (2007). *Characteristics of shared-placement child support formulas used in the fifty states* (Report to the Wisconsin Department of Workforce Development). Madison: University of Wisconsin–Madison: Institute for Research on Poverty.

Cancian, M., & Costanzo, M. (2019). Comparing income-shares and percentage-of-income child support guidelines. *Children and Youth Services Review, 96*(1), 451–462.

Cancian, M., Meyer, D. R., Brown, P. R., & Cook, S. (2014). Who gets custody now? Dramatic changes in children's living arrangements after divorce. *Demography, 51*(4), 1381–1398.

Carlson, M. J., & Meyer, D. R. (2014). Family complexity: Setting the context. *The Annals of the American Academy of Political and Social Science, 654*(1), 6–11.

Cashmore, J., Parkinson, J., Weston, R., Patulny, R., Redmond, G., Qu, L., Baxter, L., Rajkovic, M., Sitek, T., & Katz, I. (2010). *Shared care parenting arrangements since the 2006 family law reforms* (Report to the Australian Government Attorney-General's Department). Sydney: University of New South Wales: Social Policy Research Centre.

Child custody and maintenance. (2017). Helsinki: National Institute of Health and Welfare.

Claessens, E., & Mortelmans, D. (2018). Challenges for child support schemes: Accounting for shared care and complex families. *Journal of European Social Policy, 28*(3), 211–223.

Cook, K., & Skinner, C. (2018). Gender equality in child support policy: Fathers' rhetoric of "fairness" in a parliamentary inquiry. *Social Politics: International Studies in Gender, State & Society, 26*(1), 164–187.

Corden, A. (1999). *Making child maintenance regimes work*. London: Family Policy Studies Centre.

Convention on the Rights of the Child (CRC). (1989). United Nations.

Fehlberg, B., Smyth, B., Maclean, M., & Roberts, C. (2011). Legislating for shared time parenting after separation: A research review. *International Journal of Law, Policy and the Family, 25*(3), 318–337.

Flaquer, L., Escobedo, A., Garriga, A., & Moreno, C. (2017). A igualdade de género, o bem-estar da criança e a residência alternada em Espanha. In Sofia Marinho e Sónia Vladimira Correia (Eds.), *Uma família parental, dues casas* (pp. 87–105). Edições Sílabo: Residência alternada – Dinâmicas e práticas sociais. Lisboa.

Hakovirta, M., & Eydal, G. B. (2020). Shared care and child maintenance policies in Nordic countries. *International Journal of Law, Policy and Family, 34*(1), 43–59.

Hakovirta, M., & Rantalaiho, M. (2011). Family policy and shared parenting in Nordic countries. *European Journal of Social Security, 13*(3), 247–266.

Haugen, G. M. D. (2010). Children's Perspectives on Everyday Experiences of Shared Residence: Time, Emotions and Agency Dilemmas. *Children & Society, 24*(2), 112–122.

Haux, T., McKay, S., & Cain, R. (2017). Shared care after separation in the United Kingdom: Limited data, limited practice? *Family Court Review, 55*(4), 572–585.

International Network of Child Support Scholars. (2019). http://www.incss.org/. Accessed in 1 Mar 2019.

Júlíusdóttir, S. (2009). Samskipti foreldra og barna eftir skilnað. [Communication between parents and children after divorce]. In H. S. Guðmundsson & S. B. Ómarsdóttir (Eds.), *Rannsóknir í félagsvísindum X félagsráðgjafardeild og stjórnmálafræðideild* (pp. 119–131). Reykjavík: Félagsvísindastofnun Háskóla Íslands.

Kitterød, R. H., & Wiik, K. (2017). Shared residence among parents living apart in Norway. *Family Court Review, 55*(4), 556–571.

Lacroix, C. (2006). Freedom, desire and power: Gender processes and presumptions of shared care and responsibility after parental separation. *Women's Studies International Forum, 29*(2), 184–196.

Lodge, J., & Alexander, M. (2010). *Views of adolescents in separated families: A study of adolescents' experiences after the 2006 reforms to the family law system*. Melbourne: AIFS.

Melli, M. S., & Brown, P. R. (1994). The economics of shared custody: Developing an equitable formula for dual residence. *Houston Law Review, 31*(x), 543–584.

Meyer, D. R., & Skinner, C. (2016). Privileging biological or residential obligations in separated families: Child maintenance policy approaches in 12 countries. *Families, Relationships and Societies, 5*(1), 79–95.

Meyer, D. R., Skinner, C., & Davidson, J. (2011). Complex families and equality in child support obligations: A comparative policy analysis. *Children and Youth Services Review, 33*(10), 1804–1812.

Meyer, D. R., Cancian, M., & Cook, S. T. (2017). The growth in shared custody in the United States: Patterns and implications. *Family Court Review, 55*(4), 500–512.

Millar, J., & Warman, A. (1996). *Family obligations in Europe*. London: Family Policy Studies Centre.

Moreau, C., Munoz-Perez, B., & Serverin, E. (2004). *La residence en alternance des enfants de parents séparés* (Études et Statistiques Justice 23). Paris: Ministere de Justice.

Mortelmans, D., & Defever, C. (2017). Income trajectories of lone parents after divorce: A view with Belgian register data. In L. Bernardi & D. Mortelmans (Eds.), *Lone parenthood in the life course. Life course research and social policies*. Cham: Springer.

Newnham, A. B. (2010). The use of shared residence arrangements in English and Swedish family law in the child's best interests or a covert resurrection of traditional patriarchal structures? University of Sussex.

Ottosen, H. M., Andersen, D., Dahl, K. M., Hansen A. T., Lausten, M., & Østergaard, S. (2014). *Børn og unge i Danmark – Velfærd og trivsel 2014*. [Children and youth in Denmark – Welfare and well-being]. København: SFI – Det Nationale Forskningscenter for Velfærd.

Qu, L., Weston, R., Moloney, L., Kaspiew, R., & Dunstan, J. (2014). *Post-separation parenting, property and relationship dynamics after five years*. Canberra: Attorney-General's Department.

SCB. (2014). *Olika familjer lever på olika sätt – om barns boende och försörjning efter en separation* [Different families live in different ways: A survey on residence and support of children after a separation]. Örebro: Statistiska Centralbyrån.

Singer, A. (2008). Active parenting or Solomon's justice? Alternating residence in Sweden for children with separated parents. *Utrecht Law Review, 4*(2), 35–47.

Skinner, C., & Davidson, J. (2009). Recent trends in child maintenance schemes in 14 countries. *International Journal of Law, Policy and the Family, 23*(1), 25–52.

Skinner, C., Bradshaw, J., & Davidson, J. (2007). *Child support policy: An international perspective*. Leeds: Corporate Document Services.

Skinner, C., Hakovirta, M., & Davidson, J. (2012). A comparative analysis of child maintenance schemes in five countries. *European Journal of Social Security, 14*(1), 330–347.

Skinner, C., Meyer, D., Cook, K., & Fletcher, M. (2017). Child maintenance and social security interactions: The poverty reduction effects in model lone parent families across four countries. *Journal of Social Policy, 46*(3), 495–516.

Smyth, B. (2017). Special issue on shared-time parenting after separation. *Family Court Review, 55*(4), 494–499.

Soydan, H., & Stål, R. (1994). How to use the vignette technique in cross-cultural social work research. *Scandinavian Journal of Social Welfare, 3*(2), 75–80.

Trinder, L. (2010). Shared residence: A review of recent research evidence. *Child and Family Law Quarterly, 22*(4), 475–498.

Vanassche, S., Sodermans, A. K., Declerck, C., & Matthijs, K. (2017). Alternating residence for children after parental separation: Recent findings from Belgium. *Family Court Review, 55*(4), 545–555.

Wikeley, N. (2009). Child support and parental responsibility. In I. Curry-Sumner & C. Skinner (Eds.), *Persistent problems, finding solutions: Child maintenance in the Netherlands and the United Kingdom*. Nijmegen: Wolf Legal Publishers.

Mia Hakovirta is Academy Research Fellow at the Department of Social Research and Senior Research Fellow in INVEST Flagship, University of Turku, Finland. Her research has centered on family and child support policies, and the issue of the economic well-being of single-parent families. She has published on post-separation family policies, child support policies, shared care, post-separation fatherhood and child poverty and child well-being. Most of her research is cross-national. In her current project, funded by Academy of Finland, she is studying complex families and child support policy in 15 countries.

Christine Skinner is an expert in child support policy with over 20 years' experience researching the lives of separated families. She has worked on numerous projects for the UK's Economic and Social Research Council and the Department of Work and Pensions. Christine's' research has impacted on UK policy developments and she has acted as specialist policy adviser to the House of Commons Select Committee, the National Audit Office and the Ministerial 'Expert Steering Group on Relationship Support Services'. Known internationally, she has advised other policy-making bodies on child support in Korea, France and Australia and she has conducted comparative analysis of child support schemes across many countries. Most recently, she is involved in comparative analysis of shared care policies (with Dr Mia Hakovirta, University of Turku, Finland) and in exploring the impact of domestic violence on lone mothers' pursuance of child support (with A/Prof Kay Cook, Swinburne University, Melbourne).

ermissions

l chapters in this book were first published in SPCIICCA, by Springer; hereby published ith permission under the Creative Commons Attribution License or equivalent. Every apter published in this book has been scrutinized by our experts. Their significance has en extensively debated. The topics covered herein carry significant information for a mprehensive understanding. They may even be implemented as practical applications or ay be referred to as a beginning point for further studies.

e contributors of this book come from diverse backgrounds, making this book a truly ternational effort. We would like to thank all the contributing authors for lending their pertise to make the book truly unique. They have played a crucial role in the development this book. Without their invaluable contributions this book wouldn't have been possible. ey have made vital efforts to compile up to date information on the varied aspects of is subject to make this book a valuable addition to the collection of many professionals d students.

is book was conceptualized with the vision of imparting up-to-date and integrated formation in this field. To ensure the same, a matchless editorial board was set up. Every dividual on the board went through rigorous rounds of assessment to prove their worth. ter which they invested a large part of their time researching and compiling the most evant data for our readers.

e editorial board has been involved in producing this book since its inception. They have ent rigorous hours researching and exploring the diverse topics which have resulted in successful publishing of this book. They have passed on their knowledge of decades rough this book. To expedite this challenging task, the publisher supported the team at ery step. A small team of assistant editors was also appointed to further simplify the iting procedure and attain best results for the readers.

art from the editorial board, the designing team has also invested a significant amount their time in understanding the subject and creating the most relevant covers. They utinized every image to scout for the most suitable representation of the subject and ate an appropriate cover for the book.

e publishing team has been an ardent support to the editorial, designing and production m. Their endless efforts to recruit the best for this project, has resulted in the omplishment of this book. They are a veteran in the field of academics and their pool knowledge is as vast as their experience in printing. Their expertise and guidance has oved useful at every step. Their uncompromising quality standards have made this book exceptional effort. Their encouragement from time to time has been an inspiration for eryone.

e publisher and the editorial board hope that this book will prove to be a valuable piece knowledge for students, practitioners and scholars across the globe.

Index

www.ingramcontent.com/pod-product-compliance
Lightning Source LLC
LaVergne TN
LVHW080642210926
848485LV00003B/310

* 9 7 8 1 6 3 9 8 9 7 0 3 2 *